CHICK FLICKS

Also by Jo Berry and published by Orion

The Ultimate DVD Easter Egg Guide

Also by Angie Errigo

The Illustrated History of the Rock Album Cover
The Rough Guide to the Lord of the Rings (ed. Paul Simpson)

movies women love

CHICK FLICKS

JO BERRY AND ANGIE ERRIGO

ORION

First published in Great Britain in 2004 by
Orion
an imprint of Orion Books Ltd
Orion House, 5 Upper St Martin's Lane,
London WC2H 9EA

A CIP catalogue record for this book is
available from the British Library

ISBN 0 75286 832 2

Printed and bound in Italy

PHOTOGRAPH CREDITS

back cover: (clockwise from right) *Bridget Jones's Diary* Twentieth Century
Fox/the Kobal Collection; *Thelma and Louise* Miramax/Universal/the Kobal
Collection/Alex Bailey; *The Heiress* MGM/Pathe/the Kobal Collection; *An
Affair to Remember* Paramount/the Kobal Collection

Plates: [Page 1] Universal/ the Kobal Collection;[Page 2] RKO/ the
Kobal Collection;[Page 3] Warner Bros/ the Kobal Collection, MGM/
the Kobal Collection/ Laszlo Willinger;[Page 4] Paramount/ the Kobal
Collection; [Page 5] Twentieth Century Fox/ the Kobal Collection [Pages 6 –7]
UGC/ Studio Canal+/ the Kobal Collection, Columbia/ the Kobal Collection,
Twentieth Century Fox/ the Kobal Collection/ Nicholas, Randee St; [Page 8]
Vestron/ the Kobal Collection; [Page 9] Paramount/ the Kobal Collection,
Castle Rock/ Nelson/ Columbia/ the Kobal Collection;[Pages 10 and 11]
Universal/ the Kobal Collection [Page 12] Merchant Ivory/ Goldcrest/ the
Kobal Collection, Twentieth Century Fox/ Paramount/ the Kobal Collection /
Merie W. Wallace;[Page 13] Twentieth Century Fox/ the Kobal Collection;
[Page 14] MGM/Pathe/ the Kobal Collection;[Page 15] Twentieth Century
Fox/ the Kobal Collection, Columbia/ the Kobal Collection;[Page 16]
Selznick/ MGM/ the Kobal Collection

Contents

Acknowledgements and Dedications

Thanks to Ian Preece for being a supportive, and very patient, commissioning editor, and to Mark Rusher for his enthusiasm. Also to Robin, Richard, Dad and Bill for revealing their inner new-men for the Male Weepies list.

This is for Mum, Janey, Anita, Helen, Deryn, Debbi, Nicki M, Claire D, Ndidi, Mewe and especially Lirl. Most of all, so much love to Steve, my angel from heaven – I promise the next book will have a lot more explosions and aliens in it.

Jo Berry

In memory of my dear mother Dorothy Errigo and my sweet friend Margaret Foster, with both of whom I shed many happy tears at the movies.

Angie Errigo

Introduction

What is a chick flick? Traditionally, it's a film made specifically to appeal to a female audience. That used to mean a weepy melodrama (the so-called 'woman's picture'), a girlie costume drama (especially if it was an adaptation of a much-loved romantic novel), or an escapade for bosom buddies.

We think it's a term we can use more liberally. This book is intended as a fun, irreverent appreciation of the many kinds of movies women love – movies that are romantic, tearful, sexy, exciting; contain handsome men and gorgeous frocks; and feature women who are sassy, smart or sympathetic.

We wrote this book because it's the kind of guide we wanted to read but couldn't find. Most film reference books and guides take a critical stance, and that's obviously important. But sometimes what a woman wants has nothing to do with artistic merit. Now and then we just want a movie in which the girl gets the guy, the girl doesn't get the guy and dies, or the girl gets a wardrobe to die for. Great acting, brilliant direction and a masterful screenplay would be lovely, but some of the films we love can boast none of these. It's about time we confessed: we might love the great and good, but we can also adore the cute and the ridiculously bad, as long as the leading man is handsome or the story – no matter how cheesy – makes us laugh, makes us cry or makes us hot.

How did we decide what to include? First, we asked ourselves, 'Would a man go to see this alone or with his mates?' If the answer was yes, we decided it wasn't a chick flick. Then we promptly broke that rule with some classic films, such as *Casablanca* and *Bonnie And Clyde*, in which there is a strong element in the movie that is particularly appealing or of interest to a woman. Next, we considered whether a film was either so great that every woman should see it at least once, or really bad in a shamelessly entertaining way. Then we felt we should cover the middle ground, too – those pictures aimed at women that are neither terrific nor terrible but may be perfect to while away a wet

Sunday afternoon. Men won't necessarily run a mile from all of these films. There are plenty of great date movies included here that men enjoy too – although don't expect to hear them waxing lyrical about them down the pub.

Films that made it into this book include classics that defined or influenced a genre. Then there are smash hits, movies as familiar as old friends, and some fabulous but neglected gems, past and present. You'll also find movies that are solid examples of their kind, and some stinkers that merit a mention for their star power or inexplicable popularity. Not every entry in this book is complimentary. We may go easy on a dumb movie because its heart (or something else) is in the right place, but we've tried to save you time and money by steering you away from films that are *so* bad that they deserve the trashing we give them.

Chances are there might be something you love that isn't in here. We all have our quirks and guilty pleasures. Our own were the cause of some heated discussions, tantrums and hair-pulling sessions: Jo is still sulking because *Spartacus* – despite its weepy ending – wasn't allowed in while Angie won the argument for *Beastmaster*'s inclusion, on the basis of Marc Singer's loincloth.

Finally, if you're thinking it's sexist, old-fashioned and all man-hatey to distinguish between a woman's picture and a man's movie, you've clearly never tried to drag a man to *How To Make An American Quilt*. Equally, we could have raved about plenty of movies women enjoy just as much as men, from *Alien* to *Pulp Fiction* to *Zulu*. But that's another book. *This* book is for women who want to wallow on their own in front of the TV with a box of chocolates and a fistful of tissues, or have a laugh at the movies with a couple of girlfriends and a pizza.

Jo and Angie, August 2004

25 Chick Flicks Every Woman Should See Before She Dies

An Affair To Remember

Amélie

Annie Hall

Breakfast At Tiffany's

Bridget Jones's Diary

Dirty Dancing

Ghost

Gone With The Wind

The Heiress

His Girl Friday

The Joy Luck Club

Letter From An Unknown Woman

Like Water For Chocolate

Little Women

Love Story

Magnificent Obsession

My Big Fat Greek Wedding

Now Voyager

Pillow Talk

Pretty In Pink

Terms Of Endearment

Thelma And Louise

The Way We Were

When Harry Met Sally

Working Girl

The Top 10 Female Movie Icons Of All Time

Bette Davis

Doris Day

Goldie Hawn

Audrey Hepburn

Katharine Hepburn

Diane Keaton

Julia Roberts

Meg Ryan

Barbara Stanwyck

Meryl Streep

Chapter 1: Meeting Mr Right
Romantic Comedies and Comedies

Two people meet. They exchange witty banter with each other. Despite an obvious attraction, there is some barrier to them getting together (one is already involved perhaps, or on the surface they think they hate each other) and comic moments on the road to happiness ensue before they finally realise what we have known all along – that they belong together.

That's the basic formula of a romantic comedy – seen in everything from the works of Shakespeare (*Much Ado About Nothing*, for example) to the Farrelly Brothers – although we wonder what the Bard would have made of the 'hair gel' scene in *There's Something About Mary*. They're funny and they're romantic, which is why we girls love them – and why, if they're not too sappy, we can also get guys to watch them, too … reluctantly.

There are, of course, many romantic comedies we haven't included here; if we had featured them all, there wouldn't be much room for anything else. The ones that are equally appealing to men didn't make the grade (this is a book on flicks for *chicks*, after all) but we still love them. Once you've checked out the girliest of the romantic comedies we review below, check out some more male-friendly gems like *Roxanne* (the *Cyrano de Bergerac* update starring Steve Martin) or the Coen Brothers' *Intolerable Cruelty* with George Clooney. Then there are the adorable *Ed TV* with Matthew McConaughey, and the Frank Capra classics *You Can't Take It With You* and *Mr Deeds Goes To Town*. And don't forget the legion of semi-romantic comedies: Billy Wilder's *Ball Of Fire* and *Some Like It Hot*, *Shallow Hal*, the aforementioned *There's Something About Mary*, Jack Nicholson in *As Good As It Gets*, the twisted, blackly comic *The War Of The Roses* and many of Woody Allen's films (and we have featured the closest film he has made to a girlie romantic comedy, *Annie Hall*).

We've also excluded some comedies that are less about a girl finding love and more about a geeky boy getting laid by the hot girl who lives down the street. Those are male fantasies, not female ones – but check out the box on page 38 for a few that, while aimed at men, appeal to us either because the leading man, while deluded, is cute, or because, despite his lecherous intentions, everything turns out sweetly in the end.

Some of the more fantastical romantic comedies are in Chapter 3. There you will find the rom-coms that aren't exactly wholly in touch with reality (although we have to admit that films casting cuties like Hugh Jackman, William Holden and Keanu Reeves as single and available aren't too realistic, either!), movies in which one half of the couple is, for example, a ghost, an angel or a princess. Lovely as it is to believe that Prince Charming is waiting just around the corner, we've grudgingly decided that he belongs alongside all the other fantasies.

So this chapter instead features the girliest of the real-world rom-coms, those in which the love part is as important as the comedy part, if not more so. These are films featuring gorgeous men, to-die-for frocks, romantic kisses, and sometimes that ultimate movie repellent for men, weddings. Here you'll find the classic (and the not-so-classic, but still enjoyable) romantic comedies about finding love, losing it, finding it again, getting married and, of course, living happily – or, just occasionally, not so happily – ever after …

BRINGING UP BABY (1938)

Directed by Howard Hawks
Starring Katharine Hepburn, Cary Grant, Charlie Ruggles, May Robson

Screwball comedy is distinguished from straightforward romantic comedy by eccentric characters, unconventional situations, slapstick, misunderstandings and snappy repartee. All of these are superb in Howard Hawks's breakneck, maniacally funny jape. The screenplay, by top thirties writer Dudley Nichols, established favourite genre ingredients: an absent-minded professor, a madcap heiress, contrary animals, a large sum of money sought, pratfalls, cocktails, mistaken identity, a chase, an unwanted fiancée and absurd confusion.

Earnest, easily muddled palaeontologist Dr David Huxley (Grant)

is awaiting the last bone to complete the brontosaurus he has been reconstructing for years. It is to arrive the next day, his wedding day. Fiancée Alice (Leona Roberts), a prim nag, sends him off to play golf with the lawyer of a potential benefactor and clinch a million-dollar grant. But Huxley's golf session becomes a shambles when he encounters blithe, playful scatterbrain Susan Vance (Hepburn). And that's just the first five minutes. Give her twenty-four hours and Susan is going to turn David's life upside down.

Susan's secret weapon is Baby, the leopard her brother has shipped from his expedition in Brazil (which was the sort of thing the idle rich did all the time in thirties films, when it didn't seem to matter that there are no leopards in Brazil). The only information that comes with him is that Baby likes dogs and is soothed by music, particularly 'I Can't Give You Anything But Love'. Baby also enjoys mauling the hapless Huxley, as does Susan, determined to have him after discovering how handsome he is without his glasses. Thus he is shanghaied to convey Baby to Susan's aunt's country house where, among many misadventures, the aunt is revealed as the potential philanthropist, her fiendish fox terrier steals Huxley's precious bone, Susan frees a man-eating leopard she's mistaken for the runaway Baby, and most of the ensemble are jailed in noisy pandemonium.

Countless films have imitated *Bringing Up Baby* but it has never been topped for romantic hilarity. Hawks, a master in any genre, was one of the great innovators of frantic, overlapping dialogue; only his own journalism farce *His Girl Friday* can claim faster talking. Hepburn and Grant, who made four films together, are a peerless partnership, both gorgeous, charming and expert at comic timing. Throughout her career Hepburn was rarely sexy, but with Grant the chemistry is sensational. Highlights include: Susan, unaware that David's foot is on her hem, stomping off minus the back of her lamé gown; Susan and David serenading an unhappy Baby; and an enraged David accosting stately Aunt Elizabeth (Robson) while he's wearing a marabou-trimmed negligée.

Bizarrely, *Bringing Up Baby* did not find its audience on its first release. Branded Hepburn's latest flop, it ended her work at RKO. She went to New York for two years, returning with the film rights to her stage smash *The Philadelphia Story*, for which she chose Grant to partner her in a triumphant comeback – at MGM. Ironically, as RKO declined, *Bringing Up Baby*'s popularity grew alongside its reputation as *the* definitive screwball comedy.

WHEN HARRY MET SALLY (1989)

Directed by Rob Reiner
Starring Billy Crystal, Meg Ryan, Carrie Fisher, Bruno Kirby

One of the most popular and imitated modern movie moments comes from this film. Harry (Crystal) and Sally (Ryan) are chewing over sandwiches and sexual politics in a crowded lunchroom when Sally noisily demonstrates that a man can't tell a faked orgasm from the real thing. All that's required to conjure up the scene for anyone is to moan and scream 'Yes!' fifteen times and throw in some table banging. Her atypically uninhibited display rocketed Ryan from winsome ingénue to star. But the fantastic punchline, the funniest in the entire movie, is given not to its stars but to the director's mother, Estelle Reiner, who looks at the waiter after Sally's perform-ance and deadpans, 'I'll have what she's having'. This is even funnier to women for whom food can be as good as sex.

When Harry Met Sally typifies the modern thirtysomething rela-tionship romantic comedy, preoccupied with personalities and pop analysis rather than situation or plotting. A couple meet and don't hit it off, but in the course of their separate searches for love they reconnect to become confidants, endlessly discussing their feelings and friendship. The joke is always on them; the audience never loses confidence that their cute, companionable chumming around with their honesty, late night phone calls and strolls through Central Park will take them eventually into bed and up the aisle.

The angle is the question 'Can men and women ever really be just good friends?' This is rather spuriously pushed as a burning contem-porary issue (have none of them read, oh, say, Jane Austen's *Emma*?). Harry's contention that 'Men and women can't be friends because the sex part always gets in the way' is presumably shared with the famously embittered screenwriter Nora '*Heartburn*' Ephron, whose divorce from journalist Carl Bernstein fuelled her new career as gender-differences savant. The 'sex part' does indeed get in the way here, a consoling kiss escalating into a tumble, after which Sally goes into full-on commitment-demanding mode.

Thanks to the engaging leads, amusing dialogue and urban fairy-tale depiction of Manhattan, it's a charming, populist, Woody Allen-lite affair, less sophisticated or angst-ridden, in which goddess of cute Sally Albright and cynical, wisecracking Harry Burns play out their relationship to classic love songs by the Gershwins and Rodgers and Hart. Meanwhile, their best friends – Carrie Fisher (hers) and Bruno Kirby (his) – pair off effortlessly to provide a balanced, two-person chorus for confidences, encouragement, and the story's most appealingly humorous element: the smart and knowing commentary on how eighties men view women and vice versa. The timely script and the film's huge success propelled Ephron into directing her own films, for which *WHMS* was the blueprint. *Sleepless In Seattle*, *You've Got Mail* and other, non-Ephron imitations have made regular features of the recurring movie reference among characters (for *WHMS*'s *Casablanca* substitute *An Affair To Remember*, *The Dirty Dozen* and *The Godfather*), the easy listening soundtrack to underline scenes, and the helpfully instructive best friends. Its influence can also be discerned in nineties sitcoms *Friends* and *Will And Grace*, and in the Richard Curtis British romcom hit machine. Harry Burns is a gnomic Hugh Grant without the tics; Sally Albright is Bridget Jones's spiritual big sister, only without the worries about her thighs.

10 THINGS I HATE ABOUT YOU (1999)

Directed by Gil Junger
Starring Heath Ledger, Julia Stiles, Joseph Gordon-Levitt, Larisa Oleynik

This is an adorable and clever romantic comedy inspired by Shakespeare's *The Taming Of The Shrew*, but it also owes a debt to the popular John Hughes teen pics of the eighties. Two daughters have to contend with an overprotective dad obsessed by the menace of teen pregnancy. Flirty, in-demand younger sister Bianca (Oleynik) can't date unless her self-contained, abrasive elder sister Katerina (Stiles) does. So Ledger's Padua High School bad boy is paid by a gang of would-be Romeos to woo the stroppy Kat, enabling them to vie for Bianca.

There's plenty of smart comic plotting and incident – unsurprising, since the film was crafted by top US TV sitcom veterans. It is also full of juicy characters, even in minor roles (*The West Wing*'s Allison Janney as the school guidance counsellor writing an erotic romance novel is priceless, as is Daryl Mitchell's English teacher, who hits the nail on the head when he tells his class, 'Shakespeare may be a dead white guy, but he knew his shit'). But it's most irresistible when it gets mushy and the cute mating game takes its inevitable course (with pop songs), as when Ledger's Patrick publicly serenades Kat on the athletic field with a high-stepping 'Can't Take My Eyes Off You'. And, unlike Shakespeare's 'shrew', this contemporary independent heroine comes out on top.

50 FIRST DATES (2004)

Directed by Peter Segal
Starring Adam Sandler, Drew Barrymore

The Wedding Singer's Adam Sandler and Drew Barrymore are reteamed for this fun romantic comedy set in photogenic Hawaii. He's a marine vet who only romances tourists (because, of course, they leave after two weeks) but finally falls in love with local gal Drew. The only problem is that she suffers from a type of short-term memory loss that means when she wakes up she can't remember the events of the day before. So how will she remember him?

After *There's Something About Mary* six years earlier, romance seems destined always to be accompanied by stomach-turning comedy involving bodily fluids, and this film is no exception (most of it supplied by co-star Rob Schneider or Sandler's main patient, a large walrus). *50 First Dates* is nevertheless quite restrained for a Sandler movie, and is a surprisingly bittersweet comedy thanks to the chemistry between the leads, a warm, charming idea, and Barrymore's winsome performance.

AMÉLIE / a.k.a. LE FABULEUX DESTIN D'AMÉLIE (2001)

Directed by Jean-Pierre Jeunet
Starring Audrey Tautou, Mathieu Kassovitz

This disarming, enchantingly offbeat romance captivated international audiences and saw the gamine Tautou hailed as the new Audrey Hepburn. In the hands of kooky Swiss filmmaker Jeunet (*Delicatessen*), the waifish Amélie's mission to bring happiness to the sad, wistful and lonely people around her in Montmartre has qualities of magical fantasy as she busily manipulates fate and contrives serendipitous accidents. But her own loneliness, shy yearning and inarticulate, nervous reaction to a young mystery man (Kassovitz) who could be the one for her are amusingly and painfully rooted in realism – even as the lengthy process of their meeting takes daft, excruciatingly suspenseful and maddening turns. The best romantic gambit is the trail of clues leading a potential lover up, down and around the scenic landmark of the church of Sacre Coeur. (We must try it next time we're in Paris.) And to emphasise there are many kinds of love, there is a hilarious running gag involving Amélie's apathetic dad and a well-travelled garden gnome.

THE AMERICAN PRESIDENT (1995)

Directed by Rob Reiner
Starring Michael Douglas, Annette Bening, Michael J. Fox, Martin Sheen

You won't find a much more perfect Mr Right than President of the United States Andrew Shepherd (Douglas). A good-looking widower with a daughter (as well as being leader of the free world), he certainly catches the eye of lobbyist Sydney Ellen Wade (Bening, at her most luminous), but their romance is complicated by politics, press interest, and the machinations of Shepherd's political rival (Richard Dreyfuss).

Snappily written by Aaron Sorkin, this is filled with terrific dialogue and sparkling scenes and has a warm, charming romance at its heart. Douglas gives one of his most winning performances, and director Reiner fills his White House with a superb supporting cast, including Martin Sheen (who went on, of course, to star as another President in Sorkin's TV series *The West Wing*), Michael J. Fox, Samantha Mathis and David Paymer.

ANIMAL ATTRACTION (2001)

Directed by Tony Goldwyn
Starring Ashley Judd, Greg Kinnear, Hugh Jackman

Also known as *Someone Like You*, this romantic comedy is short on laughs and not exactly brimming over with romance, either, but deserves a mention simply because it stars that slice of Australian hunkiness Hugh Jackman in one of his first romantic leading roles.

Based on Laura Zigman's novel, the film stars Judd as Jane Goodale, a TV talent booker enjoying a romance with suave Ray (Kinnear). That is until he dumps her, and she bitterly works on the theory that you can guess a man's behaviour simply by looking at the mating ritual of bulls, which explains why men find it so hard to be monogamous. Her new roommate, womanising co-worker Eddie (Jackman), seems to provide proof of her theories, but, darn, do you think in the end she might discover he has a soft centre after all?

Hideously predictable and overlong, the movie coasts along on the charm of Judd and Jackman, and some nice supporting performances from Kinnear, Marisa Tomei and Ellen Barkin.

ANNIE HALL (1977)

Directed by Woody Allen
Starring Woody Allen, Diane Keaton, Tony Roberts, Paul Simon, Carol Kane

Paranoid, angst-ridden Alvy (Allen) is a stand-up comic trading on Jewish neuroses. He meets Annie (Keaton), a sweetly insecure, tense, Midwestern WASP, and is enchanted by her awkward charm. The progress of their 'nervous romance' is combined with memories of childhood, family and failed relationships, and an avalanche of inspired jokes, from escaping lobsters fleeing their fate as a romantic supper to Alvy sneezing away the cocaine served at a party.

This funny, philosophical and wistful post-mortem of a love affair was the Academy Awards' first comedy Best Picture since 1960's *The Apartment*. Also an Oscar winner for its direction, screenplay and Keaton as Best Actress, it stands out as a refreshing change of pace in a decade in which the important film trends were in hard-hitting dramas that took advantage of a new permissiveness to explore violence, sexuality and conspiracies, while blockbuster adventures and disaster movies reaped the big box-office rewards. Allen was unique, quietly turning out an idiosyncratic oeuvre full of wit and invention. His sixth effort as a writer–director, this is particularly warm and romantic, if bittersweet. He drew inspiration from his relationships with both New York and Keaton (whose real name is Hall), and the film has the realistic intimacy of a home movie – albeit a beautifully filmed one. It is now recognisable as the major turning point in his work, from broad, absurdist comedy to something sweeter, richer and deeper. Keaton, much to the dismay of the film's costume designer, brought her own wardrobe, setting a fashion for baggy, eccentrically mannish ensembles. 'La di dah, la di dah'!

AUNT JULIA AND THE SCRIPTWRITER / a.k.a. TUNE IN TOMORROW ... (1990)

Directed by Jon Amiel
Starring Barbara Hershey, Keanu Reeves, Peter Falk

Jon Amiel's offbeat, at times wildly funny comedy romance has hip credentials (it's based on a novel by Mario Vargas Llosa and features a funky score by jazz great Wynton Marsalis, who also appears in the film). But the heart-warming appeal in this tale of an impressionable young thing (the delectable, twenty-five-year-old Reeves) discovering life in fifties New Orleans lies in his ardent pursuit of his sexy, wary 'aunt' (the incontestably lovely forty-two-year-old Hershey). The film didn't set the box-office tills ringing since predominantly young audiences tend to find the age-gap romance a turn-off. But – surprise, surprise – the older we get, the more receptive we become to rom-coms in which the sophisticated, mature woman gets the dishy younger man! Once upon a time such a coupling was exclusively the domain of tearful melodrama (see *All That Heaven Allows*), but here it's handled with charm, some suspense and a credible outcome. Meanwhile, Reeves's involvement with Peter Falk's crazy/wise scriptwriter for a radio soap opera provides the side-splitting, spellbinding influence for embracing life.

THE BACHELOR (1999)

Directed by Gary Sinyor
Starring Chris O'Donnell, Renée Zellweger

A weak update of the 1925 Buster Keaton film *Seven Chances* has Chris O'Donnell cast as the young man who has to get married by his thirtieth birthday (little more than twenty-four hours away) if he is to inherit $100 million from his deceased grandfather. His girlfriend (Zellweger) has already given up on him, so it's up to Chris to try all his stereotypical ex-girlfriends (the rich bitch, the obsessive, etc.) to see whether any will take him on. This is a tall order indeed as the deal doesn't end with the ceremony – the potential bride has to live with him for ten years and bear his children.

Unfortunately, no matter how pretty he is, O'Donnell lacks both the charisma and the comic timing to hold this unfunny film together, and, despite a nicely bitchy turn from Brooke Shields as one of his exes and the well-choreographed scene in which O'Donnell is chased through San Francisco by a horde of wedding-dress-wearing women, the movie has very few either romantic or amusing moments. Which is something of a drawback for a romantic comedy.

THE BACHELOR AND THE BOBBY-SOXER (1947)

Directed by Irving Reis
Starring Cary Grant, Myrna Loy, Shirley Temple

An Oscar winner for Sidney Sheldon's entertaining screenplay, this film showcases one of Cary Grant's irresistible charm offensives. Shirley Temple's schoolgirl Susan develops a passionate crush on Grant's playboy artist Richard, to the disgust of her much older sister Margaret (Myrna Loy), a judge. After Susan sneaks into Richard's place and is caught, he's the one who ends up in court, where the judge sentences him to date Susan in the belief that her baby sister will swiftly outgrow her fixation. The talented Temple is delightful, trying desperately to act grown-up and sophisticated, while Grant hilariously affects adolescent goofiness to put her off. Even funnier are the accumulating, disastrous misunderstandings that convince Margaret that Richard is a degenerate until everyone realises who should be matched with whom. It's sparkling fun thanks to the skilled, light-handed playing.

BENNY & JOON (1993)

Directed by Jeremiah S. Chechik
Starring Johnny Depp, Mary Stuart Masterson, Aidan Quinn

Joon (Masterson) is a mentally unstable young woman living happily with her big brother Benny (Quinn), who looks after her and tries to stop her from getting into trouble in this quirky comedy-drama. One thing Benny can't prevent, however, is Joon falling for eccentric Buster Keaton-loving Sam (Depp), a quiet loner who is just as much of an outsider as she is.

With charming comic scenes – Depp demonstrates a new way to make cheese on toast by ironing it, and does a Chaplin-esque turn with a couple of forks and dancing bread rolls that display a previously untapped skill at physical comedy – and a sweet romance between a very unlikely couple, this is one movie that proves love truly does conquer all ... even the female romantic lead's tendency to set things on fire. Watch out for an early appearance by Julianne Moore as Benny's potential love interest.

BLIND DATE (1987)

Directed by Blake Edwards
Starring Bruce Willis, Kim Basinger

Poor Bruce Willis is having an even worse day than the bad ones he has in the *Die Hard* movies in his first (and pretty much only) romantic comedy post-*Moonlighting*. He's everyday guy Walter, who watches his life fall apart over the course of a single night when he takes Nadia (Basinger) on a blind date. Unfortunately, she gets wild and crazy when she drinks, and Walter also has to contend with her psycho ex-boyfriend David (John Laroquette), who wants to marry her, and his humourless father, who just happens to be a judge (William Daniels).

A series of comic set pieces rather than a true comedy romance, this has some very funny moments (especially when Walter tries to crash Nadia and David's nuptials, and comes up against ferocious dogs and an even scarier butler) and terrific performances from Willis and the supporting cast. Basinger is somewhat annoying, however, and while director Edwards knows how to deliver a sight gag, we never really learn enough about the characters to empathise with them as well as laugh at them.

BORN YESTERDAY (1950)

Directed by George Cukor
Starring Judy Holliday, William Holden, Broderick Crawford

Here's one for the record books: the heroine gets the guy when she puts her glasses *on*! The not-so-dumb blonde has never been more hilariously and lovably personified than by Judy Holliday, reprising her Broadway *tour de force* in writer Garson Kanin's smash about a diamond in the rough, the immortal Billie Dawn. When boorish self-made millionaire crook Harry (Crawford) decides to make a splash in Washington, DC political circles he hires cash-strapped writer Paul (a suave Holden) to tutor Billie, his ditsy, uneducated ex-showgirl mistress. She proves a more than able pupil, eagerly soaking up history, making a hit with the 'swellegant' set, and using her newly independent, informed thinking to expose Harry's corruption. The inevitable match between Billie and Paul is just as likeable as the humorously delivered message that education matters.

Interestingly, the real-life vulgarian Harry Cohn of Columbia Pictures was intent on Rita Hayworth for the Billie Dawn role, crudely rejecting Holliday as a 'fat Jewish broad'. Director Cukor won his fight for Judy, who starved for months to look glamorous in her Jean Louis costumes. Take that, Mr Cohn. Holliday also beat off Bette Davis (in *All About Eve*) and Gloria Swanson (in *Sunset Blvd.*) to win the Oscar for Best Actress.

The well-cast 1993 remake starring Melanie Griffith, Don Johnson and John Goodman is not bad at all, but it was simply overshadowed by the classic stature of the original. Then married, Melanie and Don had obvious real-life chemistry, and a cute highlight is Griffith leading a dinner party of Washington VIPs in a rousing mnemonic of US Constitutional amendments, sung to the tune of 'The Twelve Days Of Christmas'!

THE BRIDE CAME C.O.D. (1941)

Directed by William Keighley
Starring James Cagney, Bette Davis, Jack Carson

The only teaming of screen legends Davis and Cagney demonstrates star power big time. Davis's runaway heiress Joan and Carson's Allen, a bandleader she's known for only four days, hire Cagney's broke pilot Steve to fly them to Las Vegas. Her father gets wind of the elopement, however, and agrees to pay Steve ('$10 a pound'!) to kidnap her and bring her back single. Of course the plane goes down in the desert, the duo battle all the way, and Father winds up with a different son-in-law along with a bill for $1180. The comic highlight comes when Joan convinces herself she and Steve are about to die romantically together after becoming trapped in a mine cave-in, unaware that he's been able to sneak in and out to enjoy meals. How like a man!

BRIDGET JONES'S DIARY (2001)

Directed by Sharon Maguire
Starring Renée Zellweger, Colin Firth, Hugh Grant

Everyone's favourite single thirtysomething Brit jumped from the pages of Helen Fielding's novel to become flesh and blood in the form of American actress (shock, horror!) Renée Zellweger. But once you get used to her rather stiff English accent, she does a pretty good job as the slightly podgy girl trying to cut down her cigarette and alcohol intake while blindly staggering through the perilous world of dating.

On hand to make it even more tricky are Hugh Grant as her boss/lover/all-round cad Daniel Cleaver, and Colin Firth as family friend Mark Darcy, both of whom are terrific – especially Grant, who should ditch all those romantic male leads and plump for some more devilishly dishy roles like this instead. Well played and often rib-ticklingly funny – especially during Grant and Firth's hilariously pathetic street fight – this modern-day homage to *Pride And Prejudice* is a must for any girl who has ever sat alone in her bedroom dramatically singing along to the definitive singleton's anthem 'Without You' (with glass of cheap plonk in hand, of course).

BRIDGET JONES: THE EDGE OF REASON (2004)

Directed by Beeban Kidron
Starring Renee Zellweger, Colin Firth, Hugh Grant

Almost four years on from *Bridget Jones' Diary*, Renee Zellweger once again piled on the pounds and put on the big support knickers to play English singleton Bridget Jones. Actually, as the movie starts (about six weeks after the original left off), Bridget is no longer a singleton but the girlfriend of serious, rather stuffy human-rights lawyer Mark Darcy (Firth). Of course, their blossoming romance doesn't stay blissful for long, or this would be a very short movie. Our heroine is hardly the most graceful of ladies, so embarrassment soon occurs when she accompanies Mark to a society dinner, and their relationship is further fractured when Bridget suspects one of Mark's female colleagues may be a bit friendlier to him than she would like.

Much of the comedy here is in the same vein as the original movie – Bridget bumbling around on a series of escapades that include parachuting into a pigsty and hurtling helplessly down a ski run – while the formulaic moments that made *Diary* a success are repeated. There's the recognisable pop soundtrack, another public fight between stiff-upper-lipped male characters played for laughs, the supporting cast of British TV favourites (Neil Pearson, Sally Phillips, etc) and, of course, the return of Hugh Grant's hilarious cad Daniel Cleaver at just the right moment.

So far, so enjoyably predictable. The main hiccup in the proceedings is a bizarre detour to Thailand that can be blamed on Helen Fielding's lacklustre source novel, as Bridget – with gal pal and Cleaver in tow – goes on a business trip and then is arrested at the airport on her way home. Once Bridget is thrown into a Thai jail so friendly and fun it makes a Club 18-30 holiday look sedate, any shred of credibility the film has is thrown out of the window, leaving the audience to hope that Mark Darcy will rescue her as soon as possible so the pair can fall in love again and we can all go home happy.

BULL DURHAM (1988)

Directed by Ron Shelton
Starring Kevin Costner, Susan Sarandon, Tim Robbins

Men like this offbeat, madly sexy sporting comedy a lot, too, but we're particularly keen on Sarandon for wittily demonstrating the appeal of lusty older women. She is the central character, baseball groupie Annie, who is devoted to screwing, baseball and philosophy, in roughly that order. Each season Annie selects a promising player from the Durham Bulls baseball team to benefit from her sexual favours and life wisdom. This year she chooses 'Nuke' LaLoosh (Robbins, Sarandon's real-life partner ever since), a dim-witted young pitcher 'not cursed with self-awareness'. But she really fancies the veteran at the end of his career, Crash Davis (Costner). Crash is also occupied with teaching Nuke about the big game of life so he and Annie deny their attraction until a fabulous, explosively erotic recognition of their rightness together. Naturally, by the end of the season everyone has learned a little something – we adore Crash's speech listing the things he believes in, which include the small of a woman's back, prolonged foreplay, chocolate cookies and long, slow, deep kisses that last for days. This really has nothing to do with baseball and everything to do with the irresistible excellence of a woman who ties men to the bedposts and reads them the poetry of Walt Whitman.

CACTUS FLOWER (1969)

Directed by Gene Saks
Starring Walter Matthau, Ingrid Bergman, Goldie Hawn

Julian (Matthau) tells his girlfriend Toni (Hawn) that he can't leave his wife because of the children. Trouble is, he doesn't actually have a wife and kids – it's a line he uses on all women to avoid commitment – so when he finally realises he wants to marry Toni and she insists on meeting the missus, he has to conjure one up in the form of his receptionist Stephanie (Bergman).

Hawn, in her first major film role, won an Oscar for her performance as the perky, dippy blonde, but Bergman is equally enjoyable as the bristly woman who blossoms in her guise as Matthau's wife, and she displays a terrific sense of comic timing. Who knew the ice maiden from *Casablanca* could be so funny?

A CINDERELLA STORY (2004)

Directed by Mark Rosman
Starring Hilary Duff, Chad Michael Murray

The *Cinderella* fairytale gets updated for the twenty-first century, with the general idea intact but the magic (both literal and otherwise) missing. Following the death of her dad, young Sam (Duff) is forced to share her home with his gold-digging widow Fiona (Jennifer Coolidge) and her two nasty, dim-witted daughters. When she's not working at Fiona's diner, Sam is running around after her stepmother and stepsisters at home. The only bright spot in her life is the email and text relationship she is having with a mystery boy at school – little does she know, however, that it's dreamy high-school hunk Austin (Murray) that she's been communicating with.

Instead of a ball there's a high-school dance; and instead of a glass slipper Sam leaves behind her mobile phone. Adults will puzzle over some of the plot twists that keep Sam and Austin apart, but if you're fifteen or under this is inoffensively sweet fare that doesn't strain the brain.

CLUELESS (1995)

Directed by Amy Heckerling
Starring Alicia Silverstone, Paul Rudd, Brittany Murphy

Jane Austen's classic novel *Emma* (see page 175) gets updated for the MTV generation with a dash of *Beverly Hills 90210* thrown in for good measure in this genuinely funny comedy that made a star of Silverstone. She plays Cher, a cool Valley Girl teen who knows everything about the most important things in life: boys and fashion (she has a computer detailing the contents of her extensive wardrobe). But, of course, Cher soon discovers she doesn't know as much as she thought she did, as she tries to turn her new friend Tai (Murphy) into a boy-magnet, and matchmake her friends and teachers, while ignoring the guy with eyes only for her who's right under her nose.

Deliciously daft stuff from *Fast Times At Ridgemont High* director Amy Heckerling, this is a fun jab at those girls who think Calvin Klein and American Express are the most important phrases in the English language. Great soundtrack (Radiohead, World Party, Counting Crows) too.

COUSINS (1989)

Directed by Joel Schumacher
Starring Ted Danson, Isabella Rossellini, Sean Young, William Petersen

Based on the 1975 French movie *Cousin Cousine*, this enjoyable Americanised version is as much about family and its intertwining relationships as it is about the romance between the two leads. Larry (Danson) and Maria (Rossellini) discover that his wife Tish (Young) and her husband Tom (Petersen) are having an affair. Commiserating together while their spouses sneak off for a quickie at a family wedding, the pair become friends and eventually begin to fall in love.

While the inevitable happens, we get to know more about their other halves, as well as Larry's grumpy old codger of a father (Lloyd Bridges, who enjoys all the best lines), Maria's mother (Norma Aleandro), and Larry's son (Keith Coogan), whose video of one of the family get-togethers is enough to bring the event to a stunned halt. The romantic sections are a bit sappy, but the disastrous family gatherings that pepper the film are a treat.

CROSSING DELANCEY (1988)

Directed by Joan Micklin Silver
Starring Amy Irving, Reizl Bozyk, Peter Riegert, Jeroen Krabbé

In this sweet affair the independent, thirtyish singleton Isabelle (Irving) is a Manhattan literary groupie and uptown girl who lives a world away from her beloved grandmother's traditional Jewish world downtown. But her old Bubbie (Bozyk) gets a matchmaker (Sylvia Miles) on Isabelle's case, anxious to find her a nice Jewish husband. Smitten with an arrogant, womanising poet (Krabbé), Isabelle turns her nose up at Peter Riegert's Sam, a kind, amiable, down-to-earth pickle-maker who's ready to commit. Clearly she needs a few disappointments and reality checks to appreciate his worth. The flaw in this cute comedy (nearly stolen by the two old dears, Bozyk and Miles) is that no woman in New York would be so fast to dismiss an attractive, self-employed, single, straight man; they'd be queuing up to get their hands on his pickles.

DESPERATELY SEEKING SUSAN (1985)

Directed by Susan Seidelman
Starring Madonna, Rosanna Arquette, Aidan Quinn

Bored suburban housewife Roberta (Arquette) is intrigued by a regular personals advert headlined, 'Desperately seeking Susan,' through which quirky couple Susan (Madonna) and boyfriend Jim (Robert Joy) arrange to meet. So Roberta decides to go along to their latest rendezvous, but a nasty bump on the head means that when she wakes up she thinks she *is* Susan; as does Dez (Quinn), a friend of Jim, who has never met Susan before and finds himself drawn to his pal's girl. To complicate matters even further, there's a bad guy on Roberta's trail who thinks she's Susan, too.

Madonna – who became a star while the movie was being filmed (rumour has it much to the annoyance of her co-stars) – effectively plays herself, and delivers the most enjoyable performance of her acting career as free-spirit Susan. Her dangling earrings, numerous necklaces and bracelets and eclectic fashion sense spawned a trend, so while Rosanna Arquette is officially the star of the film, it's Madonna you really remember. A fun adventure, the soundtrack features Madonna's hit single 'Into The Groove'.

DOWN WITH LOVE (2003)

Directed by Peyton Reed
Starring Ewan McGregor, Renée Zellweger

A delightful attempt to recreate those candy-coloured, fashion-filled romantic comedies of the 1960s (which usually starred Doris Day) in all their frivolous, superficial glory.

It's New York in 1962 and Barbara Novak (Zellweger, in her most engaging performance since *Jerry Maguire*) has just written a book that tells women to ignore love and romance (casual sex, however, is fine) in order to further their careers. (She suggests eating chocolate as a way to quell those romantic stirrings.) Smooth-talking journalist and ladies' man Catcher Block (Ewan McGregor) isn't convinced, however, and decides to expose Barbara as a fraud who secretly wants to ditch her feminist views and fall girlishly in love.

Packed with sexual innuendo, zippy dialogue and Technicolor fashion, this battle of the sexes also boasts terrific performances from McGregor (who comes across as even more charming and sexy than Sean Connery's James Bond), Sarah Paulson (as Barbara's editor) and *Frasier*'s David Hyde Pierce (as Catcher's envious boss). Of course, it's as frothy as a cappuccino with extra foam, but if you enjoy a bit of movie silliness every now and then, and have a soft spot for films in which the costume department have obviously received the lion's share of the budget, then this sweet confection is guaranteed to make you smile.

FORCES OF NATURE (1999)

Directed by Bronwen Hughes
Starring Sandra Bullock, Ben Affleck

Affleck is the husband-to-be, travelling from New York to Savannah to marry his fiancée (Maura Tierney) who gets sidetracked by the weather and kooky Sandra Bullock in this thirties-style romantic comedy which relies heavily on the appeal of its two stars. The pair do have a certain chemistry as they bicker and then bond while being beset by travel trouble en route, but Ben's dilemma (should he marry his patient girl-friend or get involved with been-around-the-block Bullock?) has an obvious resolution from the start which makes it all a bit predictable.

Bullock looks extremely uncomfortable playing a wild child, but Affleck is more successful (and appealing) in his role as the dependable, strait-laced guy whose world has unexpectedly turned upside down. There's fine support from Steve Zahn and Blythe Danner – but it's a shame the movie doesn't match their talents.

FRENCH KISS (1995)

Directed by Lawrence Kasdan
Starring Meg Ryan, Kevin Kline

When her fiancé (Timothy Hutton) phones her from Paris to say he's fallen in love with someone else, Kate (Ryan) flies to France in an attempt to win him back. However, when her luggage is stolen she accepts the aid of mysterious (and rather slimy) Frenchman Luc (Kline), unaware that he is helping her only because he has hidden something suspicious in one of her bags. The mismatched pair then set off together through the picture-postcard French countryside.

A predictable comedy at best, matters are not helped by Kline's daft impersonation of a Frenchman which must have Peter Sellers doing pirouettes in his grave. And Ryan, who showed some real depth the previous year in *When A Man Loves A Woman*, disappoints here as she simply reprises her cute but ditzy *When Harry Met Sally* persona. Tedious, unfunny and as romantic as frog's legs, this is one trip to Paris on which you'll wish you'd stayed at home.

GIDGET (1959)

Directed by Paul Wendkos
Starring Sandra Dee, James Darren, Cliff Robertson

Sandra Dee was the perfect, bubbly all-American innocent teen. In a publicity department's dream match she married pop idol Bobby Darin, and she was even immortalised in a song in *Grease*. She was never more charming than in this coming-of-age beach comedy as the petite girl who discovers surfing, love and her womanliness all in the summer when she turns seventeen. Based on novelist Frederick Kohner's own daughter, Dee's spirited Frances, unlike most California girls of her day, eschews sunbathing alluringly to ride the waves with the boys ('Honest to goodness, it's the absolute ultimate!'). Attaching herself to the local surf bums, she becomes their mascot, is nicknamed Gidget – short for girl midget – and falls for Darren's errant college boy Moondoggy. While the dudes party with the curvier, easier girls (generically known as beach bunnies), Gidget's lack of artifice and her relationship with elder statesman surfer the Big Kahuna (Robertson) promote the blossoming of our heroine. A cute cultural artefact (including the terrifically dated beach slang of the time), this hit launched a franchise – sadly, minus Dee – including *Gidget Goes Hawaiian*, *Gidget Goes To Rome* and the TV spin-off series that launched Sally Field.

THE GOODBYE GIRL (1977)

Directed by Herbert Ross
Starring Richard Dreyfuss, Marsha Mason

Neil Simon's bittersweet play about two mismatched people learning about relationships and taking chances translated nicely if not brilliantly to the screen, although Richard Dreyfuss won an Oscar for his role as struggling actor Elliot, who sublets a New York apartment but doesn't have the heart to kick out divorced mother Paula (Mason) and her daughter (Quinn Cummings), who are already living there. Instead, the three try to coexist despite the fact that Elliot and Paula initially hate each other. Surely they'll never fall in love, will they?

The funniest moments are when Dreyfuss's actor attempts to play Richard III as an extravagantly camp homosexual in an off-Broadway play (which garners him reviews saying he was 'the Betty Boop of Stratford-upon-Avon'), and when he and Cummings get to swap some of Simon's wittiest one-liners. Mason is less successful, coming across as a bit of a pain, but all in all this is a fun comedy from Herbert Ross (who also made *Footloose* and *Steel Magnolias*).

HOPE SPRINGS (2003)

Directed by Mark Herman
Starring Colin Firth, Heather Graham, Minnie Driver

Hugh Grant seems to star in just about every British romantic comedy, but since he was busy making *Two Weeks' Notice* and *Love Actually* in 2003, his old sparring partner from *Bridget Jones*, Colin Firth, got the chance to show he can be just as funny and romantic in this comedy.

While the film isn't exactly on a comedic par with *Four Weddings And A Funeral* or *Notting Hill*, Firth makes the best of his role as Colin, who flees London for the American town of Hope (he chooses the destination because he likes the name) after his fiancée Vera (Driver) dumps him to marry someone else. Then, just as it looks as if he may have found happiness in the pretty town and romance in the form of local Mandy (Heather Graham), Vera turns up to try to win him back.

Based on the book *New Cardiff* by Charles Webb (who also wrote the novel on which *The Graduate* is based), this is warm and cute rather than laugh-out-loud hilarious, but it is pleasant enough thanks to three polished lead performances (Driver's bitchy turn is a treat) and a terrific supporting cast (including Mary Steenburgen and a woefully underused Oliver Platt) who bring the oddball townspeople to life.

HOW STELLA GOT HER GROOVE BACK (1998)

Directed by Kevin Rodney Sullivan
Starring Angela Bassett, Taye Diggs, Whoopi Goldberg

She got laid, in short. Not that there are any shortcuts taken in a women's picture that takes its time meandering from comedy to romance to weepy and back to comedy again. Based on a novel by Terry McMillan (who also wrote *Waiting To Exhale*), this is TV movie material masquerading as cinema on the back of the always superb Bassett. Her Stella is a super-successful stockbroker and single mother with everything but a love life. On a break in Jamaica with her raucous best buddy (Goldberg), she gets it on (and on and on) with a studly trainee chef (Diggs) who is about half her age. And why not?

When the holiday is over, will the romance survive? It won't if Stella's self-doubt and shocked, jealous social circle get to her. It will if she heeds the 'seize the day' urgings of Whoopi, who contracts a terminal illness and therefore is an unimpeachable source of life wisdom. The film gets by because Bassett is a stunner who brings inviolable class to potentially tasteless material, and Diggs is sexier and considerably more poised than the average callow youth.

DORIS DAY: WHO SAID NICE GIRLS FINISH LAST?

When we're talking fifties and sixties romantic comedies, the First Lady is indisputably the eternally adorable Doris Day. As fresh-faced as a milkmaid, perfectly groomed and dressed like an original Barbie, Doris was the ideal role-model for nice girls who loved pastels and didn't have the oomph to impersonate Marilyn Monroe.

The pretty blonde born Doris von Kappelhoff in 1924 trained as a dancer until she was badly injured in a car crash. She had a voice, however, and hit the road at sixteen, scoring on radio and in clubs, particularly with her youthful signature song 'Day By Day' – hence her stage name – and her first million-seller 'Sentimental Journey'. In 1948 she got her big break as the last-minute replacement for Betty Hutton in the escapade *Romance On The High Seas*. A tireless trouper, Doris notched up over a dozen films in five years, becoming America's favourite musical sweetheart playing bouncy gals, including her immortal, whip-cracking Calamity Jane. She also made occasional forays into drama, most successfully in *Young At Heart* and *Love Me Or Leave Me*, and while she was out of her element in Hitchcock's *The Man Who Knew Too Much* (1956), it gave her the enormous hit song 'Whatever Will Be Will Be (*Que Sera Sera*)'. Day was always at her best expressing exuberant joy (as in 1957's delightful *The Pajama Game*) and radiant charm (as when directed at Clark Gable in 1958's journalism rom-com *Teacher's Pet*).

At the age of thirty-five, career twilight for most leading ladies in those days, Doris was rewarded for her years as one of America's most professional stars with an Academy Award nomination for *Pillow Talk*. Its phenomenal success launched her into a succession of popular farces that epitomised the not-so-swinging first half of the sixties – for example, *Lover Come Back* (1961) and *Send Me No Flowers* (1964), both of which reunited Day with Rock Hudson, her improbable but glossy battle to retain her virtue against a persistent Cary Grant in *That Touch Of Mink* (1962), and two bubbly outings apiece with dreamboats James Garner and Rod Taylor. These were styled sex comedies but contain no overt sex, airily conveying sexual suggestion through glamour, sophisticated flirtation, crossed wires and slapstick. On screen, the thrice-married Doris remained cheerfully wholesome and pure well into her forties, forever victoriously holding out for marriage. As the decade wore on, the incongruity prompted the Hollywood wit Oscar Levant's oft-quoted boast: 'I knew Doris Day before she was a virgin!'

HOW TO LOSE A GUY IN 10 DAYS (2003)

Directed by Donald Petrie
Starring Kate Hudson, Matthew McConaughey

Andie (Hudson) is a magazine journalist writing a feature about the things women do that scare off men, who picks unsuspecting ad exec Ben (McConaughey) to try her theories out on. For the article, she's got to drive him away within ten days by doing all the crazy things women do (like becoming clingy and needy), but what she doesn't know is that Ben's got his own hidden agenda – he's just dating her to prove he is in tune with women so he can win a big jewellery ad campaign.

Yes, the premise to this romance is completely ludicrous, and there are more holes in the plot than you'd find in a piece of Swiss cheese (trust us, magazine writers don't usually go to such lengths for a story), but the couple are so likeable that you'll be won over by their onscreen charm. There's also good support from Bebe Neuwirth as Andie's editor and Robert Klein as Ben's boss.

HOW TO MARRY A MILLIONAIRE (1953)

Directed by Jean Negulesco
Starring Betty Grable, Marilyn Monroe, Lauren Bacall

This is the story of three broke models – Grable's good-natured Shatze, Monroe's near-sighted Pola and Bacall's pragmatic Loco – who stake their all on renting a plush Manhattan apartment long enough to lure and land rich husbands all round. Unfortunately, the movie falls down in its lacklustre male casting: David Wayne, Rory Calhoun and Cameron Mitchell collectively can't hold a candle to polished thirties idol William Powell, who plays the older, bona fide millionaire in the pack of suitors. What's better is the fifties fashion show, with the high-voltage trio of actresses parading scads of outfits by designer Travilla (who regularly costumed Marilyn, including her famous pink strapless number for 'Diamonds Are A Girl's Best Friend' in *Gentlemen Prefer Blondes* and the celebrated white pleated halter-neck dress in *The Seven Year Itch*). The film captures the forties' top pin-up girl, Grable, at the precise moment her successor, Monroe, was overtaking her in popularity. But there's no hint of rivalry or torch-passing in the fun interplay; all three women are smashing together.

I KNOW WHERE I'M GOING (1945)

Directed by Michael Powell and Emeric Pressburger
Starring Wendy Hiller, Roger Livesey

Nothing particularly hilarious happens in this beguiling romance, but it has a simple charm that is quite magical. Pragmatic, unsentimental Joan Webster (Hiller) is bound for a remote Scottish isle where she is to marry a wealthy man. Stranded by stormy weather, she finds the wild beauty of the coast, the welcome of warm-hearted locals, and the attractive values and life view of Livesey's penniless local laird Torquil MacNeil bringing out her good and noble romantic side. The film is unforgettable for the quiet emotional power it exerts on the heart.

IT COULD HAPPEN TO YOU (1994)

Directed by Andrew Bergman
Starring Nicolas Cage, Bridget Fonda, Rosie Perez

A likeable romantic comedy loosely based on the true story of a cop who shared his lottery winnings with a waitress (although, in real life, he was happily married and didn't fall for her as he does here). When NY cop Charlie Lang (Cage) realises he doesn't have any cash to pay diner waitress Yvonne (Fonda) a tip, he promises that if he wins the lottery, he will give her half. And – surprise, surprise – he does win: a rather impressive $4 million, and much to his screeching wife Muriel's (Perez) annoyance, he duly hands over $2 million to Yvonne.

While Perez's nasal twang is usually infuriating, here it's spot on, as Muriel goes from nagging wife to money-grabbing nightmare, suing Charlie for his half of the money while decking out his former home in the type of lurid decor that would make the House Doctor faint. Cage, in one of his more restrained performances, is sweet as Charlie, while Fonda delivers a nice turn as the waitress who can't believe that guys can sometimes be honourable, especially in light of her experiences with her ape of an ex-boyfriend, played to perfection by Stanley Tucci. Cute stuff.

IT HAPPENED ONE NIGHT (1934)

Directed by Frank Capra
Starring Clark Gable, Claudette Colbert

This seminal road movie was the first to sweep the Big Five of Oscars – for Best Picture, Direction, Actor, Actress and Screenplay – and age has not diminished its charm or light-hearted sex appeal. Gable is Peter Warne, a gruff, wisecracking, unemployed reporter. Colbert is runaway heiress Ellie Andrews, fleeing from Miami to New York to rendezvous with her fortune-hunting groom in defiance of her controlling tycoon father. Warne recognises the snooty society princess on a bus and attaches himself to her for the sensational scoop. (This plot is always a winner and recurs in *Roman Holiday*.) The delight is in the misadventures of Peter and Ellie as they traverse Depression-era America, sparring verbally all the way and encountering all types of people on their travels.

Memorably, he teaches her how to hitch-hike, how to dunk a doughnut and – in a scene that inspired the creation of Bugs Bunny, no less – how to gnaw raw carrots. The 'Walls of Jericho' scene, in which the duo virtuously divide a motel room by hanging up a blanket, famously caused undershirt sales to plummet when audiences saw Gable wasn't wearing one. What makes the film forever special is the deft, witty romantic spark between Gable's hard nut and Colbert's good sport, enjoying her first taste of real freedom.

LAWS OF ATTRACTION (2004)

Directed by Peter Howitt
Starring Julianne Moore, Pierce Brosnan

Audrey Miller (Moore) and Daniel Rafferty (Brosnan) are two high-flying Manhattan divorce lawyers who find themselves on opposite sides of the courtroom during a high-profile case in which a philandering British rock star (Michael Sheen) is attempting to end his marriage to an eccentric clothes designer (Parker Posey). Of course, the two lawyers may be at loggerheads during the day but they secretly fancy each other, and when they have to travel to Ireland to gather evidence they wind up in bed together and, after too much Irish hospitality, hitched.

Brosnan is perfect as the roguish, dishevelled male lead and Moore is a great foil as the career girl who is grudgingly attracted to him. But you can't help wishing their terrific partnership had been in a different movie, as here they are surrounded by wincingly awful clichés, two over-the-top supporting performances from Posey and Sheen, dull dialogue and, worst of all, the terrible detour to Ireland. At that point the film plummets from 'average' to 'barely watchable'.

LOVE ACTUALLY (2003)

Directed by Richard Curtis
Starring Hugh Grant, Colin Firth

Notting Hill and Four Weddings writer Curtis delivered an unashamedly sentimental movie – actually ten intertwining stories – for his directorial debut. Among the tales, there is widower Liam Neeson mourning the death of his wife while trying to connect with his son, Keira Knightley as the bride trying to befriend her husband's best man (Andrew Lincoln), and, loveliest of all, Hugh Grant as the new British prime minister who finds himself falling for his maid (Martine McCutcheon).

There are, perhaps, too many storylines thrown into the mix – one featuring Laura Linney could have been cut for starters – which detract from the funnier and more moving ones. However, the Who's Who of British acting talent – including Martin Freeman, Emma Thompson, Bill Nighy and Alan Rickman – all deliver terrific performances in a soppy, moving, unashamedly slushy but often very funny film.

MAID IN MANHATTAN (2002)

Directed by Wayne Wang
Starring Jennifer Lopez, Ralph Fiennes

A *Pretty Woman*-style vehicle for superstar Jennifer Lopez in which she stars as single mum Marisa, who works as a maid in a top New York hotel. Coerced by a pal to try on a rich-bitch guest's outfit while she's cleaning a room, Marisa meets handsome politician Christopher Marshall (Ralph Fiennes) while in the swanky get-up, and then doesn't have the heart to tell him who she really is when he starts making googly eyes at her.

It's fluffy stuff that should be avoided by anyone with an aversion to J-Lo, as she is in every scene. But it's also kind of cute, with fine support from Stanley Tucci (as Marshall's campaign manager), Natasha Richardson (as the bitch) and Bob Hoskins (as Marisa's boss). And, best of all, it's also possibly the only opportunity we'll ever get to see Fiennes in a completely unsinister, non-disfigured romantic leading man role.

MANY RIVERS TO CROSS (1955)

Directed by Roy Rowland
Starring Robert Taylor, Eleanor Parker

This raucous frontier comedy romance – a cable TV staple which is always a welcome treat on a dull afternoon – has hunky Taylor and ravishing redhead Parker equally fetching in their matching fringed buckskins and excellent raccoon hats. Love 'em and leave 'em Kentucky trapper Bushrod Gentry is forced at gunpoint to marry amorous pioneerwoman Mary Stuart Cherne and spends the rest of the film trying to escape from her, but the Indians don't call her Steppin' Woman for nothing! She's impossible to shake off, but saves his bacon more than once before he surrenders to the inevitable.

Parker's ball-of-fire Mary is a spirited miss who scrubs up a treat in her early nineteenth-century frock but she can also thread a needle with a bow and arrow, and her whip-cracking method of seeing off a Shawnee war party is priceless. This is timeless fun if you love a spunky, dogged, Calamity Jane kind of gal.

MOONSTRUCK (1987)

Directed by Norman Jewison
Starring Cher, Nicolas Cage, Vincent Gardenia, Olympia Dukakis

Self-sufficient widow Loretta Castorini (Cher), a Brooklyn book-keeper, finally agrees to marry her dull, ageing mama's boy suitor, Johnny Cammareri (Danny Aiello). But while he's at his mother's alleged deathbed in Sicily Loretta seeks out his estranged younger brother, Ronny (Cage), to invite him to the wedding – and sparks fly sky high.

This magical, Oscar-winning vehicle for Cher is a treat, full of rich characters, memorable dialogue and the atmosphere of enchantment cast over proceedings by an extraordinary full moon. Cage's passionate oddball Ronny is a brilliant creation, a one-handed baker tortured by anger, resentment and despair until his yearning for Loretta effects the healing power of love. Even the potential clichés – like Cher's make-over from greying drudge to glamour puss and the volatile Italian-American family – are handled with affectionate observation. Among many marvellous, bittersweet and joyous vignettes the high-light is a heart-stoppingly dreamy date at the opera. Funny and warm, John Patrick Shanley's script gives every character at least one life-enhancing moment, and there were Oscars for him, Cher and Dukakis.

MY MAN GODFREY (1936)

Directed by Gregory La Cava
Starring William Powell, Carole Lombard

The immortal Carole Lombard's dizzy society girl Irene finds a home-less man while on a scavenger hunt and hires him as butler to her idle-rich and completely dotty family, the Bullocks. A Harvard graduate with more intelligence and dignity than all of them put together, William Powell's Godfrey saves them from financial ruin and teaches them all valuable life lessons while vainly attempting to fend off Irene's amorous designs. One of the screwball classics, with a marvellous ensemble, it was remade in 1957 with June Allyson and David Niven, but the later film lacks the sharp Depression-era observation that makes the original so rich and witty.

NEVER BEEN KISSED (1999)

Directed by Raja Gosnell
Starring Drew Barrymore, Michael Vartan

In this enjoyable teen comedy Barrymore is Josie Geller, a bumbling twentysomething journalist who gets a chance to prove herself when her editor sends her undercover at a school to lift the lid on the nefarious activities of teenagers. A brainy geek during her own school years (her nickname was Josie Grossie), Josie sees this as the perfect opportunity to rewrite history, become a popular kid and get the kiss she never enjoyed first time round. In the process she falls for her English teacher (Vartan), who is, of course, unaware of her assignment.

It's a simple but fun romance in the *Clueless* vein, enlivened by a great central performance from the infectiously cute Barrymore, and a wacky supporting turn from *Scream*'s David Arquette as her older brother.

NINOTCHKA (1939)

Directed by Ernst Lubitsch
Starring Greta Garbo, Melvyn Douglas

A cold, austere Soviet female emissary arrives in France to remonstrate with three errant junior diplomats who have been making whoopee while they should have been reclaiming Romanov jewels. But the persistent seduction of a 'decadent capitalist' ladies' man and the equal temptation of frivolous Parisienne hats melt her socialist stoicism.

The result is a sparkling, divine comic clash of ideologies. As Ninotchka, the ravishing Garbo exploits her own icy mystique and explodes it to reveal a warm, humorous humanity. Suave Melvyn Douglas matches her all the way as her aristocratic admirer, Count Leon, and a brilliant gang of émigré character actors enliven, hinder and help the starry romantic relationship through its geopolitical travails. The satirical swipes at communism in the wicked screenplay by Billy Wilder, among others, are now showing their age, but the Westernisation of Ninotchka through *amour* is as adorable as ever. The story was charmingly transformed into the stylish musical *Silk Stockings* (1957), in which Fred Astaire's man-about-town defrosts leggy Cyd Charisse's Soviet stunner with the aid of a Cole Porter score.

NOTTING HILL (1999)

Directed by Roger Michell
Starring Hugh Grant, Julia Roberts

Written by Richard Curtis and produced by Duncan Kenworthy (the team behind *Four Weddings and a Funeral*), the premise of this romantic comedy is simple enough – huge Hollywood star Anna Scott (Roberts) walks into the Notting Hill bookshop of William (Grant), and the pair embark on a funny, frustrating and problematic romance. But *Notting Hill* becomes a classic, infectious comedy because of the chemistry between two perfectly cast stars, the seemingly endless flow of spot-on jokes, and, as in *Four Weddings*, an excellent supporting cast of characters. Rhys Ifans steals every scene in which he appears as Spike, William's gross Welsh lodger, while Tim McInnerny and Gina McKee also shine as Grant's married best friends. And London has never looked better (or cleaner).

Trivia fans should note the book Anna is reading at the end of the movie – it's *Captain Corelli's Mandolin*, which was an early plug for director Michell's next film project.

THE OBJECT OF MY AFFECTION (1998)

Directed by Nicholas Hytner
Starring Jennifer Aniston, Paul Rudd

An interesting but uneven romantic comedy in which *Friends* star Aniston plays a pregnant single girl named Nina who wants rid of the boyfriend who put the bun in her oven, so she asks her gay flatmate George (Rudd) to help her raise the child instead. Problems arise, of course, when she falls in love with him, and matters are further complicated when the father of the baby insists on being involved and George finds a new boyfriend. Unsurprisingly, with all that going on, Aniston dissolves into tears at every possible opportunity.

While the underlying theme of falling in love with someone who loves you back (but not in the way you want them to) will strike a chord with many hanky-clutching viewers, director Hytner never injects much warmth into the central relationship. In fact, the most affecting relationship in the film is between George's aging colleague

Rodney (Nigel Hawthorne) and his young friend Paul. Still, this is much better fare than Aniston's previous big-screen outing (the tedious *Picture Perfect*), and a welcome return to a leading role for *Clueless*'s Paul Rudd.

ONE FINE DAY (1996)

Directed by Michael Hoffman
Starring Michelle Pfeiffer, George Clooney, Mae Whitman, Alex D. Linz

The charms of Michelle Pfeiffer and George Clooney go a long way (and need to) in this relentlessly nice cute-a-thon of strangers who meet, dislike each other and change their minds within a hectic twelve hours. It's a catalogue of catastrophes that befall a stressed single mother and divorced father who are both childcare challenged on a critical day in their careers. He's a newspaper columnist with a little girl; she's an architect with a maddening little boy. All day they cross paths, taking turns minding the kids while the other tackles a professional crisis. So will they ever kiss before watching women everywhere go crazy? Clooney is sexy and funny with Pfeiffer, and natural with the kids. Pfeiffer plays the smart but vulnerable caregiver who is determined to cope with her usual grace. Issues of parenthood, careerism and love in the nineties are belaboured, but the end result is modestly appealing due to the leads' charisma.

ONLY YOU (1994)

Directed by Norman Jewison
Starring Marisa Tomei, Robert Downey Jr

Faith (Tomei) believes in soul mates and true love, so when a Ouija board and a carnival fortune-teller both tell her she'll meet and fall in love with a man named Damon Bradley, she believes them. However, years later, she's on the verge of marrying a nice, dull man when she takes a phone call from one of her fiancé's old friends, called – you guessed it – Damon Bradley. Damon has phoned to apologise: he can't make it to the wedding as he will be in Italy. Faith, naturally enough, ditches her plans and her poor groom and heads off to Rome with her sceptical sister (Bonnie Hunt) in tow to find him. There she meets Downey Jr's travelling shoe salesman, who may or may not be the Damon of her dreams.

The film is most enjoyable not for the rom-com antics of the two leads (and Billy Zane as another possible Damon), but for the beautiful Italian scenery as Faith's quest leads her down the coast. Jewison packs so much of the film with scenes of the sun twinkling on the Tyrrhenian Sea, gorgeous flowers and pristine architecture that you can almost imagine yourself skipping down the cobblestones in high heels just as Faith does.

OVERBOARD (1987)

Directed by Garry Marshall
Starring Goldie Hawn, Kurt Russell, Roddy McDowall

A charming, old-fashioned movie, this teams real-life couple Goldie Hawn and Kurt Russell in a 1930s-style screwball comedy. She's rich-bitch Joanna Stayton, who with imbecilic husband Grant (Edward Hermann) docks their impressive yacht at the run-down port of Elk's Cove for repairs. There she hires local widowed handyman Dean (Russell) to fit some new shoe racks on the vessel, but when she's displeased with the work she throws him overboard and refuses to pay him. It's completely understandable, then, that when Dean sees on the news that Joanna has washed up in the local hospital with amnesia (and her husband sensibly decides not to claim her), he goes to collect her, saying she is his wife and mother to his four wayward kids.

Much of the humour comes from watching this snooty woman attempt to live the rural life. Goldie has always been best in comic roles, but Kurt also shows a deft romantically comic touch and there is terrific support from Hermann, McDowall (as the Staytons' weary butler) and, best of all, Katherine Helmond as Joanna's equally over-privileged mother. Simply terrific.

MALE FANTASIES

While most romantic comedies are aimed at us girls, there are some that appeal to the more testosterone-fuelled members of the audience (usually those featuring a very hot girl and a very lucky, nerdy young man). But we can love them too, of course, so here are a few of the best male fantasy romantic comedies …

THE APARTMENT (1960)

This Billy Wilder classic has the adorable Jack Lemmon starring as life's loser C. C. Baxter. To get in with his bosses, he lets them use his apartment for afternoon and evening trysts with the girls from the typing pool, but matters are complicated when he falls for elevator operator Fran (Shirley MacLaine), who is having an affair with his smarmy boss (Fred MacMurray). It's a male fantasy because it's more about C. C.'s feelings for Fran than about hers for him, but we like it because it's hilarious, touching and just lovely.

RISKY BUSINESS (1983)

Tom Cruise's first leading role casts him as Joel, a teenager whose life unravels when his parents go away for the weekend, and he somehow manages to get involved with a hooker (Rebecca De Mornay) and, even worse, her pimp Guido (Joe Pantoliano). We love it, of course, for Tom's infamous pants, shirt and sunglasses dance around the house; guys, equally obviously, like it for Rebecca. Check out 2004's similarly themed *The Girl Next Door*, starring *24*'s Elisha Cuthbert.

SPLASH (1984)

Another movie in which the man gets the innocent, incredibly sexy and very amenable woman of his dreams. Tom Hanks is the cute guy who for some reason doesn't have women falling all over him, and Daryl Hannah is the gorgeous blonde mermaid who washes up in New York. We love it because virtually the first word Daryl utters when she learns English is 'Bloomingdales'. Sensible girl.

THE SURE THING (1985)

Four years before *When Harry Met Sally*, Rob Reiner directed this terrific romantic comedy. Stuck in a cold, North-Eastern college, Gib (John Cusack) is tempted by his pal to travel to California for the holidays to hook up with a promised 'sure thing' (a girl who won't say no). His journey there is a succession of disasters, especially as snooty Alison (Daphne Zuniga) – who refused Gib a date – is along for the ride. Every scene is funny, and Cusack has never been cuter.

MANNEQUIN (1987)

A decade before *Sex And The City*, Kim Cattrall was the department-store dummy who comes to life at night and falls for shop assistant Andrew McCarthy. Desperately silly, and with a godawful theme song ('Nothing's Gonna Stop Us Now' by Starship), this nevertheless has some kitsch charm.

CHASING AMY (1997)

Writer–director Kevin Smith's ode to love is a boy's dream come true as Ben Affleck's Holden fulfils the ultimate male fantasy by falling in love with and then 'converting' lesbian Alyssa (Joey Lauren Adams). Affleck has never been better, there's terrific support from Jason Lee as his cynical friend, and Smith's sharp, witty bloke dialogue is priceless.

THE WEDDING SINGER (1998)

Adam Sandler and Drew Barrymore's first onscreen teaming (see *50 First Dates*, above) casts him as the wedding singer and her as the waitress who often works at the same receptions. Set in the mid-eighties, it's packed with jokes about the decade that taste forgot, and even features a cameo from rocker Billy Idol.

PICTURE PERFECT (1997)

Directed by Glenn Gordon Caron
Starring Jennifer Aniston, Jay Mohr, Kevin Bacon

A flimsy romantic comedy that's little more than a vehicle for Aniston and her cleavage, which is displayed on a regular basis throughout the proceedings in a variety of low-cut numbers. She stars as an advertising exec named Kate who is not taken seriously by her boss because she's single. So, naturally, she pretends she's engaged to a guy named Nick (Jay Mohr) whom she was photographed with at a wedding. Of course, things get complicated, especially when Nick becomes a local hero and everyone at Kate's work wants to meet him.

Many of the cast are terrific – especially a slimy Kevin Bacon as the office Lothario and Illeana Douglas as Kate's work pal – but, despite Aniston's spot-on comic timing, she can't disguise the fact that she's saddled with a dull leading man in Mohr. Perhaps with better casting this could have been a really good romantic comedy instead of an average one.

PILLOW TALK (1959)

Directed by Michael Gordon
Starring Rock Hudson, Doris Day, Tony Randall, Thelma Ritter

The imaginative, influential and still delightful first teaming of Doris Day with Rock Hudson is a definitive romantic comedy which won an Oscar for screenwriters Stanley Shapiro and Maurice Ricklin. Although undeniably coy, it's beautifully constructed, timed, played … and dressed. Day's Manhattan interior decorator Jan is pert and chic, but her one big headache (unimaginable now) is having to share a phone line with Hudson's womanising songwriter Brad. He has the archetypal swinging bachelor's pad and is forever tying up the line with his hectic seduction arrangements. Jan's complaints infuriate Brad, who's convinced she's a drab, eavesdropping spinster, unaware she's a babe and being pursued by Randall's dapper millionaire, Jonathan. In a neat reveal we discover Brad and Jonathan are buddies. When Brad realises Jonathan's Jan is his telephone harpy he resolves to put one over on her and introduces himself to her as courtly Texan country boy Rex Stetson.

Much of the subsequent fun and romantic confusion come from voiceovers of their contrasting perceptions. He's gloating, 'Five or six dates ought to do it!' while she's sighing, 'It's so nice to meet a man you can trust!' This is whipped into the perfect light and frothy confection with lustrous stars, mildly saucy split-screen scenes, physical comedy, cynical one-liners from Day's hard-drinking maid Ritter, Randall's man-about-town laments ('As many times as I'll be married I'll never understand women'), and good visual jokes (vengeful Jan's transformation of Brad's apartment from playboy *moderne* to tacky bordello). Its style and tone inspired a stream of sixties 'sex' comedies, and forty-odd years later was paid lavish homage in *Down With Love*.

PRETTY IN PINK (1986)

Directed by Howard Deutch
Starring Molly Ringwald, Andrew McCarthy, James Spader, Jon Cryer

If you were a teenage girl in the eighties, chances are you have seen this John Hughes-produced teen classic at least twice. You probably own the soundtrack, too, which includes OMD's 'If You Leave' and, of course, the Psychedelic Furs' theme tune.

Andie (Ringwald) is a poor gal from the wrong side of the tracks who lives with her dad and makes her own, eclectic clothes. Her best pal is Duckie (Cryer), but while he quietly lusts after her, she only has eyes for rich kid Blaine (McCarthy). Will Blaine ask her out, despite the attitude of his snobby friend (Spader)? Will it be Blaine or Duckie who takes Andie to the prom? And, most importantly, when Andie's pal Iona (Annie Potts) gives Andie her nice old pink prom dress, why does Andie cut it up and turn it into something even more hideous than what she started with?

Legend has it that the ending was changed after test audiences hated who Andie originally ended up with, but whether you're a Duckie or a Blaine fan this is still a cute slice of adolescent angst with terrific performances, especially from Ringwald (who later found it hard to shed her teen image), Cryer and Potts.

PRETTY WOMAN (1990)

Directed by Garry Marshall
Starring Julia Roberts, Richard Gere

Ah, yes, we are sure many a young hooker believes that a millionaire who looks like Richard Gere is going to sweep her off her feet as happens in this preposterous – but completely loveable – romantic comedy.

The original idea for this film was actually a serious look at prostitution in Los Angeles, based on a script called *$3000*. Of course, the end result is far more frivolous than that, as business mogul Edward Lewis (Gere, looking dishy in his first big hit since the mid-eighties) gets lost downtown and seeks directions to his Beverly Hills hotel from hooker-with-a-heart-of-gold Vivian (Roberts). If there was a shred of realism in this movie, she would have mugged him and stolen his swish sports car, but here she sensibly offers to take him there herself for a small fee. Then she charms him into hiring her for the week to be his 'beck and call girl', accompanying him to posh society events and hanging around for cosy nights in the penthouse suite.

The film works best as a comedy when Roberts shares the screen with the terrific supporting cast: bitchy shop assistants who refuse to serve her, the hotel's helpful concierge (Hector Elizondo) and Edward's sleazy lawyer Philip (Jason Alexander). Her charm glitters from every frame (and garnered her a Best Actress Oscar nomination) and, while neither she nor Gere can hide the fact that this *Pygmalion*-meets-*Cinderella* tale is highly improbable, the beautiful stars are completely convincing as two lonely people falling in love. Just yummy.

SABRINA (1954)

Directed by Billy Wilder
Starring Humphrey Bogart, Audrey Hepburn, William Holden

This classic, funny *Cinderella* variation of a chauffeur's daughter being wooed in the interests of his business by workaholic tycoon Linus Larrabee (Bogart), who doesn't want her embroiled with his younger playboy brother David (Holden), is elevated by Audrey Hepburn at her most enchanting. It lingers in the collective consciousness for the iconic style marriage of Hepburn and designer Hubert de Givenchy – *that* little black dress, *those* capri pants with ballet pumps, defining fifties chic – not for the pairing of Hepburn with a tired, disinterested looking Bogey. We'd all take Holden's feckless dreamboat she's had a crush on all her life, imagining we could change him, now wouldn't we?

The overlong 1995 remake starring Harrison Ford, Julia Ormond and, making a surprisingly creditable film debut, former talk-show host Greg Kinnear, benefits from Ford being happier in the Linus role and delivering his quips with dry relish. Ormond is pretty, sweet and vulnerable as the gawky teen transformed by her sojourn in Paris, but doomed to be judged merely adequate compared to Hepburn.

SHE'S ALL THAT (1999)

Directed by Robert Iscove
Starring Freddie Prinze Jr, Rachel Leigh Cook

A slight but enjoyable teen comedy that's another twist on *Pygmalion*, *She's All That* follows popular kid Zach (Prinze) after he's dumped by his vacuous girlfriend Taylor (Jodi Lynn O'Keefe) a few weeks before the prom. Instead of moping, Zack rises to his pal's challenge of finding the most unlikely (in other words, ugly) girl in school and turning her into a prom queen. Of course, the girl he picks, Laney (Cook), may *look* dowdy but she's an absolute stunner underneath, and it doesn't take much (glasses off; make-up on) to turn her into a babe.

Naturally, Laney will find out she's the subject of a bet and Zack will discover there's more to life than popularity – but with some likeable performances (including supporting roles for Usher, Lil' Kim, Anna Paquin and Kieran Culkin), it's fun nonetheless.

SHIRLEY VALENTINE (1989)

Directed by Lewis Gilbert
Starring Pauline Collins, Tom Conti, Julia McKenzie, Alison Steadman

Liverpudlian mousewife Shirley Valentine Bradshaw (Oscar nominee Pauline Collins) talks to the walls (and the camera) while she's serving up everything with chips for her uninterested husband Joe (Bernard Hill). Shirley's monologues on life, love and domestic servitude are basically feminist stand-up comedy: screenwriter Willy Russell adapted his one-woman stage show that had been a *tour de force* for Collins. On screen her *bons mots* are uneven, from witty to frankly banal. When her pal Jane (Steadman) wins a trip for two to Greece, however, things open

up in seductive Mykonos, where Shirley gleefully succumbs to the caricature Greek waiter Costas (Conti). He may or may not be Mr Right;
what's more important is that 'St Joan of the kitchen sink' has seized
the day, reclaimed her life, and so on. A gaggle of British actresses,
including Joanna Lumley and Sylvia Syms, add to the fun, which is
firmly aimed at frustrated fortysomethings.

THE SHOP AROUND THE CORNER (1940)

Directed by Ernst Lubitsch
Starring Margaret Sullavan, James Stewart, Frank Morgan

This all-time great romance – adapted from the European period play
Parfumerie – is so cute and lovely that it's been revamped into a 1949
musical vehicle for Judy Garland (*In The Good Old Summertime*),
updated into sixties play *She Loves Me* and been given a modern, inter-
net-age reworking by Nora Ephron for 1998's *You've Got Mail*. None of
the later versions improved on the original film, though, which boasts
the fabled 'Lubitsch Touch', mingling charm, amusing conflict, bittersweet anticipation and absolute joy.

Snippy Budapest shopgirl Klara Novak (the radiant Sullavan) gets off
on the wrong foot with assistant manager Alfred Kralik (Stewart), both
unaware they are lonely-heart pen pals conducting a romantic corre-
spondence via post office boxes. The development is sublimely
excruciating, even when Alfred arrives for their long-awaited rendezvous and realises his sweetheart's identity. After recovering from the
shock, instead of owning up he lets her think her soulmate has stood
her up, prolonging her (and our) agony of suspense. Vivid supporting
characters add to the dramedy, and the Christmas Eve climax
enshrined the holiday as the perfect cinematic setting for romance.

SIXTEEN CANDLES (1984)

Directed by John Hughes
Starring Molly Ringwald, Anthony Michael Hall

The first of writer–director John Hughes's teen comedies, this was also
eighties teen queen Molly Ringwald's first starring role. She's Saman-

tha, and it's her sixteenth birthday, but it's anything but sweet. The school geek (Hall) is ardently pursuing her, the boy she has a crush on is the most popular guy in school, her sister's getting married to an Italian hood, and the rest of her family have forgotten it's her birthday.

While it's not as well known as *Pretty In Pink* or *The Breakfast Club,* *Sixteen Candles* was considered ground-breaking in 1984, when most teen movies involved female students bouncing around in tight tops for teenage boys' amusement (*Porky's, Spring Break,* etc). This film showed what it was like to be a teenager from the awkward girl's perspective, and, despite some broader, coarser moments (the foreign-exchange student's name is 'Long Duk Dong'), it remains a sweet tale in which the girl may even get her Prince Charming at the end. Note: the cute kid from *Kramer Versus Kramer,* Justin Henry, is certainly not cute anymore as Sam's nightmare brother.

SLEEPLESS IN SEATTLE (1993)

Directed by Nora Ephron
Starring Tom Hanks, Meg Ryan

This may be the warm, fuzzy movie to end all warm, fuzzy movies. Annie (Ryan), lonely and depressed despite having a cute fiancé (Bill Pullman), hears a young widower from Seattle named Sam (Tom Hanks) on a phone-in radio show talking about how much he loved his wife. His monologue – 'I'm gonna get out of bed every morning … breathe in and out all day long. Then, after a while, I won't have to remind myself to get out of bed every morning and breathe in and out' – prompts hundreds of women to write to him and makes Annie wonder whether he could be her destiny. The only trouble is, she has to find him first, and she spends the rest of the movie doing just that.

The fact that this is a romantic comedy in which the two protagonists don't meet until the final scene is a bit of a first, but we get plenty of humour leading up to that point, as Sam reluctantly re-enters the dating scene, much to the disgust of his precocious young son Jonah (Ross Malinger) and Annie debates modern romance with her cynical pal Becky (Rosie O'Donnell) over a viewing of classic weepy *An Affair to Remember.* It's far mushier than Ephron's script for *When Harry Met Sally* of course, so it's one to watch with just the girls, a good supply of tissues (you'll need them during Hanks's radio lament for his wife) and a big box of chocolates.

SLIDING DOORS (1998)

Directed by Peter Howitt
Starring Gwyneth Paltrow, John Hannah, John Lynch, Jeanne Tripplehorn

Ex-*Bread* TV star Howitt debuted as a writer–director with this ingenious concept movie in which the delicious Gwyneth Paltrow's character, Helen, lives out two alternative plots from the moment she catches/misses a London tube train. One Helen gets chatted up by John Hannah's charming apparent Mr Right, arrives home to catch her cheating boyfriend with his other woman, and moves on from there. Helen Number Two does *not* meet Hannah's James, gets home too late to discover she's being two-timed, and heads downhill from there. The contrivance is by turns engaging and annoying, although we doff our hats to the continuity team and the actors for keeping their places in what must have been an unusually confusing shoot. And the unattractiveness of Lynch and Tripplehorn's duplicitous supporting characters sours the proceedings too much. But by the time the parallel stories work their way to a surprising, dovetailing conclusion, the romantically inclined have to go with the picture's touchingly stubborn insistence that you are fated to be with one right person and, somehow, some day, somewhere, he'll find you. Awwww.

SOME KIND OF WONDERFUL (1987)

Directed by Howard Deutch
Starring Eric Stoltz, Mary Stuart Masterson, Lea Thompson

The enduring appeal to women of producer–screenwriter John Hughes's eighties teen comedies lies in the humanity of his characters. His adolescent outcasts speak to our insecure inner ugly ducklings, and their emotional growing pains remind us what it feels like having dreams and trying to realise potential. In this gender-reversal of *Pretty In Pink* the odd ones out at school – named after the members of the Rolling Stones, incidentally – are Mary Stuart Masterson's tomboy Watts and her best friend, aspiring artist Keith (Eric Stoltz), who has a crush on the It Girl Amanda (Lea Thompson). The characters and the situation (who is going with whom to the big dance) are standard, but the development is sweet. And Masterson is captivating, so caring and selfless that she presents herself as chauffeur for her secret love's dream date with the sexpot. We also appreciate that the boy is, of course, too thick to grasp the real feelings of his confidante. Naturally, everyone learns a little more about life and love, and they do so in an affecting way.

SOMETHING'S GOTTA GIVE (2003)

Directed by Nancy Meyers
Starring Jack Nicholson, Diane Keaton, Keanu Reeves

Jack Nicholson and Diane Keaton prove you can still be sexy – and *have* sex – when you're over sixty in this romantic comedy. He's Harry, the loveable, ageing rogue who dates much younger women; she's Erica, the wound-too-tight mother of his latest girlfriend (Amanda Peet). When Harry keels over while at Erica's beach house, hunky local doctor Julian (Reeves) suggests that Harry should stay put while he recuperates, and soon there's a romantic triangle as Erica finds herself pursued by both dishy Julian and her craggy house guest. (While she finds this a tough choice, we all know that in the real world every sane woman would go for Keanu, especially as he looks even sexier than usual in scrubs.)

Keaton garnered an Oscar nomination for her performance – perhaps as much for her bravery in doing a nude scene as for anything else – and both Nicholson and Reeves are warm and charming. Like Nicholson himself, the movie is a bit flabby around the middle, but it's often very funny and is a welcome, all-too-rare example of a rom-com not aimed at teenagers or thirtysomethings.

SWEET HOME ALABAMA (2002)

Directed by Andy Tennant
Starring Reese Witherspoon, Josh Lucas, Patrick Dempsey

There's one small problem when dashing mayor's son Andrew (Dempsey) proposes to successful fashion designer Melanie (Witherspoon): he doesn't know she's already married. It seems Melanie ran away from her childhood sweetheart Jake (Lucas) and her small, poor Alabama home town seven years ago to make a name for herself in New York, and the couple never divorced. So Melanie has to go home, get the divorce papers signed and return to Manhattan before Andrew discovers her dilemma, and before his disapproving mother (Candice Bergen) learns the secrets of Melanie's past.

This hugely successful comedy suffers from the same flaw as *The Wedding Planner* (see page 61): for Melanie to find happiness, one of the men in her life has to be dumped, which isn't very romantic … or very comical. The reason the film still works – and why it was such a big hit – is Witherspoon, who delivers a classy, sassy and very watchable performance.

TAMMY AND THE BACHELOR (1957)

Directed by Joseph Pevney
Starring Debbie Reynolds, Walter Brennan, Leslie Nielsen

This endearing charmer is as corny as Kansas, but it's mighty sweet corn. Tirelessly cheerful, sunny Debbie Reynolds is barefoot backwoods tomboy Tammy, who lives with her kind, incorrigible, moonshine-making grandpa (Brennan). When handsome, rich sophisticate Peter Brent (Nielsen) crashes his plane into their swamp, Tammy saves his life and nurses him back to health. After Grandpa is incarcerated, Tammy is taken in by the Brent swells at their mansion, where she dispenses country home cooking and homespun wisdom. Naturally, it's only when a decrepit auntie turns Tammy into a belle that Peter realises she's not a funny little girl any more and duly sheds the obligatory snooty fiancée. Unpretentious and very cute, this notched up a hit theme tune for Debbie, two sequels starring Sandra Dee, and a TV spin-off series.

THEY MIGHT BE GIANTS (1971)

Directed by Anthony Harvey
Starring George C. Scott, Joanne Woodward

Ever since his wife died, Justin (Scott) has believed he is Sherlock

Holmes. His brother wants him committed, but then Justin meets a psychiatrist named Dr Muriel Watson (Woodward), who wants to study him. He, inevitably, decides she is *the* Dr Watson, Holmes's famous sidekick. Part romantic comedy, as Watson becomes drawn to Justin/Holmes, part drama, as Holmes attempts to find his arch nemesis Moriarty, this is a delightful, quirky adventure that muses on perception and reality. Does it really matter that Justin thinks he is someone else?

THE TRUTH ABOUT CATS AND DOGS (1996)

Directed by Michael Lehmann
Starring Uma Thurman, Janeane Garofalo, Ben Chaplin

This girlie variation on the *Cyrano de Bergerac* theme is very funny, warm-hearted *and* sharp, capped with a trio of winning performances. Although the title refers to a phone-in pet-advice show, it also plays nicely on the eternal differences between men and women. Abby (Garofalo) is short, dark and cuddly. Her friend Noelle (Thurman) is tall, blonde and thin. Abby is a smart, witty vet who dispenses sense and sassibility on her radio show. Noelle is a model. Guess who all the boys go for?

When photographer Brian (Chaplin) rings Abby's show with a dog crisis he is seduced by her personality and attempts to meet her. But he mistakes her babe buddy for the voice of his dreams, and the women sustain the deception to prove that what you see is not always what you get. This creates all manner of complications of the heart, friendship and self-esteem – ranging from the wrong gal forced to give a turtle a rectal examination to an awfully embarrassing phone-sex marathon. Former DJ Audrey Wells's screenplay is full of telling observations on what, whom and why we love, as well as great lines (nearly all for Garofalo) and great business for Thurman's half-starved, dizzy waif. There's plenty to make you purr.

TWENTIETH CENTURY (1934)

Directed by Howard Hawks
Starring John Barrymore, Carole Lombard, Walter Connolly, Roscoe Karns

Egocentric theatre luminary Oscar Jaffe (the great matinée idol of his generation, John Barrymore) discovers Carole Lombard's pretty Mildred, renames her Lily, and makes her a star. Weary of his abuse and megalomania, she heads for Hollywood and becomes a superstar. Some years later, his career on the ropes, Jaffe encounters her on the Twentieth Century Limited cross-country train and stops at nothing to win her/trick her/woo her back to Broadway – most memorably with a monstrously hammy, phoney death scene that has her tearfully grabbing to sign the contract he's foxily clutching. A wonderful, timeless screenplay (later adapted into the stage musical *On The Twentieth Century*) and brilliant performances (including Connolly and Karns as Barrymore's sidekicks) make for peerless screwball hilarity.

TWO WEEKS' NOTICE (2002)

Directed by Marc Lawrence
Starring Hugh Grant, Sandra Bullock

Apparently, Hugh and Sandra spent a couple of years looking for a joint project before this comedy romance came along. It's a shame they didn't wait a bit longer. This isn't awful, but you can't help wishing that the first pairing of one of America's top comic actresses and Britain's most suave comic actor was, well, funnier and more romantic.

Grant plays George Wade, a wealthy British businessman in New York who treats his lawyer Lucy (Bullock) as a servant/nanny. It's only when she finally hands in her notice that the pair realise they may have feelings for each other. Unfortunately, as there's nothing on screen to suggest that George and Lucy have harboured any emotion for each other apart from mild amusement, the romantic conclusion seems a bit odd. That said, there are some laughs, mainly from Hugh, who can now do the adorable upper-class Englishman routine in his sleep, and good support from David Haig as his brother and Alicia Witt as Lucy's rival at work.

ROMANTIC COMEDY CLICHÉS

1 The ugly duckling none of the boys notices gets her hair done/removes her glasses/has a make-over and (gasp!) turns out to be beautiful ...

2 The best male friend who dispenses advice to our lovelorn heroine should be gay ...

3 While half of the rom-com couple knows they are in love almost instantly, the other realises the same thing only five minutes before the end of the movie. They then have to run through the streets (it's New Year's Eve/Christmas Eve/Valentine's Day, so all the cabs are taken) to declare their love before it's too late ...

4 The main character in a romantic comedy always has a gorgeous, spacious, beautifully designed apartment (perfect for two). Even in New York. And, if it is in Paris, the apartment invariably has a view of the Eiffel Tower ...

5 The heroine has a fiancé from Dullsville who has to be let down. Alternatively, the hero has a domineering, snotty or uptight fiancée who has to be fobbed off on to someone equally unpleasant, but usually rich. (Note the contrast here with dramas, in which fiancées can be nice; but, if they are, they die in the first reel.)

UNDER THE TUSCAN SUN (2003)

Directed by Audrey Wells
Starring Diane Lane

This isn't exactly meeting Mr Right – the romance that newly divorced fortysomething Frances (Lane) has is with a house, a rundown villa she first spots on a ten-day sightseeing trip to Tuscany.

Based on Frances Mayes's memoirs of buying a house in Tuscany (the romantic subplot of Frances meeting a hunky Italian is entirely fictional), the film evolves like an episode of *Wish You Were Here* mixed with *A Year In Provence* as our floatily-dressed heroine struggles to renovate the property with the help of local builders who don't speak English. An excuse for miles of lingering footage of the beautiful Tuscan scenery, this comedy is packed with more clichés that a pizza has pieces of pepperoni, but features a warm performance from Lane, and a quirky one from Lindsay Duncan as her free-spirited English ex-pat pal. We guarantee you'll be booking a holiday to Italy before the end credits have rolled.

WHAT WOMEN WANT (2000)

Directed by Nancy Meyers
Starring Mel Gibson, Helen Hunt, Marisa Tomei, Lauren Holly, Alan Alda

Macho advertising exec Nick (Gibson) loses a promotion to more deserving rival Darcy (Hunt) because of his offensive sexism. When a freak accident gives him the ability to hear women's thoughts he misuses the gift for seduction and career sabotage, but finds himself inadvertently becoming a better, more understanding man.

Whatever else women may want – world peace, a cure for cancer, no-calorie chocolate – clearly Mel still features high on some wish lists. And he is utterly delightful even as a womanising boozehound and unrepentant arsehole unwittingly heading towards redemption. So it is no surprise that this sporadically cute, screwy rom-com was a smash hit, despite sloppy direction, the frankly non-flammable pairing of Gibson with a colourless Hunt, and a screenplay littered with highly predictable inconsequentials. It is, after all, a great little comic concept in a society that keeps buying *Men Are From Mars, Women Are From Venus*. When Nick takes his 'problem' to a shrink (Bette Midler in an uncredited cameo), she shrieks, 'Just think of the possibilities! You can rule the world!' Unfortunately, the women in Nick's world don't have much on their minds save for the state of their thighs and the location of their G-spot to guide him on his journey from oaf into Mr Sensitive. However, an unexpected highlight is the spectacle of Mel dancing like Astaire around his apartment to Sinatra crooning 'I Won't Dance': a bit of movie magic that we definitely want.

WHAT'S UP, DOC? (1972)

Directed by Peter Bogdanovich
Starring Barbra Streisand, Ryan O'Neal, Madeline Kahn, Kenneth Mars

A musicologists' convention in a San Francisco hotel brings together academics, thieves and spies who get all hot and bothered mixing up four identical suitcases – one stuffed with a socialite's stolen jewels, one containing top-secret government documents, one holding igneous rock samples and one just packed with clothes. The stage is set for Peter Bogdanovich's modern farce, an elaborate homage to *Bringing Up Baby* and the screwball comedy canon of thirties Hollywood. Streisand, in one of her funniest, most likeable performances, is mischievous researcher Judy Maxwell, who develops an obsession for absent-minded professor Howard Bannister (O'Neal) despite the presence of his domineering fiancée Eunice (a hilarious Madeline Kahn). The frantic efforts to win him amid baggage burglaries and zany chases produce delightful mayhem which pauses just long enough for Babs to sing a smashing version of Cole Porter's 'You're The Top'.

WHERE THE BOYS ARE (1960)

Directed by Henry Levin
Starring Dolores Hart, George Hamilton, Jim Hutton, Paula Prentiss

It's spring break, which means teenagers from across America descend on Fort Lauderdale, Florida, for a vacation packed with fun, sun, parties and, well, you know. The film follows four gal pals – Hart, Prentiss, Yvette Mimieux and Connie Francis (who sang the film's hit theme song) – as they look for boys and try to find love. It's fluffy stuff that's occasionally overly moralistic: the one gal prepared to do *anything* to snag an Ivy League boyfriend ends up wandering down the highway in a daze and is hit by a car, which seems a slightly drastic turn of events in what is essentially a sex comedy.

This was the first onscreen teaming of Paula Prentiss and Jim Hutton, who went on to appear together in a series of sixties comedies, including *Bachelor In Paradise* and *The Horizontal Lieutenant*. (Note: There was a dreadful 1984 remake of *Where The Boys Are* co-starring Hamilton's and Rod Stewart's ex-wife Alana, that should be avoided at all costs.)

WHILE YOU WERE SLEEPING (1995)

Directed by Jon Turtletaub
Starring Sandra Bullock, Bill Pullman, Peter Gallagher

An absolutely adorable romantic comedy. Lucy (Bullock) is a hopeless romantic who's in love with Peter (Gallagher), a man she sees every day from the ticket booth where she works, but whom she has never spoken to. One day, though, she saves his life after he falls on the tracks, and then stays with him at the hospital while he lies in a coma, only to find herself being mistaken for his fiancée when his family comes to visit. She goes along with the charade, but her situation becomes even more complicated when Peter's brother Jack (Pullman) appears, and she starts to fall for him instead.

Bullock proved to be a delightful and funny leading lady, while Bill Pullman, who had almost gone unnoticed in everything from *Sleepless In Seattle* to *The Accidental Tourist*, finally got the chance to play a sexy, charismatic leading man (and he sure is sexy!). Turtletaub's direction is spot on, the supporting cast (including Peter Boyle, Jack Warden and Glynis Johns) are superb, and the hilarious script knocks spots off anything written by Nora Ephron.

WIMBLEDON (2004)

Directed by Richard Loncraine
Starring Paul Bettany, Kirsten Dunst

Tennis movies are usually execrable, and the only other one involving romance was the dire *Players* (1979), starring Ali McGraw and Dean Paul Martin. But this sporting romantic comedy gets a few more balls over the net.

Peter Colt (Bettany) is a British tennis player whose best years are behind him. He's received a wild-card entry into Wimbledon, and no one – including himself – expects him to get much further than the first round. Then he meets hot, young American prospect Lizzie Bradbury (Dunst), who has a chance at the Ladies' Singles title, and Peter's game begins to improve. Could he make it to the final? And have he and Lizzie found love, despite her well-meaning father's (Sam Neill) interference?

It's all pretty predictable stuff that has far too much tennis and not enough laughs (Jon Favereau as Peter's ruthless agent and Bernard Hill and Eleanor Bron as Peter's parents deserve more screen time), but it's worth a look simply for the novelty of seeing a British player walking on to Centre Court on finals day.

YOU'VE GOT MAIL (1998)

Directed by Nora Ephron
Starring Meg Ryan, Tom Hanks

Sleepless In Seattle stars Ryan and Hanks reunite with director Nora Ephron for another cute romantic comedy, a nineties update of *The Shop Around The Corner*.

Thirtysomething New Yorkers Kathleen (Ryan) and Joe (Hanks) have been communicating (and falling in love) by email, unaware of each other's identity. And little does corner-bookshop owner Kathleen know that the man with whom she's sharing her innermost thoughts is the owner of a mega-bookstore chain, which is opening a branch near by that will drive her out of business.

The conclusion is obvious from the get-go, but thanks to the chemistry between the leads, getting there isn't as painful as it could have been. More annoying is Ephron's sledgehammer use of an overbearing soundtrack which signals (and spoils) every emotion and plot twist before it arrives.

WEDDINGS

BETSY'S WEDDING (1990)

Directed by Alan Alda
Starring Alan Alda, Molly Ringwald, Madeline Kahn, Joe Pesci

When Eddie (Alda) and Lola's (Kahn) daughter Betsy (Ringwald) prepares to tie the knot with a spoiled rich kid (Dylan Walsh), they and their extended family are sucked into the emotional cyclone that is the extravagant modern wedding. Construction workers, blue-blooded financiers and the Mafia collide as soon-to-be in-laws, while the ceremony and reception have to accommodate Catholics, Jews and vegetarians. Inspired by his own daughter's wedding, writer–director Alda's funny, truthful social comedy pays less attention to Ringwald's battle of the bulge with her dress than to the fraught relationships, financial blight, intense nerves and random couplings that spring up around the big event. The highlight is the bride's policewoman sister Connie (Ally Sheedy) falling for hunky young mafioso Stevie Dee (Anthony LaPaglia), a subplot that steals the show.

FATHER OF THE BRIDE (1991)

Directed by Charles Shyer
Starring Steve Martin, Diane Keaton

There have been two versions of this idea. In the charming 1950 original Spencer Tracy was the harassed father, Joan Bennett his wife and Elizabeth Taylor their soon-to-be-wed daughter. Then there was this surprisingly watchable remake that's essentially a vehicle for Steve Martin's crazed family-man persona, first seen in *Parenthood*.

George Banks (Martin) isn't happy. His daughter Annie has just announced she wants to get married, and his wife Nina (Keaton) is determined to pull out all the stops for her little girl. Then, just as George realises the happy day is going to bring him to the brink of bankruptcy, Annie decides she doesn't like her fiancé after all …

The comedy centres on the chaos of the big day itself, with George going quietly insane as hilarious wedding co-ordinator Franck (Martin Short) runs riot through his house, installing marquees, removing doors and planting fake geese in the garden. Although sentimentality rears its ugly head a little too often, there are some great laughs to be had as one disaster follows another. A weak sequel, *Father Of The Bride Part II*, followed in 1995, while the 1950 original was followed in 1951 by *Father's Little Dividend*.

FOUR WEDDINGS AND A FUNERAL (1993)

Directed by Mike Newell
Starring Hugh Grant, Andie MacDowell, Kristin Scott Thomas, Simon Callow

In this modern fairytale the charming prince (called Charles, possibly coincidentally) is an archetypal English, upper-middle-class twitterer who struggles with fears of intimacy and commitment before babbling a stammering declaration of love. Hugh Grant is Charles, in this, the definitive British rom-com of the nineties. It became the top-grossing British film of all time, and set forth the winning formula for writer Richard Curtis's subsequent films: a sophisticated but boyish, bemused, self-mocking Grant; an American leading lady for the US market; witty or wacky chums; and a romance fraught with mistiming and misunderstandings.

Wedding Number One is introductory, allowing Charles to give a great best man's speech and be lovestruck at first sight of MacDowell's Carrie, who engineers their one-night stand despite his diffidence. The plot thickens at Wedding Number Two, at which Charles is harassed by old girlfriends, discovers his dream girl has become engaged and gets trapped in the newlyweds' bedroom. A month later Charles runs into Carrie for the film's sole non-ceremonial social encounter, the justly famous, David Cassidy quoting, 'I think I love you' highlight. Another month on sees Carrie's rites and Gareth's (Callow) demise, an occasion devised to provide a pause for sober reflection before another leap of ten months takes us to the climax: Charles's own nuptials.

This is comedy that knits together superior sitcom sketches, so blithely unencumbered by back story or reason that it doesn't bear reality checks but still works. How did this disparate group – including the *soignée*, acerbic Scott Thomas, the flamboyant Callow and the younger, kooky Charlotte Coleman – become inseparable? Does anybody have a job? Does nobody have parents? Why would Carrie marry the pompous, aged politician, and why would she invite these people she scarcely knows to her wedding? And can anyone make sense of the final conversation in the rain? That this good-natured jape transcends its blatant contrivance to cajole and continually amuse is testimony to Curtis's hilarious take on insecure thirtysomethings and the delightful performances.

MURIEL'S WEDDING (1994)

Directed by P. J. Hogan
Starring Toni Collette, Rachel Griffiths

This is an original, very funny and affecting tale about learning to love yourself. Small-town lump Muriel (Collette) obsesses over ABBA songs and bridal gowns, dreaming of a wedding that will wow all the pretty, popular girls and ghastly relatives who have belittled her. But how is she ever going to snare a groom? The story of how she wreaks her revenge on everyone, makes a splash in Sydney and in the process finds herself is a frequently side-splitting odyssey of misbehaviour, outlandish clothes, high kitsch, two weddings and a funeral.

Muriel's all-too-common delusion is that finding a husband will turn her life around, a fixation by turns hilarious and deeply pitiful in writer–director Hogan's smart mix of bizarre satire and warm sympathy for life's little people. She is a classic underdog, a person seemingly with nothing going for her, who learns how to make herself the heroine of her own story.

And Toni Collette as Muriel is sensational, progressing from the girl no one would want to be seen dead with into a new woman, as surprisingly dark and sobering twists in the quirky plot transform goofy grotesques into real human beings.

MY BEST FRIEND'S WEDDING (1997)

Directed by P. J. Hogan
Starring Julia Roberts, Dermot Mulroney, Rupert Everett, Cameron Diaz

A career-resurrecting movie at the time for both star Julia Roberts and comic foil Rupert Everett, this has the former *Pretty Woman* starring as someone who (for once) may not get the guy. Following a pledge made years before that they would marry each other if they were both still single at twenty-eight, Julianne (Roberts) is shocked to discover her old friend Michael (Mulroney) is about to get hitched. Determined to break up his wedding to the beautiful Kimmy (Diaz) and win him for herself, Julianne sets about disrupting the big day with the reluctant help of her gay pal George (a wonderful, hilarious Everett).

This is a frothy, incredibly girlie affair that isn't completely satisfying as director Hogan (*Muriel's Wedding*) can't quite decide where our sympathies should lie – with the poor bride who may get jilted or with ditzy, I-just-want-someone-to-love-me Julianne. And matters are not helped by the casting of Mulroney – surely a guy no woman in her right mind would be fighting over in the first place. Roberts goes through the motions, and in the end it's Diaz – especially good in an embarrassing karaoke scene – and the deliciously camp Everett (don't miss his rendition of 'Say A Little Prayer' – it's a scream) who make this romantic comedy fun.

MY BIG FAT GREEK WEDDING (2002)

Directed by Joel Zwick
Starring Nia Vardalos, John Corbett

The story behind this mega hit is almost as enjoyable as what unfolds on the screen. American-Greek actress Vardalos, tired of being offered one-dimensional ethnic roles in films and TV, wrote about her life and performed it as a one-woman stage show in Los Angeles. Rita Wilson – Tom Hanks's wife – saw the show and suggested to her husband that they finance a film version. This is the result, and it went on to become the most successful independent film of all time (only losing that title when Mel Gibson's *The Passion Of The Christ* was released two years later).

It's easy to see why it was such a hit. Like *Moonstruck* over a decade earlier, it's the tale of a supposedly on-the-shelf girl who finds true love amid a warm, eccentric supporting cast of family and friends. Vardalos, who wrote the script, stars as Toula, a young Greek woman who works in her father Gus's (Michael Constantine) restaurant and still lives at home. When she meets handsome teacher Ian (*Sex And The City's* Corbett), she falls in love but has to face the wrath of her proud father, who always imagined – if Toula got married at all! – that she would end up with a nice Greek boy.

Toula and Ian's courtship is sweet – and surprisingly chaste for a twenty-first-century film – while the laughs come from her extended Greek family and the manic wedding preparations that should bring a knowing smile to the face of every former bride.

THE PHILADELPHIA STORY (1940)

Directed by George Cukor
Starring Cary Grant, Katharine Hepburn, James Stewart

Aloof, disdainful society girl Tracy Lord (Hepburn) is anticipating her tasteful wedding to an uptight square when her disreputable ex-husband C. K. Dexter Haven (Grant) crashes the party to dispense wit and comic wisdom. Even worse, Dexter has brought a tabloid team along to cover the society event of the season, the deal being they won't expose Tracy's errant father's sexcapades. Hijinks with heart abound as the misunderstood, vulnerable bride-to-be is desperate to love and be loved for the woman she wants to be.

Arguably the most sparkling gem of the entire romantic comedy genre, Philip Barry's Broadway hit was written for Hepburn, and she owned the rights (a gift from billionaire admirer Howard Hughes). The film version provided her with a triumphant Hollywood comeback, winning over audiences by playing on her own 'impossible' image. The entire ensemble is perfect – Virginia Weidler as kid sister Dinah is a hoot. But abetted by her most sympathetic director and her most charming regular leading man, Cary Grant (who wisely opted to play laidback playboy Dexter, giving James Stewart his Oscar-winning opportunity as the cynical reporter in need of a hug, Macaulay 'Mike' Connor), Hepburn's class shines radiantly through a perfectly timed, masterly mélange of slapstick, farce, romantic confusion and posh frocks.

Hepburn's sophisticated prancing between Grant and Stewart is more classic, snappy screwball, but *High Society*, the 1956 musical remake with Cole Porter songs, is also a 'swellegant' party that never ceases to delight, either (see review, p235).

RUNAWAY BRIDE (1999)

Directed by Garry Marshall
Starring Julia Roberts, Richard Gere

Roberts is the bride-to-be who has already left three grooms at the altar and Gere is the cynical New York reporter sent to see if she'll finally go through with it this time in this extremely girlie (there are enough bridal moments to put the fear of God into even the most commitment-friendly male viewer) romantic comedy which reunited the stars of *Pretty Woman* with the film's director, Garry Marshall.

It took a decade for the stars to find a project they wanted to work on together, and while the film isn't exactly packed with razor-sharp humour, it's nicely done, with the usual winning lead performances and a supporting cast which includes Joan Cusack and Marshall-favourite Hector Elizondo (the scene-stealing concierge in *Pretty Woman*). Most of the laughs come from Gere's chats with the unfortunate men Roberts has dumped over the years: the wonderful Donal Logue is one former fiancé who was so devastated that he turned to the priesthood. Julia has little to do except look lovely in a series of wedding gowns and flash that brilliant smile of hers, which, of course, she does perfectly.

THE WEDDING PLANNER (2001)

Directed by Adam Shankman
Starring Jennifer Lopez, Matthew McConaughey, Bridgette Wilson

Wedding co-ordinator Mary (Lopez) thinks she has found the man of her dreams when she meets hunky doctor Steve (McConaughey, whose yumminess is a good enough reason to watch this), but it turns out he's the groom at the next ceremony she's planning. Should she try to stop his nuptials or realise it's not nice to steal someone else's fiancé, and settle for family friend Massimo (Justin Chambers) instead? That's the conundrum that stymies this romantic comedy from the outset.

While J-Lo does all the patented romantic comedy moves – laughing coquettishly, crying beautifully without her mascara running in such an expert fashion Meg Ryan would be proud – she can't hide the film's big flaw. The essential rule of romantic comedy is that we must want the leading characters to live happily ever after. For that to happen here, Mary must crush Massimo, who has been in love with her since they were kids, while Steve has to dump likeable fiancée Fran (Wilson), whom he must love to have proposed to her in the first place. The fact that Mary and Steve's flirtation continues after she realises he's engaged, *and* that she remains his wedding planner, shifts all our sympathy to the bride-to-be and makes us even less accepting of any Mary/Steve romantic denouement. Add in an ill-advised and awkward 'comedy' scene involving a statue's broken-off penis and some super-glue, and you begin to wonder whether this is one wedding movie that should have been left at the altar.

THE AWFUL TRUTH (1937)

Directed by Leo McCarey
Starring Irene Dunne, Cary Grant, Ralph Bellamy, Molly Lamont

This sublime, classic screwball comedy romance that won McCarey the Best Director Oscar sees sophisticates Lucy (Dunne) and Jerry (Grant) suspecting each other of infidelity and, lamenting their loss of trust, filing for divorce. By the time Lucy realises she doesn't want to marry her new country-boy fiancé (Bellamy), Jerry is about to tie the knot with Lamont's heiress. A series of hectic set pieces eventually halts the wedding plans and undoes the divorce proceedings. Of four screen versions of this story (including a fun 1953 musical, *Let's Do It Again*, starring Jane Wyman and Ray Milland), this is unmatched for chemistry, inspiration and brilliant timing. They really don't make 'em like this any more, which is a crying shame.

BAREFOOT IN THE PARK (1967)

Directed by Gene Saks
Starring Robert Redford, Jane Fonda, Charles Boyer, Mildred Natwick

This film version of Neil Simon's hit play about newlywed New Yorkers (with Robert Redford and Mildred Natwick reprising their Broadway roles) is forever charming, even without the benefit of much in the way of a plot. After a hot honeymoon the kooky, high-spirited, wildly emotional Corie (Fonda) and her tidy, square lawyer hubby Paul (Redford) move into a tiny, horrid flat up five flights of stairs to begin their married life. Cue trials and tribulations: the young couple are quickly rubbing each other up the wrong way, their personality clashes aggravated by a colourful old roué of a neighbour (Boyer) and mediated by Corie's wise old mother (Natwick). Can Corie calm down? Will Paul learn to unwind? That would be yes, as when Redford lets his hair down in a hilarious drunken scene. Gorgeous stars and a bubbly mood keep this fun.

THE EGG AND I (1947)

Directed by Chester Erskine
Starring Claudette Colbert, Fred MacMurray, Marjorie Main, Percy Kilbride

Based on Betty MacDonald's autobiographical bestseller, this is a cute comic treat in which reality and worse things hit city girl Colbert squarely in her pretty face after she marries chicken farmer MacMurray. While mucking in on the farmyard, hardship, poultry crises and colourful neighbours seem to be vying to drive her back to the life she knew. Good thing she's full of love and good-humoured pluck! The film not only inspired a TV series but nine lucrative spin-off comedies centring on Main and Kilbride's folksy characters, raucous Ma and timid Pa Kettle.

FOOLS RUSH IN (1997)

Directed by Andy Tennant
Starring Matthew Perry, Salma Hayek

Friends star Matthew Perry got his first big-screen leading role in this amiable romantic comedy, playing preppy (some would even say Chandler-esque) New Yorker Alex, whose life is turned upside down after he has a one-night stand on a business trip to Las Vegas. Three months later, luscious Mexican girl Isabel (Hayek) tracks him down to let him know that their night of passion has resulted in pregnancy, and they rashly agree to get married. Of course, this would be a very short film if they then lived happily ever after, so the pair suffer various mis-understandings, the problems of radically different lifestyles, and disapproving families before they inevitably find true happiness.

There are, then, no surprises, but Perry's comic timing is just as perfect as when he's in Central Perk, and with an agreeable lack of slop-piness the film zips along quite merrily. Perry and the sultry Hayek have great onscreen chemistry, and they are ably supported by Jill Clayburgh, Jon Tenney and Matthew's real-life dad John Bennett Perry (playing, of course, Alex's dad).

GREEN CARD (1990)

Directed by Peter Weir
Starring Gérard Depardieu, Andie MacDowell

When earnest health-freak Manhattan gardener Brontë (MacDowell) gets a shot at her dream apartment with a rooftop greenhouse, she learns it's a 'couples only' crib. Meanwhile, carefree slob and bon vivant Georges (Départdieu) needs to marry an American to get legal residency. An arranged wedding and relieved parting swiftly ensue, but the immigration authorities are rightly suspicious and the at-odds duo have to live together for a crash course in partnership. Gee, do you think they'll warm to each other before he gets deported?

Yes, it's improbable and cutely contrived. It's also a soupçon more sophisticated than the average rom-com, with the great French star Depardieu madly delightful – cellulite and all – in his English-language debut. The comic highlight has to be the insistence of Brontë's snobbish friends that he play something for them at a party (he's allegedly a composer), and while we know hostilities will eventually turn into affection, the affair bounds along with irresistible *joie de vivre*.

JUST MARRIED (2003)

Directed by Shawn Levy
Starring Ashton Kutcher, Brittany Murphy

Everything that can go wrong does go wrong on Tom (Kutcher) and Sarah's (Murphy) honeymoon. Crumbling *pensions*, snowdrifts, mad hoteliers and Sarah's persistent ex-boyfriend all conspire to turn what should be a romantic getaway into a disaster that threatens to end their marriage almost before it's started. It's like *Planes, Trains And Automobiles* with wedding bells as the not-so-happy couple bicker around Europe, and thanks to fun turns from Kutcher and Murphy – who were real-life partners at the time – it's enjoyable to watch them bounce from one unlikely mishap to another. Christian Kane, as Tom's rival for

Sarah's hand, and David Rasche and Veronica Cartwright, as her disapproving parents, shine in the supporting cast.

MARRIED TO THE MOB (1988)

Directed by Jonathan Demme
Starring Michelle Pfeiffer, Alec Baldwin, Matthew Modine, Dean Stockwell

One of director Demme's best movies – and certainly his funniest – gave Michelle Pfeiffer one of her most enjoyable screen roles. She plays Angela DeMarco, a mob wife tired of husband Frank 'The Cucumber's (Baldwin) hot-blooded ways, and none too pleased with living in a house where all the furniture has fallen off the back of a truck. She wants a divorce, he tells her she'll never escape the mob, but an opportunity arises when he is killed. With son in tow, Angela heads for Long Island, unaware a besotted mafioso (Stockwell) and a dogged government agent (Modine) are watching her every move.

Baldwin, Stockwell and especially Pfeiffer are superb, but special mention should also go to Mercedes Ruehl, who will bring tears of laughter to your eyes as Stockwell's heavily hair-sprayed, manic missus. The only let-down is the casting of bland Modine as the good guy/romantic interest. He's less sexy than the Cucumber's corpse.

MR WONDERFUL (1993)

Directed by Anthony Minghella
Starring Matt Dillon, Annabella Sciorra, Mary-Louise Parker, William Hurt

This has a terrifically funny if improbable notion. Matt Dillon's divorced electrician Gus has an opportunity to realise his dream job by buying into a bowling alley with a few of his buddies. But he can't raise the funds because he's paying alimony to his ex-wife Leonora (Sciorra). She is attending university, chasing after her own dreams, and needs Gus's cash for her tuition. His bright idea is to find her a new husband to support her, someone so perfect she can't resist. That she sportingly agrees to the blind dates he arranges is a tad mystifying since she's already having an affair with an arrogant professor (Hurt). However, the scheme really falls down because Gus doesn't have a clue about what constitutes a wonderful man: each and every blind date is a non-starter. And we are never in any doubt that childhood sweethearts Gus and Leonora will prove to be made for each other. His hapless new girlfriend (Parker) is too clearly a ruse. Attractive, expressive leads make it modestly appealing.

SHE'S HAVING A BABY (1988)

Directed by John Hughes
Starring Kevin Bacon, Elizabeth McGovern

The great Kevin Bacon's nervous Jake and Elizabeth McGovern's serene Kristy are madly in love when they have their classic wedding. In the years that follow they still love each other, but domestic routine, with its pressures of mortgage, work and in-laws, capped with the anxiety of pregnancy, sees the less mature Jake feeling trapped and fantasising wildly about life's missed opportunities.

Told from the young, panic-prone husband's point of view, writer–producer–director John Hughes's partly autobiographical 'what happened next' tale shows what it takes to be a perfect couple. Funny, poignant and honest, with appealing stars, the film isn't hurt by having the then smouldering, young Alec Baldwin as Jake's envious, devilish 'best friend' – wisely predicting, 'You'll be happy; you just won't know it.' Like Hughes's earlier teen flicks, this has a cool, eighties time-capsule soundtrack.

SOMETHING TO TALK ABOUT (1995)

Directed by Lasse Hallström
Starring Julia Roberts, Dennis Quaid, Robert Duvall, Gena Rowlands

Julia Roberts's Grace has had her entire life mapped out for her, first by her parents (Duvall and Rowlands) and then by her husband Eddie (Quaid). But when she catches him cheating she surprises them all by taking control of her destiny. Her emancipation from wronged and angry victim to rebellious heroine exposing other women's follies certainly sets the town talking, while also inconveniencing her traditionalist parents' and husband's shared interests in the family stud farm (the metaphor of women as brood mares is no coincidence). Callie '*Thelma And Louise*' Khouri's script has its moments, particularly when the women unite to question paternalistic authority and revolt. But the Roberts–Quaid relationship loses focus amid the antics of her colourful family (especially sister Kyra Sedgwick), who collectively steal the show. Nevertheless, there are smart and funny points about 'being bred to have low expectations', and Roberts plays one of her more rounded characters.

SWEET HEARTS DANCE (1988)

Directed by Robert Greenwald
Starring Don Johnson, Susan Sarandon, Jeff Daniels, Elizabeth Perkins

Life after the 'happily ever after' is the hardest part as Wiley Boon (Johnson) knows all too well. His marriage to high-school sweetheart, Sandra (Sarandon) is crumbling just as his best friend Sam (Daniels) embarks on a romance with a teacher (Perkins). Unfortunately, Wiley has no idea why he feels the need to leave his wife and move into a mobile home: he's just confused, unhappy, perhaps suffering from a mid-life crisis or a need for freedom. His inner turmoil (superbly portrayed by Johnson, better known as slick Sonny Crockett in *Miami Vice*) and friendship with Sam are at the heart of this modest, sweet film that explores both the good and the bad sides of love, often with humour and always with charm. The insightful script is by Ernest Thompson, who also penned the family weepy *On Golden Pond*.

Chapter 2: *Life's a Bitch*
Romantic Dramas and Melodramas

If there is a single defining chick flick, it has to be a sob story. Girlies are quintessentially women's pictures. You might be able to drag a man into a romantic comedy, but threaten him with a tear jerker that promises heartache and histrionics and you risk a scrap outside the box office (unless, of course, your partner is in touch with his feminine side or the picture has a spot of warfare or an afflicted athlete in it). On the other hand, there are few simple pleasures much more fun than lolling on the sofa with like-minded girlfriends, sharing chocolates and a box of tissues while Deborah Kerr vows she will walk again, Bette Davis climbs the stairs to die quietly, Barbra Streisand smooths back Robert Redford's stray lock of hair for the last time or Audrey Hepburn runs around in the rain searching for Cat.

Classically, a drama is a story of human conflict. Really good, compelling drama touches on the nature and the mystery of the human condition. This is true whether it's *Hamlet*, *The Godfather* or what used to be regarded as the trivial end of the dramatic spectrum, women's domestic drama. A women's drama may not be a love story but it gives a woman's point of view on birth, death and getting on with the living in between. Life's a bitch, and then you die. Women's pictures emerged early, epitomised by the films that made Mary Pickford the first female screen superstar who wasn't a sex goddess and was idolised by female fans. Pickford projected a charming, pure and innocent image, and kept her chin up in films like *Her Darkest Hour* (1911), *Tess Of The Storm Country* (1915) and *Pollyanna* (1920).

Dramatic true stories and biographical films about exceptional women – Amelia Earhart, Annie Oakley, Marie Curie, queens, singers, novelists – have always had inspirational appeal. There are almost as many pictures 'based on' or 'inspired by' a true story as there are films adapted from novels. It's hard to think of many that are comedies.

Almost invariably they involve a reversal of fortune, the rapture of a once-in-a-lifetime love affair (1955's *Love Is A Many-Splendored Thing*) or triumphs over adversity. And there are the ever-popular pictures about death, disease, disability and other hardships – many of them also based on true stories. Real-life disease-of-the-week movies made for TV have become staples of afternoon schedules (as have tales of beleaguered mothers, battered wives, rape victims and husband killers). But a big, well-done movie sob story can still pull us into cinemas to share the pain of cancer (*Terms Of Endearment*, *Shadowlands*) or love amid catastrophe (*Titanic*).

Melodrama – a word from the Greek for song and drama because in the theatrical tradition it incorporated songs or orchestral music, making it a perfect form of entertainment for cinema – is now the genre of exaggerated or sensationalised drama. It is usually romantic, always emotional, sometimes violent. A melodrama is not supposed to be realistic but reality heightened, and it may manage to effect a happy ending, however improbably. The romantic melodrama reached its pinnacle in vehicles for Hollywood's queen bees of the thirties (Greta Garbo in *Camille*, Barbara Stanwyck in *The Bitter Tea Of General Yen*) and forties, and was a particularly rich genre for actresses and audiences past their bloom of youth. Bette Davis (*Now Voyager*, etc.) and Joan Crawford (who is one of the most unbearable stars with her unsympathetic, hard-faced persona, but we'll concede that the length of her career suggests some women related to her) were at their best as women beset by torment, loss, lovelessness and regret in stories of hearts despairing, crimes punished and sins redeemed. The lush, teary melodramas of the fifties did the same for Jane Wyman and Lana Turner (after her transition from sexpot to mother). In the more modern films we still don't empathise most with the glamorous siren but with those women who could be people we know (albeit more beautiful versions): Joanne Woodward, Judy Davis, Debra Winger, Sally Field, Meryl Streep. We've chosen an assortment of women's pictures featuring trials, tribulations and tears with an emphasis on romance and self-realisation that we find particularly entertaining: the sumptuous, the wonderfully trashy and the delicately poignant. The things women experience and suffer in these pictures are things we understand. They are a pleasure because we can be happy nothing so desperate has happened to us, or because something like that *has* happened to us, or because we're simply fascinated to see what women do/ought to do/should not do/are capable of doing in tragic or merely trying situations.

NOW VOYAGER (1942)

Directed by Irving Rapper
Starring Bette Davis, Paul Henreid, Claude Rains

Of the classic forties melodramas in which Bette Davis suffered and surmounted heartbreaking, gut-wrenching emotional travails, the warm sea of soapsuds that is *Now Voyager* – classily adapted from a bestseller by Olive Higgins Prouty – is the most splendid wallow of all. Davis enjoyed her biggest hit and received her fifth consecutive Academy Award nomination for her deeply touching, empathetic performance, as self-sacrificing Bostonian heiress Charlotte Vale. She is the repressed, overweight, frumpy spinster who's understandably having an overdue nervous breakdown after a life of cruel domination by her selfish mother (Gladys Cooper). After a spell under psychiatrist Rains's gentle and understanding care, Charlotte takes control of her life, gets her eyebrows plucked and finds some happiness.

The first great rush of satisfaction comes on seeing her physical transformation, revealed with breathtaking chic as she embarks, svelte, perfectly made up and exquisitely dressed, on a cruise to South America. This is the pre-eminent make-over movie! But Charlotte is still a fearful bundle of insecurities and low self-esteem, travelling under another woman's name and wearing her borrowed finery. (A nice touch is the note pinned to one designer dainty telling her what goes well with what.) The slow-burning pleasure comes from Charlotte's inner voyage to self-confidence and her dignified assertiveness back in Boston after a shipboard romance and delicate relationship with architect Jerry (Henreid, the suavest lighter of a lady's cigarette in screen history), whose own ugly-duckling daughter Charlotte determines to transform into a swan.

This is one of the great 'if only' pieces, so unhappily but irretrievably married Jerry strews his crumbs of love to Charlotte while she finds her joy in giving. Now if only she could have had some wild sex as well it would really be a morale booster, but selflessness rules here and as Charlotte unforgettably tells Jerry: 'Don't let's ask for the moon. We have the stars.'

TITANIC (1997)

Directed by James Cameron
Starring Leonardo DiCaprio, Kate Winslet

Director James Cameron – best known for action movies like *Aliens* and *The Terminator* – seemed an unlikely helmsman for this shamelessly romantic love story. But as the romance takes place aboard the most famous sinking ship in history, this epic, effects-filled film isn't just about two people finding each other on the high seas; it's also an impressive reconstruction of what happened on the night when *Titanic* fatefully collided with an iceberg in 1912.

It remains one of the most expensive productions of all time. The budget was reported to have exceeded $200 million, some of which went on a 775-foot replica of the ship, and the hiring of the original companies that had provided the real *Titanic*'s furnishings, to make sure every plate, fork and chandelier was a perfect replica. But it was money well spent, as the film won an impressive eleven Academy Awards (the most since *Ben-Hur*).

If we're being mean, the movie is like a combination of *The Poseidon Adventure* and *The Love Boat*, as romance and high-seas disaster are delivered in equal measure. But while the boys are impressed by the jaw-dropping effects as *Titanic* strikes the iceberg, splits and is slowly swallowed by the water, girls fell in love with the Mills & Boon-style plot.

Rose (Winslet) is a young socialite on course to marry dastardly Cal (Billy Zane) when they dock in New York. But she falls for steerage passenger Jack (DiCaprio) en route and shares a night of steamy passion just before the ship sinks to its watery grave. Will they both survive? Will the movie have a happy ending or will we all be weeping into our tissues throughout the final hour and a half? We're sure you know the answer, as Jack and Rose's tragic, forbidden romance gives the movie its memorable heart.

A blockbuster if ever there was one, the movie made a superstar/teen heart-throb of Leonardo DiCaprio, boasted one of the biggest-selling soundtracks of all time (and a worldwide number-one hit for Celine Dion with the theme 'My Heart Will Go On') and, in terms of production size and sheer epic scale, remains one of the most impressive productions of all time.

ALICE DOESN'T LIVE HERE ANY MORE (1974)

Directed by Martin Scorsese
Starring Ellen Burstyn, Kris Kristofferson

Scorsese's only contemporary film aimed at women reflected the impact of the women's movement on disenfranchised housewives embarking on personal odysseys of self-discovery. When brow-beaten, newly widowed Alice (Ellen Burstyn in a wonderful, Oscar-winning performance) and her young son are left penniless she has to find a way to make a living. In the moving, realistically drawn process she finds herself, friendship and a chance for happiness. Heading West, she plucks up the courage to revive youthful aspirations, reject brutish attentions (from Harvey Keitel) and find understanding in the form of kind Kris Kristofferson. Alice's stint as a waitress also gives her the salty support of Diane Ladd (and inspired a spin-off TV series). Young Jodie Foster has an amusing role, and the keen-eyed might spot little Laura Dern (Ladd's daughter) in the diner.

ALL THAT HEAVEN ALLOWS (1955)

Directed by Douglas Sirk
Starring Jane Wyman, Rock Hudson

Douglas Sirk was a leftist filmmaker who fled from Nazi Germany to Hollywood, where his European sophistication and formal visual style elevated absurd, maudlin stories into deliriously entertaining, heightened-reality, multiple-hanky domestic dramas. This, one of Sirk's most memorable glossy melodramas, tackled obsessions with class and age in the older woman–younger man relationship. Affluent widow Wyman is touched by wise and gentle – not to mention hunky – gardener and woodsman Hudson, whose admiration for her grows into heart-warming love. But her selfish, grown children and her hypocritical country-club set react with shock, outrage and malice, forcing her into a shamed solitude (in which she is supposed to be content watching TV and arranging flowers). Fortunately a fateful catastrophe occurs to make her see what's important.

Beautifully dressed, *All That Heaven Allows* is still making its influence felt in films as diverse as *Far From Heaven* and the French farce

Eight Women, and did so in Rainer Werner Fassbinder's poignant German working-class melodrama of 1974, *Ali: Fear Eats the Soul*, which is essentially an earthier re-make.

BED OF ROSES (1996)

Directed by Michael Goldenberg
Starring Christian Slater, Mary Stuart Masterson

Masterson is the career girl wooed by complete stranger/sensitive new man Slater in this romantic comedy-drama from writer and first-time director Michael Goldenberg. But the path of true love never runs smooth. She's got so much emotional baggage that she's deeply suspicious of L-O-V-E, while he thinks the way to win her heart is to shower her with the finest cuts from the florist's he handily owns.

Both Slater and Masterson are winning and Pamela Segall is a scream as Masterson's best friend, but none of them can hide the fact that they're dealing with an extremely slight script and a cliché-filled plot. Sadly, the very funny moments and cutely mushy bits serve only to hint at what a good movie this could have been in a more experienced writer–director's hands. It's sweet in places, but completely unbelievable, as we all know that in the real world no woman in her right mind would turn down Christian Slater and an endless supply of flowers.

THE BITTER TEA OF GENERAL YEN (1933)

Directed by Frank Capra
Starring Barbara Stanwyck, Nils Asther

Ah, forbidden love. It's the stuff of sex fantasy, but when a missionary's prim bride-to-be (Stanwyck) is abducted by a Chinese warlord (Asther) within minutes of arriving in turbulent Shanghai, her fearful fascination comes to the fore. The drama is handled with delicacy amid treachery and moody intimations of doom in this superlative oldie. Capra conveys subtle and exotic eroticism a world away from the sentimental small-town Americana with which he is associated. He was also instrumental in shaping Stanwyck's career, and she rewarded him here with a beautiful intensity. Nowadays, of course, it would be totally unacceptable to have a Swedish actor made up as Chinese, but Asther, a suave and accomplished star of silent films, plays the part with swoonsome sensitivity.

BREAKFAST AT TIFFANY'S (1961)

Directed by Blake Edwards
Starring Audrey Hepburn, George Peppard

What do men know? They usually think this charming, romantic adaptation of Truman Capote's novella is a comedy. But while it possesses an abundance of arch and broad amusements, women are more alive to the vulnerability and pathos in Audrey Hepburn's enchanting Holly Golightly, the country girl attempting to reinvent herself as a bohemian Manhattan sophisticate, dreamily staring into the glittering jeweller's window of the title. The treatment softens the sordid: Holly lives on 'gifts' from middle-aged men, and her intrigued neighbour (George Peppard's frustrated writer) has a mortifying interlude as a kept man. But what stick in the mind are the iconic images of Audrey with upswept hair and cigarette holder wearing her little black Givenchy dress, and blithe Holly dropping her pose to bare real emotion and accept love when she's lost the cat, Cat. Lovely.

THE BRIDGES OF MADISON COUNTY (1995)

Directed by Clint Eastwood
Starring Clint Eastwood, Meryl Streep

Robert James Waller's bestselling novel of middle-aged romance seemed an odd choice for tough guy actor–director Eastwood (and, indeed, Robert Redford was originally touted for the lead). But Eastwood's elegant performance matches his assured direction in a film that could have become sloppily sentimental in the wrong hands.

Instead, this story of a brief, but life-changing, affair is genuinely moving. Lonely Iowan housewife Francesca (Streep, looking atypically plump and dowdy) meets *National Geographic* photographer Robert (Eastwood) while he is on assignment, photographing the bridges on rural roads near her home. The pair are drawn to each other over a few days while her husband is away, but they are both aware that their romance will end the moment he returns. Filled with subtle, warm moments and some sweet dialogue – get the hankies out when Robert tells Francesca, 'It seems right now that all I've ever done in my life is making my way here to you' – this is one of those rare girlie movies that seem to move men, too. That can't be a bad thing, can it?

BRIEF ENCOUNTER (1945)

Directed by David Lean
Starring Celia Johnson, Trevor Howard

Perfectly pleasant and ordinary housewife Laura (Celia Johnson) and doctor Alec (Trevor Howard) meet in a railway station and fall in love within a few innocent outings remembered in flashback. Both are married and suffer torment from their furtive rendezvous for a few meals and movies. One of the all-time great British films and universally beloved tear jerkers may be dated: in the unconsummation of its romance, in the decency and guilt of the characters (which would now be called inhibition and repression), and in Johnson's quite horrendous hat. But the intensity and pain of this delicate affair is almost unbearable. Director Lean, adapting Noël Coward's one-act play *Still Life*, brought distinctive craft to the sad story, enveloping the couple in sound, lighting and music (Rachmaninov) to perfection. Crucially, the two stars are marvellous, expressing longing and loss with the merest touches and subtle but heartbreaking expressions.

CASABLANCA (1943)

Directed by Michael Curtiz
Starring Humphrey Bogart, Ingrid Bergman, Paul Henreid, Claude Rains

'Of all the gin joints in all the world' – the woman who broke his heart walks into a man's bar with her husband, instigating the most popular love triangle of all time. The problems of American exile Rick (Bogart), his lost love Ilsa (Bergman) and her Resistance leader husband Victor Laszlo (Henreid) are compounded by wartime intrigue in a dangerous, mysterious locale. A magical model of romantic melodrama, *Casablanca* received Academy Awards for Best Picture, Director and Screenplay, and it remains a universal favourite. Absolutely everything in the film's combination of patriotic wartime sentiment, desperate refugees and star-crossed lovers works beautifully, even after all this time has gone by.

The plot is a political thriller in which Bogart plays embittered, enigmatic but idealistic and ultimately heroic Rick with immortal style. And smart, cynical humour brings the supporting cast and background figures to extraordinarily vivid life. But it is the self-sacrificing love story that is the soul of the film, from the Paris flashback sequences – virtually a film within the film that reveals Rick's love affair with Ilsa and his heartache – to the immortal parting at the airport. Director Michael Curtiz unified all *Casablanca*'s elements and creative talents into its fast-paced, atmospheric, utterly captivating whole, a world in miniature in which basic human desires, sins and impulses, for bad and good, are enveloped in glamour, suspense and style.

CORRINA, CORRINA (1994)

Directed by Jessie Nelson
Starring Ray Liotta, Whoopi Goldberg

Previously known for playing psychos and cokeheads in *Something Wild* and *GoodFellas*, Ray Liotta made a radical, albeit temporary, career shift with this romantic tale. He plays a widower named Manny who is trying to raise his young daughter during the Eisenhower era. Just when things are looking really bleak, into his life steps Corrina (Goldberg), a college-educated black woman who has had to resort to cleaning and nannying jobs to make ends meet. It's all a bit predictable as Manny's too-cute-to-be-true daughter (Tina Majorino) tries to push Corrina and her dad together, but the lead performers are engaging, and the film eventually says more about the problems of interracial romance than movies like Spike Lee's *Jungle Fever* ever did.

CRAZY/BEAUTIFUL (2001)

Directed by John Stockwell
Starring Kirsten Dunst, Jay Hernandez

Dunst is the rich girl who falls for a Latino boy (Hernandez) from the wrong side of the tracks in this teen drama, but the twist here is that he is the hard-working, straight arrow getting up at the crack of dawn to travel across LA on a bus to a good school, while she is the mad, rebellious one – Daddy pays no attention, Mummy isn't around and Stepmum doesn't understand her – brimming over with trouble and teen angst.

Yes, as well as being a twenty-first-century teen romance (complete with a cool pop/rock soundtrack) this is an 'issues' movie, one of those films packed with messages ('drugs are bad'; 'studying is good') that usually star an escapee from *Beverly Hills 90210* and fill a hole in the schedules on Saturday afternoon TV. But while the script occasionally thuds with melodrama, the performances are terrific, notably from Hernandez and Bruce Davison (as Dunst's Congressman father), who give classy, moving turns. And Dunst herself – complete with addict pale face – storms through each scene with such ferocity that she instantly announces herself as one of the best young actors in Hollywood.

A CRY IN THE DARK (1988)

Directed by Fred Schepisi
Starring Meryl Streep, Sam Neill

Family grief, public outrage and a trial by media rage around Lindy and Michael Chamberlain (Streep and Neill) in this realistically distressing, true account of Australia's notorious dingo-ate-my-baby case.

After baby Azaria disappeared on a family camping trip, national horror soon turned to malice. The Chamberlains' religion (they were Seventh Day Adventists) led to them being branded as sinister, kooky cultists. Worse, Lindy's refusal or inability to weep for the cameras saw her perceived by the public as cold, unlikeable and (probably) guilty of infanticide. Writer–director Schepisi cleverly intercuts the Chamberlains' private tragedy with the gossip grapevine coiling around the nation, culminating in Lindy being tried and convicted before giving birth to another child in prison. Three and a half years later she was finally exonerated, when the baby's bloodied clothing was found, corroborating Lindy's version of events. This is thought-provoking on important contemporary issues, while Streep and Neill are both heartbreaking.

DANCE WITH A STRANGER (1985)

Directed by Mike Newell
Starring Miranda Richardson, Rupert Everett

Richardson, in her first movie role, gives a *tour de force* performance as Ruth Ellis, the last woman to be executed in Britain, in this fascinating and atmospheric *film noir*. A bleach-blonde hostess at a nightclub/brothel in fifties London, living in a small flat with her young son, desperate to make a better life for them, Ellis falls for younger aristocrat David Blakely (Everett). Their tempestuous relationship – her increasing possessiveness, his immaturity and wavering affections – ends when she shoots him outside a Hampstead pub. While we know the outcome from the beginning, Everett's and Richardson's superb performances still draw us in to this moody, gripping tale of love, jealousy, obsession and tragedy.

ENEMIES, A LOVE STORY (1989)

Directed by Paul Mazursky
Starring Anjelica Huston, Ron Silver, Lena Olin, Margaret Sophie Stein

Silver's Herman Broder, an intellectual Jewish Holocaust survivor, leads a complicated post-war life in New York. He is married to the devoted Polish peasant (Stein) who hid him from the Nazis, but he is in love with the flamboyant Russian Masha (Olin), whose passionate exuberance thinly disguises her raw pain and guilt from cheating death in Dachau. Just when Herman thinks he can't be run more ragged his supposedly dead first wife Tamara (Huston), who miraculously escaped a death camp herself, tracks him down.

Adapted from a novel by Isaac Bashevis Singer, this builds like classic farce as Herman reels between women, bewildered acquaintances and suspicious relatives. But the full horror of what happened to these people in the past gradually emerges. Humour, sex, despair and magnificent performances combine for a tragicomedy of unusual depth, a vivid testimony of life and hope for those tough enough to go on living.

FALLING IN LOVE (1984)

Directed by Ulu Grosbard
Starring Robert De Niro, Meryl Streep

This romance, starring two of the most acclaimed actors of the late twentieth century (appearing together for the first time since *The Deer Hunter*), is surprisingly low key. Streep doesn't attempt one of her accents, and De Niro didn't gain twenty pounds or lock himself away for a month in preparation for his role. Instead, they give subtle performances as Molly and Frank, who meet by chance in New York and strike up a friendship that leads to love. Trouble is, both of them are married to other people.

While the script is standard fare – and the ending a little too neat and nice – Streep and De Niro are affecting as the couple who are drawn to each other while not wanting to hurt anyone else. There's also a little light-hearted relief from Harvey Keitel and Dianne Wiest as their friends.

FAR FROM HEAVEN (2002)

Directed by Todd Haynes
Starring Julianne Moore, Dennis Quaid, Dennis Haysbert

In fifties suburbia the Whitakers (Moore and Quaid) are the perfect, popular couple. But the façade crumbles when Cathy discovers Frank's homosexual double life and begins a poignant relationship with black gardener Raymond (Haysbert). Tongues start wagging and social ruin looms.

Anyone familiar with plush fifties Technicolor melodramas will immediately recognise Todd Haynes's main inspirations for this bold experiment as *All That Heaven Allows* and *Imitation Of Life*. Another was Max Ophuls's noir classic of domesticity blown apart by dark secrets, *The Reckless Moment*. With remarkable confidence and subtlety Haynes has tackled topics never addressed openly in their day – homosexuality, racism, the oppression of women – along with the hard drinking, malice, home-wrecking and tearful sacrifice that were the stuff of vintage women's pictures. On one level, the end result is a fabulous reinterpretation of a genre by a witty filmmaker with hip credentials and connections (including Steven Soderbergh and George Clooney as executive producers). But when you get into it, the emotional experiences of the film's distant lives are timeless and powerfully affecting.

The actors are magnificent, and the picture looks good enough to eat, with exquisite art direction, costumes and cinematography all keyed to a specific and sumptuous colour palette. But the style serves the content, an unhappy observation of human nature that leaves you in no doubt that complacency over issues of sex and race is as naive now as it was then.

GIRL, INTERRUPTED (1999)

Directed by James Mangold
Starring Winona Ryder, Angelina Jolie, Clea DuVall, Brittany Murphy

Although this psychodrama might be dubbed *One Flew Over The Cuckoo's Nest: The Girlie Version*, it's still a credible, sobering yet lively movie. Susanna Kaysen's autobiography – a cult chicks' book if ever there was one – centres on her incarceration in a psychiatric hospital in the sixties, when her parents tired of coping with her endless adolescent rebellion. This film adaptation assembled a cast of talented young actresses to flesh out the stock characters of mental-ward patients as seen through the eyes of Ryder's depressed-not-crazy Susanna. Ryder co-produced the film as a moving vehicle for herself, and older actresses – including Vanessa Redgrave and Whoopi Goldberg – add weight. But it's Angelina Jolie's vibrant, Oscar-winning performance as the 'McMurphy' of the piece, a fiery habitual escapee subdued with shock treatment, that blazes with star power.

BETTE DAVIS (1908–89)

'You know what they'll write on my tombstone?' Bette Davis once cracked. '"She did it the hard way."' Certainly, the heroines she portrayed in an electrifying body of work did it the hard way. No beauty, Davis was never a favourite with men. But women adored the romantic melodramas in which she shone, admired her as a feisty, independent woman of wit, and were with her whether she was nobly being heartbroken or, even better, when she played domineering, ruthless, breathtakingly selfish women who turned men into mice.

Variously known as 'The First Lady of the American Screen' and 'Mother Goddam', the indomitable Ruth Elizabeth Davis (she adopted Bette from a Balzac novel) was the only person who believed in her star potential through years of rejection. She was fired from her first theatre job. She failed her first screen test. When she was signed by Universal, studio boss Carl Laemmle loudly deplored her lack of sex appeal. She showed them all, fighting for roles and willing herself attractive and compelling through the sheer intensity of her proud, pop-eyed gaze. She paid her dues in a string of supporting roles at Universal then Warner Bros., but when RKO borrowed her to play the brassy waitress in *Of Human Bondage* (1934), people started to sit up and take notice. She won her first Oscar for *Dangerous* (1935) as a fallen star, and her second for *Jezebel* (1938) as the tempestuous belle. She may have defied typecasting, and she constantly battled with Warners over material, but she really hit her stride by suffering or making others suffer in romantic soapers and melodramas of the late thirties and forties aimed at an appreciative women's audience.

Labelled 'box-office poison' at forty after a few flops, she made a triumphant comeback in *All About Eve* (1950). In the sixties she kept going, fearlessly playing monstrous mothers, psychotic servants and grotesques, most awesomely demented in the macabre *What Ever Happened To Baby Jane?* (1962) tormenting her detested rival Joan Crawford. With four failed marriages and no great success as a mother (daughter Barbara's memoir *My Mother's Keeper* rivalled Crawford's daughter's, *Mommie Dearest*, for scarifying revelations), Davis's work was her life, and she continued to make movies through her six-year fight with cancer, right up to her death aged eighty-one.

In addition to the range of her classic pictures we've extolled throughout this book we also dote on these definitive Davis weepies:

DARK VICTORY (1939)

Bette's spoiled socialite learns she has a terminal brain tumour, mends her wild wastrel ways and settles down sweetly with her handsome brain surgeon (George Brent) for a brief interlude of worthy domestic bliss before the light begins to dim and she climbs the stairs to die alone in peace.

THE OLD MAID (1939)

Bette's love–hate relationship with her cousin (Miriam Hopkins) takes an intense twist when her lover (George Brent again) is killed in the Civil War. Bette surrenders her illegitimate baby and has to endure her daughter growing up adoring stand-in mummy Miriam and hating Bette as the strict spinster aunt.

THE GREAT LIE (1941)

Bette's bride discovers her missing husband's ex (you've guessed it, George Brent again), a neurotic concert pianist (Mary Astor), is pregnant. Bette confines Mary with no cigarettes or booze until the birth, takes the child as her own and has some explaining to do when hubby emerges from the jungle.

OLD ACQUAINTANCE (1943)

This time Bette plays nice while Miriam Hopkins gets to be the bitch. They are childhood friends who become writers (Bette talented and literary; Miriam flashy and trashy), professional and romantic rivals during decades of cattiness. Remade not half as well as *Rich And Famous* (1981).

A STOLEN LIFE (1946)

Bette plays identical twins – one a feckless floozy, the other shy and pure. When the mean one drowns after pinching good Bette's crush (Glenn Ford), fortuitously leaving behind her wedding ring, the good girl can't resist the temptation to put it on and impersonate her sister, unaware that her unhappy hubby is gagging for a divorce.

THE HEART OF ME (2002)

Directed by Thaddeus O'Sullivan
Starring Paul Bettany, Helena Bonham Carter, Olivia Williams

A small but almost perfectly formed period melodrama tackling those most riveting subjects, love and betrayal. Free spirit Dinah (Bonham Carter) and very proper, respectable Madeline (Williams) are sisters living in thirties London who have just one thing in common – they are both in love with Rickie (Bettany). Madeline is married to him, but it is Dinah who truly has his heart and whom Rickie secretly visits for passionate trysts at her flat. Of course, a couple committing such a sin probably aren't going to live happily ever after, and it comes as no surprise when obstacles such as pregnancy, a car crash and the small matter of the Second World War pop up to block Dinah and Rickie's road to happiness.

Smartly directed by Thaddeus O'Sullivan – at ninety-six minutes long, there's no lingering, Merchant–Ivory-style camerawork dwelling on stiff upper lips here – this is also perfectly cast. Bonham Carter and Williams effectively portray the huge gulf that can sometimes separate siblings, while Bettany convinces as a man who is clearly in over his head.

HEARTBURN (1986)

Directed by Mike Nichols
Starring Meryl Streep, Jack Nicholson

Adapted from Nora Ephron's novel based on her own failed marriage to Watergate reporter Carl Bernstein, this comedy drama is a painfully funny and bitter look at a crumbling relationship. Rachel (Streep) is pregnant when she discovers her husband Mark (Nicholson) has been unfaithful; they split then attempt an awkward reconciliation.

Streep gives a quirky performance as Rachel; but because this is written from Ephron's – presumably vengeful – perspective, the character of Mark is one-dimensional, leaving Nicholson with little to work with. He's utterly believable as a philandering husband, but Ephron fails to explain what Rachel ever saw in him. Watch out for Kevin Spacey in his first screen role as a robber Streep encounters on the subway.

THE HORSE WHISPERER (1998)

Directed by Robert Redford
Starring Robert Redford, Kristin Scott Thomas, Sam Neill, Scarlett Johansson

In the aftermath of a horrific accident a traumatised girl (Johansson) and her terribly injured horse are taken to Montana by her anxious mother (Scott Thomas) for rehabilitation with a renowned horse whisperer – a trainer–healer with a near-mystical connection to horses. Nicholas Evans's phenomenal bestseller provided a perfect vehicle for the ageing Robert Redford and a serious dilemma for Scott Thomas's chic Manhattanite: torn between duty to good husband Neill and desire for animal-lover Redford, what's a woman to do?

The drama of the damaged horse and child is extremely moving, and Redford directs with his usual fine taste and craft. But the depiction of a mature romance is also particularly affecting. This is suggested more powerfully by longing and small, tender moments (especially a knee-buckling slow dance in a bar) than by explicit coupling. Redford maybe learned from Clint Eastwood's *The Bridges Of Madison County* that after a certain age a cowboy should not bare too much.

LOVE FIELD (1992)

Directed by Jonathan Kaplan
Starring Michelle Pfeiffer, Dennis Haysbert

It's 1963 and sassy Texan housewife Lurene (Pfeiffer) is obsessed with the Kennedy clan – her bleached hair is styled like Jackie's and she reads everything she can about the presidential family. So JFK's sudden death understandably devastates her, and she decides to take a Greyhound to the funeral in Washington, against the wishes of her small-town husband. It's on the bus that she meets black pharmacist Paul (Haysbert) and his young daughter Jonell, and when Lurene's incessant friendly chatter lands them in trouble and on the run, the three strangers become friends while making their way to the capital.

A small-scale film that could almost have been made for TV (it only got a video release in the UK), this becomes so much more than that thanks to two gentle, sweet turns from Haysbert and Pfeiffer, who was nominated for an Oscar for her moving performance.

LOVE IS A MANY-SPLENDORED THING (1955)

Directed by Henry King
Starring William Holden, Jennifer Jones

Where would sudsy love dramas be without forbidden love? At the outbreak of the Korean War Holden's married American war correspondent Mark Elliott and Jones's beauteous, widowed Eurasian doctor Han Suyin meet in Hong Kong and snatch a brief bit of bliss before he leaves for the front. Based on Dr Han's autobiography, this Cinemascope treat is full of intelligence, grace and sexual heat, even though Jones and Holden didn't get on and she supposedly chewed garlic before every smooching scene! The couple defy taboos of adultery and interracial romance to roll on a beach and lie in the tall grass on a windy hill, accompanied by Alfred Newman's Oscar-winning score and the killer love ballad by Sammy Fain and Paul Francis Webster. Holden's voiceover at the tragic end always turns us into puddles.

LOVE WITH THE PROPER STRANGER (1963)

Directed by Robert Mulligan
Starring Natalie Wood, Steve McQueen

When Italian-American – and Catholic – shopgirl Angie (Wood) discovers she is pregnant, she tracks down the father, Rocky (McQueen), and asks for his help in finding a doctor to carry out an abortion.

Not the most obvious plotting for a romantic comedy drama, this was quite an eyebrow-raising film back in 1963, when abortion in the USA was still illegal and certainly not the sort of subject normally dealt with on film. But it's sensitively handled by Mulligan, who manages to mix humour and drama throughout the story. Wood is perfect as the young girl trying to break free from her overprotective family, while McQueen gives one of his most subtle performances as the easygoing guy trying to do the right thing.

THE MIRROR HAS TWO FACES (1996)

Directed by Barbra Streisand
Starring Barbra Streisand, Jeff Bridges

There are two kinds of people in the world: those who love Barbra Streisand and those who don't. If you fall into the second category, you'd be best to give this film – starring and directed by La Streisand – a wide berth. But if Babs is your gal, and you yearn for those long-off romantic comedies in which the characters never indulged in anything horizontal, this could be for you.

Rose (Streisand) is a dowdy woman who lives a lonely life with her mother (a sparkling Lauren Bacall). Gregory (Bridges), meanwhile, has had a series of empty relationships with young floozies and now believes the secret to eternal happiness is to marry for companionship, with no sex involved. The pair soon get together to enjoy sexless wedded bliss – but Rose, of course, secretly wants to explore the contents of Gregory's pants, and decides to change from frumpy spinster into cleavage-revealing sex kitten to tempt him. The whole transformation is ludicrous (but hey, this is a Streisand movie – what do you expect?) and, unsurprisingly, the director has taken care to film herself in a flattering way at all times. Get past that, though, and you'll be treated to a warm and fuzzy romantic comedy with some smart performances, especially from Bacall, and George Segal as Bridges's cynical pal.

MY BRILLIANT CAREER (1979)

Directed by Gillian Armstrong
Starring Judy Davis, Sam Neill, Wendy Hughes

Judy Davis is brilliant in a touching true story of ambition in conflict with love and family expectation. Her Sybylla Melvyn (who published this autobiographical story under the pen name Miles Franklin) is part of a poor, struggling family but she longs to be independent and creative rather than the outback farmer's wife she seems destined to be. Plain, but headstrong and outspoken, she is dispatched to wealthy relatives (including Hughes's Aunt Helen) to be groomed as a nice young lady and make a match. Amazingly, she does, when rich and handsome

Harry Beecham (Neill) admires her intelligence and plucky individualism.

One of the top films of the Australian movie renaissance of the seventies (and a starmaker for Davis, Neill and debuting director Armstrong), this is charming, witty and beautifully detailed, although it still always sticks in our craw that Sybylla couldn't marry the dish *and* be a writer, too.

AN OFFICER AND A GENTLEMAN (1982)

Directed by Taylor Hackford
Starring Richard Gere, Debra Winger, Louis Gossett Jr

What girl hasn't fantasised about being swept off her feet and away by a hunky man in uniform after seeing that very thing happen in this classic drama? Debra Winger is the lucky girl, of course, as factory worker Paula, who falls for misunderstood Zack Mayo (Gere), a new recruit to the US Navy's flight school. However, before he can carry her off into the sunset, Zack has to endure rigorous training, a fellow officer's suicide and, worst of all, harassment from his malicious superior, Sgt. Foley (Gossett Jr, who won an Oscar for his performance).

It's the scenes between Gere and Gossett Jr – rather than Gere and Winger – in which sparks fly, and while the romantic finale, complete with thunderous theme song 'Up Where We Belong', is the bit everyone remembers, it's actually a scene in which Foley tries to get Zack to quit ('I got no place else to go' being Zack's anguished reply) that truly tugs at the heartstrings. Useless fact: like Gere's career-making role in *American Gigolo*, John Travolta was offered the part of Zack and turned it down. Oops.

PEYTON PLACE (1957)

Directed by Mark Robson
Starring Lana Turner, Hope Lange, Arthur Kennedy

Grace Metalious's tawdry, reputedly autobiographical, blockbuster created quite a steamy scandal in the fifties, but it was adapted into this classy melodrama with multiple plot strands weaved into a riveting exposé of the secrets and hypocrisy in a 'typical' New England town. Prim mother Constance Mackenzie (Turner) tries to hide her shameful past from sheltered daughter Allison (Diane Varsi) while romancing handsome Michael Rossi (Lee Philips). Meanwhile, town tart Betty (Terry Moore) is being bad in cars with boys like spoiled rich kid Rodney Harrington (Barry Coe).

The hanky-panky is laced with life experience and tragedy, and come-uppances are dealt out very satisfactorily. The torrid TV soap series that followed in the sixties launched the careers of Mia Farrow and Ryan O'Neal (as Allison and Rodney).

A PLACE IN THE SUN (1951)

Directed by George Stevens
Starring Montgomery Clift, Elizabeth Taylor, Shelley Winters

Theodore Dreiser's classic novel *An American Tragedy* gets plush and full-blooded treatment in a picture of romance, loss and doom that is even more heart-stopping because of the sheer gorgeousness of its stars. Beautiful Clift is poor George Eastman, who comes East in the hope of bettering himself through some distant connections. Lonely and struggling, he strikes up a relationship with the equally forlorn Alice (Winters), who expects him to marry her when she becomes pregnant. Meanwhile, George's tireless social climbing has been rewarded with the love of rich society belle Angela (Taylor). Weak of character, strong in desire for the good things in life, George contemplates killing Alice, but the plan goes awry in mounting horror and despair. The camera can't help but love Clift and a radiant Taylor, swirling around them on the dance floor and lingering on their delicious kisses, making the awfulness of their separation and George's cruelly ironic fate (not to mention that of poor, silly Alice) even harder to bear.

RACHEL, RACHEL (1968)

Directed by Paul Newman
Starring Joanne Woodward, James Olson, Estelle Parsons

Rachel Cameron (Woodward) is a lonely, repressed, thirty-five-year-old schoolteacher who still lives with her demanding mother (Kate Harrington) in the home where her late father was the local funeral director. The only person she can confide in is fellow teacher Calla (Parsons), who has yearnings of her own, and the only respite she has from the stifling dreariness of her life is in flights of fantasy. No wonder she'd like a life before it's too late. When old friend Nick (Olson) returns to their small Connecticut town from New York he seems like the answer to a spinster's prayers, but Rachel's emotional rescue isn't going to be that easy, and he proves another disappointment.

Paul Newman's directorial debut was a real family affair since Paul and Joanne's daughter Nell plays Rachel as a child. It is a tender, sensitive character study, adapted from the Margaret Laurence novel *A Jest Of God*. And Woodward is marvellous as Rachel, shyly trying to break out of her shell. You go, girl!

REBECCA (1940)

Directed by Alfred Hitchcock
Starring Laurence Olivier, Joan Fontaine

The only movie for which Hitchcock won a Best Picture Oscar, *Rebecca* is a spooky love story based on the Gothic novel by Daphne Du Maurier. A young, naive woman (Fontaine, playing a character whose name we never learn) falls for the suave charms of George 'Maxim' De Winter (Olivier) and, after a whirlwind romance, he marries her and whisks her off to his home, the beautiful but imposing Manderley. There she meets stern and severe housekeeper Mrs Danvers (Judith Anderson) and learns that Maxim has been married before, and that the house is filled with memories – and perhaps ghosts – of his dead wife Rebecca.

Rumour has it that Hitchcock told Fontaine the entire cast hated her to produce that look of unease she has throughout this melodrama. If so, his ruse certainly succeeded as poor Joan gets more uncomfortable and wide-eyed as the secrets about the first Mrs De Winter are finally revealed.

 **MALE WEEPIES**

This chapter is, of course, devoted to movies women love, and often sob all the way through. But we had to include a few screen moments that get men all mushy – and we don't mean highlights of the 1966 World Cup Final ...

SPARTACUS (1960)

Kirk Douglas certainly gets our thumbs up as the former slave who leads a revolt against the Roman Empire in this sword and sandals epic. The big weepy moment is the finale, as Varinia (Jean Simmons) shows Spartacus his child for the first and last time.

BUTCH CASSIDY AND THE SUNDANCE KID (1969)

A very boyish film about outlaws Butch and Sundance, who surely can't have been as gorgeous in real life as Paul Newman and Robert Redford are here. Many a man has been seen to shed a tear during Butch's bicycle-riding courtship of Etta (Katharine Ross) to the strains of 'Raindrops Keep Fallin' On My Head' and at the memorable finale.

THE DEER HUNTER (1978)

A harrowing movie about the Vietnam War, notable for the sequence in which American prisoners of war are forced to play Russian roulette by their Vietcong captors. Intense stuff, with superb performances from Robert De Niro, Christopher Walken, John Cazale and John Savage.

GLORY (1989)

Matthew Broderick is the colonel in command of the first black regiment during the American Civil War in this lush drama. Denzel Washington's performance as a runaway slave and the final battle provide the most heart-rending moments.

FiELD OF DREAMS (1989)

Farmer Kevin Costner hears voices that lead him to build a baseball diamond in his cornfield, where ghosts of famous players come to play, but at the heart of this beautifully played film is the theme of a man learning to love and forgive his late father.

THE SHAWSHANK REDEMPTION (1994)

This adaptation of a Stephen King novella stars Tim Robbins as inmate Andy Dufresne, a man trying to come to terms with life at Shawshank Prison with the help of old-timer Red (Morgan Freeman). The life-affirming ending causes lumps in the throat for guys everywhere.

BRAVEHEART (1995)

Mel Gibson is terrific as William Wallace, who united thirteenth-century Scots against the English in this epic that he also directed. One man's determination is stirring in itself, but apparently the death of Wallace's wife (the beautiful Catherine McCormack) is what reduces grown men to snivelling wrecks.

JERRY MAGUIRE (1996)

Down-on-his-luck sports promoter Tom Cruise's 'you complete me' declaration to Renée Zellweger has been much parodied (even by Dr Evil in *Austin Powers*) but its simplicity turns both sexes to goo.

GOOD WILL HUNTING (1997)

Matt Damon is the janitor who is a genius mathematician, as discovered by professor Stellan Skarsgaard. Two wonderfully rendered relationships – between Damon and Minnie Driver (as his girlfriend), and Damon and Robin Williams (as the psychiatrist who uncovers hidden traumas) – are the most powerful in this superb drama.

SAVING PRIVATE RYAN (1998)

Everyone was moved by Steven Spielberg's graphic depiction of the D-Day landings, but men are especially touched by the subsequent story of one group of soldiers, led by Tom Hanks, who are sent on a mission to rescue a single paratrooper (Matt Damon).

ROMEO AND JULIET (1968)

Directed by Franco Zeffirelli
Starring Leonard Whiting, Olivia Hussey

WILLIAM SHAKESPEARE'S ROMEO AND JULIET (1996)

Directed by Baz Luhrmann
Starring Leonardo DiCaprio, Claire Danes

Shakespeare's tragedy of star-cross'd young lovers has kept audiences sobbing for 400 years and has been filmed many times, including a lavish 1936 version with Leslie Howard and Norma Shearer (good, but the leads are too old), a 1954 version with Laurence Harvey and Susan Shentall (very nice), and a 1966 recording of the Royal Ballet's famous production danced by Rudolf Nureyev and Margot Fonteyn. But the most gorgeous screen version is Franco Zeffirelli's sixties smash hit, filmed on medieval Italian locations with exquisite costumes, music (by Nino Rota) and actors at least close to the correct age. Admittedly purists were dismayed by fifteen-year-old Hussey's and seventeen-year-old Whiting's lack of experience in speaking the verse, and by Zeffirelli's omission of some of the famous soliloquies. But what it lacks in poetry is richly compensated for in youthful ardour as these beautiful children of feuding families plummet passionately into love, and die unnecessarily through cruel fate and folly.

William Shakespeare's Romeo & Juliet (as opposed to *Joe Bloggs's Romeo and Juliet*, presumably) stars the considerably more accomplished young duo of Leonardo DiCaprio and Claire Danes, and director Luhrmann is faithful to the text while updating the story with electrifying wit and pizazz. The designer-dressed Capulets and Montagues are presented as corporate rivals, their minions as streetwise gangs armed with guns, and the chorus is a television newsreader. A sly bending of the conventional treatment of the suicide scene delivers an almighty, heart-rending shock, even to those who know the play well.

Shakespeare's original also inspired a cute political satire–romantic comedy, *Romanoff And Juliet* (1961), in which Sandra Dee and John

Gavin escape a Cold War diplomatic incident with their lives and love intact.

RUBY IN PARADISE (1993)

Directed by Victor Nunez
Starring Ashley Judd, Todd Field, Bentley Mitchum

Among small, independent modern dramas, this low-key, at times poetic, study of an ordinary young woman trying to make a life for herself stands out because of its deceptive simplicity and understated emotional punch. Ruby (Ashley Judd, making her name in a quiet performance) leaves her dead-end life in Tennessee and arrives in a small coastal Florida town where she finds a crummy job, reluctantly accepts the advances of her employer's arrogant son (Bentley Mitchum, Robert's grandson) and is intrigued by a gentle man she meets (Todd Field, the writer–director of 2001's acclaimed drama of family grief *In The Bedroom*). Nothing earth-shattering happens, but Ruby's loneliness, hope and sincerity make her utterly believable, and she soon earns our sympathy. Writer–director Nunez refrains from any pat resolution, instead inviting you to make up the rest of Ruby's story for yourself.

SAY ANYTHING (1989)

Directed by Cameron Crowe
Starring John Cusack, Ione Skye, John Mahoney

Sigh. If only there was a Lloyd Dobler (Cusack) for every woman on the planet. A teenager just graduating from high school with dreams of being a kickboxer, Lloyd may not have great ambitions but the way he woos dedicated student and daddy's girl Diane (Skye) is just wonderful. He takes her to a party and keeps his lovelorn eye on her all night, serenades her with a boombox outside her window playing Peter Gabriel's 'In Your Eyes', teaches her to drive, writes her a beautiful love note and even shivers with devotion when they are finally alone together in the back of his car. Unfortunately, her dad (Mahoney) doesn't approve, thinking Lloyd is an unwelcome distraction to Diane's academic career.

But we know all along that this is one guy who really deserves to get the girl. Just lovely.

SILKWOOD (1983)

Directed by Mike Nichols
Starring Meryl Streep, Cher, Kurt Russell

This drama is based on the true story of Karen Silkwood (Streep), a young woman who worked at a nuclear facility and became concerned about safety levels there for workers like her dealing with radioactive plutonium. Her attempts to blow the whistle on her employers affected her relationship with her boyfriend (Russell) and her friend (Cher), and many believe that her determination to expose what was going on also led to her death. In 1974 Karen had arranged to show a reporter evidence of malpractice, but she died in a car accident on the way to their meeting.

It's a fascinating story of big business and one woman's fight against it that ends in tragedy, and Streep gives a suitably tough-cookie performance, impressively supported by Russell and Cher.

SLEEPING WITH THE ENEMY (1991)

Directed by Joseph Ruben
Starring Julia Roberts, Patrick Bergin

A serious subject – wife abuse – is turned into an extremely daft but strangely compelling drama. On the surface, Laura (Roberts) and Martin (Bergin) seem like a happy couple. But the slightest thing can turn him from mild-mannered husband into raging psychopath, so Laura decides the only way to be free of him is to fake her own death and start again somewhere else with a new identity. But will Martin realise what she has done and come after her? What do you think?

Riddled with plot-holes and silliness – rather than throwing her wedding ring away once she has escaped, Laura flushes it down the loo so it can pop back up again for Martin to find – this has some truly unintentionally hilarious moments: Laura realises Martin has found her because the little obsessive–compulsive has taken the time to organise her cupboards and straighten the towels before hiding in a corner.

This was Roberts's first leading role after her breakthrough hit *Pretty Woman* (a scene featuring her playing dress-up with hats has strong echoes of the earlier movie) and it's a testament to her star power that this so-bad-it's-almost-good film didn't bury her career before it had truly started.

SOMEONE TO WATCH OVER ME (1987)

Directed by Ridley Scott
Starring Tom Berenger, Mimi Rogers, Lorraine Bracco

If there is such a thing as a gripping police thriller for women, this is it. For while, at its heart there is a murder case – Manhattan socialite Claire (Rogers) has witnessed the crime – it's really a tale of love and betrayal as the married cop, Mike (Berenger) assigned to protect her finds himself falling in love with her.

Stylishly directed by Ridley Scott – New York has never looked so cool and classy – the film works so well as a romantic drama because no one is painted in black and white. Down-to-earth Mike loves his wife (Bracco) and doesn't want to hurt her, but he is in love with Claire too, and she shows him a different life from the one he has always known. Heartbreaking to watch, the three leads are superb, especially Berenger and the underrated Rogers.

SPLENDOR IN THE GRASS (1961)

Directed by Elia Kazan
Starring Natalie Wood, Warren Beatly

Notable for being the first mainstream Hollywood movie to feature a French kiss (how shocking!), this also marked the first big-screen role for Warren Beatty. He looks good enough to eat as Bud Stamper, a young man from a prominent 1920s Kansas family whose sweetheart is poor schoolmate Deanie (Wood). Each has intense longing for the other – there's lots of sexual repression and deep sighing throughout –

but both his wealthy father and her strict mother disapprove of their relationship.

Not many romances feature a twist in which half the couple – Deanie – ends up in the nuthouse as a result of their secret trysts, but this is melodramatic stuff, memorably played by the handsome cast.

ST ELMO'S FIRE (1985)

Directed by Joel Schumacher
Starring Emilio Estevez, Rob Lowe, Demi Moore, Judd Nelson

One of the 'brat pack' movies of the mid-eighties featuring the hottest young actors of the time. Here, they are a group of pals finishing college and venturing out into the grown-up world of jobs, relationships and marriage. And it turns out that it's a pretty complicated world: Kevin (Andrew McCarthy) loves Leslie (Ally Sheedy) but she lives with Alec (Nelson). Kirby (Estevez) lusts after older woman Dale (Andie MacDowell in her first screen role). Jules (Moore) is a mass of insecurities and a disaster waiting to happen, while Wendy (Mare Winningham) is the dowdy girl who secretly fancies the hunk – and wannabe musician – Billy (Lowe).

The hideous theme song by John Parr may be cheesy and the naff eighties fashions date the movie horribly, but there is some kitsch appeal in this preposterous coming-of-age movie in which all the characters are so different that they could never be pals in real life. Silly stuff – but Rob Lowe and Emilio Estevez have never looked prettier.

THE STORY OF US (1999)

Directed by Rob Reiner
Starring Bruce Willis, Michelle Pfeiffer, Rob Reiner

On paper, a romantic comedy drama featuring the combined talents of Willis, Pfeiffer and Reiner – who, with *This Is Spinal Tap* and *When Harry Met Sally*, made two of the funniest films of the eighties – sounds like a potential laugh riot. Unfortunately, scriptwriters Jessie Nelson (*Stepmom*) and Alan Zweibel (*Dragnet*) produced a surprisingly downbeat tale of a fifteen-year marriage on the skids.

Essentially, it's *When Sally Divorced Harry*, as Bruce (playing Bruce) and Michelle (stuck in the unsympathetic role of whiny wife) try a temporary separation and proceed to dissect their marriage with the obligatory flashbacks (Bruce with long hair will at least raise a giggle). Then there are the chats with witty pals – Bruce gets Reiner and Paul Reiser; Michelle gets Rita Wilson – that could have been lifted straight out of a Nora Ephron film … if they'd been funnier. As it is, we're left wondering why Reiner *didn't* get Ephron to write the screenplay – it would have made for a much better film all round.

TEQUILA SUNRISE (1988)

Directed by Robert Towne
Starring Mel Gibson, Michelle Pfeiffer, Kurt Russell

Strictly speaking, this thriller about a drug dealer and his former best friend, a cop, both in love with the same girl, isn't a chick flick. But with hunks Gibson and Russell playing the two pals, and a strong central performance from Pfeiffer as the gal in the middle, it deserves a special mention. Anyway, we've yet to meet a man who likes this movie, but plenty of women do.

Mac (Gibson) seems to be a legitimate businessman, but his old friend Nick (Russell) is convinced he is still a drugdealer. So when Nick sees Mac spending a lot of time at icily gorgeous Jo Ann's restaurant, he assumes he's using it for his deals, not realising that Mac hangs out there because he is in love with Jo Ann (Pfeiffer).

There's a complicated subplot about a forthcoming major drug deal, but more interesting is the simmering chemistry between Pfeiffer and Russell *and* Pfeiffer and Gibson (lucky girl). All three stars are terrific and exceedingly sexy, and the sultry Californian locations make them all the more attractive.

TIM (1979)

Directed by Michael Pate
Starring Piper Laurie, Mel Gibson

Mary Horton (Laurie) is a successful middle-aged businesswoman whose relationship with her young, retarded gardener Tim (Gibson) develops from pity and friendship into warm, mutual love. When Tim's parents die Mary is torn: should she bow to society's taboos or follow her heart? Since the twenty-three-year-old Gibson in his little shorts looks like a god, we're never in much doubt about which path she'll choose.

This sensitive adaptation of Colleen '*The Thorn Birds*' McCullough's novel is irresistibly sweet corn, almost entirely saved from mawkishness by the delicate playing of its stars – although we have to hide our blushes when the adorably innocent Tim shows Mary he can hop like a bunny. Gibson's startling diversion from *Mad Max* won him the Australian Film Institute's Best Actor award. An American TV remake of 1996, *Mary And Tim*, starring Candice Bergen, can't hold a candle to the original.

TROP BELLE POUR TOI (1989)

Directed by Bertrand Blier
Starring Gérard Depardieu, Josiane Balasko, Carole Bouquet

Bernard (Depardieu) is a successful car dealer with a coolly beautiful and cultured wife, Florence (Bouquet). So when he falls for Colette (Balasko), the plain, plump temp at his office, no one can quite believe it. But the perfect wife is not all she seems (there's a jaw-dropping scene in which Florence upbraids her dinner guests for hating her because she's so beautiful), and we come to see why Colette's honest delight with the ordinary guy is catnip to him. The passion, the fantasy and the great, undeniable love that passes between Bernard and Colette with simple looks are palpable. And since Colette is a bit of a Bridget Jones who doesn't fret about her thighs and doesn't undergo a miraculous make-over, we're hoping against hope that the affair will work out.

A WALK IN THE CLOUDS (1995)

Directed by Alfonso Arau
Starring Keanu Reeves, Aitana Sánchez-Gijón, Anthony Quinn

Like candyfloss, this movie is a soft, fluffy confection that is almost too sweet to digest, but it's just about palatable thanks to the casting of Keanu Reeves at his most rugged.

Returning from the Second World War, Paul (Reeves) discovers his wife (*Will & Grace*'s Debra Messing in an early role) has been less than faithful and wants a divorce. Understandably disappointed, he heads out of town, and meets a young Mexican-American woman, Victoria (Sánchez-Gijón), on the bus. She's distraught because she is unmarried and pregnant – which won't please her traditionalist father when he finds out. So Paul, being the decent sort of bloke he is, offers to pretend to be her husband and travel with her to the family's vineyards to face the music.

Of course, eventually the pair fall in love for real, but before then Paul and Victoria have to deal with the family's animosity, learn some deep, dark secrets, harvest and press the grapes and deal with an inevitable family disaster. Arau directs the collecting and pressing of the grapes as if it were some sort of Bacchic rite, while all the major events are emphasised by lovingly filmed scenery, swirling music and, best of all, lots of shots of a brooding Keanu. Let's just hope all that sweetness doesn't rot our teeth …

A WALK ON THE MOON (1999)

Directed by Tony Goldwyn
Starring Diane Lane, Viggo Mortensen, Liev Schreiber

It's 1969, and while the rest of America is experiencing Vietnam and the sexual revolution, Pearl Kantrowitz's (Lane) life plods along as she plays wife to dependable Marty (Schreiber) and mother to Daniel (Bobby Boriello) and Alison (Anna Paquin). Things change, however, when she and the kids spend the summer at a Catskills resort and Pearl embarks on a torrid affair with smouldering hippy Walker (Mortensen), which forces her to choose between her old life and one without inhibitions.

Tony Goldwyn (best known as the bad guy in *Ghost*) directs this realistic, tender and moving comedy drama that works well thanks to superb performances and a script that portrays every point of view without damning either Marty or Walker (or Pearl, for that matter). Everyone here wants love, and it's heartbreaking to know that at least one of them will ultimately be disappointed.

WELCOME TO THE DOLLHOUSE (1995)

Directed by Todd Solondz
Starring Heather Matarazzo, Eric Mabius, Brendan Sexton Jr

This sharp, truthful comedy drama provides a painful insight into puberty for anyone who has forgotten the absolute hell of being twelve. Dawn Wiener (the sensational Matarazzo) has neglectful parents, a smarter older brother and a prettier younger sister who does ballet. Dawn has bad glasses, bad clothes, bad skin, and no good hair days. Whether she's enduring the jeers of the cool kids, being bullied by a nasty 'admirer' in classmate Brandon (Sexton) or ignored by her heart-throb Steve (Mabius), clever Dawn soldiers on with interesting coping mechanisms. Writer–director Solondz's debut film is horribly, cruelly funny, but your heart will ache just as much as your ribs.

A WORLD APART (1988)

Directed by Chris Menges
Starring Barbara Hershey, Jeroen Krabbé, Jodhi May, Linda Mvusi

Screenwriter Shawn Slovo, whose lawyer father Joe was a leading figure in the African National Congress and whose mother Ruth was a political journalist assassinated by the secret police, courageously evoked family history for a deeply personal, moving account of anti-apartheid activists (fictionalised as the Roth family) in sixties South Africa.

Gus and Diana Roth (Krabbé and Hershey) are branded communist subversives, and while Gus is in exile Diana is repeatedly, tortuously detained in prison. The story is seen through the eyes of their unhappy thirteen-year-old daughter Molly (the outstanding May), who respects their cause but resents coming a distant second to it in her parents' attentions. The impact of political abuse, social injustice and parental idealism on a conflicted child is powerfully rendered, both intellectually and emotionally.

WRITTEN ON THE WIND (1956)

Directed by Douglas Sirk
Starring Rock Hudson, Lauren Bacall, Robert Stack, Dorothy Malone

Texan poor-boy Mitch Wayne (Hudson) has grown up on the super-rich Hadleys' ranch and now works for their oil company. He and his lifelong chum, dissolute playboy Kyle Hadley (Stack), both fall for poised New Yorker Lucy (Bacall) but she weds Kyle. His wild, wanton sister Marylee (Malone, in an Oscar-winning performance) bitterly nurses unrequited love for Mitch, and jealously leads the fitfully impotent Kyle to believe Lucy is pregnant by his rival. Naturally, all hell breaks loose in this lusciously overwrought melodrama of billionaires, booze, incest, homoeroticism and nymphomania. *Dallas* and *Dynasty*, eat your hearts out!

Sirk's inimitable blend of art and artifice, trash and style, wallows in the depraved depths with subversive enjoyment. It would be hard to find anything more luridly entertaining.

DEATH, DISEASE AND OTHER PROBLEMS

AT FIRST SIGHT (1999)

Directed by Irwin Winkler
Starring Val Kilmer, Mira Sorvino

Loosely based on factual events as recorded by doctor-turned-writer Oliver Sacks (whose case notes were the basis of the movie *Awakenings*), this is the story of a blind man named Virgil (Kilmer). Hunky, brooding and the best masseur you'll ever find, his magic touch reduces client Amy (Sorvino) to tears (lucky girl). The pair fall in love, but rather than accept Virgil as he is, Amy is soon setting up doctors' appointments in a bid to give Virgil sight. Of course, once he can see, things become really complicated – Virgil can make out objects but understands what they are only when he touches them. Winkler clearly has some interesting ideas about what life is like for someone who can suddenly see, but he spends too much time on a very formulaic romance with a disappointingly cheesy ending.

AUTUMN IN NEW YORK (2000)

Directed by Joan Chen
Starring Richard Gere, Winona Ryder, Anthony LaPaglia

When ageing restaurateur and man-about-town Will (Gere) meets young hat designer Charlotte (Ryder), he finally seems to shed his womanising ways and falls in love. But it would be a very short film if they lived happily ever after, so it comes as no surprise to learn that Charlotte is suffering from a terminal illness, and the affair that changes Will's life is going to end in inevitable tears.

Unfortunately, what could have been a three-hankie weepie is instead a rather tedious tale, mainly because Gere and Ryder have about as much onscreen chemistry as a pair of cold, dead fish: her character comes across as icy and unappealing, while his is arrogant. But an even bigger stumbling block is that Will is so much older in years and experience than Charlotte, so he comes across as a dirty old man. Only LaPaglia (as Will's friend) and Elaine Stritch (as Charlotte's confidante) go some way towards saving the day, but your interest in the film will still expire long before Charlotte does.

BEACHES (1988)

Directed by Garry Marshall
Starring Bette Midler, Barbara Hershey

Barbara Hershey's freshly poofed-up lips make the biggest impression here. They're certainly more fascinating than many of the sketchy characters in this episodic tale of lifelong bosom buddies. Hershey's classy, privileged girl and Midler's poor, raucous one meet at the seaside as children and keep their special connection through a roller-coasting three decades of bad marriages, triumphs, tantrums, bust-ups and recriminations. But Midler is terrific in this turning point in her career (she also co-produced), making a winning transition from comedies to tear jerkers. Once a terminal illness rears its head the two stars bear us off with them on a sea of sobs. Barbara suffers bravely, and Bette rises to the occasion with solidarity and selflessness while belting out her now-classic 'Wind Beneath My Wings'.

CHILDREN OF A LESSER GOD (1986)

Directed by Randa Haines
Starring William Hurt, Marlee Matlin

Hurt here gives his warmest, most generous performance, as a teacher at a school for the deaf. He is drawn to Matlin's isolated but fiercely independent young deaf woman, and his understated performance allows her Oscar-winning fireworks in first-time director Randa Haines's moving version of Mark Medoff's internationally successful play. Matlin's character is particularly intriguing because she chooses to work as the school janitor and disdains speech classes, rejecting the idea that she is 'disabled' and must fit in with hearing people's expectations. This is a remarkably confident screen debut from Matlin (who is herself deaf, of course), playing an uncompromising woman with intelligence, a strong sense of self-worth, and vulnerability.

DYING YOUNG (1991)

Directed by Joel Schumacher
Starring Julia Roberts, Campbell Scott

Well, the title certainly lets you know that this vehicle for Julia Roberts isn't going to be a barrel of laughs. She plays working-class girl Hilary, who – despite having no nursing qualifications – is hired by rich-boy Vic (Scott) to tend to him while he endures chemotherapy for his leukaemia. Presumably she got the job thanks to her short skirt. Soon the pair are making gooey eyes at each other and falling in love while he teaches her about art and manners. And – joy! – it even looks like Vic's health may be improving between their smooching sessions. Or is it? Perhaps he is just overdosing on the treacle that is liberally spread all over this contrived film, which ends up as a turgid mix of *Pretty Woman* and *Love Story*.

HERE ON EARTH (2000)

Directed by Mark Piznarski
Starring Chris Klein, Leelee Sobieski, Josh Hartnett

Arrogant college-kid Kelley (Klein, surely one of the least charismatic young actors around) smashes his car into a small-town restaurant and is charged with helping to rebuild the diner over the summer vacation. While boarding in the town he falls for Sam (Sobieski), much to the annoyance of her devoted boyfriend Jasper (Hartnett). But just as Kelley's love turns him into a much nicer, new man, Sam reveals that she's not quite the healthy girl she appears to be …

Hartnett and Klein don't do much except strut about trying to decide who has the most testosterone, but Sobieski is lovely as the saintly girl stricken with the disease that afflicted Ali McGraw in *Love Story* – it may be called cancer but movie sufferers of the disease get more beautiful as they get sicker. It's not a great weepy, but if you're in the mood for a good sniffle, this may do the trick.

JOHNNY BELINDA (1948)

Directed by Jean Negulesco
Starring Jane Wyman, Lew Ayres

Deaf–mute Belinda McDonald (Wyman) lives in a remote village where her family (Charles Bickford and Agnes Moorehead) have tried to shelter her from the narrow-minded fishing and farming community. But when new doctor Robert Richardson (Ayres) arrives in town and recognises the sensitive intelligence in her haunting eyes, Belinda matures, discovers new things and develops as an individual. When Belinda is attacked and impregnated the tongues wag cruelly and a crisis erupts with the birth of her son Johnny. Love triumphs, of course, in a powerful adaptation of a hit play, notable for its strong atmosphere and the fine playing, particularly from Wyman, who won an Oscar without uttering a word.

LORENZO'S OIL (1992)

Directed by George Miller
Starring Nick Nolte, Susan Sarandon

The true story of Augusto and Michaela Odone is harrowing and heart-breaking, but also inspirational, showing the courage and will-power people can find in adversity. When the Odones discover their son Lorenzo (Zack O'Malley Greenburg) is suffering from a rare disorder called ALD – which is always fatal – they cannot accept the prognosis and set about fighting for the boy's life with demanding questions and a worldwide search for answers. Exhausting and challenging, this is far superior to routine disease-of-the-week dramas, with Nolte and Sarandon both magnificent, and writer–director Miller (himself a doctor) indicting the medical profession for the patronising attitude that it often takes to those suffering from terminal illness. The postscript is that Michaela died in 2000, but Augusto still cares for Lorenzo, now in his twenties, although he is unable to move or speak. The olive-oil treatment they helped develop is credited with preventing or slowing the progress of ALD.

LOVE STORY (1970)

Directed by Arthur Hiller
Starring Ali McGraw, Ryan O'Neal

A three-hanky weepy with one of the most famous taglines of all time: 'Love Means Never Having To Say You're Sorry'. Harvard law student Oliver (O'Neal, looking simply scrumptious) is the man who utters those words to music student Jennifer (McGraw) in this classic romance where the obstacles to true happiness come first from his rich and disapproving father (Ray Milland) and then from her falling tragically ill. There are no cheap plot twists, though, since the movie's first line is Oliver's voice-over: 'How do you describe a twenty-five-year-old girl who died?' O'Neal is charming, sensitive and sweet (a new man a couple of decdes before that phrase had been invented), while McGraw is a tough cookie who looks inappropriately gorgeous in the deathbed scenes. The film was almost instantly castigated for being manipulative and a bit cheesy, but we bet you'll still sob as soon as you hear the first strains of the memorable theme. It was followed by a forgettable sequel, *Oliver's Story* in 1978, in which O'Neal found love again, this time with Candice Bergen.

MAGNIFICENT OBSESSION (1954)

Directed by Douglas Sirk
Starring Jane Wyman, Rock Hudson

Sirk's first teaming of Wyman with Hudson is terrifically compelling twaddle, adapted from a Lloyd C. Douglas novel. Wyman is genteel widow Helen Phillips, pursued by Rock's spoiled playboy Bob Merrick – right into the path of a car when he is trying to apologise for inadvertently being the cause of her husband's death! Helen is blinded by the accident, so remorseful Bob goes back to school, becomes a doctor and woos her anonymously while devoting himself to one end – restoring her sight. *Wow!* Along with a spiritual-redemption theme of repaying good deeds by anonymously passing them on, this has everything you could want in a glossy melodrama: tears, suffering, selfless love, nice costumes, an overwrought soundtrack. A smash hit, it made Hudson a star and is still perfection of its type.

THE MIRACLE WORKER (1962)

Directed by Arthur Penn
Starring Anne Bancroft, Patty Duke

Bancroft and sixteen-year-old Duke (so diminutive she could play a nine-year-old) both won Oscars reprising the bravura roles they first took in William Gibson's Broadway play. The former is inspirational teacher Anne Sullivan; the latter her pupil, the deaf, blind Helen Keller. Duke's Helen is a wild, savage child whose genteel Southern family treat her pityingly like an untamed pet or a dangerous doll. The no-nonsense Sullivan, herself partially sighted and raised in hellish circumstances, is having none of that and embarks on a combative regime with determination and tough love. Keller, of course, eventually became a famous educator and American icon, so we know the outcome of this battle of wills, but when Helen finally speaks her first word it is an electrifying moment in a film that disdains sugary sentiment to deliver extraordinary emotional power.

MY LIFE (1993)

Directed by Bruce Joel Rubin
Starring Michael Keaton, Nicole Kidman

Expect gushy sentiment aplenty – and have at least one box of tissues to hand – as Michael Keaton discovers he's got cancer just as wife Nicole Kidman learns she's pregnant. He decides to videotape his life for his unborn child, and in the process becomes a much more likeable fellow, coming to terms with the rage he feels towards his disease. Written and directed by Rubin, who wrote the equally weepy *Ghost*, this might all sound absolutely hideous, and would have been without the casting of Keaton, who rises above the schmaltz to give a funny, truly outstanding performance.

MY LIFE WITHOUT ME (2003)

Directed by Isabel Coixet
Starring Sarah Polley, Mark Ruffalo, Scott Speedman

And this is another film about someone coming to terms with their terminal illness. But when young wife and mother Ann (Polley) discovers she's going to die of ovarian cancer, she doesn't tell her high-school sweetheart husband (Speedman), her mother (Deborah Harry) or her friend (Amanda Plummer). Instead, she decides to experience the life she was never going to have by embarking on an affair (with brooding Ruffalo) while trying to put her affairs in order before ovarian cancer claims her life.

Polley is outstanding as the twenty-three-year-old in love with both of the men in her life, and she's matched by Ruffalo, Harry and Speedman in their supporting roles. Surprisingly uplifting, when you consider it's a movie about dying, this was based on the novel *Pretending The Bed Is A Raft* by Nancy Kincaid.

THE OTHER SISTER (1999)

Directed by Garry Marshall
Starring Juliette Lewis, Giovanni Ribisi

Returning home after years in a 'special' school, mentally challenged Carla (Lewis) is determined to go it alone in the world. However, she faces resistance from her wound-too-tight mother (Diane Keaton), who isn't exactly supportive of Carla's insistence on getting her own apartment or too keen on her budding romance with a slightly retarded marching-band enthusiast (Ribisi).

This cute, romantic comedy drama clearly has its heart in the right place, but *Pretty Woman* director Marshall gets hopelessly bogged down in predictability and political corrrectness. Nevertheless, there are good, understated performances from Lewis – in her first role for two years following the dire *Terms Of Endearment* sequel, *Evening Star* – and *Saving Private Ryan*'s Ribisi, and well-meaning support from Tom Skerritt (as Carla's dad) and Juliet Mills.

A PATCH OF BLUE (1965)

Directed by Guy Green
Starring Sidney Poitier, Shelley Winters, Elizabeth Hartman

Get the hankies ready for this bittersweet story that was one of the first mainstream Hollywood movies to deal with interracial romance. Gordon (Poitier) befriends young white blind girl Selena (Hartman) in a city park. Almost kept as a slave by her horrendous mother (Winters, who won an Oscar) and grandfather, Selena warms to this stranger, whom she determines is kind by the calm sound of his voice. Naturally, as this is the essence of the story, she doesn't know he is black. Poitier is wonderful as Gordon, while the Oscar-nominated Hartman, in her movie debut, is heartbreaking as the innocent, isolated woman he helps out of her shell. Sadly, she committed suicide in 1987 at the age of 43.

RANDOM HARVEST (1942)

Directed by Mervyn Leroy
Starring Ronald Colman, Greer Garson

Where would the movies be without amnesia? The same year Garson won an Oscar for *Mrs Miniver* she also scored in this emotionally turbulent doozy of memory loss, adapted from James Hilton's novel. Colman, a shell-shock victim of the First World War, wanders from an asylum into the arms of Garson's saintly, flame-haired singer Paula, with whom he starts a new, peaceful life as John 'Smithy' Smith. Alas, during a business trip, he gets a knock on the noggin and remembers he's fabulously rich and important Charles Rainier, but forgets where he's been since the war. Long-suffering is a wholly inadequate description for the tragically bereft Paula, who reinvents herself to win him back, and endures a series of hanky-wringing blows with dignity and devotion. This is just fabulous, with splendid performances.

RETURN TO ME (2000)

Directed by Bonnie Hunt
Starring David Duchovny, Minnie Driver

Poor old David Duchovny has yet to find a film that gives him the success he had on TV with *The X-Files*. However, he fares quite well in this odd little romantic comedy drama as widower Bob, who finds himself falling for free-spirited gal Grace (Driver). Trouble is, he doesn't know that Grace was the recipient of his own dead wife's heart, a secret that threatens to derail their romance from the outset.

Unfortunately for Duchovny, who is enjoyably cute as the bewildered hero and touching in the scenes following the loss of his beloved wife (played, briefly, by Joely Richardson), the film doesn't quite match his talents, being instead a mess of clichéd scenes and situations. One can't help thinking that if Grace had just told Bob about her heart transplant immediately, they could have lived happily ever after without any complications, and could have saved us all a lot of turmoil.

ROSEANNA'S GRAVE (1997)

Directed by Paul Weiland
Starring Jean Reno, Mercedes Ruehl, Polly Walker

Roseanna (Ruehl) has a heart condition that is going to kill her any time now. She has a single wish: to be buried in the village churchyard next to the cherished daughter she lost. But there are only three plots left in the cemetery, so her anxious husband Marcello (Reno), desperate to fulfil his promise to her, makes himself the town's unofficial protector. Oblivious to everything else going on around him, he frantically races around preventing accidents, donating blood and going to insane lengths to conceal a fatal unpleasantness he's stumbled across – all to save Roseanna's space. Hilarity and heartache rub along together charmingly in an offbeat story of heartfelt love with improbable but pleasing twists.

STANLEY AND IRIS (1990)

Directed by Martin Ritt
Starring Robert De Niro, Jane Fonda

A sweet if slightly bland little drama, this film was the last Fonda made before she took a fifteen-year leave of absence from the movies (her long-awaited return to the screen being the 2005 Jennifer Lopez comedy *Monster-in-Law*). She stars as newly widowed Iris, who certainly has a tough life: dead-end job, sullen son, pregnant daughter, annoying and dependent relatives and too many bills to pay. To top it off, she is being pursued by cook Stanley (De Niro) – and while he appears to have all his own teeth and faculties, there is one thorn in the side of their relationship: he can't read. So Iris teaches him and love blossoms. And that's about it, really, as it's all just an excuse to unite Fonda and De Niro on screen and have them spout meaningful dialogue at each other about literacy, companionship and life. Which, admittedly, they do quite nicely.

SYBIL (1976)

Directed by Daniel Petrie
Starring Sally Field, Joanne Woodward

Originally made for US television, this harrowing drama is based on a true story. Field stars as Sybil Dorsett, a woman who has suffered horrific abuse as a child to the extent that she has blocked it out and created sixteen distinct personalities for herself. Only psychiatrist Dr Wilbur (Woodward) has the patience to help Sybil cope and come to terms with her past.

A turning point in Field's career as up to this point she had been best known for light-hearted roles, this also features superb turns from Woodward, Natasha Ryan (haunting as young Sybil in flashback scenes) and Martine Bartlett as Sybil's unbalanced, horrendous mother, who devises 'games' to torture her child.

THE THREE FACES OF EVE (1957)

Directed by Nunnally Johnson
Starring Joanne Woodward, David Wayne, Lee J. Cobb

Joanne Woodward understandably won the Oscar for, well, her several performances as a woman leading three lives in this multiple personality disorder drama.

Dowdy mousewife Eve White (Woodward), suffering from headaches and blackouts, is taken to the doctor by her clueless husband (Wayne). Under hypnosis the wild and wanton persona of Eve Black emerges. Eventually, Dr Luther (Cobb) also coaxes out Jane, Eve's nice, normal, articulate and attractively poised inner self. *Sheesh!* In keeping with fifties thinking, a severe psychiatric problem is the result of childhood trauma, and, although we may regard the 'cure' as unsophisticated and simplistic now, the dedicated sleuthing and analysis required to winkle out that secret horror of Eve's is gripping stuff and a *tour de force* for Woodward. In 1976 Woodward switched to the shrink's role, treating the similarly showily afflicted Sybil.

UNTAMED HEART (1993)

Directed by Tony Bill
Starring Christian Slater, Marisa Tomei

A weepy of the highest order, *Untamed Heart* stars Christian Slater in one of his most low-key performances, as shy, sensitive Adam. A quiet dishwasher at a Minneapolis diner, he worships cynical-about-love waitress Caroline (Tomei) and comes to her rescue when two men try to attack her on the way home from work. Finally noticing him, she lets their friendship blossom into love, and Adam tells her his secret – to explain the scar on his chest, the orphanage nuns who raised him told him he had been given a baboon's heart. In fact, he has a regular, but very weak, human one.

Subtly played by the two leads, and with a fine turn from Rosie Perez as Caroline's brash best friend, this is an achingly poignant love story that ends in tears – not only for the characters but for the audience too. Slater makes your heart ache, but Tomei ultimately breaks it as the woman who finally finds love but has to suffer tragedy with it.

A WALK TO REMEMBER (2002)

Directed by Adam Shankman
Starring Mandy Moore, Shane West, Peter Coyote

A teen weepy that's a bit of a guilty pleasure for anyone over the age of fifteen, *A Walk To Remember* stars beautiful singer Mandy Moore as gawky (yeah, right) schoolgirl Jamie, who is thrown together with cool guy Landon (West) when he is punished for a minor crime by having to appear in the school musical alongside her. She's quiet, devout (her dad, played by Coyote, is the town preacher) and, of course, a bit of a stunner when she puts on a gown and performs. So it's no surprise that Landon falls for her and aspires to be a better man because of her. But she has a tragic secret … (cue lots of fainting and fluttering of eyelashes by Moore).

Surprisingly innocent for a contemporary teen movie, this is incredibly sweet and sincere (and a real sob-fest at the end), with two lovely performances from West and Moore, and great support from Coyote, and Daryl Hannah as Landon's single mum. You'll figure out the ending long before the characters do, but by then you'll have come over so warm and fuzzy that you won't care.

WHEN A MAN LOVES A WOMAN (1994)

Directed by Luis Mandoki
Starring Andy Garcia, Meg Ryan, Ellen Burstyn

Meg Ryan bravely bucked her cute image to play Alice Green, a drunk who hides the vodka in the linen cupboard, hits her children when she remembers where she put them and rages at her nice husband Michael (Garcia), who only wants to help her beat the bottle and hold them all together. Interestingly, it's after rehab and in recovery that a new set of problems emerges, as Michael is reluctant to surrender any control to the newly assertive Alice, and he, uncomfortably, has to shoulder some blame as the unwitting enabler of an alcoholic. It's an ambitious attempt to deal with love in bad times, with sympathy for both points of view and a particularly moving performance from the gorgeous Garcia. The children, Tina Majorino and Mae Whitman, are also terrific. It's tempting to wonder what the heck Alice's problem is, but the movie pushes all the right buttons and demands a hanky.

 TRUE-ISH TALES OF TORTURED ARTISTS

There must be writers, painters, composers, thespians and other creative artists who lead happy and fulfilled lives, but the movies certainly aren't interested in them. The cinema likes art at the high price of dramatic personal pain. The more alcoholism, insanity, doomed love, sexually transmitted disease and suicide there are, the better, which is why poor Vincent Van Gogh has graced so many biopics. When it comes to female creativity, literary figures with more talent than good times are particularly popular subjects. Of course, historically, women were allowed to write novels, poetry and journals after they'd finished their needlepoint more often than they were encouraged to sculpt, paint or compose symphonies. Among our favourite tormented creative talents to have been treated to movie mythologizing:

84 CHARING CROSS ROAD (1987)

Directed by David Hugh Jones
Starring Anthony Hopkins, Anne Bancroft

Based on Helene Hanff's autobiographical book – which was then made into a play and a BBC *Play For Today* in 1975 – this is a delicate love story in which the two protagonists don't even share the screen. American Hanff (Bancroft) contacts Frank Doel's (Hopkins) bookshop at the address of the title to locate a copy of Pepys's diary, and so begins a pen-pal friendship that continues for two decades without the pair ever meeting. By the way, romantics beware: 84 Charing Cross Road is now a Pizza Hut.

AN ANGEL AT MY TABLE (1990)

Directed by Jane Campion
Starring Kerry Fox, Alexia Keogh

Warming up for *The Piano*, director Campion tackles the life of important New Zealand novelist and poet Janet Frame (Fox), whose travails and internal struggle – chronicled in the three autobiographies on which this arresting picture is unflinchingly based – are unusually well captured. Solitary, overweight and marching to the beat of a different drum, unhappy young Janet is misdiagnosed as schizophrenic rather than recognised as exceptionally gifted. And as a result she is consigned to a psychiatric hospital for eight years. Kerry Fox is superbly sympathetic, getting to the heart of a woman finding herself and making her voice heard.

THE BARRETTS OF WIMPOLE STREET (1934)

Directed by Sidney Franklin
Starring Norma Shearer, Fredric March, Charles Laughton

MGM's lavish production of the ever-popular love story of Victorian poets Elizabeth Barrett (Shearer) and Robert Browning (March) is a divinely romantic melodrama in which Laughton looms large as Elizabeth's tyrannical papa. Invalid Elizabeth reclines prettily on a chaise longue in gigantic hoop skirts, sympathising with her tribe of oppressed siblings, recoiling from the obsessive attentions of her father and receiving the impassioned addresses of Mr Browning, whose vitality inspires her to elope. Franklin's own 1957 remake with Jennifer Jones, Bill Travers and John Gielgud doesn't come close.

CAMILLE CLAUDEL (1988)

Directed by Bruno Nuytten
Starring Isabelle Adjani, Gérard Depardieu

French sculptress Claudel (Adjani) is celebrated in this biodrama for being a singularly driven, ambitious artist whose 'madness of mud' as she slaps, smooths and kneads her work is her entire *raison d'être.* We have to say, though, that the hands-on art sessions are *un peu* dull. The film really takes off whenever Depardieu rears his big head as the greater sculptor Auguste Rodin, with whom the jealous and frustrated Camille enjoys and bewails an inspiring, maddening love affair. Evidence, if it were needed, that artists of either sex are better off with a supportive consort who cooks and cleans rather than a rival talent, no matter how hot they are.

CARRINGTON (1995)

Directed by Christopher Hampton
Starring Emma Thompson, Jonathan Pryce

A rather lifeless portrayal of some minor members of the Bloomsbury Set (see *The Hours*, below, for the major players). Short-haired, boyish painter Dora Carrington (Thompson) had an unconventional relationship with author Lytton Strachey (Pryce): he was over a decade older than her and a homosexual; she was heterosexual with a string of lovers; yet they became very close platonic friends. Their friendship lasted longer than the other relationships in their lives, even when it became complicated by the arrival of Ralph Partridge (Steven Waddington), whom Strachey loved but Dora married. Worth watching for a superb performance from Pryce, and good support from Rufus Sewell, Jeremy Northam and Waddington.

FINDING NEVERLAND (2004)

Directed by Marc Forster
Starring Johnny Depp, Kate Winslet

A fine weepy about the relationship between *Peter Pan* author J. M. Barrie (Depp) and the Llewellyn Davies family, who inspired him to write the famous story about the boy who never grew up. Barrie meets the boys in a London park with their widowed mother Sylvia (Winslet), and is soon enchanting them with tales of pirates, Red Indians, crocodile fights and big adventures. While his marriage to Mary (Rahda Mitchell) crumbles, Barrie spends more and more time with the family, much to the disapproval of Sylvia's mother (Julie Christie) and London society. Depp, as always, is terrific, as is young Freddie Highmore as Peter, while Dustin Hoffman (in his second *Peter Pan* movie, as he also starred in *Hook*), Kelly MacDonald and Ian Hart lend solid support.

FRANCES (1982)

Directed by Graeme Clifford
Starring Jessica Lange, Kim Stanley, Sam Shepard

Thirties film-star Frances Farmer, whose pictures include *The Toast of New York* and *South of Pago Pago*, is a tragic icon. Her disappointments in love, disdain for the silly studio fare she was offered, and aggressive, self-destructive behaviour landed her in an appalling mental hospital and ultimately lobotomised. Lange is superbly distressing as the beauty with brains and unpopular left-wing political sensibilities who became a martyr. Stanley is almost equally awesome as Frances's ambitious, domineering mother.

FRIDA (2002)

Directed by Julie Taymor
Starring Salma Hayek, Alfred Molina

Madonna was just one of artist Frida Kahlo's fans who wanted to make a biopic about her, but it was Hayek who got her version to the screen, and rumour has it that her boyfriend at the time, actor Edward Norton, tinkered with the script. Crippled in a bus accident in Mexico as a girl,

Frida (Hayek) is forced to spend hours, days and months in bed, and while there she picks up a paintbrush. As much about her tempestuous relationship with philandering fellow-artist Diego Rivera (Molina) as her art, this is an enjoyable, if not particularly revelatory movie. Hayek and Molina are both terrific.

HILARY AND JACKIE (1998)

Directed by Anand Tucker
Starring Emily Watson, Rachel Griffiths

Watson excels at the tricky task of portraying the often difficult, selfish and driven cellist Jaqueline du Pré in this controversial biopic of the unusual relationship between her and her sister Hilary (Rachel Griffiths). Loosely based on Hilary's and their brother Piers's biography *A Genius In The Family*, the film is a fascinating, no-holds-barred account of Jackie's musical career and private life.

While many column inches have been devoted to the most eyebrow-raising portion of the film – Jackie, in a time of need, asks Hilary whether she can sleep with her husband, and then does so – the movie, thanks to Watson's mesmeric performance, should be lauded for its fascinating realisation of Jackie's talent and almost self-destructive personality. You may not like her by the end, but you will certainly be glad you had the chance to meet her.

THE HOURS (2002)

Directed by Stephen Daldry
Starring Julianne Moore, Nicole Kidman, Meryl Streep, Ed Harris

This is a slow, mannered drama (you will either love its subtlety or gnash your teeth in boredom) focusing on a few hours in the lives of three women living in different decades of the twentieth century. The link between the trio is Virginia Woolf's novel *Mrs Dalloway*. First, we see Woolf herself (Kidman, almost unrecognisable with a pronounced prosthetic nose) as she sits down to write her most famous novel. Then we shift to the fifties, where Laura (Moore) is reading the book as she prepares for her husband's birthday, and wrestles with the pressures of her domestic life. Finally, we meet Clarissa (Streep) as she organises a party (much as Mrs Dalloway does) for her friend (Harris), who is dying of AIDS. Michael Cunningham's book was always considered too literary to be made into a movie, but screenwriter David Hare cleverly interweaves the three stories, and Daldry teases fabulous performances from the leads. Nicole Kidman won an Oscar for her performance.

IMPROMPTU (1991)
Directed by James Lapine
Starring Judy Davis, Hugh Grant, Mandy Patinkin

An undeservedly neglected treat depicts the cream of Europe's nineteenth-century artistic celebrities enjoying scandals, duels and *bons mots* during a pretentious French country-house weekend. At the centre of this galaxy is the revolutionarily liberated, trouser-wearing, cigar-smoking novelist Georges Sand (a delicious Davis). She revels in her tempestuous affairs, particularly with younger superstar composer Frédéric Chopin (floppy-haired Grant), whom she has apparently frightened into submission. 'You promised to love me!' accuses Sand's ex, Mallefille (Georges Corraface). 'I didn't promise to succeed,' retorts Georges. Historically, it's complete hooey, but it makes for a really amusing, fun romp.

IRIS (2001)
Directed by Richard Eyre
Starring Judi Dench, Kate Winslet

Kate Winslet gets to swim naked, ride bicycles at great speed and drive bumbling suitor John Bayley (played as a youth by Hugh Bonneville) to distraction as the buoyant, eccentric and bursting-with-ideas novelist Iris Murdoch. Judi Dench gets the far meatier, Oscar-worthy scenes as the older Murdoch falls apart due to Alzheimer's, in spite of the devotion of John (now her husband, played by the always wonderful Jim Broadbent). Unfortunately, if you watch this in the hope of learning something about Murdoch, Richard Eyre's drama will leave you disappointed. The author's accomplishments are glossed over, and the film doesn't seem to know whether it's coming or going as it darts unevenly between her free-spirited youth and troubled later life without focusing fully on either.

MRS PARKER AND THE VICIOUS CIRCLE (1994)

Directed by Alan Rudolph
Starring Jennifer Jason Leigh, Campbell Scott, Matthew Broderick

This portrait of legendary wit, writer and critic Dorothy Parker, and the acid-tongued clique of literary and theatrical celebs who lunched and bitched together at the Algonquin Round Table in twenties New York, is handsome but disappointingly overlong and dreary. However, Leigh, though too pretty, is magnificently mannered as the brilliant, eccentric, troubled Dorothy. She loves, loses, and when she isn't contemplating suicide effortlessly comes up with lines like, 'A girl can get splinters sliding down a barrister.'

SHADOWLANDS (1993)

Directed by Richard Attenborough
Starring Anthony Hopkins, Debra Winger

A deeply moving drama, based on the romance between *The Lion, The Witch And The Wardrobe* author C. S. Lewis (Hopkins) and American divorcee Joy Gresham (Winger). Lewis – known as Jack to colleagues and his brother Warnie (Edward Hardwicke) – was a shy Oxford professor in the 1950s, uncomfortable with his success as a novelist, when he met the louder, brasher Joy and her young son Douglas (*Jurassic Park*'s Joseph Mazzello). The pair fall in love, much to their and everyone else's surprise, but his love and Christian faith are both tested when Joy is diagnosed with cancer. Beautifully played out against the pretty Oxfordshire countryside, this is a tender tale, featuring two heart-rending performances from Hopkins and Winger.

SYLVIA (2003)

Directed by Christine Jeffs
Starring Gwyneth Paltrow, Daniel Craig

The relationship between poets Sylvia Plath and Ted Hughes was tempestuous and tragic, ending in her suicide in 1963, and many Hollywood players probably thought it was perfect for the screen – a sort of real-life, literary *A Star Is Born*. Unfortunately, while Paltrow gives a stunning performance as Plath, the movie itself is disappointing. Throughout, there are moments that make you feel like you are watching edited highlights of the Virginia Woolf section of *The Hours*, as composite characters pop up, supposed events are added, and Plath's children disappear from the screen when they are not necessary to the plot. Like a cinematic GCSE reader on Plath's life, the film rarely does more than skim the surface. Both Plath and Paltrow deserved better.

TOM AND VIV (1994)

Directed by Brian Gilbert
Starring Willem Dafoe, Miranda Richardson

The tortured marriage of poet T. S. Eliot (Dafoe) and aristocratic muse Vivienne Haigh-Wood (Richardson) is explored from their wide-eyed Oxford courtship in 1914 through literary fame and erratic behaviour to Viv's last years in an asylum in the forties. The Bloomsbury Set are beautifully dressed, but their activities go by in something of a baffling blur, and the transformation of Eliot from sensitive, honourable carer to cold egocentric is as mystifying as it is contentious with his admirers. Nevertheless, Dafoe does a fastidious impersonation, and Richardson is extraordinary as tragic, unpredictable Viv, whose misunderstood and wickedly treated gynaecological problems will make any woman's hair stand on end.

CLASSIC WEEPIES

AN AFFAIR TO REMEMBER (1957)

Directed by Leo McCarey
Starring Deborah Kerr, Cary Grant

One of the most famous tear jerkers of all time, this was a remake of 1939's *Love Affair* (made by the same director), and it was remade yet again in a lifeless 1994 version with Warren Beatty and his real-life wife

Annette Bening in the leading roles.

This version – the one that Meg Ryan and pal Rosie O'Donnell sob over in *Sleepless In Seattle* – is without doubt the loveliest, as charmer Nickie (Grant) and luminous Terry (Kerr) meet on an ocean liner and fall in love. Because they both already have partners and he has a reputation as a lazy playboy, they agree to test their love by parting at the end of the trip and then meeting up six months later once they have sorted out their complicated personal lives – at the top of the Empire State Building in New York. You probably know what happens next, but that won't stop the tears flowing as Grant and Kerr's romance warms the heart and turns even the most stoical viewer into a quivering pile of mushiness. Simply gorgeous.

THE BODYGUARD (1992)

Directed by Mick Jackson
Starring Whitney Houston, Kevin Costner, Gary Kemp

'I-iiii-iiiiiiiiii-iiiiii will always love you,' warbled Whitney on the soundtrack of this phenomenally successful movie, in which she starred as pop singer Rachel Marron. When Rachel gets death threats, former presidential bodyguard Frank Farmer (Costner) is hired by her manager (ex-Spandau Ballet star Gary Kemp) to protect her. They have a few rows about his overprotective security measures, then inevitably fall in love. But can a brooding bodyguard and a millionairess pop star be together for ever? And who's that lurking in the bushes?

Incredibly glossy and more than a little daft – can anyone explain why Frank and Rachel don't just fly off into the sunset together after the first kiss? – this is still an entertaining drama, in part thanks to the soundtrack, which went on to become one of the bestselling CDs of all time. Kev looks cute with his short haircut, and he suits the role originally intended two decades earlier for Steve McQueen, when Diana Ross was pencilled in for the Whitney role.

CAMILLE (1936)

Directed by George Cukor
Starring Greta Garbo, Robert Taylor

Arguably, this is Garbo's finest hour, and legend has it, her favourite film. She shines in this adaptation of Alexandre Dumas's (son of the Alexandre Dumas who wrote *The Count of Monte Cristo*) novel as Marguerite, a courtesan in nineteenth-century Paris known as Camille for her love of camellias, who falls for the young and handsome nobleman Armand (Taylor). Of course, their love is complicated – first by a jealous rival, then by Camille's other men friends and Armand's disapproving father. And, to make matters worse, she also suffers from tuberculosis. Have you got your hankies ready?

Filled with romantic dialogue ('Fate must have had something to do with this. I've hoped for it for so long,' Armand declares when he first speaks to Camille), this is really a gorgeous soap opera. Taylor – and in supporting roles Lionel Barrymore, Elizabeth Allan and Henry Daniell – are all wonderful, but Garbo, elegant even when she's coughing and swooning, is simply perfect. The story also provided the basis for Verdi's opera *La Traviata*.

IMITATION OF LIFE (1959)

Directed by Douglas Sirk
Starring Lana Turner, John Gavin, Sandra Dee

Miraculously, Sirk turned Fannie Hurst's tosh blockbuster into this lavishly moving melodrama, in which the daughter of Lana Turner's black housekeeper passes as white with heart-rending consequences. Turner's down-on-her-luck, would-be-actress Lora Meredith and her young daughter Susie meet homeless Annie Johnson (Juanita Moore) and her child Sarah Jane at the beach. The penniless single mothers decide to form an alliance: Annie cooking and cleaning in exchange for room and board. When Lora's star rises everything should be rosy for all of them, but she and her daughter (Dee) fall for the same man (Gavin), while bitter Sarah Jane (Susan Kohner) runs away and sinks into a dissolute life. Cue much soaking of tissues and a spectacularly upsetting funeral scene. Turner waived her salary for a percentage of

the profits and netted $2 million, which made her the highest-paid
actress in history at the time.

KRAMER VERSUS KRAMER (1979)

Directed by Robert Benton
Starring Dustin Hoffman, Meryl Streep

A terrific example of a late twentieth-century tear jerker if ever there
was one, this isn't about the beginning of a romance, but the end of
one, and the fallout that occurs when a family disintegrates. Joanna
Kramer (Streep) walks away from her unsatisfying marriage, leaving her
bewildered husband Ted (Hoffman) to raise their young son Billy
(Justin Henry). Previously a working dad who had contributed more
money than time to his child, Ted has to learn by trial and error how to
raise his son alone, but eventually the pair begin to bond and finally
become a self-contained family. Then Joanna returns and decides she
wants to sue Ted for custody of their son.

Streep has a tough job making her character sympathetic, but she
largely succeeds, and won a Best Supporting Actress Oscar for her
trouble. It's Hoffman's film, though (he won an Oscar for Best Actor),
and his natural depiction of a father slowly getting to know, and love,
his son is heart-warming.

LETTER FROM AN UNKNOWN WOMAN (1948)

Directed by Max Ophuls
Starring Joan Fontaine, Louis Jourdan

One of the greatest women's pictures ever made, and the ultimate 'if
only ...' romance, is a heart-rending tale of unrequited love with all the
yearning, remorse and redemption one could desire.

An ageing roué (Jourdan) receives a confessional letter from a
woman on her deathbed. He reads her story, which he learns too late
has been *their* story. In turn-of-the-century Vienna shy, awkward fourteen-year-old schoolgirl Lisa Bernal (Fontaine) develops a hopeless
crush on a neighbour, the dashing rake Stefan Brand. After years of
watching, waiting and hoping she attracts his attention for a brief,

blissful interlude of single white roses, carriage rides and seduction, only to be abandoned, forgotten and pregnant. Years later they meet again and Lisa leaves her husband, but she is devastated to realise Stefan doesn't even remember her. Disaster, death, more death and an impending duel at dawn ensue as Stefan discovers his mute manservant knew the truth all along. Lyrical visuals, poignant details and Fontaine's delicate, tremulous performance combine to make this a dreamy heartbreaker.

MESSAGE IN A BOTTLE (1999)

Directed by Luis Mandoki
Starring Kevin Costner, Robin Wright Penn, Paul Newman

Based on Nicholas Sparks's bestselling novel, this is a rather manipulative weepy, with Costner trying to bring tears to the audience's eyes as a widower who has written a heartfelt letter to his late wife, put it in a bottle and sent it out to sea. Luckily, reporter (and divorcée) Robin Wright Penn happens upon it, and sets out to find the man who wrote it. Of course, these two lonely souls are going to find love.

While Penn and Costner's on-screen chemistry fizzles rather than sizzles, the slushy script still manages to tug a few heartstrings. And there are more light-hearted moments than you might imagine, provided by Newman as Costner's wise but sarcastic dad. At seventy-four (as he was when this was made), he is still sexier, more handsome and more enthralling on screen than Costner could ever hope to be.

THE NOTEBOOK (2004)

Directed by Nick Cassavetes
Starring Gena Rowlands, James Garner, Ryan Gosling, Rachel McAdams

An old-fashioned tale of love across the years, this movie is based on a Nicholas Sparks novel. In the present day, an old man (Garner) reads a story of young love to an elderly woman (Rowlands), who is suffering with Alzheimer's. The tale he tells is of a 1940s summer romance between rich-girl Allie (McAdams) and local-boy Noah (Gosling), who fall in love but are then separated when circumstance – and her parents – intervene.

Director Cassavetes – Rowlands's son – mixes the teenage love story with the present-day relationship between Garner and Rowlands (they are the ageing Noah and Allie, though she doesn't remember). It's sentimental stuff – all luscious scenery and lakes filled with beautiful swans – that's pretty predictable, but perfect for anyone who's a sucker for slushy romance.

SWEET NOVEMBER (2001)

Directed by Pat O'Connor
Starring Charlize Theron, Keanu Reeves

Based on the 1968 movie of the same name that starred Sandy Dennis, this is one of those mushy romantic dramas that are best enjoyed on a wet and wintry Saturday afternoon with a pile of tissues and a large box of chocolates. Keanu Reeves is Nelson, a brash advertising executive who is obviously very successful because he has one of those massive apartments with no furniture in it. Although he seems perfectly happy living his yuppie life, we know that deep down he has a softer side, and it will no doubt come to the surface if he meets the right woman. And that woman is hippy chick Sara (Theron), who crashes into Nelson's life and asks him to come and live with her for a month, promising it will change his life. It seems that Sara does this kind of thing all the time: the guy can stay just long enough to find his inner man, but he must leave before any major romantic attachments have had time to develop.

It doesn't take Einstein to work out that this time her plan will fall apart when they fall in love. And the film's major plot twist, which involves an over-stuffed medicine cabinet and much coughing, is equally obvious. But there are still some cute moments, and Theron and Reeves both look very pretty.

TERMS OF ENDEARMENT (1983)

Directed by James L. Brooks
Starring Shirley MacLaine, Debra Winger, Jack Nicholson

It's the great Cancer Movie of the eighties. And five Oscars (out of a whopping eleven nominations), for Best Picture, Director, Screenplay, Actress (MacLaine) and Supporting Actor (Nicholson), proved this offbeat hit, which combines romantic comedy, a crazy–wonderful mother–daughter relationship and heartbreaking drama, meant more to many people than the sentimental tear jerker some cynics would describe it as.

Smothering mother Aurora Greenway (MacLaine) is obsessive and controlling with daughter Emma (Winger), who is just as headstrong and stubborn. Emma strikes out on her own for a youthful, difficult marriage to the straying Flap (Jeff Daniels). Meanwhile, eccentric Aurora, a vain belle with a string of admirers, gets her panties in a twist over the large-living, womanising ex-astronaut next door, Garrett Breedlove (Nicholson, a hoot as the pot-bellied Don Juan). But through all their ups and downs, Aurora and Emma never stop talking to each other every day, fighting, laughing and crying. Gears shift dramatically when Emma is stricken with terminal cancer, and both women rise spectacularly to the situation, Aurora with protective ferocity, Emma with grace. The disappointing 1996 sequel, *The Evening Star*, catches up with Aurora and her grandchildren.

THE WAY WE WERE (1973)

Directed by Sydney Pollack
Starring Barbra Streisand, Robert Redford

The handsome, turbulent chronicle of a love affair across twenty years is a romantic heartbreaker that is polished to perfection in every department. Babs belts out Marvin Hamlisch's Oscar-winning title song. Arthur Laurents's intelligent script is packed with immortal lines (such as 'Your girl is lovely, Hubble', memorably recited by Carrie in one of her encounters with Big in *Sex And The City*). And Redford is at the peak of his gorgeousness in white naval dress uniform.

Frizzy-haired, Jewish, impassioned political activist Katy (Streisand) has a crush on the unattainable WASP golden-boy Hubble (Redford) at university in the thirties. During the Second World War – by which time she's had her hair straightened – Katy can't believe her luck when she sights a drunken Hubble on leave in New York and gets him home and into her bed. The two are opposites politically, socially and temperamentally, but she can't let go of this dreamboat or the hopes she has of shaping him as a writer. Break-ups, reconciliations and irreconcilable beliefs reach a crisis after Hubble sells out to Hollywood and chooses an easy life of not rocking the boat. Director Pollack heavily edited the McCarthy-era blacklisting sequences, which makes the final split somewhat abrupt, but its cruel inevitability and the wistful postscript are still devastating.

Chapter 3: See You in My Dreams
Fantasies, Supernatural Stories, Ghost Stories and Swashbucklers

All movies are fantasies in one way or another: in real life the girl doesn't always get the guy, the endings aren't always happy and you can never afford a swanky New York loft apartment on a secretary's wage. But some movies are more fantastical than others, and those are the ones featured here – comedies, dramas, adventures or weepies that all share an element of the magical and supernatural, or are set in mythical worlds or far-off lands.

While boys fantasise about daring feats of bravery while wearing a fedora and carrying a whip, or flying through the sky in a cape with their pants outside their tights, we want adventures filled with gallant heroes and beautiful damsels in distress. Or tales of love featuring ghosts, reincarnated husbands, exotic creatures of the night and, best of all, men who will cross time and space to find the women they love. Ah, bliss.

Fantasies and supernatural stories have been staple themes for film-makers since the first silent movies unspooled on the screen: Murnau's *Nosferatu*, the haunting and oddly romantic vampire tale, was made in 1922, while Douglas Fairbanks dashingly swashed his buckle in *The Thief of Baghdad* just two years later. Many fantasy films, of course, aren't particularly girlie – most science fiction and horror, for a start, unless you have a strange fetish for blood, guts and aliens – but others find plenty of time for romance. *King Kong* (1933) sacrificing his life rather than hurt his love (Fay Wray); Snow White being kissed by her prince in *Snow White And The Seven Dwarves* (1937); David Niven falling in love with radio operator Kim Hunter in *A Matter Of Life And Death* (1946); Princess Leia telling Han Solo she loves him just before he is frozen in carbonite in *The Empire Strikes Back* (1980); the astronaut clinging to the vision of his dead wife in *Solaris* (in both the 1972 original and the 2002 remake) – all these films are romantic in their own way, but we don't include any of them here, simply because everyone, not just us soppy gals, loves them.

Unfortunately, some of our favourite fantasies won't ever be committed to film, so they can't be featured here, either. We want to play treehouse with a loincloth-clad Brendan Fraser from *George Of The Jungle*. We want to eat oysters with Albert Finney's Tom Jones and play baccarat with Sean Connery's James Bond. If none of this is possible, maybe someone could arrange for us to be rescued by Orlando Bloom's hero from *Pirates Of The Caribbean*, or spend the hereafter with *Beetlejuice*'s Alec Baldwin.

Impossible, all of them. But we can dream …

ROMANCING THE STONE (1984)

Directed by Robert Zemeckis
Starring Michael Douglas, Kathleen Turner, Danny De Vito

We gals had been waiting a mighty long time for a decent romantic adventure movie before *Romancing The Stone* came along, so it came as no surprise when the movie was a big box-office hit. A modern twist on the matinée romps of the thirties and forties, in which the girl is in danger and the hunky man comes to her rescue, the film has also been credited with revitalising Michael Douglas's career (he went on to make *Fatal Attraction* and *Basic Instinct*, and won an Oscar for *Wall Street*) and putting Kathleen Turner on the A-list of Hollywood leading ladies.

The story, written by Diane Thomas, is terrific. Romance novelist Joan Wilder (Turner), a lonely, self-proclaimed 'hopeful romantic' who doesn't expect a real man to live up to her heroic ideal, receives a package from her sister containing a treasure map. It transpires that the sister has been kidnapped in Colombia, and the bad guys want the map in exchange for her, so Joan heads to South America and straight into trouble. But, luckily, she meets fortune hunter Jack Colton (Douglas) – a man as rugged as her novels' heroes – who is prepared to help her, for a fee.

Their adventures are like a girlie version of *Raiders Of The Lost Ark* as the duo – who alternately loathe and fancy the pants off each

other – deal with mud slides, river rapids, drug barons and two inept kidnappers (the hilarious Danny De Vito and Zack Norman) while tossing witty banter back and forth. The dialogue sizzles ('What did you do, wake up this morning and say "Today I'm going to ruin a man's life"?' asks Jack when yet another disaster occurs) almost as much as the two leads, as they tumble around in the mud and try to outwit the kidnappers.

Turner, best known at the time as the sex siren from *Body Heat*, is superb as the wallflower who blossoms into a sexy adventuress, while Douglas is absolutely gorgeous as the tough, sarcastic 'hero' we'd all want to come to our rescue. As well as the double-act from De Vito and Norman, there's nice support from Alfonso Arau (now better known as the director of *Like Water For Chocolate*), as Colombian businessman Juan. But in the end, of course, it's the chemistry between Douglas and Turner that makes this a funny, smart and adorable adventure. They later teamed up for a sequel, *The Jewel Of The Nile*, and also reunited for the Danny De Vito-directed black comedy *The War Of The Roses*.

13 GOING ON 30 (2004)

Directed by Gary Winick
Starring Jennifer Garner, Mark Ruffalo

This is sort of a *Big* body-swap fantasy for girls. It's 1987, and thirteen-year-old Jenna, after being humiliated by a bitchy schoolfriend at her birthday party, makes a wish that she was older. Thanks to some magic sprinkles, she wakes up seventeen years in the future to find she is a successful thirty-year-old women's magazine editor in New York (*Alias* star Garner playing the adult Jenna). Unsurprisingly confused about what has just happened, she goes in search of her old pudgy school-mate Matt (who has blossomed into the sexy, gorgeous Mark Ruffalo), hoping he will help her figure it out.

While the plot of this romantic comedy is extremely obvious – gee, could Jenna and Matt possibly have hidden feelings for each other? – both Garner and Ruffalo are infectiously charming. Andy Serkis (best known as icky Gollum in *The Lord Of The Rings*) as Jenna's boss and Judy Greer as her bitchy co-worker provide witty support.

ALWAYS (1989)

Directed by Steven Spielberg
Starring Richard Dreyfuss, Holly Hunter, John Goodman, Brad Johnson

Dreyfuss plays devil-may-care firefighting aviator Pete, who regularly brushes off the anxieties of his dispatcher girlfriend Dorinda (Hunter). However, as she always feared, he is killed in a fiery crash and she is left bereft. Then an elegant angel (Audrey Hepburn in her last screen role) assigns Pete's spirit to watch over his replacement (in more ways than one), Ted (Brad Johnson). Helplessly, Pete looks on as Dorinda and Ted fall in love.

This is a sweet remake of Victor Fleming's much-loved but equally rather drab Second World War fantasy *A Guy Named Joe* (1943), starring Spencer Tracy and Irene Dunne as the lovers not completely parted by death. Both Spielberg and Dreyfuss had seen that film dozens of times and longed to make their own version; *Always*'s dated tone is perhaps an unwelcome consequence of their repeated viewings. A tough-yet-vulnerable Hunter is the real star, cute and heartachingly credible.

BELL, BOOK AND CANDLE (1958)

Directed by Richard Quine
Starring James Stewart, Kim Novak, Jack Lemmon

Publisher James Stewart moves in above an art gallery owned by Kim Novak's sultry, bohemian Gillian and experiences an instant animal magnetism, even though he is about to be married. The poor sap is not to know that Gillian is a powerful witch, her cat Pyewacket is her familiar, and her oddball relations are Manhattan's hippest coven. Gillian can't resist trying to enchant the man *without* using magic, but his obnoxious fiancée is a tempting target, and Gillian risks losing her powers if she falls in love herself. (The title refers to the ritual 'Ring the bell, close the book, quench the candle' that supposedly undoes a witch.) Jack Lemmon, as Novak's mischievous warlock brother, Ernie Kovaks as an investigative writer and Elsa Lanchester and Hermione Gingold as comic crones all add to the fun.

LA BELLE ET LA BÊTE (1946)

Directed by Jean Cocteau
Starring Jean Marais, Josette Day, Marcel André

This is not only an exquisite masterpiece of world cinema but a profound fairytale/fable for adults, motivated by poet and filmmaker Jean Cocteau's post-war conviction that any man can be transformed into a beast. When a poor merchant falls afoul of the enchanted Beast, his devoted daughter Belle (Day) – a solitary paragon among his otherwise selfish, greedy children – sacrifices herself as a hostage, and she is whisked away to the creature's magical chateau. French matinée idol Jean Marais brings new meaning to the phrase sexy beast, being simultaneously striking, seductive and moving.

This is a classic, haunting film, full of simmering emotions, spectacular costumes and stunning, ingenious visuals – such as the candelabra held by live arms poking through the walls. Francis Ford Coppola paid homage to some of these effects in his *Dracula*.

THE BISHOP'S WIFE (1947)

Directed by Henry Koster
Starring Cary Grant, Loretta Young, David Niven

Christmas is coming and overworked bishop Henry Brougham (Niven) prays for heavenly guidance in his project to build a new cathedral. Enter an angel named Dudley (Grant), who makes it his mission not to worry about the fundraising but to raise the spirits of Henry's neglected wife Julia (Young). It's a charming fantasy in which faith is tested in an unexpected way, and, naturally, folks learn what really matters in this life.

Director Penny Marshall's less magical, overlong and more grounded contemporary remake, *The Preacher's Wife* (1996), seems primarily a vehicle to let Whitney Houston's Julia raise the church roof with some superb gospel singing. But Denzel Washington's studly Dudley and Courtney B. Vance as the disbelieving minister – beset by social ills as well as financial worries – are fine in a defiantly old-fashioned Yuletide story.

BLITHE SPIRIT (1945)

Directed by David Lean
Starring Rex Harrison, Constance Cummings, Kay Hammond, Margaret Rutherford

Noël Coward's delightful, inimitably English stage confection makes for a very funny fantasy film with an acerbic touch of the comedy of manners. Elegant Rex Harrison's well-heeled writer Charles Condomine thinks it would be great fun and valuable research to entertain his dinner guests with a séance. Enter Margaret Rutherford's divinely dotty medium Madame Arcati, who inadvertently summons the ghost of Charles's late wife Elvira (Hammond) – much to the dismay of his current wife Ruth (Cummings). The whimsical Elvira can be seen and heard only by Charles, but she certainly makes her presence felt, provoking a screamingly funny, catty battle of wills between the wives. Clever lighting and make-up achieve amusing (and Oscar-winning) ghostly effects, Madame Arcati's excited attempt to exorcise Elvira backfires, and the haunting of Charles takes a deliciously tart twist.

BRAM STOKER'S DRACULA (1992)

Directed by Francis Ford Coppola
Starring Gary Oldman, Keanu Reeves, Winona Ryder

Without doubt the sexiest and most romantic version of the Dracula legend, this is more a sad story of a man – albeit with pointy teeth and a yearning for blood – searching for his lost love than it is a horror movie. The prologue tells us that, on returning from the Crusades, Vlad the Impaler (Oldman) discovered his adored wife had killed herself. Renouncing God, Vlad rampages through fifteenth-century Transylvania, becoming a creature of the night known as Dracula who feeds on human blood. Centuries later, however, when innocent lawyer Jonathan Harker (Reeves) visits the ancient, now-immortal creature's castle, Vlad becomes obsessed with a picture of Harker's fiancée Mina (Ryder), convinced she is a reincarnation of his mourned wife, Elizabeta.

Oldman is haunting as the tortured count who, in an aching voice that's enough to make any woman melt into a girlish heap, tells Mina he has 'crossed oceans of time' to find her. Reeves, meanwhile, is as pretty as ever, and Ryder is ethereally beautiful as the woman for whom both men are prepared to die.

BUFFY THE VAMPIRE SLAYER (1992)

Directed by Fran Rubel Kazui
Starring Kristy Swanson, Donald Sutherland, Rutger Hauer, Luke Perry

Writer Joss Whedon's brilliant notion – which he would develop into a much-loved landmark in genre TV when Buffy became Sarah Michelle Gellar and moved to Sunnydale – of an all-American blonde teen cheerleader dusting vampires made for the cutest horror comedy. Popular Valley Girl Buffy's life of pom-pom-shaking and mall-shopping is overturned when a mysterious stalker (Sutherland, as Buffy's demanding 'Watcher') reveals she is the Chosen One. Her destiny as her generation's defender of the innocent and her crash course in slayage – against fanged Rutger Hauer – lays down the lore for the television series. Look out for future Oscar winners Ben Affleck (on the basketball court) and Hilary Swank (as one of the cool kids).

THE BUTCHER'S WIFE (1991)

Directed by Terry Hughes
Starring Demi Moore, Jeff Daniels

Moore went blonde for her role as clairvoyant Marina, a Carolina belle who sees signs that her true love is about to arrive by sea. When a rowing boat lands on the beach outside her home she decides it must be fate and weds the man onboard, a New York butcher named Leo (George Dzundza). Soon she is living with him in Greenwich Village, dispensing her predictions of love to his customers, but Leo isn't too keen on her psychic displays and asks her to see local psychiatrist Alex (Daniels). Can you see where this may be going?

Yes, it seems that Marina can predict love only for other people and not for herself, so perhaps her vision that Leo was her soulmate was wrong. Never mind, because everything sorts itself out in the end (there's even a woman who secretly yearns for Leo). While it's all utterly predictable, it's also quite cute, thanks mainly to Moore, and nice support from a cast that includes Mary Steenburgen, Frances McDormand, Margaret Colin and Miriam Margolyes.

CHANCES ARE (1989)

Directed by Emile Ardolino
Starring Cybill Shepherd, Robert Downey Jr, Ryan O'Neal, Mary Stuart Masterson

This is a little-known gem of a comedy romance. Corinne (Shepherd) and Louie (Christopher McDonald) are a young couple in love. On their first wedding anniversary, however, Louie is killed in a car accident on his way home. Fast forward more than two decades, and Corinne's daughter Miranda (Masterson) – Corinne was pregnant when Louie died – is bringing home her new boyfriend Alex (Downey Jr) to meet Mom. Trouble is, after a bang to the head, Alex realises he's actually a reincarnation of Louie, and hilarity really does ensue as the hapless young man discovers that he's (sort of) dating his own daughter.

There's much fun to be had from this odd state of affairs. Downey Jr is heart-warming and charming as the man with someone else's memories and affections, while Shepherd hits the right note as a widow who has never enjoyed another love. But equally good is the understated Ryan O'Neal as Philip, Louie's best friend who has carried a torch for Corinne for many years. We know he'll eventually get his happy ending, as will Corinne and Louie/Alex, and that's what makes this such a sweet and warm movie.

CITY OF ANGELS (1998)

Directed by Brad Siberling
Starring Nicolas Cage, Meg Ryan

Seth (Cage) is an angel who wanders through Los Angeles, along with scores of other heavenly messengers, listening to people's thoughts and comforting those in need. Having never been human, he doesn't know what it's like to be mortal, how it would feel to touch someone or feel their touch, and he yearns to experience both, especially after he meets heart surgeon Maggie (Ryan). Although he can reveal himself to her, he's not flesh and blood, so he must decide whether to make the ultimate sacrifice and 'fall' to earth – an act that will make him human, but also means giving up all that he has as an angel.

Based on Wim Wenders's sublime *Wings Of Desire*, this Hollywood-lite version is a somewhat slow, subtly played, low-on-slush romantic drama, featuring a mesmeric performance from Cage and a less-weepy-than-usual one from Ryan, although she doesn't convince as a surgeon. They are ably supported by Andre Braugher as Seth's celestial pal and Dennis Franz as an angel who has already 'fallen', and some haunt-ingly beautiful moments (the angels gathering on the beach to watch the sunrise; Cage and Braugher chatting atop a freeway sign) outweigh the silly ones that pop up towards the inevitable climax. Slow but a must for Cage fans.

DEATH BECOMES HER (1992)

Directed by Robert Zemeckis
Starring Meryl Streep, Bruce Willis, Goldie Hawn

A blackly comic look at vanity and the strange things we do for love, this is worth a look for the hilarious performances of the three leads. When her successful best friend Madeline (Streep) steals her plastic surgeon fiancé Ernest (Willis), Helen (Hawn) becomes a depressed blob. That is, until the mysterious Lisle (Isabella Rossellini) delivers a potion that will make her young and beautiful for ever. When it looks like the now-sexy Helen has a chance to steal back poor Ernest, Madeline decides she wants some of the potion too, but only after they have both taken the strange liquid do the pair finally twig that any damage done to their immortal bodies is permanent, and they may need Ernest's skills to keep them looking even vaguely human.

Packed with special effects as Helen and Madeline resort to desper-ate measures in their attempts to outwit each other, this is a very dark comedy that isn't to everyone's taste. But fans of Streep will enjoy seeing her lighter side, while those with a twisted sense of humour will find much to laugh at during this bizarre tale.

DEFENDING YOUR LIFE (1991)

Directed by Albert Brooks
Starring Albert Brooks, Meryl Streep, Rip Torn

Comic writer–director–actor Brooks has a cult following for his droll work, and this whimsical fantasy is the most chick-worthy of his out-of-the-mainstream treats. Brooks's Daniel is killed in a car crash and finds himself on trial in Judgment City (which looks uncannily like a Vegas resort complex), where it will be determined whether he has to return to earth in another incarnation. The veteran Rip Torn is hilarious as his defence attorney, while the divine Meryl Streep, as fresh and at home in this slight fable as she is in high drama, plays the angelic Julia, with whom Daniel learns eternal lessons about life and love while his fate beckons. The philosophy is muddled, but the film is fun and likeable.

THE DOUBLE LIFE OF VERONIQUE (1991)

Directed by Krzysztof Kieslowski
Starring Irène Jacob, Philippe Volter

Two girls, Veronika in Prague, Veronique in Paris – identical but with no discernible connection – are born at the same time and go on to have uncannily similar lives. Both have widowed fathers, a musical gift and a medical condition. In their twenties, Veronika is in love and about to make her professional singing debut, but she also has strange visions and feels that she is 'not alone'. Meanwhile, Veronique can't shake the feeling that she is 'missing someone', then falls in love with a mystery man and receives a series of puzzling objects in the post.

Acclaimed Polish filmmaker Kieslowski's eerie romantic mystery is a corker. Not all the loose ends are tied up in a bizarre and absorbing tale of love, grief and goosebumps, but one scarcely minds as the fourth-dimensional goings-on – underlined by a haunting score – are like an erotic trip into *The Twilight Zone*.

EVER AFTER (1998)

Directed by Andy Tennant
Starring Drew Barrymore, Anjelica Huston, Dougray Scott

Cute-as-a-button Barrymore is adorable as the clever, gutsy orphan Danielle in this enchanting, feminist-friendly retelling of *Cinderella*, beautifully filmed on French locations. An aged Queen of France (living legend Jeanne Moreau) reveals to the Grimm Brothers the 'real' royal family history behind their best-loved fairytale. And a thorough delight it is, as our plucky heroine foils her cruel, scheming stepmother (Anjelica Huston in handsome, malevolent fettle) and captivates the charming prince (Dougray Scott), who has much to learn from his mystery girl about courage, honour, goodness and true love. Replacing the magical intervention of the traditional fairy godmother we get the benevolent assistance of Renaissance genius Leonardo da Vinci, but a smashing cast with good script, direction and technical team make romantic magic without the 'bibbidi bobbidi boo' or a pumpkin in sight.

FIRST KNIGHT (1995)

Directed by Jerry Zucker
Starring Richard Gere, Sean Connery, Julia Ormond

Many think 1981's darkly wonderful *Excalibur* is the last word on Camelot films, but that hasn't stopped Hollywood rehashing the story numerous times since, including here, in the girliest version. Arthur (Connery) is a wise old sort who lays eyes on Guinevere (Ormond), and decides that, although she's about as animated as a plank of wood, she'll do quite nicely, thank you. She's happy with the deal too, especially because Arthur and his knights promise to save her from Malagant (Ben Cross), a dastardly dude who's trying to kidnap her. But then Guinevere meets Lancelot (Gere) en route to the altar, and decides to indulge in a bit of adulterous tonsil hockey before (and after) her nuptials.

Unfortunately, Gere and Ormond lack any sexual chemistry, so it's hard to believe she'd betray sweet, sexy Sean for a man mainly interested in his own hairdo. And *First Knight* is similarly lacking all over: Ben Cross is not given enough time to perfect his Alan Rickman/Sheriff of Nottingham impersonation; director Zucker unwisely dumps the magic usually associated with the tale; and the action sequences are used only briefly to spice up the slushy bits. All in all, it's an unromantic romance.

FOREVER YOUNG (1992)

Directed by Steve Miner
Starring Mel Gibson, Jamie Lee Curtis, Elijah Wood

In despair when his fiancée is left in a coma after a car wreck, Mel Gibson's 1930s test pilot volunteers to be the guinea pig in a cryogenics experiment that is subsequently abandoned and forgotten. Over fifty years later he is accidentally defrosted by cute kiddy Elijah Wood, who takes him home to single mom Jamie Lee Curtis for a crash course in the brave new world and a race against time to reunite with his lost love.

Men simply don't get this unashamedly romantic fantasy twaddle, but we have no problem cheering on our charismatic hero's quest for his geriatric girl. The fish-out-of-water/man-out-of-his-own-time comedy is nicely done, the sentimentality is as yummy as a chocolate truffle, and the three leads are all very appealing as they champion emotional rescue, a second chance in life and eternal love.

FREAKY FRIDAY (2003)

Directed by Mark Waters
Starring Jamie Lee Curtis, Lindsay Lohan

Tess is a widowed psychiatrist getting married on Saturday. Her resentful fifteen-year-old daughter Anna has problems at school and an audition with her rock band on Friday. Then the two are magicked into each other's bodies for a fraught twenty-four hours of unfamiliar challenges and new mutual understanding.

This amusing body-swap fairytale, adapted from Mary Rodgers's juvenile classic of comedic life lessons, is a much-improved update of Disney's 1976 Jodie Foster version, in which a girl not knowing how to operate a washing machine was about as wacky as it got.

Here Tess in Anna's body neatly tackles school bullying and young lurve, while Anna as Tess lets rip with demanding patients, amorous fiancé and the wedding arrangements. It's very cute and innocently funny, with Jamie Lee Curtis beautifully silly and Lindsay Lohan feisty.

GHOST (1990)

Directed by Jerry Zucker
Starring Patrick Swayze, Demi Moore, Whoopi Goldberg

This romantic supernatural thriller was the surprise box-office smash of its year, when women turned off by big-bang flicks stormed back into cinemas for one of the all-time-great date movies. *Ghost* has it all: sex, ghosts, guns, roses, fun gags *and* dance routines. Swayze – satisfyingly shirtless for a fair share of the running time – plays Sam Wheat, a Wall Street banker (well, it *is* a fantasy), while Moore, in her star-making break, is his great love Molly. They scarcely have time to do erotic things over her potter's wheel (memorably to 'Unchained Melody') or enjoy a smoochy twirl around their apartment before Sam is killed in reel one. Sam then has to get to grips with ghost-dom: solving his own murder, devising a revenge sting and haunting his honey. He does all this with the reluctant assistance of Whoopi Goldberg in her Oscar-winning turn as Oda Mae Brown, a phoney medium aghast to discover she is Sam's personal instrument of communication.

The first 'straight' solo film from Jerry Zucker, one of the perpetrators of *Airplane* and *Naked Gun*, this has fab special effects, a subway spectre whose shtick is positively inspired, and black-cloaked critters from hell who look like rejects from *Fantasia*. But what really makes it are the sweet, credible performances from Swayze and Moore, the theme of love beyond death, and Whoopi mugging it up amusingly for light relief. For one incredible moment we also appear to be heading for an interracial lesbian love scene when Oda Mae is possessed by Sam for a posthumous clinch with Molly. It's still a hugely entertaining hanky-wringer.

THE GHOST AND MRS MUIR (1947)

Directed by Joseph L. Mankiewicz
Starring Gene Tierney, Rex Harrison, George Sanders

Around 1900 impoverished young widow Lucy Muir (Tierney) and her little daughter Anna (Natalie Wood) move into a lonely English seaside dwelling called Gull Cottage. The reason for its neglect becomes clear when the irascible ghost of its former occupant, seafarer Captain Gregg (Rex Harrison), employs his usual spooky tactics to scare off intruders. But he's impressed by Lucy's pluck and a rich relationship develops. After ensuring the Muirs' future by dictating his colourful memoirs to Lucy (who becomes a bestselling author as a result), the crusty Gregg finds himself jealous of her fellow-author and suitor Miles (suave George Sanders in a rare non-caddish role). This fantasy romance is gentle, atmospheric (with a memorable score by Bernard Herrmann) and utterly charming.

THE GRIMM BROTHERS' SNOW WHITE / a.k.a. SNOW WHITE: A TALE OF TERROR (1997)

Directed by Michael Cohn
Starring Sigourney Weaver, Sam Neill, Monica Keena, Gil Bellows

The classic fairytale of Snow White and her seven vertically challenged pals gets a decidedly un-Disney reworking in this grown-up drama. Gone are the cute dwarves, to be replaced by a group of disfigured outsiders who risk their lives mining for the gold they need to survive, and rather than an evil queen who's wicked just for the sake of it, we have a beautiful woman (Weaver), twisted and bitter after a gruesome miscarriage, who finds refuge in black magic when she believes her husband (Neill) loves his daughter Lili (Keena) more than her.

While the fifteenth-century Black Forest setting is all dense, dark trees and atmospheric flickering candles, this never quite gets beyond slightly creepy, despite a deliciously seething performance from Weaver. Director Cohn may have been trying for a *Company Of Wolves*-style bloody fairytale to have you hiding behind the cinema seats, but instead he's made a well-acted, beautifully photographed but ultimately small-screen version of a well-loved tale, best suited to a rainy night in front of the telly.

HEART AND SOULS (1993)

Directed by Ron Underwood
Starring Robert Downey Jr, Kyra Sedgwick, Alfre Woodard, Charles Grodin

Have the hankies at the ready because this fantasy comedy drama is a major tear jerker. A bus containing four troubled people crashes in San Francisco in 1959 on the same night as a baby boy named Thomas Reilly is born. The passengers – played by Grodin, Woodard, Sedgwick and Tom Sizemore – become ghosts because they all need to resolve issues in their lives before they can go to heaven. To do this they must each enter the body of now-grown Thomas (Downey), whom they have haunted since infancy.

A skilful mix of comedy and tears as the four take turns inhabiting the relucatant Thomas's body, this works brilliantly, thanks to a superb performance from Downey Jr and a script that makes you laugh and cry without ever ladling on the syrup too thickly.

HEAVEN CAN WAIT (1978)

Directed by Warren Beatty, Buck Henry
Starring Warren Beatty, Julie Christie, James Mason

In this remake of 1941's *Here Comes Mr Jordan* Beatty stars as Joe Pendleton, a football player who dies too soon. As a result, he is sent back to earth in the body of a millionaire called Leo, whose wife (Dyan Cannon) and partner (Charles Grodin) are both trying to kill him. The only bright spot on Leo/Joe's horizon is a beautiful woman named Betty (Christie), who comes to see Leo to persuade him to save her small town from ruin.

Corny and sentimental this may be, but Beatty is charming, and there is some delicious humour from Cannon and Grodin. Surprisingly, the film – best described as cute but slight – was nominated for a whopping *nine* Academy Awards, including Best Actor for Beatty, Best Picture and Best Direction. Sanity was restored at the ceremony itself, as it won only one Oscar, for Best Art Direction. A further, more comedic remake of the story – *Down to Earth* with Chris Rock – was made in 2001.

I MARRIED A WITCH (1942)

Directed by René Clair
Starring Fredric March, Veronica Lake, Cecil Kelloway, Susan Hayward

Years before Samantha twitched her nose in *Bewitched* (inspired, as were *Bell, Book And Candle* and *Practical Magic*, by this film) or the Halli-well sisters became *Charmed*, Veronica Lake was a sexy and mischievous screen witch. Jennifer, burned at the stake alongside her father in the seventeenth century, returns in the twentieth still intent on carrying out her bad-marriage curse on the male descendants of the Puritan who condemned her and Daddy. In this generation that scion is quite a catch, though, and he manages to crack her resolve on the eve of his wedding to snippy Estelle (Susan Hayward).

Adapted from the novel *The Passionate Witch* by Thorne Smith, who was also the source for the classic ghost comedy *Topper* (1937) and the original body-swap tale *Turnabout* (1940), this remains a delight. Elegant Fredric March plays gubernatorial candidate Wallace Wooley (and three of his ancestors) in what is a wonderfully sly, witty, romantic comedy fantasy in which love potions are swallowed by the wrong people, Lake slides *up* banisters and, alas, the witch must surrender her powers to get her man.

INTERVIEW WITH THE VAMPIRE (1994)

Directed by Neil Jordan
Starring Tom Cruise, Brad Pitt, Antonio Banderas, Kirsten Dunst

The seductive, immortal characters from Anne Rice's much-loved Gothic novels *The Vampire Chronicles* were finally brought to the big screen in this luscious adaptation of the first book in the series. We are introduced to lonely, reluctant vampire Louis (Pitt, looking just as porcelain-skinned and contemplative as he is described in the book) and the egotistical, arrogant creature who made him, the vampire Lestat (Cruise).

In the present day Louis tells his epic, centuries-long story to a young interviewer (Christian Slater, in a role originally meant for River Phoenix). We learn of his human days as a plantation owner, his travels around Europe with Lestat and the child vampire Claudia (Dunst) they make as a companion. While Pitt's, Banderas's (as older, wiser vampire Armand) and especially Dunst's performances are spot on, many fans – and at one point Rice herself, although she later recanted – were unhappy with the casting of Cruise as the (on paper at least) sexy, utterly amoral, seductive blond vamp. Cruise certainly isn't quite right – he captures the evil well enough, but he's not so successful with the seductive. However, he's not as bad as you might imagine, and Pitt and Banderas more than make up for Tom's lack of sex appeal here.

KATE AND LEOPOLD (2001)

Directed by James Mangold
Starring Meg Ryan, Hugh Jackman

Kate (Ryan) has given up on men until she meets dashing Leopold (Jackman) in this romantic fantasy. Little does she know that he is an English duke from the 1870s who has travelled through a rip in time to the present day; or that at some point he'll have to go back or risk screwing up his future bloodline.

Logic is thrown out of the window pretty early on – there's a head-scratching subplot in which it transpires that Kate's ex-boyfriend (Liev Schreiber) is a direct descendant of Leopold, causing all sorts of problems. And Mangold expects us to believe that a nineteenth-century duke would understand all of Kate's modern babbling without pausing to ask what the hell she is talking about. Ryan's girl-next-door routine, which she has been doing since *When Harry Met Sally*, is starting to grate by now, but the movie is saved by a truly winning, sexy and suave performance from Jackman that's well worth taking a trip back in time for.

LADYHAWKE (1985)

Directed by Richard Donner
Starring Matthew Broderick, Rutger Hauer, Michelle Pfeiffer

This gorgeous medieval fantasy of lovers under an evil spell, ravishingly filmed on Italian locations, is one of the most absurdly neglected romantic adventures. Broderick's escaped thief Philippe 'The Mouse' Gaston is befriended by mysterious knight Etienne Navarre (Hauer), also a fugitive from the wicked Bishop of Aquila (John Wood). The bishop desired Navarre's love, Lady Isabeau d'Anjou (Pfeiffer), and has put them under a curse that turns Navarre into a wolf by night, and Isabeau into a hawk by day. Heart-meltingly, they can share a fleeting touch only at sunrise and sunset.

Broderick is inescapably contemporary as the lively rogue eager to assist Navarre in taking down the villain and breaking the spell, and the rock music score is a big mistake. But charismatic Hauer and lovely Pfeiffer are perfect.

MADE IN HEAVEN (1987)

Directed by Alan Rudolph
Starring Timothy Hutton, Kelly McGillis

Hutton and McGillis are two souls who meet and fall in love in heaven. Unfortunately, she is sent down to earth to be born, so he pleads with the higher power (named Emmett, and played by an almost unrecognisable Debra Winger) to be allowed to follow her. Emmett gives him thirty years to find his love and be reunited, but there's a catch: down on earth neither of them will remember the other from their previous life in heaven.

Like the leads' relationship, the film works best when they are in heaven but then falls to earth with a bit of a bang. Sweet in places, it would be incredibly sappy if it weren't for Hutton's terrific performance and some fine support from Maureen Stapleton as his aunt, who is already dead and up in heaven to act as his guide.

MEET JOE BLACK (1998)

Directed by Martin Brest
Starring Brad Pitt, Anthony Hopkins, Claire Forlani

Susan (Forlani) thinks she's met the man of her dreams when she starts chatting to a young hunk (Pitt) in a coffee shop, but she's surprised when she turns up at her father's home to find the very same man sitting at the dinner table. He's introduced to her as Joe Black, but he's actually Death in mortal guise, who took over the body of her new acquaintance after he was hit by a car. Joe's on earth to learn about life, and he has selected Susan's millionaire dad (Hopkins) as his tour guide, in exchange for a few more days of life. However, matters are complicated when Joe and the blissfully unaware Susan fall for each other.

Unlike the 1934 movie *Death Takes A Holiday*, on which this is based, *Meet Joe Black* is a whopping three hours long, which is a tad excessive for a romantic drama. Director Brest piles on the clichés, throws in an unnecessary business subplot about a hostile takeover, cues up sweeping orchestral music for every romantic scene, and has nothing original to say in Pitt's fish-out-of-water scenes. That said, we do get three hours of Brad looking absolutely yummy, so it isn't all bad.

PEGGY SUE GOT MARRIED (1986)

Directed by Francis Ford Coppola
Starring Kathleen Turner, Nicolas Cage

A surprisingly whimsical movie from *Godfather* director Coppola, this asks the question, 'If you could live your life again, knowing what you know now, would you do things differently?' That's the problem housewife Peggy Sue (Turner) has to resolve. When she collapses at her high-school reunion, she wakes to find herself back at school in her own past and has to decide whether to continue the teen romance that she knows will lead to a disappointing marriage to cute-but-dim Charlie (Cage).

Filled with fun jokes as Peggy Sue uses her present-day knowledge in the past, this meanders somewhat in the middle, but it benefits from a charming performance from Turner and a hilarious one from Cage. Also, watch out for Jim Carrey in an early role as one of Charlie's pals.

13 ACTORS WHO HAVE PLAYED ANGELS

John Travolta in *Michael*
Nicolas Cage in *City Of Angels*
Holly Hunter and Delroy Lindo in *A Life Less Ordinary*
Jessica Lange in *All That Jazz*
Cary Grant in *The Bishop's Wife*
Denzel Washington in *The Preacher's Wife*
Frankie Avalon in *Grease*
Michael Caine in *Mr Destiny*
Isaac Hayes in *It Could Happen To You*
Ben Affleck, Matt Damon and Alan Rickman in *Dogma*

A FEW WHO HAVE PLAYED GOD ...

Debra Winger in *Made In Heaven*
Alanis Morrisette in *Dogma*
George Burns in *Oh God*
Morgan Freeman in *Bruce Almighty*
Val Kilmer (as the voice of God) in *The Prince Of Egypt*

AND SOME WHO HAVE PLAYED THE DEVIL ...

Al Pacino in *The Devil's Advocate*
Jack Nicholson in *The Witches Of Eastwick*
Robert De Niro in *Angel Heart*
Harvey Keitel in *Little Nicky*
Peter Cook in the original *Bedazzled*
Elizabeth Hurley in the remake of *Bedazzled*
Mickey Rooney in *The Private Lives Of Adam and Eve*
Terence Stamp in *The Company Of Wolves*
Gabriel Byrne in *The End Of Days*

PHENOMENON (1996)

Directed by Jon Turteltaub
Starring John Travolta, Kyra Sedgwick, Robert Duvall

Following three he's-a-bad-guy-but-we-love-him roles in *Pulp Fiction*,

Broken Arrow and *Get Shorty*, Travolta opted for a mushier role in this sweet drama, that of small-town car mechanic George Malley. He lives an everyday life fixing cars, growing veggies and pursuing reluctant divorcee Lace (Sedgwick), until the night of his thirty-seventh birthday, when he sees a bright light in the sky that knocks him off his feet. When he comes round, George finds he has an insatiable thirst for learning, and can understand in a matter of minutes concepts that he could never have grasped in a whole lifetime before. He's soon beating old pal Doc (Duvall) at chess, devising a new fuel source for cars, moving objects with his mind and learning languages in an afternoon.

George's experiences with this knowledge, and how he's treated by friends who think he saw a UFO, are at the centre of this tale, with the romance with Lace being pushed to the fore only at the end. Although peppered with a few unnecessary soundtrack moments, and slightly drawn out towards the three-hankie conclusion, this is still a superbly performed, sweet, tear-jerking, enchanting movie that showcases Travolta's more sensitive side.

PORTRAIT OF JENNIE (1948)

Directed by William Dieterle
Starring Jennifer Jones, Joseph Cotten

This classic romantic fantasy melodrama stars Cotten as struggling artist Eben Adams. Walking home one day he meets a young girl named Jennie (Jones), and is so touched by her that he is inspired to paint her portrait. Over the next few months, Eben and Jennie cross paths several times, and each time she seems to have mysteriously aged a few years, while the events and people she talks about all seem to have existed years before. *Oooooh* – do you think she could be a ghost? Yes, it's all a bit obvious, but Jones is just gorgeous as Jennie (almost convincing as a child, going from pigtails to an adult hairdo as she ages) while Cotten is at his most debonair.

PRACTICAL MAGIC (1998)

Directed by Griffin Dunne
Starring Nicole Kidman, Sandra Bullock, Aidan Quinn

Nicole Kidman and Sandra Bullock are sisters Gillian and Sally, who also happen to be descended from witches *and* are cursed to see the men they love die in this uneven romance. Kidman is the wilder sibling, turning up on the run from her abusive boyfriend (*ER*'s Goran Visnjic), while Bullock is the more home-loving one, running a herb store in the local village and falling for the hunky cop (Quinn) who comes to investigate when Gillian's ex disappears.

Unfortunately, this is *The Witches Of Eastwick* with all the humour and sizzle removed and a bit of tepid romance mixed in to make a somewhat disappointing witches' brew. There are good supporting performances from Stockard Channing and Dianne Wiest as the siblings' equally witchy aunts, Bullock and Kidman both look great, but director Dunne ultimately fails to make either a moving romantic drama or a funny romantic comedy.

PRELUDE TO A KISS (1992)

Directed by Norman René
Starring Alec Baldwin, Meg Ryan, Sydney Walker

New Yorkers Peter (Baldwin) and Rita (Ryan) meet at a party, fall head over heels and marry despite her depressive, pessimistic outlook on life. But when a mysterious little old man (Walker) crashes the wedding party and claims a kiss from the bride, Peter finds himself on honeymoon in Jamaica with an eccentric ball of fire. Yes, the pretty young woman and the frail stranger have exchanged souls, for a body-swap love fable that proves most testing for the new husband.

Baldwin (in a role he first played on stage in Craig Lucas's play) is terrific as the comically bewildered, then desperate lover who eventually figures it out and takes his vows to heart. Ryan is amusing as an old man in selfish possession of a young woman's body, but she's outshone by stage veteran Walker as the girl learning about the beauty of life and love imprisoned in a failing shell.

THE PRINCE AND ME (2003)

Directed by Martha Coolidge
Starring Julia Stiles, Luke Malby

Ah, the perils of being a young twenty-first-century woman. There you are, concentrating hard on your studies at the University of Wisconsin, determined to become a doctor and help the needy, when along comes a hunky European to sweep you off your feet. And – wouldn't you just know it? – he turns out to be Edward, Crown Prince of Denmark (Malby, doing a passable Prince William impersonation). Life just isn't fair, is it?

This *Cinderella*-style romantic comedy has a feminist twist – young Paige (Stiles) doesn't need rescuing, nor does she particularly dream of being smothered in jewels – but deep down it has a slushy, sentimental heart. The incognito 'Eddie' escapes his princely duties and playboy lifestyle for a year at an American college, finds true love there with Paige and in the process grows from boy to man. Aimed at a teen-girl audience supposedly easily enchanted by pretty dresses, a handsome boy and a pop soundtrack, this is very cute and silly, but a funny turn from Ben Miller (as Eddie's long-suffering butler) goes some way towards rescuing it.

THE PRINCESS DIARIES (2001)

Directed by Garry Marshall
Starring Julie Andrews, Anne Hathaway

Every little girl dreams of becoming a princess, and that is exactly what happens to fifteen-year-old Californian Mia (Hathaway) in this *Cinderella*-style story. Raised by her single mother, she discovers her grandmother is Clarisse Renaldi (Andrews), the queen of European principality Genovia, who wants Mia to take her rightful place as Crown Princess.

Of course, Mia is a gawky, modern teenager, so her transformation from average American gal to tiara-wearing princess is fraught with frustration and hilarious moments as Clarisse attempts to teach her the finer points of royal etiquette. Andrews gives a classy, luminous performance in a surprisingly amusing comedy designed to appeal to the little girl in all of us. Hugely successful, it spawned a sequel in 2004, *The Princess Diaries 2: The Royal Engagement.*

THE PURPLE ROSE OF CAIRO (1985)

Directed by Woody Allen
Starring Mia Farrow, Jeff Daniels, Danny Aiello, Dianne Wiest

An unhappy movie fan's heartthrob steps out of a 1930s Depression-era adventure serial and off the screen, offering her romance in this whimsical flight of fancy from writer–director Woody Allen. It's a deft blend of philosophical comedy and bittersweet fantasy.

Allen created a great role for Mia Farrow as Cecilia, the mousewife dreamer married to a good-for-nothing brute, and Jeff Daniels does a fun double act as the screen hero, decent, cheery, square-jawed archaeologist Tom, and his 'real-life' counterpart, self-centred actor Gil, who arrives on the scene to rescue his career. The laughs are witty – particularly as innocent Tom struggles to cope with the real world while the characters he has abandoned on the screen go to pieces. But at the heart of the film is Cecilia's dilemma as she yearns for a happy ending, caught between bleak reality and artificial glamour.

ROMAN HOLIDAY (1953)

Directed by William Wyler
Starring Audrey Hepburn, Gregory Peck

Hepburn got her first big film break and took the Oscar for Best Actress with an absolutely charming performance in Wyler's still fresh and delightful romance. She is the perfect princess who slips away from her chaperones and duties during an official visit to sample real life, paint Rome red and have a heart flutter with handsome Gregory Peck's cynical but smitten reporter. He, in the tradition of Clark Gable's reporter in *It Happened One Night*, is aware of her identity and plans to make a lucrative scoop out of her innocent escapades on the town, but he becomes too enchanted to betray her.

Proving that gallantry doesn't begin and end in the movies, in real life Peck insisted that his virtually unknown co-star receive top billing over him because, he said, it was obvious she was going to have exactly the same enchanting effect on audiences. His panache and her grace, good humour and sheer loveliness make for magic.

SIMPLY IRRESISTIBLE (1999)

Directed by Mark Tarlov
Starring Sarah Michelle Gellar, Sean Patrick Flanery

Despite two personable leads with sex appeal and designer clothes, this gastronomic rom-com fantasy is half-baked. Bad cook and failing restaurateur Amanda (Gellar) encounters an angel who gives her a crab – yes, a *crab*! – which is an agent of supernatural intervention. No sooner has it run loose in Amanda's kitchen than she becomes the master chef of Manhattan. In a shameless steal from *Like Water For Chocolate*, her emotions are expressed in her recipes, so her desire for uptown restaurant manager Tom (Flanery) turns her caramel eclairs into aphrodisiacs.

Contrived when it wants to be charming, embarrassingly clumsy when it tries to be endearing, this even has a dance routine in which the hapless stars appear to have left feet to spare. It's simply excruciating.

SOMEWHERE IN TIME (1980)

Directed by Jeannot Szwarc
Starring Christopher Reeve, Jane Seymour

A shameless weepie that's like a big tub of rich chocolate ice-cream: you know you shouldn't indulge, but as long as no one else is watching, why not just let yourself melt into its gooeyness?

Reeve – in his first major role after megahit *Superman* – stars as playwright Richard. Visiting a hotel, he sees a portrait of Elise (Seymour), a beautiful actress who performed there in 1912. Instantly obsessed, he learns everything he can about her and then discovers he can hypnotically transport himself back in time to meet her. However, while the pair begin to fall in love, Richard discovers that any reminder of the late twentieth century immediately pulls him back to the present day.

An old-fashioned movie that wasn't much of a success when it was released, this has become a popular favourite for girls wanting to have a good old sob in front of the telly. Seymour never looked more ethereal, Reeve never more handsome, and while plot-holes abound you can't help but have a sniffle at the sheer unashamed romance of it all.

STARMAN (1984)

Directed by John Carpenter
Starring Jeff Bridges, Karen Allen, Charles Marin Smith

Horror specialist Carpenter's only really girlie flick, this is that great rarity, a sci-fi love story. Alien beings made of energy accept the *Voyager II* probe's invitation to visit Earth, only for the emissary Starman to be shot down. Using genetic material from a shed hair to create a living body, Jeff Bridges's extra-terrestrial shocks Karen Allen's grieving, childless widow Jenny Hayden, whose late husband he has duplicated. Pursued by government agents, the very odd couple flee across country towards Starman's mothership. As they do so, Jenny herself develops from hostage to intense sympathiser to lover.

Emotional, nostalgic, enjoyable, this is a multiple-hanky fable. Bridges's remarkable, Oscar-nominated performance as the curious, sensitive alien growing accustomed to humanity elevates the film to something deeper and more touching than anyone could have suspected from the plot.

TRULY MADLY DEEPLY (1991)

Directed by Anthony Minghella
Starring Juliet Stevenson, Alan Rickman, Michael Maloney

The British answer to *Ghost* is a truly madly offbeat, at times deeply touching fantasy, created by writer–director Minghella as a showcase for stage veteran Stevenson. Her Nina is bereft after the death of her cellist lover Jamie (Rickman) until her grief brings him back to haunt her in the nicest possible way. Amusement arises from her friends' bewilderment at her sudden transformation from despair to joy, and from the arrival of Jamie's new dead pals in Nina's flat. ('I can't believe I have a bunch of dead people watching videos in my living room!' Nina complains.) The introduction of Maloney's gentle charmer Mark – a new, living suitor for Nina – triggers deep thoughts about life, death and difficult choices.

THE WITCHES OF EASTWICK (1987)

Directed by George Miller
Starring Jack Nicholson, Cher, Susan Sarandon, Michelle Pfeiffer

Let's face it, with that grin and those wicked twinkling eyes, Jack Nicholson makes a perfect 'horny little devil'. He's Daryl Van Horne, the vile, but somehow strangely irresistible, mysterious man who comes to Eastwick at the behest of amateur witches Alexandra (Cher), Jane (Sarandon) and Sukie (Pfeiffer).

Soon the three women are fighting for his attention, while odd things start happening in the formerly peaceful New England town as their cravings for sex, food and magic spiral out of control. A quirky mix of supernatural scariness and humour (Daryl asks of God: 'Women … a mistake? Or did He do it to us on *purpose*?'), this zings thanks to great performances from Cher and Sarandon (Pfeiffer seems less comfortable as a satanic reveller) and a movie-stealing, scene-chewing one from Nicholson.

SWASHBUCKLERS

THE BEASTMASTER (1982)

Directed by Don Coscarelli
Starring Marc Singer, Tanya Roberts, Rip Torn, John Amos

We'll have no arguments! This is, uniquely, a girl-friendly sword and sorcery fantasy. Singer, in his only big outing besides saving Earth in TV's *V*, is hunky hero Dar, whose people are massacred by Rip Torn's evil priest in a tale of revenge, rebellion and romance.

Unlike Arnold the Barbarian and other he-men of brutish sagas, though, Dar is a deeply sensitive dish, who has a telepathic bond with animals. As a result, there are lots of 'ahh' moments: Dar's dog dying to save him; Dar acquiring his eyes (in the form of an eagle scout), his strength (a panther sidekick) and his cunning (a pair of comedy-relief ferrets); and Dar rescuing small children, as well as, for some reason, former *Charlie's Angel* Tanya Roberts. And it should be noted that Singer's perfect, broad-shouldered, narrow-waisted bod is advantageously displayed throughout. *Whoo hoo!* Sadly, the 1991 sequel missed the point entirely by transporting Dar to the twentieth century and replacing his loincloth with clothes.

THE COUNT OF MONTE CRISTO (2002)

Directed by Kevin Reynolds
Starring Jim Caviezel, Guy Pearce

There have been numerous versions of Alexandre Dumas's famous tale of betrayal and revenge, most memorably the classic 1934 version with Robert Donat and the camp 1974 one with Richard Chamberlain and Tony Curtis. This 2002 version is more camp than classy, and is thoroughly entertaining for it, as all the cast swash their buckles with unconcealed glee.

Caviezel is Edmond Dantes, the gullible sailor tricked by his pal Fernand (Pearce) and sentenced to life in the island prison of Chateau d'If. With the help of another inmate (Richard Harris, looking suitably gruff and grubby), he plots to escape, and after thirteen years finally manages it, returning home as the mysterious Count of Monte Cristo with the intention of wreaking revenge on Fernand and everyone else who betrayed him. Smartly directed by Kevin Reynolds – best known for the critical disaster that was *Waterworld* – this never tries to be anything more than a period romp, and it wholeheartedly succeeds because of it. Terrific fun.

CYRANO DE BERGERAC (1990)

Directed by Jean-Paul Rappeneau
Starring Gérard Depardieu, Anne Brochet, Vincent Perez

Edmond Rostand's Cyrano has fascinated filmmakers almost as much as Dumas's Monte Cristo – including Steve Martin, who gave the story a funny spin in *Roxanne*. But no other version is as lovely as this lavish French adaptation.

Depardieu – at his most vulnerable and hunky – is Cyrano, the soldier with a huge nose and an even bigger heart who lends his words of love about the beautiful Roxane (Brochet) to Christian (Perez), who is also in love with her. Of course, Roxane is charmed by Christian's letters, unaware that they were written by the heartbroken Cyrano. A truly girlie swashbuckler, this is lusty, luscious, passionate, funny and moving stuff.

D'ARTAGNAN'S DAUGHTER (1994)

Directed by Bertrand Tavernier
Starring Sophie Marceau, Philippe Noiret, Sami Frey

In their heyday swashbucklers came a bit swashier than this meandering but still fun escapade. It's a light-hearted vehicle for Sophie Marceau, in which she sparkles as the *fille* determined to step into the thigh boots of her legendary Musketeer papa (Noiret).

As idealistic convent girl Eloïse, her blood boils when a dastardly *duc* and his wicked paramour, 'the Lady in Red', launch a fiendish conspiracy which gets her beloved Mother Superior killed. Fortunately, Eloïse possesses equine and duelling skills not usually acquired during a convent education. Cue clashing blades and much dashing about the taverns and chateaux of seventeenth-century France as Eloïse foils baddies and rouses the aged Musketeers back into droll action. En route she also collects a smitten poet (Nils Tavernier) as a sidekick for her jaunty heroics. *Vive la romp!*

DON JUAN DE MARCO (1995)

Directed by Jeremy Leven
Starring Marlon Brando, Johnny Depp, Faye Dunaway

Johnny Depp continued to corner the market in quirky roles with an enjoyable turn as a young man who is convinced that he is that legendary lover of over a thousand women, Don Juan.

He comes to the attention of psychiatrist Dr Mickler (Brando) when he tries to jump off a building after being rejected by his one true love. Mickler has ten days to decide whether Juan is delusional and should be committed or actually is who he says he is. Over the next few days we and the doctor learn of Juan's many adventures, which helps Mickler rekindle the romance that has vanished from his relationship with his wife (Dunaway).

It's a lush, swashbuckling, comic tale, with Depp perfectly cast as the sexy seducer. But it is Dunaway and Brando who bring unexpected charm to the film (Brando giving one of his best performances in ages). Delightful.

HIDALGO (2004)

Directed by Joe Johnston
Starring Viggo Mortensen, Omar Sharif

An enjoyable piece of old-fashioned filmmaking, this desert-set Western is packed with clichés, eyebrow-raising adventures, manly heroics and enough corn to fill a field. At the centre of it all is the chiselled Mortensen, dashing and studly, which is why this could become a girl's best-kept movie secret.

He stars as Frank Hopkins, a nineteenth-century cowboy, who, with his mustang Hidalgo, has become champion of many a long-distance horse race across the wilds of America, before succumbing to booze and a side job as an entertainer in Buffalo Bill's Wild West Show. (The real Hopkins was apparently not as lovely as he is portrayed here, being best remembered as a consummate liar, but we will gloss over that, just as this rose-tinted film does.) So when Frank is asked by horse breeder Sheikh Riyadh (Sharif) to race Hidalgo in a 3,000-mile epic trek across the Arabian Desert, our hero has nothing to lose and sets off for the Middle East to prove his steed is worthy of the prize money. Naturally, that's when his problems really begin. No one wants Hopkins and Hidalgo to win, or expects them to, since they will have to endure intense heat, sandstorms, traps, locusts, vengeful Arabs (yes, racial stereotypes abound) and even hungry leopards before they reach the finish line.

Packed with picture-postcard landscapes, action and many loving shots of photogenic Mortensen and his adorable mustang, this is like a feature-length Milk Tray advert. The behind-the-scenes story is cute, too: five horses were used for the role of Hidalgo, but Mortensen loved one so much that at the end of filming he bought it for himself. Ahhhh.

KING SOLOMON'S MINES (1950)

Directed by Compton Bennett, Andrew Marton
Starring Deborah Kerr, Stewart Granger, Richard Carlson

The beautiful woman teamed with the misogynistic tough guy on safari in search of a legendary diamond mine/lost civilisation/missing husband is always an appealing adventure. Here all three objects are combined into one quest. This version of the evergreen H. Rider Haggard classic is the girliest probably because the screenwriter was Helen Deutsch (whose credits include *National Velvet*, *I'll Cry Tomorrow* and *Valley Of The Dolls*). She gave equal emphasis to Haggard's perennially popular, swaggering hero Allan Quatermain (Granger) and the dainty but fiercely determined heroine (Kerr). We appreciate that Quatermain simply *has* to rip her bodice when the stifling heat gets to her, and we can also relate to the stressful problems she has with her hair. If the impressive tribal warriors, crocodiles and spectacular stampeding herds all look familiar, that's because the footage was borrowed many times afterwards and stuck into cheaper safari sagas.

The rather splendid 1937 adaptation starring Paul Robeson is far more butch. But the 1985 version starring Richard Chamberlain and a young Sharon Stone is just a disappointingly feeble *Indiana Jones* wannabe.

THE MAN IN THE IRON MASK (1998)

Directed by Randall Wallace
Starring Leonardo DiCaprio, Jeremy Irons, John Malkovich, Gérard Depardieu, Gabriel Byrne

Alexandre Dumas's classic swashbuckler gets another airing with a top-flight, multinational cast. Young King Louis (DiCaprio) is a spoiled brat who is letting the French lower classes starve while he lives a life of decadence. This unacceptable state of affairs inspires three of the now-retired Musketeers – priestly Aramis (Irons), Lothario Porthos (Depardieu) and moody Athos (Malkovich) – to reunite in a quest to rescue the imprisoned Man in the Iron Mask, Philippe (DiCaprio again), who bears an uncanny resemblance to the King. Their plan is to substitute Philippe for the unbearable Louis under the noses of the courtiers and their former friend but now King's guard D'Artagnan (Byrne).

While this isn't as camp as the TV version starring Richard Chamberlain there is still a fair amount of silliness (mostly in the script) mixed with tongue-in-cheek performances (notably Depardieu having fun as the skirt-chasing, wine-swilling pudgy Porthos) and a little swashbuckling. An enjoyable romp that's a must-see for DiCaprio fans.

THE MASK OF ZORRO (1998)

Directed by Martin Campbell
Starring Antonio Banderas, Anthony Hopkins, Catherine Zeta-Jones

The masked swordsman of old California, Zorro (Spanish for fox) first appeared in a pulp novel in 1919. Within a year silent-movies superstar Douglas Fairbanks had donned the mask and created a screen legend. Roughly every twenty years since then Zorro has been reborn, notably in the forms of Tyrone Power (in 1940's *The Mark Of Zorro*) and Alain Delon (in 1975's *Zorro*), and always to a swoonsome welcome from women.

In this witty retelling Zorro becomes not a single man but an ideal and a destiny to be passed on from one generation to the next. Hopkins (whose panache with whip and sword is surprisingly sexy) is the aristocratic Don Diego de la Vega, who has been unmasked as Zorro and captured, his life destroyed. Twenty years later his nemesis returns with the daughter (Zeta-Jones) he stole from Diego and a new scheme to plunder the land. Thus roused to action once more, the greying fox grooms his scruffy *bandito* protégé (Banderas) to take over the mantle.

This has it all: romance, thrills, laughs, glamour, magnificent black stallions to be ridden like the wind, duels to the death, a saucy, spirited heroine *and* a hot dance number. Swashbuckling Banderas is beyond sexy, with the grace and humour to cut a dash without being too tongue-in-cheek or too stolid. *Ariba!*

HEROIC DREAMBOATS

A film doesn't have to be aimed at women to reel us in if there's a sufficiently hunky hero in armour or leather, riding a mighty steed, barking at the helm or clasping the hilt of his sword. Some of the men we'd most like to cut a swash with or unbuckle:

ERROL FLYNN in CAPTAIN BLOOD (1935)

One flash of that insolent grin and the fencing duel with Basil Rathbone are enough to show what made sexy Flynn a star overnight and the pirate we'd still most like to abduct us. If you prefer your heroes in green tights, Errol in *The Adventures Of Robin Hood* (1938) is the man.

TYRONE POWER in CAPTAIN FROM CASTILE (1947)

His dashing pirate in *The Black Swan* (1942) is a contender, too, but we opt for beautiful Ty as our *numero uno* conquistador, fleeing the Spanish Inquisition with flashing blade for revenge, plunder and a barefoot wench.

BURT LANCASTER in THE CRIMSON PIRATE (1952)

Handsome, strapping Burt exercises his skills (he was a professional acrobat before turning to the movies) with a twinkle in his eye and plenty of animal magnetism as he swings from masts in a thrilling, funny cult classic.

PETER O'TOOLE in LAWRENCE OF ARABIA (1962)

Lawrence's homosexuality and sado-masochism don't enter the picture for women who dote on this epic historical biopic because the young blue-eyes sweeping across the sands in his Arab robes is belated heir to the swoonsome desert dish, an erotic fantasy icon originated by Rudolph Valentino in *The Sheik* (1921).

HARRISON FORD in RAIDERS OF THE LOST ARK (1981)

Archaeologist Indiana Jones may be a *Boys' Own* hero, inspired by children's Saturday matinée serials of yesteryear, but for women who like the leather-jacketed, whip-cracking type he's the treasure we'd most like to globe-trot with.

VIGGO MORTENSEN in THE LORD OF THE RINGS (2001–2003)

Women didn't sit through nine hours of Tolkien's epic trilogy for hairy-footed Hobbits and CGI battles with the forces of evil, but for rugged, manly Aragorn in his fight for right, kingship and love.

THE PRINCESS BRIDE (1987)

Directed by Rob Reiner
Starring Cary Elwes, Mandy Patinkin, Robin Wright, Chris Sarandon

Beauteous maiden Buttercup (Wright) is being forced to wed an evil prince when she is abducted by brigands. Meanwhile, her reportedly dead true love, farm boy Westley (Elwes), has become an infamous pirate who eventually joins forces with one of the kidnappers – passionately dashing swordsman-in-search-of-vengeance Inigo Montoya (Patinkin) – to rescue her and right sundry wrongs.

This unique romantic spoof of the sword and sorcery genre, adapted by William Goldman from his witty novel, has all the spellbinding charm of a classic fairytale wedded to swashbuckling adventure. It also delivers a string of funny dialogue and sight gags along with the perils as our hero and heroine scale the Cliffs of Insanity, endure the Pit of Despair and encounter a host of colourful, crazed characters (from André the Giant to Billy Crystal's wizened wizard). Lovingly filmed in England and Ireland, and narrated by Peter Falk (told as a story to his initially bored grandchild), it's consistently amusing and as pretty, smart and sweet as can be. And there's kissing.

THE PRISONER OF ZENDA (1937)

Directed by John Cromwell
Starring Ronald Colman, Douglas Fairbanks Jr, Madeleine Carroll

There have been numerous adaptations of Anthony Hope's classic novel – including 1979's spoof with Peter Sellers, and the lavish Stewart Granger/Deborah Kerr adventure from 1952 – but we are rather partial to the 1937 original, in which buckles are swashed by the suave Ronald Colman.

He's the British commoner who is asked to impersonate his cousin, the king of the small European country of Ruritania, to foil a plot. Of course, once there, he falls for the charms of the beautiful Princess Flavia (Carroll), as well as being the target of the scheming Rupert (a deliciously evil Fairbanks). One of the truly great swashbucklers, thanks to a terrific cast that also boasts David Niven and Raymond Massey.

ROBIN AND MARIAN (1976)

Directed by Richard Lester
Starring Sean Connery, Audrey Hepburn

A quirky rethink of the classic tale of Robin Hood has Connery starring as the ageing Robin, who returns from the Crusades after many years away with a barking-mad King Richard (Richard Harris). While Robin has been away, Marian (Hepburn) has entered a nunnery, and on his arrival back home he discovers that the Sheriff of Nottingham (Robert Shaw) is up to no good yet again. What's a poor old former hero to do?

With Ronnie Barker, Denholm Elliott and Nicol Williamson on hand to play Friar Tuck, Will Scarlett and Little John respectively, this is an odd, occasionally brutal, little film, but a sweet one, largely thanks to tons of chemistry between Connery and Hepburn. A tale of tarnished legends and long-lost love, this certainly has the saddest ending of any Robin Hood movie – we recommend at least two boxes of tissues should be within arm's reach when viewing.

ROBIN HOOD: PRINCE OF THIEVES (1991)

Directed by Kevin Reynolds
Starring Kevin Costner, Morgan Freeman, Alan Rickman

This daft frolic through Sherwood Forest is definitely a guilty pleasure, complete with the endlessly-at-number-one theme song 'Everything I Do (I Do It For You)' from Bryan Adams. Costner wisely doesn't even attempt an English accent as Robin of Locksley, who lands in England at Dover with trusty Moor Azeem (Morgan Freeman) at his side, and heads home to Nottingham – via Hadrian's Wall, for some strange reason – only to find that a new sheriff (Rickman) has taken over, forcing Robin to become an outlaw.

With Will Scarlett (Christian Slater), Little John (Nick Brimble) and a rag-tag bunch of forest dwellers reluctantly on his side, Robin attempts to outwit the Sheriff and romance lusty young maiden Marian (Mary Elizabeth Mastrantonio). Costner and Mastrantonio may look a tad out of place in Ye Olde England, but they're clearly having a ball, while Alan Rickman steals the show from both of them as the pantomime-villain, leather-clad Sheriff. ('… And call off Christmas!' he decrees) who gets all the best lines.

VALLEY OF THE KINGS (1954)

Directed by Robert Pirosh
Starring Robert Taylor, Eleanor Parker

Maybe not every little girl possesses a youthful passion for archaeology, but we all love romances featuring people in khaki linens and those hats with scarves tied round the crown. And this one positively throbs.

Parker's plucky, scholarly Victorian lovely is trotting around Egypt with her mysterious French husband (blatantly a bounder). She recruits Taylor's manly Egyptologist to help her search for evidence that the Bible's Joseph converted the Pharaoh to monotheism. It's a load of historical hooey, of course, but boasts authentic locations, suitably sinister tomb-robbing heavies, and one of our all-time favourite fantasies: trapped in a Saharan sandstorm, our twosome find refuge in a remarkably luxurious Bedouin tent and surrender to forbidden love. Oh yeah, and then they find the tomb, treasures beyond their wildest dreams, etc.

Chapter 4: Bustles and Bullets
Period Movies, Costume Dramas and Women at War

And now we come to the scrumptiousness that is the period film, those romantic and ripping yarns of yesteryear. Period movies – apart from the Westerns, most war movies and sword 'n' sandals epics – usually scream, 'Women's Picture!' Men run from the cinema at the first sight of the big frocks, the tear-jerking turmoil, the relationship conflicts and the extravagant hats that bedeck the classic literary adaptation or the historical romance.

By 'period film', we don't mean films of their own time. If it was made in the fifties and set in the fifties, it may by now have acquired a period patina, but a true period picture is one that sets out to transport us back to another time. We have classified many period films as fantasies, adventures or timeless weepies in other chapters, so the emphasis here is on movies that are so specifically of a period that the set decoration and fashions are seriously important. Also, it is immediately apparent that most of them are literary adaptations. While a high percentage of all films are based on a novel, a short story, a magazine article or even a Christmas card (the inspiration for *It's A Wonderful Life*), period films rely particularly heavily on acknowledged classics of literature and their imitators, books that were required reading at school, and chunky romantic bestsellers. And if they aren't based on a book – *The Piano*, for instance, is from Jane Campion's original screenplay – they still look as if they have been, as they draw from a literary tradition.

The films featured here are distinctive because they place the emphasis firmly on the female characters, not on a macho gladiator, Achilles at Troy or gangsters in turn-of-the-century New York. But while they save money by not having to stage elaborate battle scenes and gunfights, these stories, set in castles and manor houses or on rolling Southern plantations, are still an expensive business. Done properly, they cost far more to make than a typical contemporary drama (as long as it doesn't involve a lengthy car chase, an asteroid collision or a computer-generated cast of thousands). Thus, bringing a well known book to the screen has a 'brand value' supposed to attract readers or people who suspect they ought to have read the book. Plus, old books are out of copyright, so filmmakers don't have to negotiate deals with demanding celebrity authors. Jane Austen, for example, is in no position to hold out for cast approval or a piece of the box-office gross. There is also an intention of achieving prestige, aspiring to class, and what better way to achieve this than by turning a respected novel into a dignified film? When it works, Academy Awards rain down. When the result is corny, cheesy or just plain bonkers, well, we can live with that too, especially if there are marabou trimmings, hobble skirts or Fortuny silk pleats on display.

Of course, not all the staples of English, American and World Literature courses are women-only zones. The ever-popular Charles Dickens, whose vividly descriptive novels have been adapted for the screen more often than those of any other writer, is enjoyed by men and women equally. Men can also be steered without too much difficulty into epics of the land and its labourers, such as the sweeping adaptations of Pearl Buck's *The Good Earth*, Marcel Pagnol's *Jean De Florette/Manon Des Sources* and Emil Zola's *Germinal*. Nor will they kick too hard if promised a robust spot of roistering (so pencil in Sir Walter Scott's romps and Alexandre Dumas's *The Three Musketeers*), martial arts mayhem (practically any Japanese period film) or alcohol, gambling and lusty peasants (ah, don't you just love those Russian novels?). However, we are not here for them, but to celebrate the sniffle spectacles with a special female appeal.

Finally, we look at those rare beasts: war movies that focus on women. They, too, are period films, but of a very different stamp to the literary epics. Nevertheless, a large box of tissues remains mandatory for successful viewing. Wars are waged by men over the bodies of women and children, and films of women in war are hardly ever about the combat itself, but rather deal with the misery and suffering. Unsurprisingly, these tend to be based on true stories of survival, quiet heroism and self-sacrifice. They are less confrontational than inspirational.

There have been lavish and ludicrous literary adaptations for as long as there have been feature films. Of the innumerable 'costumers' that have been made, we present some of the handsomest, most curious, most fun and most moving.

GONE WITH THE WIND (1939)

Directed by Victor Fleming
Starring Clark Gable, Vivien Leigh, Leslie Howard, Olivia de Havilland

This is the grandmother of all romantic historical epics.

The saga of bringing Margaret Mitchell's hugely successful best-seller to the screen has passed into movie legend. As has its appeal as one of the most entertaining wallows in cinema history. Yes, *GWTW* is dated, its depiction of slavery false, its glorification of the Old South ('a civilisation gone with the wind ...') baldly sentimentalised. But it is still the most gorgeous load of tosh ever committed to cellu-loid, and a blueprint for storytelling on a grand scale.

The plot follows the progress of wilful Georgia Peach Scarlett O'Hara (the simply terrific Leigh) from spoiled, compulsively flirta-tious belle on the family cotton plantation Tara after aristocratic heart-throb Ashley Wilkes (Howard) rejects her to marry his kind and gentle cousin Melanie (de Havilland). Hardened by disappoint-ment, war and poverty, thrice-married, ever selfish and shrewd, Scarlett endures and surmounts enough romantic, socio-economic and life-threatening vicissitudes to fill several seasons of a uniquely tumultuous, exquisitely costumed soap opera. But all this has been condensed into a thundering three and three-quarter hours. Para-mount, of course, is her turbulent relationship with sexy and sardonic Charleston rake Rhett Butler (the fabulous Gable).

The showcase images still pack a wallop. Scarlett, in mourning black, capers like a merry crow through a shocked, pastel assem-blage at a fundraising ball. Searching for the doctor during frail Melanie's labour, she arrives on a staggering panorama of wounded and dying men. Rhett and the women's hair-raising flight through burning Atlanta remains thrilling. His farewell kiss as he abandons Scarlett to join the futile 'cause' still weakens the knees. After the harrowing journey back to Tara, where Scarlett has learned her mother is dead, her father has gone mad, the Yankees have taken everything, and the frightened little band of survivors are starving, her reaction is immortal. Reduced, sobbing and retching, to grubbing in the soil for a root, she lifts herself, silhouetted against a fiery sky, to shake her fist at heaven and famously vow, 'As God is my witness, I'll never be hungry again!' It's all just divine.

But such classic set pieces are only part of the winning formula. The film is such a treat because of its unflagging passion, the range of great, perfectly cast characters, and the precision, intensity and wit with which they are propelled through life. The tone turns hushed and grim with the grief and devastation of war, exuberant again with Scarlett's resurrected fortunes, moody when – daringly – love does not conquer all but is blasted by pragmatism, misunderstanding and tragedy. All the secondary characters are excellent foils for Leigh, none more so than Hattie McDaniel's archetypally indomitable Mammy, whose reactions to Scarlett's outrages are priceless, while her scene with Melanie, sobbing out the details of Rhett's and Scarlett's darkest day, is heart-rending.

Its long-held record of eight Oscars may have been overtaken, but, in Rhett's famous last words, 'Frankly my dear, I don't give a damn.' *Gone With The Wind* is America's most loved women's picture and always will be.

THE ABDUCTION CLUB (2002)

Directed by Stefan Schwartz
Starring Daniel Lapaine, Alice Evans, Sophia Myles, Matthew Rhys

An enjoyable jaunt through eighteenth-century Ireland, this is essentially a romantic comedy filled with pretty boys, and girls in big skirts. The story tells us that, back then, a family's wealth and titles would be inherited by the eldest brother, leaving the younger sons penniless or destined for a life in the priesthood. To avoid this fate, many became members of an 'abduction club', where each member would steal an heiress from her home for one night in an attempt to woo her into marriage, knowing that, if she agreed, all her inheritance would be shared by her lucky husband.

Unfortunately, when Byrne (Lapaine) and Strang (Rhys) kidnap the Kennedy sisters, Anne (Myles) and Catharine (Evans), they run up against unexpected resistance from the two ladies. Soon they are on the run from the authorities and Anne's slithery and persistent suitor, John Power (Liam Cunningham).

It's all very daft – like a more romantic version of *Plunkett And MacLeane* – and has some rough edges (check out the huge hairsprayed chunk of Evans's hair that a stylist must have failed to notice had come adrift), but it's packed with robust performances and beautiful Irish scenery.

THE AGE OF INNOCENCE (1993)

Directed by Martin Scorsese
Starring Daniel Day Lewis, Michelle Pfeiffer, Winona Ryder

Edith Wharton's Pulitzer Prize-winning novel of forbidden passion and emotional repression is a penetrating record of the tribal customs of nineteenth-century New York's elite. Refined attorney Newland Archer (Day Lewis) is engaged to fresh blossom May (Ryder) when he is irresistibly drawn to her scandal-tainted cousin, Countess Olenska (Pfeiffer), a divorcee whose sophistication and independence outrage their rigidly conformist set.

In a radical departure from his violent chronicles of men who walk mean streets, Scorsese's first foray into classical literary adaptation is a ravishing, poignant, sensuous epic of romantic grandeur. In a perfect cast, Day Lewis looks divine and displays unsurpassed nostril-flaring, Ryder is demure yet cunning, and Pfeiffer is more exquisite than ever. The screenplay is highly literate, and the movie is fastidiously dressed (with Oscar-winning velvets, feathers and furs) and scores for its highly charged looks of longing, hopeless embraces and desperate kisses. Self-sacrifice has never been more sumptuous.

ANASTASIA (1956)

Directed by Anatole Litvak
Starring Ingrid Bergman, Yul Brynner, Helen Hayes

In 1949 Bergman had scandalised society by having an affair with Roberto Rossellini and then giving birth to their son. For seven years she made films only in Europe , returning to American screens in 1956 with this 'comeback' that won her a Best Actress Academy Award.

She stars as a young, haunted and destitute woman – picked by

Russian exiles in Paris to pose as the missing heir to the Russian throne, Anastasia, who was believed to have survived the execution of the Romanovs in 1918. General Bounine (Brynner) doesn't think this suicidal woman could possibly be the real Anastasia, but he grooms her for the role in order to claim her £10 million inheritance, aware that she will have to convince the Dowager Empress (Hayes) that she is who she claims to be for them to succeed.

Romantic fiction rather than historical drama, *Anastasia* is a charming film about a woman looking to belong, and it benefits from a luminous central performance from Bergman. Brynner, too, gives one of his most well-rounded and appealing portrayals, while Helen Hayes is at her acerbic best.

There was also a missable animated version of the story in 1997 that plays even more loose with the historical facts (Rasputin pops up as an undead corpse), featuring the voices of Meg Ryan, John Cusack and Kelsey Grammer.

ANNA KARENINA (1935)

Directed by Clarence Brown
Starring Greta Garbo, Fredric March

Tolstoy's classic tragedy has been filmed several times with varying degrees of success. This Garbo version (which was her second: in 1927 she had starred in a silent, modern-dress adaptation titled *Love*) is still far and away the best, tearful but yummy, with brilliant cinematography.

In 1880s Russia beautiful Anna is married to wealthy stick Karenin (Basil Rathbone). However, she is helplessly gripped by a consuming passion for dashing cavalry officer Count Vronsky (March), which leads to the loss of her cherished son, social ruin and, ultimately, suicide. Garbo is gorgeous and poignant from beginning to despairing end. This is always labelled a tragic love story, but Anna is betrayed by her *need* for love. The real tragedy is that, as a woman in her society, she has no personal rights and is made an outcast for her transgression. The sexy but weak Vronsky, by contrast, is unharmed by his reputation as an aristocratic stud.

A 1948 version starring Vivien Leigh is disappointingly stodgy, while *Leo Tolstoy's Anna Karenina* (1997), directed by Bernard Rose and starring Sophie Marceau and Sean Bean (now there's a man in uniform most of us would leave home for!), is more faithful to the novel and boasts authentic Russian locations, but it has more artifice than heart.

THE BALLAD OF LITTLE JO (1993)

Directed by Maggie Greenwald
Starring Suzy Amis, Bo Hopkins, Ian McKellen

Writer–director Greenwald's interesting drama is loosely based on the true story of Josephine Monaghan (Amis), a young woman living in the late nineteenth century who is thrown out of her family home when she gives birth to an illegitimate child. Of course, being young, female and homeless in the Wild West is not a good combination, but instead of marrying for safety (or becoming a prostitute, the only other real option), Josephine disguises herself as a man named Jo and settles down outside Ruby City with the intention of leading a quiet life. Unfortunately, after she rescues a Chinese man named Tinman (David Chung) from a lynch mob and hires him to be her housekeeper, then discovers she has decidedly womanly feelings for him, her peace is bound to be shattered.

While it's hard to imagine anyone mistaking pretty Suzy Amis for a man, the actress settles into the role by the halfway mark and manages to convince us that such a ruse could go undiscovered by the towns-folk. However, while her restrained performance is worthy of praise, more acclaim should go to Bo Hopkins as her brutal, cursing neighbour Frank, who steals every scene in which he appears.

THE BEGUILED (1971)

Directed by Don Siegel
Starring Clint Eastwood, Geraldine Page, Elizabeth Hartman

While the oeuvres of Siegel and Eastwood don't boast too many women's pictures, this rare gem was a radical departure for the two tough guys, and it provides a cautionary tale that creeps out the menfolk. An unusually offbeat and artistic costumer set in the Confederacy during the American Civil War, it's no war film but a dark psychological fable of confined women assuming power and exacting revenge, while overreacting just a tad to their claustrophobic situation.

Wounded Union soldier Eastwood is given sanctuary and is nursed back to health in an isolated girls' boarding school where the frustrated spinster headmistress (Page), pretty young teacher (Hartman), hormonal adolescents and admiring little girls vie for his attentions in an increasingly heated, unwholesome atmosphere. Initially the man plays each of the women and girls, imagining he's in control and will be sitting out the war in a gracious harem. *Big* mistake. Desire, jealousy and spite simmer slowly into a rich stew of uniquely feminine malevolence. Think *Jezebel* meets *Misery*.

BELOVED (1998)

Directed by Jonathan Demme
Starring Oprah Winfrey, Thandie Newton, Danny Glover

Despite some impressive performances, Toni Morrison's bestselling novel about the aftermath of slavery in the 1870s is turned into a complete snore-fest by the usually reliable Demme (*The Silence Of The Lambs, Philadelphia*).

Sethe (Winfrey) is a freed slave, tortured by the past which forced her to murder her own child so the baby wouldn't be taken into slavery. Now living with her surviving daughter Denver (Kimberley Elise) in her own home, she discovers a strange, drooling and murmuring young woman on her doorstep who says her name is Beloved (Newton). Taking her in, Sethe soon realises this bizarre girl could have some other-worldly connection to the daughter she sacrificed years before. Unfortunately, Demme takes so long to relate Morrison's fascinating story that you are past caring well before the film's three-hour running time is up. A missed opportunity that even Winfrey, Glover (as Sethe's lover) and Elise's fine performances can't save.

THE COLOR PURPLE (1985)

Directed by Steven Spielberg
Starring Danny Glover, Whoopi Goldberg

At the time, Alice Walker's novel about an African-American woman seemed like a strange choice for director Spielberg. He had yet to direct *Schindler's List*, and was best known for the *Boys' Own* adventures *Jaws*, *Raiders Of The Lost Ark* and *Close Encounters Of The Third Kind*, but he successfully delivered a moving, if somewhat glossy, tale of life in the American South of the early twentieth century.

Whoopi Goldberg (in her movie debut) stars as Celie, a young woman we first meet when she is just fourteen, and pregnant by her own father. The film is the story of her triumph over life, and what a life it is. She is married to a cruel man she must address as 'Mister' (Glover), she gives away her children only to discover she can have no more, and she is separated from her beloved sister. Goldberg eloquently portrays Celie's inner strength with her smile (she rarely speaks) in a performance that remains the most restrained and interesting of her career.

Incredibly moving, and featuring a terrific supporting cast (Oprah Winfrey, Akosua Busia and Margaret Avery among them), *The Color Purple* was nominated for an impressive eleven Academy Awards but it became the most talked about film at the ceremony when it, and Spielberg, went home empty handed.

DANGEROUS LIAISONS (1988)

Directed by Stephen Frears
Starring Glenn Close, John Malkovich, Michelle Pfeiffer

This adaptation of Christopher Hampton's runaway stage success, itself based on Choderlos de Laclos's eighteenth-century novel, is a heady brew of rampant sex, bitchy repartee, beautiful silk gowns, heaving cleavage and malevolent seductions among jaded French aristocrats. Pfeiffer suffers terribly prettily as the good woman fatally seduced on a bet by Malkovich's oddly sexy, dastardly Valmont. Meanwhile, junior eye candy Keanu Reeves and Uma Thurman also lose their innocence. People die for love, and Close's magnificently cruel, decadent villain gets an awesome come-uppance, as well as all the best lines and hats.

A fastidious but more playful adaptation of Laclos's novel – *Valmont* – directed by Miloš Forman appeared a few months after Frears's effort. It had its own attractions, including a sexy young cast featuring Colin Firth, Annette Bening and Meg Tilly, but was destined to remain in *Les Liaisons'* shadow. Earlier, Roger Vadim had made a jazzy, modern-dress (make that undressed) version in 1959 with Jeanne Moreau, and a second adaptation in 1976. *Cruel Intentions* (1999), starring Ryan Phillippe, Sarah Michelle Gellar and Reese Witherspoon, shifts the action to a modern American high school. It's a fascinating idea but ends up being uncomfortably debauched.

DRAGONWYCK (1946)

Directed by Joseph L. Mankiewicz
Starring Gene Tierney, Vincent Price, Glenn Langan

In this atmospheric adaptation of Anya Seaton's novel, it's the 1840s and we're with the Dutch-descended swells in upstate New York. Tierney's beautiful Miranda is packed off up the Hudson River to the suitably gloomy, Gothic mansion of well-to-do cousin Nicholas Van Ryn (Price) as the companion to his daughter. Once his wife is conveniently disposed of, wide-eyed Miranda welcomes Van Ryn's suave attentions and a new wardrobe until it becomes obvious that she's the love slave of a frock-coated nutter. Rebellious tenant farmers and servants muttering darkly of curses should have given her a heads-up a bit earlier.

This is an honourable entry in the governess/companion/poor-relation mini-genre (all of them massively indebted to *Jane Eyre* and/or *Rebecca*), and Price rocks as the aristocratic Edgar Allan Poe devotee who smokes dope and goes homicidal in his locked tower room. As you will have noticed, where there is a handsome, kindly doctor on the scene it is invariably he who rides heroically to the damsel's rescue. And the house *always* burns down!

DOCTOR ZHIVAGO (1965)

Directed by David Lean
Starring Omar Sharif, Julie Christie, Geraldine Chaplin

Period love stories don't get much more tragic than this luscious epic (it runs at over three hours) based on Boris Pasternak's novel. Set in the decades before and after the Bolshevik Revolution, it's beautifully directed by Lean, who fills the screen with icy Russian landscapes (although, amazingly, it was filmed in Spain), women in luxurious fur, and memorable set pieces, such as the cross-country rickety train ride and the attack by the Tsar's troops on a group of protestors, to name just two. However, while it catalogues a fascinating chunk of Russian history, at its heart is a tortured love story that has yet to be equalled.

Sharif is beautiful, brooding and tortured as Zhivago, the doctor and poet who marries his childhood sweetheart (Chaplin) but is drawn to the stunning Lara (Christie). Theirs is a poignant and heartbreaking love as they are brought together and then torn apart against the wintry, snowy scenery, as she is caught between two other men, aristocrat Komrovsky (Rod Steiger) and idealist Pasha (Tom Courtenay), the man she eventually marries.

This grand yet delicately beautiful film won Oscars for Best Screenplay, Art Direction, Costume Design and Cinematography, and for Maurice Jarre's memorable score, which included the famous 'Lara's Theme'.

ELIZABETH (1998)

Directed by Shekhar Kapur
Starring Cate Blanchett, Joseph Fiennes

Australian Blanchett is charismatic as Britain's most famous female monarch, as she transforms from spirited princess to remote queen held captive by her own sense of destiny. This is a flashy, intriguing vision of Tudor history as a conspiracy thriller: Her Majesty can barely move for all the assassins, spies and perverts thronging her court. A host of famous thespians (and Eric Cantona) slink around in doublets, conniving like medieval mafiosi. Geoffrey Rush is spookiest of the lot as Elizabeth's cold-blooded hitman, Walsingham, while Fiennes cuts a handsome dash as her ambitious, overconfident lover, Dudley. But the most ingenious and spellbinding element is the Queen's insight into how to command the hearts and minds of men in a man's world by submerging her inner woman beneath the white-faced guise of the Virgin Queen.

Spectacular pageantry, bloody deeds and a provocative theory of how a shrewd young woman turned herself into a powerful icon make the sixteenth century much more gripping than it was in the schoolroom.

EMMA (1996)

Directed by Douglas McGrath
Starring Gwyneth Paltrow, Jeremy Northam, Toni Collette

A charming, frothy adaptation of Jane Austen's novel has Gwyneth Paltrow (complete with passable English accent) as the bossy heroine who, with a radiant smile, attempts to interfere with neighbours' lives in the name of charity, matchmaking and friendship. Rather than allow her friend Harriet (Collette) to find happiness with the farmer (Edward Woodall) who loves her, Emma decides the local vicar (Alan Cumming) would be a far more suitable beau. She also fumbles with relationships involving Frank Churchill (Ewan McGregor, sporting the scariest wig ever seen in a period movie) and Mr Knightley (Northam), the only man who seems a proper match for Emma herself.

Director McGrath captures the very early nineteenth-century period nicely, and fills the screen with luscious English countryside, to-die-for frocks and a superb supporting cast including Phyllida Law and Sophie Thompson (Emma Thompson's mother and sister), Juliet Stevenson and Greta Scacchi. The story, of course, was also updated in 1995 by Amy Heckerling for the romantic comedy *Clueless* (page 20).

THE ENGLISH PATIENT (1996)

Directed by Anthony Minghella
Starring Ralph Fiennes, Juliette Binoche, Willem Dafoe, Kristin Scott Thomas

'Intoxicated' by Michael Ondaatje's poetic Booker Prize-winning novel, writer–director Minghella restructured it for the cinema, greatly expanding the tale of doomed love recounted in the middle of the book.

A critically burned, disfigured pilot (Fiennes, suitably tormented and unrecognisable in prosthetics) is found in the wreckage of his biplane in North Africa. Apparently amnesic but presumed to be English, he nears death as the Second World War draws to a close, cared for by a French-Canadian nurse, Hana (Binoche), in a derelict Italian monastery. They are then joined by Dafoe's vengeful torture victim and two bomb-disposal experts for intimate, emotional explorations of memory, yearning, loss, betrayal and healing. The mystery patient – who it transpires is actually Hungarian, Count Laszlo Almasy – gradually reveals his past to Hana, and his intricate story is pieced together. His Saharan love affair with married Englishwoman Katharine (Scott Thomas) is the centrepiece as his tale unfolds with tragic and far-reaching consequences.

The story is unconventionally convoluted but classically, desperately romantic. And the production is meticulously, elaborately composed, from dreamlike aerial sequences and a dramatic sandstorm to arresting love scenes, complementing an emotive script that contains numerous references to art, culture and a much-fingered volume of Herodotus' *Histories*, which itself received a boost in sales from the film. This cool, arty class bagged the film nine Oscars, including Best Picture.

FAR AND AWAY (1992)

Directed by Ron Howard
Starring Tom Cruise, Nicole Kidman, Thomas Gibson

Real-life husband and wife (well, they were at the time) Tom and Nicole teamed up for this frothy, fun and often downright silly nineteenth-century romantic drama. He's the poor Irish boy tired of digging up spuds, so, with dreams above his station, he heads off for a new life in America with rich-bitch Nicole in tow. (She's escaping a life of boring privilege with handsome but dull Gibson.) When they arrive, though, they discover that the New World is an even tougher place than back home. Along the way there's some bare-knuckle fighting (Cruise fans should get hot under the collar at the sight of their hero, both muscular and shirtless) and a macho horse race across the plains to secure the piece of land he has always dreamed of.

Tom's Oirish accent is a hoot, and the hate-you/love-you tensions between Cruise and Kidman are a bit daft, but Howard wisely directs this as a rip-roaring flouncy-skirted adventure rather than a serious historical piece. Desperately stupid, perhaps, but also deliciously fun.

FAR FROM THE MADDING CROWD (1967)

Directed by John Schlesinger
Starring Julie Christie, Peter Finch, Terence Stamp, Alan Bates

Poor shepherd Bates, rich farmer Finch and handsome, caddish soldier Stamp are all profoundly drawn to Christie's beauteous heiress Bathsheba in Schlesinger's superb adaptation of Thomas Hardy's Wessex country tale. This is a tale of unrequited love, blasted romantic dreams, scandal, disaster, tragedy, the politics of nineteenth-century marriage and sheep ailments set in the rolling Wessex hills. Given three such admirers and so much turmoil, what's a girl to do?

While Bates's stalwart Gabriel loves Bathsheba doggedly from afar and the inarticulate longing of Finch's lonely, uptight neighbour is desperately painful to behold, the young woman struggles to assert herself after inheriting the responsibilities of a farm and its slack-jawed workforce. Stamp's devilishly seductive bad boy Frank loves another but, in his red coat and with his flashing sword, it's no wonder he's the one who steals her heart and purse.

A classy period drama of the highest order, this is gorgeous and absorbing, with an enigmatic final look hinting at the limited scope of this woman's options in life.

FOREVER AMBER (1947)

Directed by Otto Preminger
Starring Linda Darnell, Cornel Wilde, Richard Greene

This was condemned on its release by the Catholic Legion of Decency for its glamorisation of immorality and licentiousness, which, we reckon, is reason enough to watch it. Based on the racy novel by Kathleen Winsor, it stars Darnell as the seventeenth-century poverty-stricken girl of the title who shags her way through society, bedding numerous men (including John Russell's highwayman, and Richard Haydn's earl) in search of wealth and happiness, before winding up with the ultimate symbol of power, King Charles II (George Sanders). Of course, given the era when it was made, poor Amber has to be punished for her slutty, wayward ways, so the only man she ever loved is the one she will never have. Sigh.

A luscious adaptation (check out the frocks!) from Preminger, this was a sanitised version of the book to keep the censors happy, but it nonetheless features a sultry performance from Darnell who risks all for her true love against the backdrop of a London decimated by plague and the Great Fire. Disease, death, betrayal and a feisty strumpet – what more could you ask for?

THE FRENCH LIEUTENANT'S WOMAN (1981)

Directed by Karel Reisz
Starring Meryl Streep, Jeremy Irons

Harold Pinter adapted John Fowles's novel for this Oscar-nominated drama. Sarah (Streep) is a young, tortured Englishwoman, scorned by her neighbours because she has had an affair with a French military officer. She spends her time taking lonely walks and gazing off the end of the windswept Cobb in Lyme Regis, until she is spotted by scientist Charles (Irons), who – despite being engaged – becomes entranced by this dark, haunted figure.

Rather than simply focus on the forbidden lovers at the movie's heart, Pinter and director Reisz also introduce a parallel story of two present-day actors (also played by Streep and Irons) playing the characters Sarah and Charles in a movie while having an affair off-camera. Confused?

A slow-burner of a romantic drama that works best in the period scenes and less well in the contemporary ones, this nevertheless cemented Streep as the queen of Hollywood and gave Irons his first leading-man role. So go ahead and blame this movie for his subsequent skin-crawling turns as lusty men in *Damage*, *Stealing Beauty* and *M Butterfly*.

THE FIVE BEST QUEENS OF THE SCREEN

ANNE OF THE THOUSAND DAYS (1969)

Geneviève Bujold's Anne Boleyn beguiles Richard Burton's Henry VIII in a gripping, magnificent-looking version of the love affair that rocked a nation, sparked religious schism and ended as badly as possible when his demand for a male heir proved the lady's undoing.

LA REINE MARGOT (1994)

The forced marriage of Isabelle Adjani's wilful, sluttish French princess to Daniel Auteuil's Protestant King of Navarre is her spectacularly dysfunctional sixteenth-century royal family's cue to stage the St Bartholomew's Day Massacre in a smart, sexy epic of doomed romance and murderous intrigue.

MARIE ANTOINETTE (1938)

Norma Shearer hopes they'll start the Revolution without her and Robert Morley's endearingly bewildered King Louis when her lover Tyrone Power plans their escape from the guillotine. But not even MGM had the gall to save her neck in this, one of the most super-sumptuous historical biopics ever, from the towering white wigs on down.

MARY OF SCOTLAND (1936) / MARY, QUEEN OF SCOTS (1971)

Mary, another celebrated beauty who was beheaded, features in two superior costumers. Katharine Hepburn regally battles treachery in the thirties adaptation of Maxwell Anderson's eloquent play, while Vanessa Redgrave fatally provokes Glenda Jackson's jealous Elizabeth I. Both stately stars look great in black.

QUEEN CHRISTINA (1933)

Greta Garbo vanquishes all-comers to screen queendom, and she was never better or more like a goddess than as Sweden's isolated seventeenth-century monarch, who abdicated for a man (played here by Garbo's matinée idol great love, John Gilbert) but lost him, as well as her country. The last, lingering fix on her face is one of the most famously haunting final shots in cinema history.

GIRL WITH A PEARL EARRING (2003)

Directed by Peter Webber
Starring Scarlett Johansson, Colin Firth

A film big on silent expression and small on words, *Girl With A Pearl Earring* is based on the acclaimed novel by Tracy Chevalier. Like the novel, it imagines the story behind seventeenth-century Dutch artist Vermeer's painting. Who was the girl in the picture? No one knows, but here it is suggested that she may have been a maid in the artist's household who captured his eye.

Young Griet (Johansson), trying to support her disabled father, goes to work as a maid in Vermeer's (Colin Firth) house, where he lives with his children, whining wife and disapproving mother-in-law (aside from Griet, the women around Vermeer are portrayed as stereotypes rather than fully realised characters). Griet stumbles upon and is transfixed by the artist's studio, carefully cleaning his windows and daringly moving a prop that she believes is out of place in one of his compositions. An almost silent relationship develops between the maid and the artist as he begins to paint her. This annoys his wife, but is heartily encouraged by his mother-in-law, who knows a financial opportunity when she sees one. Anyone expecting this relationship to erupt in an explosion of hormones will be disappointed, however, as the affair is subtle, limited to lingering glances, which are beautifully captured in moments bathed in sunlight or furtively sought in darkened rooms.

Unfortunately, despite elegant direction and Johansson's aching performance, not every aspect of the film is a success. Firth, complete with long, dark, tousled locks, seems to think he is *Wuthering Heights'* Heathcliff – all snarls, brooding silences and lurking in doorways. Tom Wilkinson, meanwhile, as the smarmy patron with an eye for troublemaking and for Griet, struggles with a role that is akin to a pantomime villain.

THE GOVERNESS (1998)

Directed by Sandra Goldbacher
Starring Minnie Driver, Tom Wilkinson, Jonathan Rhys-Meyers

Minnie Driver has never looked more depressed (except, perhaps, when the camera caught her expression as ex-boyfriend Matt Damon won Best Screenplay at the Academy Awards) than in this grim nine-teenth-century drama in which she plays a penniless Jewish woman who disguises herself as a Protestant to secure a job as the governess to a quirky Scottish family. While the matriarch of the household (Harriet Walter) rules the place with an iron fist, Mary finds herself drawn to her charge's father (Wilkinson), a scientist fascinated with photography with whom she begins an affair.

Driver is a little too contemporary in her acting style to convince as a sexually awakened woman of the 1840s, but the rest of the cast – especially Wilkinson, tortured by guilt and desire – are terrific. Goldbacher, in her directorial debut, delivers an interesting, somewhat bleak, but beautifully photographed film.

GREEN DOLPHIN STREET (1947)

Directed by Victor Saville
Starring Lana Turner, Van Heflin, Donna Reed, Richard Hart

With a drunken slip of the pen, Hart's lonely colonial somehow manages to confuse his sweetheart's name with her sister's when he writes the eagerly awaited letter home sending for his bride. An over-joyed Turner pitches up in nineteenth-century New Zealand, to the ill-disguised chagrin of the bridegroom at the dockside who is expecting Reed.

In the 1940s MGM launched a novel competition with a whopping $200,000 prize as a cunning way to nab the rights to blockbusters before their publication. The studio pulled out all the stops for this, their first winner (and, it turned out, the only one they ever filmed). Elizabeth Goudge's tumultuous family saga boasts enough love trian-gles to construct a dodecahedron, a Maori uprising, an earthquake, a tidal wave and a heartbroken Reed finding true happiness in a convent. Only a woman could love this fantastically ridiculous costume twaddle, a corker among the more turgid *Gone With The Wind* wannabes and unusual for presenting Turner in an unsubmissive but wifely role quite different from her habitual seductresses.

THE HEIRESS (1949)

Directed by William Wyler
Starring Olivia de Havilland, Montgomery Clift, Ralph Richardson

Wyler's screen version of Henry James's *Washington Square* is one of the all-time-great, five-hanky women's pictures, although men with taste, such as Martin Scorsese, have the grace to admire it, too. De Havilland, setting the trend for pretty actresses to win Oscars by making themselves look homely, is Catherine, the painfully plain, sweetly childlike spinster whose wealthy, cold-hearted father (Richardson) goes out of his way to trample whatever meagre crumbs of self-confidence and happiness his ugly duckling can gather. Worse, Father proves sneeringly right about fortune-hunter Morris Townsend (Clift), who abandons Catherine after learning she will be disinherited. De Havilland's face as she slowly climbs back up the stairs to her lonely room, exhausted and destroyed by Townsend's failure to arrive for their carefully planned elopement, is forever haunting. And when the cad has the gall to return, renewing his charm offensive, her revenge is both brilliantly satisfying and gut-wrenching as the foiled suitor pounds on the door beseeching, 'Catherine! Catherine!' When her eternally naive, matchmaking auntie (Miriam Hopkins) asks how she can be so cruel, Catherine coolly replies, 'I have been taught by masters.' Heartbreak of the highest order, this is perfectly realised in every department, from cinematography to the wonderful Aaron Copland score.

A pointless 1997 remake titled *Washington Square* (see below) stars Jennifer Jason Leigh who, however gauche and hideously costumed in modes reminiscent of lampshades, was blatantly too pretty for pitiable Catherine.

THE HOUSE OF MIRTH (2000)

Directed by Terence Davies
Starring Gillian Anderson, Eric Stoltz

Audiences who thought Scorsese's *The Age Of Innocence* was downbeat will find this adaptation of another Edith Wharton novel even more grim, as social climber Lily Bart (Anderson) falls foul of New York society at the beginning of the twentieth century. A beauty who makes other women jealous, she loves Lawrence Seldon (Stoltz), but he isn't wealthy enough to be considered marriage material, so Lily opts to find a rich husband. Her attempts to secure a niche in upper-class Manhattan society go horribly wrong, however, as she alienates socialite Bertha Dorset (a scathing turn from Laura Linney), and is accused of the ultimate scandalous activity: having an affair with a married man.

Anderson, best known as Scully in *The X-Files*, may seem a surprising choice for the role of Lily, but she delivers just the right amount of strength and poise, saying more in the lighting of a cigarette than many actresses can muster from a whole page of dialogue. Stoltz looks more out of place, but thanks to superb supporting turns from a cast including Dan Aykroyd, Anthony LaPaglia and Eleanor Bron, and Davies's gloomy but assured direction, this is an interesting, if very sombre, period piece.

HOWARDS END (1992)

Directed by James Ivory
Starring Emma Thompson, Anthony Hopkins, Vanessa Redgrave, Helena Bonham Carter

E. M. Forster's novel of social class is lovingly brought to the screen by screenwriter Ruth Prawer Jhabvala and the producing–directing team of Ismail Merchant and James Ivory.

Matriarch Ruth Wilcox (Redgrave) writes a note on her deathbed bequeathing her country home, Howards End, to her friend Margaret Schlegel (Thompson). However, Ruth's family tears it up after her death before anyone can know about it. Feeling some remorse, Ruth's widower Henry (Hopkins) goes to visit the Schlegel family in London, and while he disapproves of their chaotic lifestyle and friendship with lowly clerk Leonard Bast (Samuel West), he is bewitched by Margaret and promptly proposes to her.

Thompson is superb as the quiet but steely Margaret, and is ably supported by Hopkins, a memorable Redgrave and Bonham Carter, as Margaret's hot-headed sister Helen. It's a luscious adaptation of a terrific novel, beautifully made and performed.

THE IMPORTANCE OF BEING EARNEST (2002)

Directed by Oliver Parker
Starring Rupert Everett, Colin Firth, Reese Witherspoon

Oscar Wilde's deliciously witty play is here dusted off for another movie adaptation, following 1952's Michael Redgrave/Edith Evans effort and numerous TV versions. This time Rupert Everett and Colin Firth are the two nineteenth-century English gentlemen both using the same pseudonym to impress their respective amours, Cecily (Witherspoon) and Gwendolen (Frances O'Connor).

A comedy of mistaken identities and manners, this has always worked best on the stage, but director Parker (who had already adapted Wilde's *An Ideal Husband* in 1999) moves things along merrily against a luscious countryside setting. He also wisely packs the film with the cream of British acting talent, including a simply perfect Dame Judi Dench as the formidable Lady Bracknell, Tom Wilkinson as Dr Chasuble and Anna Massey as Miss Prism. A shame, then, that he felt the need to use an American (Witherspoon) and an Australian (O'Connor) for his two female leads, but both are fair, and they work nicely enough with Everett and Firth.

The end result is a fun, if not spot-on, adaptation, and it's worth a look for Everett's delightful performance and that classy supporting cast.

THE INN OF THE SIXTH HAPPINESS (1958)

Directed by Mark Robson
Starring Ingrid Bergman, Curt Jurgens, Robert Donat

Based *very* loosely on a true story, this missionary drama has more exotic charm than most because the missionary in question is a woman. Furthermore, her passion for the people and their culture gives this movie a touching warmth.

Bergman's tender but indomitable Gladys Aylward is a servant girl in England, rejected as unsuitable for her dream of missionary work. Unperturbed, she sets off on her own to China. Once there, she inherits the responsibilities of a rural outpost, forms close bonds with the locals and falls in love with Jurgens's dashing Eurasian soldier. In a suspenseful second half of the film, she courageously conducts a hundred starving children on a terrifying march to safety through the lines of the invading Japanese. Yes, when she and the ragged tykes come marching down from the mountains (which were actually Welsh!) singing 'With A Knick Knack Paddywack' it's absurdly sugary, but lovely and ever watchable all the same.

JANE EYRE (1944)

Directed by Robert Stevenson
Starring Joan Fontaine, Orson Welles

There have been numerous screen adaptations of Charlotte Brontë's classic novel – including Franco Zeffirelli's dull and woefully miscast 1996 version, starring Charlotte Gainsbourg and (shudder) William Hurt as an exceedingly unsexy Rochester. Susannah York and George C. Scott, Zelah Clarke and Timothy Dalton, and Samantha Morton and Ciaran Hinds also all tried to capture one of literature's most haunting love stories on screen, but none succeeded in eclipsing Fontaine and a simmering Welles of the 1944 version.

Jane, of course, is an orphan (look for a young Elizabeth Taylor as her tragic schoolmate), deprived of love and comfort at the forbidding school where she grows up. Once she comes of age, she takes a position as governess at Thornfield Hall, where she falls for her employer, the mysterious and brooding Rochester. A happy ending seems possible, until you realise there are strange noises in the house and a room that Rochester is determined to keep locked.

Stevenson directs this black and white film as a Gothic romance (all dimly lit hallways and flickering candles), and garners terrific performances from Fontaine, and especially Welles, who storms around to maximum effect. It's unlikely anyone will ever do this tragic hero better.

JEZEBEL (1938)

Directed by William Wyler
Starring Bette Davis, Henry Fonda, George Brent

Although it made it to the screen well ahead of *Gone With The Wind*, this ripe ante-bellum melodrama of a headstrong Southern belle was tailored specifically as a compensatory vehicle for Davis when it became clear she would not be cast as Scarlett O'Hara. But Warners and Wyler did her proud with a shimmering production. Davis, always superlative as fiery, liberated women, duly picked up her second Academy Award for her spiteful vixen Julie. She scandalises New Orleans and scares off her sombre fiancé Pres (Fonda) when she insists on wearing a scarlet satin gown to the society ball at which all young ladies must wear white. When he returns from up 'Nawth' with a Yankee wife, Julie stirs up a hornets' nest of jealousy, scheming and fateful duels by the time a yellow fever epidemic intrudes.

Julie, of course, is not allowed complete success as a temptress. Instead – in something of a groundbreaker for a woman's character study – she performs a grand redemptive gesture. She sacrificially accompanies the feverish Pres into squalid quarantine without even pausing to change out of her party gown and into something a tad more practical. She nobly vows to restore him to the arms of his loving wife. And we'd like to bet she makes good on her promise.

JULIA (1977)

Directed by Fred Zinnemann
Starring Jane Fonda, Vanessa Redgrave, Jason Robards

This prestigious adaptation of Lillian Hellman's memoir *Pentimento* prompted contentious sleuths to deny that the dramatic events of the thirties she described ever took place. But they were possibly missing Hellman's point: that her youthful friendship with the fearless Julia (Redgrave) inspired her life and work.

The movie ambitiously, if sketchily, interweaves Hellman's (Fonda) long-time love affair with fading novelist Dashiell Hammett (Robards), her struggle to find her voice as a writer and her politicisation. The story's dramatic centre is an atypically timorous Lillian's high-anxiety train journey through Nazi Germany, smuggling funds from underground activist Julia to procure the release of Jewish prisoners. Around this, snotty socialites (including a young Meryl Streep) and witty literary figures (the Dorothy Parker set) swirl and swill cocktails in a vivacious, wonderfully dressed evocation of pre-war whoopee.

Rock Hudson's dishy gardener and Jane Wyman's older widow find love (and tragedy) in ALL THAT HEAVEN ALLOWS.

Katharine Hepburn (and Baby) in the definitive screwball comedy, BRINGING UP BABY.

(left) 'Don't let's ask for the moon. We have the stars.' Bette Davis and
Paul Henreid in classic melodrama NOW VOYAGER; (right) 'Simply
divine': the bitchy, scheming, fighting and gossiping 'friends' that make
up THE WOMEN.

Audrey Hepburn and co-star Gregory Peck check out the sights of Rome in the delicious romantic comedy ROMAN HOLIDAY.

Jennifer Jones and William Holden enjoy forbidden love in 1955's
Cinemascopic LOVE IS A MANY-SPLENDORED THING

(main photo) *Audrey Tatou brings happiness to Paris in* AMELIE; *(top right)
Barbra Streisand's Katy and Robert Redford's Hubble embrace in classic
weepie* THE WAY WE WERE; *(below right – and from left to right) Loretta
Devine, Whitney Houston, Angela Bassett and Lela Rochon search for their
Mr Rights in* WAITING TO EXHALE.

(left and below) Jennifer Grey falls, like any sensible girl would, for Patrick Swayze's sexy, hip-swivelling moves in DIRTY DANCING.

(top right) Molly Ringwald is the Cinderella who gets to go to the prom in teenage chick flick PRETTY IN PINK (here with costars Andrew McCarthy and Jon Cryer); (below right) 'It Had To Be You': Meg Ryan and Billy Crystal are the friends who find sex gets in the way in WHEN HARRY MET SALLY.

Doris Day and Rock Hudson share comedy and romance in their first on-screen teaming, the classic PILLOW TALK.

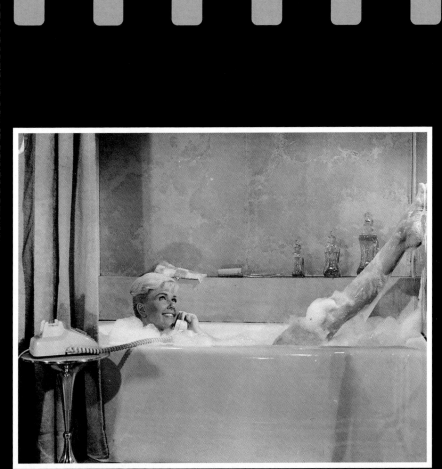

(top left) Helena Bonham Carter finds love (and Julian Sands) in the Italian countryside in Merchant Ivory's adaptation of EM Forster's novel A ROOM WITH A VIEW.

(below left) Mega-budget, mega-effects and mega-romance for Kate Winslet and Leonardo DiCaprio aboard the doomed Titanic.

(above) Michael Douglas and Kathleen Turner get up close and personal during their wild adventure in ROMANCING THE STONE.

Susan Sarandon and Geena Davis are gun-toting, law-dodging gal pals Thelma and Louise in Ridley Scott's ultimate chick-flick adventure.

(top) Backstabbing, love, betrayal and laughs are all in a day's work for Harrison Ford and Melanie Griffith in WORKING GIRL; (above) Stop the presses! Ace reporter Hildy Johnson (Rosalind Russell) and editor/ex-husband Walter Burns (Cary Grant) fight the battle of the sexes in screwball romantic comedy HIS GIRL FRIDAY.

The grandmother of all historical epics: Vivien Leigh's Scarlett and Clark Gable's Rhett share a tempestuous moment in GONE WITH THE WIND.

LADY JANE (1986)

Directed by Trevor Nunn
Starring Helena Bonham Carter, Cary Elwes

Here we have the tragic tale of teenager Lady Jane Grey, a cousin of the short-lived boy king Edward VI, and on his death set up by Protestant nobles as Queen of England. Nine days and an abortive rebellion later, Catholic Queen Mary claimed the throne and Jane lost her head.

Nunn's beautifully shot romantic drama of star-cross'd lovers presents Jane and her hastily obtained husband Dudley (Elwes) as sulky teens, she a thoughtful scholar and he a party animal, who surprise their scheming parents by falling in love and becoming virtuous conspirator–martyrs. In real life the ill-fated young couple apparently couldn't stand the sight of each other. And it's fun to ask the question, 'Who is prettier in their velvet Tudor splendour, period princess Bonham Carter or Elwes?'

THE LAST OF THE MOHICANS (1992)

Directed by Michael Mann
Starring Daniel Day Lewis, Madeleine Stowe

There had been previous adaptions of James Fennimore Cooper's novel, including 1936's adventure starring Randolph Scott, and an animated one. But it was ex-Miami Vice director Mann who delivered the most luscious version, an epic tale of romance and war set in eighteenth-century America as the French, British colonists and Native Americans battled for their piece of the frontier country.

Daniel Day Lewis, better known for character roles such as Christy Brown in *My Left Foot*, was an unlikely choice for leading man, but he embraced the role with gusto. Taking the 'Method' to extremes, he spent weeks prior to shooting living on the land, hunting and fishing to prepare himself for playing Hawkeye, a settler with flowing locks raised by Mohicans who becomes reluctantly embroiled in the rising conflicts. As well as defending his people, he finds time to come to the rescue of beautifully coiffed damsel in distress Cora Munro (Stowe) – giving her some very twentieth-century snogs behind a romantic waterfall while he's at it. Mann's version is far cornier than the source novel, and it takes all of Day Lewis's skill to make his promise to Stowe – 'I will find you, no matter how long it takes, no matter how far!' – not sound *too* cheesy.

It's a hugely enjoyable romp packed with breathtaking scenery and set pieces (including the final, gruesome battle), brimming over with passion, tension and the brooding stares of Day Lewis. Yummy.

LEGENDS OF THE FALL (1994)

Directed by Ed Zwick
Starring Brad Pitt, Anthony Hopkins, Aidan Quinn, Julia Ormond

Hearts are broken, chests are heaving and honours are challenged in this romantic saga of three brothers growing up in turn-of-the-century Montana. Alfred (Quinn) is the dutiful son who runs his father's ranch; Samuel (Henry Thomas) is the idealistic young man who wants to fight in the Great War; and Tristan (Pitt) is their wayward, untamed sibling who roams the neighbouring forest looking for bears to wrestle in his spare time.

Thrown into this clash of egos is Samuel's bride-to-be Susanna (Ormond), who seems to be under the impression that being engaged to one brother doesn't necessarily mean you can't lust after the other two. Matters are further complicated when the brothers go off to war and young Sam is the one who returns home in a body-bag, leaving the two surviving siblings to fight over the fickle former fiancée.

It's thoroughly enjoyable and well-played hokum from *Glory* director Zwick, with beautiful scenery that makes you want to book the next flight to Montana. Pitt, Quinn and Hopkins (as their father) obviously relish their roles as macho heroes, but Ormond fails to convince. Would babe-magnets Pitt and Quinn really be fighting over this vacuous female? Surely there are some other gals in town who'd have them. Still, *Legends Of The Fall* never pretends to be *Hamlet*: it's simply an entertaining drama with enough romance to turn even the hardest heart to mush.

A LITTLE PRINCESS (1995)

Directed by Alfonso Cuaron
Starring Liesel Matthews, Eleanor Bron

Just as her *Secret Garden* is an evergreen favourite, Frances Hodgson Burnett's other childhood classic of a plucky young heroine's travails and triumphs translates on the screen into ripping, gorgeous, girlie stuff. Transplanted from London in the Boer War to New York in the First World War, it's the tale of Sara Crewe (Matthews), a wealthy darling at a snooty girls' school until she is forced by evil headmistress Miss Minchin (Bron) into wretchedly abused servitude when Papa goes missing at the front and she is left penniless. Courage, imagination and friendship triumph over cruel adversity in this very pretty, spirited tale which insists, 'All women are princesses; it is our right!'

The Little Princess, a 1939 adaptation featuring child superstar Shirley Temple, follows the book more faithfully, if more sentimentally, and is also lavishly enjoyable.

LITTLE WOMEN (1994)

Directed by Gillian Armstrong
Starring Winona Ryder, Susan Sarandon, Gabriel Byrne, Christian Bale, Trini Alvarado, Samantha Mathis, Kirsten Dunst, Claire Danes

Louisa May Alcott's oft-filmed girlie classic of loving sisters growing up with high spirits and heartache in New England during America's Civil War was beautifully realised in George Cukor's superb, most faithful, 1933 version. That movie received the Academy Award for its screenplay and still glories in feisty Katharine Hepburn's headstrong Jo. A 1949 remake starring June Allyson and Peter Lawford has glossy colour trimmings that outshine the leads, although the young Elizabeth Taylor and Margaret O'Brien are terrific as vain Amy and frail Beth.

Almost half a century later, Armstrong's film respects the sentimentality of the novel while presenting it with a confident realism. Her feminist accent is more pronounced even than ahead-of-her-time Alcott's, emphasising a progressively emancipated influence from warm and wise Marmee (Sarandon) on her brood, played by a perfectly cast clutch of outstanding young actresses. This version is also the first to give us a handsome, genuinely romantic Professor Bhaer (Byrne). Finally, Jo's yearning makes perfect, sexy sense.

MANSFIELD PARK (1999)

Directed by Patricia Rozema
Starring Frances O'Connor, Jonny Lee Miller, Alessandro Nivola

A smart screen version of the classic novel has an enchanting O'Connor as Jane Austen's heroine, Fanny Price. She's a penniless young girl sent to live with her snobbish wealthy relatives, the Bertrams. There she befriends their son Edmund (Miller), but as they grow up her adoptive family push Fanny towards shallow but handsome Henry (Nivola), whom they believe to be a more suitable husband.

Rozema took inspiration from Austen's own journals and letters, as well as the novel, to deliver this nicely realised take on the story, in fact the only film version of the book (though there was a 1983 BBC series). It's well performed by a cast that also includes Embeth Davidtz as Henry's seductive sister, Lindsay Duncan as her laudanum-addled aunt and Harold Pinter as Sir Thomas Bertram, and provides a witty, interesting twist on the well-known romance.

MADAME BOVARY (1991)

Directed by Claude Chabrol
Starring Isabelle Huppert, Jean-François Balmer, Christopher Malavoy

Jean Renoir's 1932 version of Flaubert's ever-popular romantic classic of discontent and longing was tediously dreary. Unfortunately, Chabrol's isn't any better. Huppert is too mature and colourless to convince as the frustrated, adulterous dreamer Emma, whose craving for romance, excitement and expensive clothes dooms her and everyone around her to ruin. And what happened to all the passion?

Vincente Minnelli's 1949 Hollywood version, starring Jennifer Jones, Van Heflin and Louis Jordan, is the one to look out for – even though literary purists have long sneered at its deviations from the book. Jones's lovely Emma leaves a trail of broken hearts and suffering in her wake, but, boy, she pays for it in grand, tragic style. A swirling ballroom scene, when Emma giddily waltzes her cares away, is heady cinematic stuff, even by today's standards.

MARY REILLY (1996)

Directed by Stephen Frears
Starring Julia Roberts, John Malkovich

Did the world really need another Jekyll and Hyde movie? *Dangerous Liaisons* writer Christopher Hampton and director Frears obviously thought so, as they concocted this Gothic insomnia cure that focuses on the effect working for a split personality has on Jekyll's chambermaid Mary (Roberts). Still suffering from a childhood in the care of an abusive father (Michael Gambon), Mary finds herself drawn to her master and to the sexy/sinister Mr Hyde (both Malkovich). However, after Jekyll sends her on errands to Mrs Farraday's (Glenn Close) bordello, she realises Hyde may be responsible for a series of gruesome murders.

A tedious plod through the swirling, dank mists of Olde London Towne, this version of the tale – based on Valerie Martin's novel rather than the Robert Louis Stevenson classic – offers little in the way of scares or eroticism. Malkovich appears bored throughout, and Roberts, looking pale and on the verge of passing out, can't convey the emotions of a woman supposedly both attracted to and frightened by Hyde. While it's nice to see a classic story from the female perspective, it would have been even nicer if someone other than Roberts had been given the pivotal role.

MRS BROWN (1997)

Directed by John Madden
Starring Judi Dench, Billy Connolly, Geoffrey Palmer

'Their extraordinary friendship transformed an empire,' said the ads for this romantic period drama about the relationship between Queen Victoria (Dench) and commoner John Brown (Connolly). Based on historical fact, the film – wittily scripted by Jeremy Brock – begins in 1864, with Victoria continuing to mourn the death of her beloved Prince Albert two years before. Her household thinks maybe horse-riding will improve her mood, so rough Scotsman John Brown is sent for from Balmoral, to be available whenever the Queen decides she wants to ride. His outspoken ways eventually melt the monarch, and the pair become friends – much to the annoyance of the court and especially the Queen's heir, the Prince Of Wales, as whispers abound that Brown, with his matter-of-fact opinions, has become the power behind the throne.

Dench, as ever, is superb as the monarch whose court dubbed her 'Mrs Brown' amid much speculation that she and Brown were having an affair, portraying Victoria as a strong-willed, formidable, intelligent queen. But it is Connolly – best known, of course, for his stand-up comedy – who is the revelation here, delivering a strong, moving performance as the servant who touched the heart of a royal.

MRS SOFFEL (1984)

Directed by Gillian Armstrong
Starring Mel Gibson, Diane Keaton, Matthew Modine

Loosely based on a true story, this dark, sombre period drama has Keaton looking very prim and proper as prison warder's wife Kate Soffel. She dispenses prayers and compassion to the inmates, including murderer Ed Biddle (a young and yummy Gibson) and his mentally handicapped brother Jack (Modine). Stifled in her marriage to Peter (Edward Hermann), it's not long before she realises what a hottie is in the jail downstairs, and she's soon conspiring to help the brothers escape so she can break free herself (and enjoy some rumpy-pumpy with Ed, of course).

Unfortunately, while this had the potential to explore the liberation of Kate's repressed passion, Armstrong instead delivers a bleak, detached film. We mainly recommend it here for the beautiful wintry landscapes ... and Gibson's seriously seductive performance, of course.

ORLANDO (1993)

Directed by Sally Potter
Starring Tilda Swinton, Billy Zane, Lothaire Blutheau

Director Potter's globe-trotting vision of Virginia Woolf's valentine to her adventurous lover Vita Sackville-West is a stylish, witty romp. It's also an ingenious assortment of snapshots of 400 years of social history, as seen from both sides of the gender divide.

Swinton's Orlando is initially a feminine-looking man, introduced as an aristocratic Elizabethan youth who never ages. After being taken up by a raddled Queen Elizabeth I and going on to learn quite a bit about the world, wooing and war, he undergoes a metamorphosis into a woman some time in the eighteenth century. The piece playfully but cleverly blasts the absurdities of sex and class that divide people across time, locales and cultures. Things get particularly perky halfway through the nineteenth century with the arrival of a Byronic Zane to impregnate Lady Orlando, before she hits her modern-day stride as a boyish-looking woman. Very jolly, smart and moving too, this makes its points with panache.

OSCAR AND LUCINDA (1997)

Directed by Gillian Armstrong
Starring Ralph Fiennes, Cate Blanchett

Fiennes is atypically endearing as the repressed, twitchy, oddball dreamer Oscar in director Armstrong's eccentric adaptation of Peter Carey's Booker Prize-winning novel.

Devout minister Oscar is en route to Australia as a missionary when he meets independently minded heiress Lucinda (the delightful Blanchett), 'a proud square peg' in the Victorian society of round holes. Soon the two lonely, colourful soulmates discover their mutual addiction to gambling. With scandal and confusion threatening their perfect match, Oscar is inspired to transport a church made entirely of glass across the Blue Mountains as a grand poetic expression of his love and devotion. This undertaking unsurprisingly proves to be an epic misadventure with tragic, surreal and fantastic consequences.

The narration by *Shine*'s Geoffrey Rush adds dry humour to a handsome picture that moves between hilarity and heartache with a defiantly offbeat sensibility and some wild twists. This is a *Fitzcarraldo* for females with a taste for the bizarre.

OUT OF AFRICA (1985)

Directed by Sydney Pollack
Starring Meryl Streep, Robert Redford, Klaus Maria Brandauer

Another chance for Streep to display her foreign-accent skills as Danish Karen Blixen in this romantic drama based on Isak Dinesen's memoirs. Married to a man she doesn't love (Brandauer), Karen travels with him to Kenya to establish a plantation. There she meets and falls in love with the tanned and rugged adventurer Denys (Redford). Their romance is not a sappy, Mills & Boon affair (she contracts syphilis from her husband, for starters, while Denys never wants to give up his freedom, even for love), although it's ultimately a weepy with an ending guaranteed to turn most hearts to mush.

Pollack photographs the Kenyan locations lovingly, which is apt, because this story is as much about Karen's love affair with Africa as it is about her love for Denys. Sweeping in scale, and nearly three hours long, the film won seven Oscars, including Best Picture, Best Cinematography and Best Director.

PERSUASION (1995)

Directed by Roger Michell
Starring Amanda Root, Ciaran Hinds

This was originally made for television, but it is so strong in its impeccable Regency detail, its handsome, candlelit design and the perfectly pitched performances that it received a well-deserved theatrical release. It's right up there with the very best Jane Austen adaptations, from her novel with the most romantic suspense and the most alarms for older female fans.

Root's gentle, selfless, perennially put-upon Anne has never got over her love for the penniless young naval officer her snobbish family insisted she give up. Years later, when her youthful bloom is long gone and her foolish father has squandered his wealth, dashing Captain Wentworth (Hinds) reappears – now a man of means and a prize catch. He is eager to marry, and a flock of eager young things flutter hopefully around him. Poor Anne seems well out of the running and is still up to her neat bonnet in obnoxious relatives, conniving connections and worrying complications, but highly ingenious plotting and eventual recognition of a good woman's worth finally secure a deliciously happy ending.

THE PIANO (1993)

Directed by Jane Campion
Starring Holly Hunter, Harvey Keitel, Sam Neill, Anna Paquin

Writer–director Campion proved she followed the beat of a different drum with a triumphantly original, erotic and ultimately uplifting film. She created a story that deliberately harks back to passionate nine-teenth-century novels but also contains contemporary feminist attitudes to sexuality and self-realisation.

When mute Scot Ada (Hunter) arrives in Victorian New Zealand for an arranged marriage to dour, repressed Stewart (Neill), she brings along her illegitimate daughter (Paquin) and her cherished piano. Failing to comprehend either her depth of emotion or the piano's significance to headstrong Ada, who could speak if she wanted to but has chosen the instrument as her means of expression, Stewart sells it to his uncouth estate agent (Keitel, getting in touch with his hitherto well-hidden feminine side). This sets off a triangle of longings, sexual power games and defiance as Ada grudgingly barters her 'favours' to redeem her precious piano, one key at a time.

Set against evocative, wild landscapes, and beautifully acted, this is a dark, strange, complex piece that haunts those in whom it strikes a deep chord. The astonishing Hunter received an Academy Award, as did young Paquin, and Campion for her screenplay.

SUPERMODEL JANE AUSTEN

Jane Austen (1775–1817) is, of course, one of the world's greatest and best-loved writers. But her work also rivals *Cinderella* as the ideal model for feminine entertainment. All six of her novels have been adapted into period costume comedy dramas, and all provide an irresistible mix of great characters, wit, realistic dialogue and shapely plotting. If she were alive today, every studio head and agent in Hollywood would be vying to take her to lunch.

Pride And Prejudice alone has been turned into a classic film and *four* TV adaptations, including the cultural phenomenon that was the BBC's 1995 production in which Jennifer Ehle was prejudiced against proud Colin Firth. More recently, on the big screen *Bridget Jones's Diary* cheerfully borrowed from Austen's plot; and *Pride And Prejudice: A Latter Day Comedy* (2003) tried to repeat the *Clueless* concept (which ingeniously relocated *Emma* to Beverly Hills) by making Elizabeth Bennett an American college girl. But there is scarcely a girl-friendly film made that doesn't have some elements inspired by Miss Jane.

FIVE BASICS FOR A MOVIE À LA AUSTEN

1 Make the heroine intelligent, good-humoured and loyal to other women, but also judgemental, stubborn and a bit of a smarty-pants.

2 Make the hero seemingly unavailable, and certainly beyond the heroine's reach in status, wealth, looks or eligibility.

3 Give the heroine embarrassing relatives, talkative friends, rich-bitch rivals and an unwanted suitor.

4 Create a reversal of fortunes and a misunderstanding that has ongoing complications but is quickly cleared up once the heroine says what's on her mind.

5 Include come-uppances for everyone who's been mean to the heroine in or before the happy ending.

THE PORTRAIT OF A LADY (1996)

Directed by Jane Campion
Starring Nicole Kidman, John Malkovich, Viggo Mortensen

An extremely gloomy adaptation of Henry James's novel that's most notable for its impressive cast: as well as Kidman, Malkovich and Mortensen, Richard E. Grant, Christian Bale, Martin Donovan, John Gielgud and Shelley Duvall all add class to the proceedings.

Kidman's first period drama since the infinitely flightier *Far And Away* has her pale, blotchy-faced and weepy for most of the time as Isabel Archer. An orphaned young woman in nineteenth-century Europe, she rejects the attentions of a suitable man (Grant) only to be seduced and trapped into a loveless marriage by cad Gilbert Osmond (Malkovich). Quite why she takes this course of action is anyone's guess, as Gilbert is so slimy you can almost hear him slither.

Unfortunately, the film skips over the many nuances in James's novel that explain Isabel's decisions. And, while Campion skilfully recreates the period (at least, we think she does – most of the scenes are too damn dark to tell), she can't quite bring the book's characters to life.

PRIDE AND PREJUDICE (1940)

Directed by Robert Z. Leonard
Starring Greer Garson, Laurence Olivier

'It is a truth universally acknowledged that a single man in possession of a fortune must be in want of a wife.' It is also a TUA that Jane Austen's flirtatious, fraught, brilliantly observed comedy of manners about five sisters in want of husbands never loses its appeal. Of numerous adaptations, this is the most delicious, with a pacy, wickedly witty screenplay (by a team of writers, including Aldous Huxley) that revels in dreamy Olivier's aloof, snooty but terribly misunderstood Mr Darcy and sparkling Garson's playful, utterly charming Elizabeth.

This is perfection in every department, from a spectacular supporting cast – such as Edna May Oliver's contemptuous grande dame and Ann Rutherford's outrageously silly Lydia – to Oscar-winning art direction and outstanding period flavour (taken some crafty licence with, since fashion-wise they've been propelled several decades forward from Georgian England to early Victorian to cap it all with some wonderfully absurd hats).

Even though it necessarily streamlines the story, the movie includes all the important plot points and the best lines. And it's faithful to Austen's tone even in invented scenes – memorably an innuendo-laden encounter when Elizabeth and Darcy compete at archery – which the author herself would probably have enjoyed.

THE REMAINS OF THE DAY (1993)

Directed by James Ivory
Starring Anthony Hopkins, Emma Thompson

Having run out of E. M. Forster novels to adapt, producer Ismail Merchant, director Ivory and their regular screenwriter Ruth Prawer Jhabvala turned their masterful, loving attention to Kazuo Ishiguro's Booker Prize-winning novel of duty, class and betrayal. It's like a deep *Upstairs, Downstairs* … with Nazis.

Hopkins heads a sterling British cast as Stevens, the rigidly suppressed and dutiful butler commanding the vast household of His Lordship James Fox, whose deluded admiration for all things Teutonic points to treason and tragedy as war and sweeping social change loom. Thompson is the brisk, yearning, younger housekeeper at touching odds with Stevens.

As a multi-layered, ultra-restrained period piece this isn't to everyone's taste, but it is a beautifully detailed, intricately structured, perfectly crafted drama. Hopkins's performance is nothing short of brilliant, and Thompson is at her most affecting in her clumsy flirting and futile eagerness to break through a lonely man's shell.

THE RETURN OF MARTIN GUERRE (1982)

Directed by Daniel Vigne
Starring Gérard Depardieu, Nathalie Baye

In sixteenth-century France, soldier Martin Guerre (Depardieu) returns after nine years away on the battlefields. His wife (Baye) is happy to discover he is a changed man: while he was a bit of a pig before he left, now he is attentive and loving. So when rumours abound in the village that maybe this Martin is an impostor, she doesn't want to believe them.

Based on a French legend and court records of a similar incident, this is a compelling story, made all the more intriguing by Depardieu's winning performance. Vigne captures peasant life perfectly (you can almost smell the manure), and the film deservedly won a César (French Oscar) for production design. The director and cast also maintain the tension in a climactic courtroom scene. The film was ineffectively remade in the US in 1993 as *Sommersby* (see page 202).

A ROOM WITH A VIEW (1985)

Directed by James Ivory
Starring Maggie Smith, Helena Bonham Carter

Producer Ismail Merchant, director James Ivory and writer Ruth Prawer Jhabvala revitalised the period drama with this luxurious adaptation of E. M. Forster's novel. (The trio later reteamed, of course, for acclaimed movies like *Remains of the Day* and *Howards End*.)

Bonham Carter stars as Lucy, a young woman who discovers much about life and love in the Tuscan countryside as she decides between prospective suitors George (Julian Sands) and Cecil (Daniel Day Lewis). Sands, in his best screen performance, is all passion and youthful lust, kissing the demure Lucy in a yellow-tinted field. Day Lewis also hits just the right note as priggish Cecil, to whom Lucy is reluctantly engaged. But it is Maggie Smith, as Lucy's dotty companion, and Denholm Elliott, as George's forward-thinking father, who stand at the mast.

This beautiful film was nominated for eight Oscars (including Best Director and Best Picture, losing in both categories to Oliver Stone's *Platoon*), and won three, for Best Adapted Screenplay, Best Costume and Best Art Direction.

SARATOGA TRUNK (1945)

Directed by Sam Wood
Starring Ingrid Bergman, Gary Cooper

Conniving and exquisitely chic minx Clio Dulaine (Bergman), the illegitimate daughter of a well-to-do man and his Creole mistress, returns to her native New Orleans from Paris in the latest nineteenth-century modes (how she got the money for them is presumably best not asked). Her plan is to avenge herself on her father's acknowledged family and extort money from them to spare their blushes. Then she'll happily leave town. Dismayed by her avariciousness, but busy with a revenge scheme of his own, Texan Clint Maroon (Cooper) is helplessly smitten by the time they remove to the swanky hot-springs resort of Saratoga for romantic complications and more money scams.

Director Wood really made an interminable meal of Edna '*Show Boat*' Ferber's bestseller, and the studio knew it: the film wasn't released until two years after it had been completed. But nowadays, in the age of fast-forward buttons, Coop and Bergman look so gorgeous together in the flirtatious and smoochy scenes that they are worth an admiring peek.

THE SECRET GARDEN (1993)

Directed by Agnieszka Holland
Starring Kate Maberly, Maggie Smith, John Lynch

Orphaned in India, the understandably temperamental Mary (Maberly) is sent to England to live with her cold, hunchbacked uncle (Lynch) and his querulous, neglected, invalid son Colin (Heydon Prowse) in their ramshackle Victorian mansion. Her discovery of a forbidden, abandoned garden and her secret visits there with green-fingered country lad Dickon (Andrew Knott) transform all their lives.

What has always made Frances Hodgson Burnett's classic fun for all children is that Mary and Colin are both bad-tempered sprogs who relish screaming matches. But what makes it precious to the girlie faction is its emphasis on affection, healing and redemption. And Polish director Holland, always a winner with child actors, conveys this aspect of the story beautifully.

The 1949 version starring Margaret O'Brien and Dean Stockwell is also enchanting, arguably more dramatic, and borrows a neat trick from *The Wizard Of Oz*: it's in black and white until Mary brings love to the garden, whereupon a burst of Technicolor heralds life revived.

SENSE AND SENSIBILITY (1995)

Directed by Ang Lee
Starring Emma Thompson, Kate Winslet, Hugh Grant, Alan Rickman

Thompson and Winslet are the sisters looking for love in the English countryside in this yummy adaptation of Jane Austen's novel.

After their father dies, the Dashwood girls – Elinor (Thompson), Marianne (Winslet) and little Margaret (Emilie François) – are forced, along with their mother, to leave their gentrified life behind and move into a cottage kindly lent by a relative. The only way to improve the family's social and financial standing is for the two older sisters to marry well, which is exactly what they set out to do. Into their lives comes Edward (Grant), who is interested in Elinor but departs as quickly as he arrived, while Marianne has the attentions of Colonel Brandon (Rickman) and the far more dashing Willoughby (Greg Wise).

Snappily scripted by Thompson herself (who won an Oscar for her screenplay), this is part drama and part Regency comedy of manners as Elinor and Marianne attempt to make sense of the men in their lives. Lovingly directed by Ang Lee (his second non-Asian film), it is packed with handsome men galloping on horseback through scrumptious countryside, and is such a sweet picture-postcard of a movie that it should come wrapped in a big red bow.

SHAKESPEARE IN LOVE (1998)

Directed by John Madden
Starring Gwyneth Paltrow, Joseph Fiennes, Geoffrey Rush

It's 1593, and Will Shakespeare (Fiennes) is suffering from writer's block as he struggles to compose his latest play, 'Romeo And Ethel: The Pirate's Daughter', in this delicious romantic comedy. Inspiration comes in the form of the beautiful Viola (Paltrow), who, fascinated by the playwright, dresses up as a man so she can audition for his play. When he discovers her secret, the pair fall head over heels, but the path of true love does not run smooth. Viola is already betrothed to the Earl of Wessex (Colin Firth), and he demands to marry her before Will's play, by now wisely retitled, makes it to its premiere.

Madden's film – scripted by Marc '*Waterworld*' Norman and Tom Stoppard – is packed with the latter's patented in-jokes and terrific period details. It also successfully combines the fictional romance between Will and Viola with the genesis of Shakespeare's most romantic play. Paltrow and Fiennes are both sexy and superb, and they are surrounded by a stellar cast: Rush and Martin Clunes as rival theatre owners, Ben Affleck as actor Edward Alleyn, Judi Dench as Elizabeth I and Rupert Everett as Christopher Marlowe. Fabulous, fabulous stuff.

SOMMERSBY (1993)

Directed by Jon Amiel
Starring Richard Gere, Jodie Foster, Bill Pullman

A Hollywood reworking of acclaimed French movie *The Return Of Martin Guerre*, this is only worth watching if you are unable to read subtitles or if you are determined to see absolutely every film Richard Gere ever made, including the bad ones.

At the end of the American Civil War, Laurel Sommersby (Foster) believes her abusive husband Jack has died in the fighting, so she has agreed to marry the far more reliable Orin (Pullman), who in the interim has helped raise her son. But Jack (Gere) returns and isn't the boorish man she remembers – while his face looks familiar, he's now a poetry-reading, warm and fuzzy version of the man she married. In fact, he's so different that she starts to think that maybe he's not the real Jack at all.

Unfortunately, Foster and Gere have about as much onscreen chemistry as a pair of dead kippers, and this movie's court scene (unlike the French one) delivers too many twists to be even remotely plausible. In fact it's all completely daft and utterly miscast, but at least Gere looks hunky throughout.

TESS (1979)

Directed by Roman Polanski
Starring Nastassja Kinski, Peter Firth, Leigh Lawson

Tess of the D'Urbervilles is arguably the most tragic heroine in all of Thomas Hardy's Wessex tales of woe, and Polanski's gorgeous film is appropriately anguished.

Tess Durbeyfield (a star-making performance from the young Kinski) is packed off by her farmer father to the hoity-toity d'Urbervilles, whom he believes are distant, nobler kin. Lawson's handsome rake Alec is a sham (the ancient name having been bought) but he has his way with Tess and casts her out, pregnant. This being rural nineteenth-century England, the guilt and shame are all hers, so she's driven from pillar to post to dairy farm. Firth's beautiful, upright Angel Clare marries her, only to abandon her when she opens her heart and confesses her past to him. When all illusions have been shattered she kills the man who ruined her, taking flight to Stonehenge for the saddest and most scenic police arrest ever.

This is an introspective business which men tend to describe as 'a bit long'. So it is, but it's also so full of empathy for a woman eternally at the mercy of men that it's entirely absorbing. It deservedly won Oscars for cinematography, art direction and costumes.

THAT HAMILTON WOMAN (1941)

Directed by Alexander Korda
Starring Vivien Leigh, Laurence Olivier

Winston Churchill's favourite film was clearly intended to instil some British pride into its beleaguered wartime audience. It tells the tale of Lord Horatio Nelson's (Olivier) affair with Lady Emma Hamilton (Leigh), following their first meeting in Naples. She was married to the British envoy, and he had a wife at home, so their romance was scandalous, and ended tragically, of course, with Emma disgraced and Nelson killed on the deck of the *Victory* at the Battle of Trafalgar in 1805.

Told in flashback as Emma relates her story to a young woman while in jail for theft, penniless and alone after Nelson's death, *That Hamilton*

Woman remains a moving and dramatic tale thanks to a superb performance from a luminous Vivien Leigh. Her real-life husband at the time is less effective as Nelson, but this is still an enjoyable, lavish costume drama.

WASHINGTON SQUARE (1997)

Directed by Agnieszka Holland
Starring Jennifer Jason Leigh, Ben Chaplin, Albert Finney

Henry James's classic novel set in nineteenth-century New York is transferred to the screen for the second time (the first being William Wyler's superior *The Heiress*, page 182) in a faithful, slow adaptation. Catherine Sloper (Leigh) is an awkward, plain young woman, the daughter of a wealthy physician (Finney) who regards his offspring as lacking the charm and beauty ever to win a husband. So they are both surprised when the handsome but impoverished Morris Townsend (the delicious but sadly wooden Chaplin) begins to call. But while her father suspects Morris is only in love with Catherine's inheritance, she believes he loves her for herself, and realises she may have to choose between these two men in her life.

Leigh – best known for more headstrong roles in *The Hudsucker Proxy* and *Single White Female* – unfortunately looks utterly out of place here. Nevertheless, she portrays her character's gaucheness quite well, and is ably supported by Finney, and Maggie Smith as Catherine's hopelessly romantic Aunt Lavinia. It's a well-made, well-performed tale of manners, values and emotions, but is somewhat pointless, given the earlier adaptation's perfection.

WESTWARD THE WOMEN (1951)

Directed by William Wellman
Starring Robert Taylor, Denise Darcel, Hope Emerson, Julie Bishop

For once a band of women – young, not so young, small, medium and extra large – get to do the rootin' tootin' stuff. They crack whips, fight off Indians, tumble down cliffs, bicker, bond, cry, die and traverse scorching desert … and one of them is in labour!

Sardonic wagon-train guide Taylor anticipates disaster leading a diverse group of gals on an arduous, eventful odyssey to pioneer husbands they haven't met, acts tough with plucky immigrant minx Darcel, and acquires respect for the women's true grit. It's terrific stuff, but we particularly admire how the ragged survivors sensibly withhold their charms until their menfolk provide scraps of material, bandannas and tablecloths with which the ladies run up an interesting collection of wedding ensembles.

THE WINGS OF THE DOVE (1997)

Directed by Iain Softley
Starring Helena Bonham Carter, Linus Roache, Alison Elliott

Kate (an unusually sultry Bonham Carter) has been taken in by a rich aunt (Charlotte Rampling) and groomed for a society marriage, but she is in love with impoverished reporter Merton (Roache). Torn between a life of passion and one of wealth and social standing, she searches for a solution, and it comes in the form of wilful but lonely American heiress Milly (Elliott).

A sensual tale of romantic intrigue and betrayal, selfishness and selflessness based on Henry James's novel and set against a backdrop of fashionable London and dreamy Venice, *The Wings Of The Dove* boasts terrific performances from Bonham Carter, Roache and especially Elliott. Iain Softley – director of the decidedly more modern *Backbeat* and *Hackers* – delivers the period feel with aplomb. Only a somewhat rigid Elizabeth McGovern, as Milly's travelling companion, lets the film down.

WUTHERING HEIGHTS (1939)

Directed by William Wyler
Starring Merle Oberon, Laurence Olivier, David Niven

Emily Brontë's passionate tale of doomed love on the Yorkshire Moors has been filmed numerous times. Luis Buñuel came up with a Mexican version in 1953; Anna Calder-Marshall and Timothy Dalton had a good go in 1970; and, oh dear, a ham-fisted 1992 production cast Ralph

Fiennes (suitably tortured but far too grubby) and the inexplicably French Juliette Binoche. But Wyler's magnificently atmospheric and emotional film is iconic: a perfect Gothic sob-fest, with Olivier divinely handsome as brooding, moody gypsy Heathcliff, Oberon lovely as headstrong Cathy and Niven sympathetic as wan Edgar, the mug she marries.

The stirring script confines itself to the first half of the book, but that's fine because all that stuff about Heathcliff cruelly avenging himself on the next generation is so mean. This cinematically cuts to the chase, sketching out the unhappy years after Cathy's death, to haunt us with the image of Heathcliff hanging out of the window, frozen to death, still crying her name.

WOMEN AT WAR

BRIDGE TO THE SUN (1961)

Directed by Etienne Perier
Starring Carroll Baker, James Shigeta

This tame but sincere romantic drama, an American–French co-production, is unusual for offering a glimpse of what it was like being a blonde enemy alien in Japan during the Second World War. Baker stars in the true story of Gwen Terasaki, an all-American Southern girl who fell in love with a handsome young Japanese diplomat (Shigeta) in Washington, DC in 1935 and defied 'polite' society's racism to marry him. Gwen's struggles to fit in with Teri's family and tradition-bound social circle when they are in his country are humorous (the unisex bath-house and Gwen in a geisha wig), stormy (Gwen raging at being banished from the dinner table and men-only conversations), saddening and educational. But these are trivial in the aftermath of Pearl Harbor, when the Terasakis' exile in rural Japan becomes a struggle for survival punctuated by the loss of loved ones, a sombre encounter with Allied prisoners, and betrayal. Baker and Shigeta are both attractive and touching.

CAPTAIN CORELLI'S MANDOLIN (2001)

Directed by John Madden
Starring Nicolas Cage, Penelope Cruz, Christian Bale

Louis de Bernières's soppy novel is translated to the screen by *Shakespeare In Love*'s John Madden. It ends up as a sweet and slightly sickly confection that's so fanciful it should begin with 'Once upon a time ...' and end with 'And they all lived happily ever after ...' Well, almost.

Cage overdoes it on the operatic gestures as the Italian soldier of the title, who falls for babe Cruz on the war-torn Greek island of Cephalonia during the Second World War. She has a fiancé (Bale), who looks as if he's been dipped in Bisto, he's so buff and tanned. But she conveniently forgets about him once Nic flashes that big smile, while her dad (John Hurt) doesn't seem too bothered that his daughter is getting friendly with one of the men who invaded his home.

Fans of the novel may be disappointed that the story has been squashed into a couple of hours of nice scenery, but the main let-down is that it isn't even very moving any more. Sit armed with a box of tissues expecting a sob-fest and you're likely to be throwing them at the screen in frustration at Cage's hamming instead.

CARVE HER NAME WITH PRIDE (1958)

Directed by Lewis Gilbert
Starring Virginia McKenna, Paul Scofield

McKenna is a lovely mix of delicate femininity and fierce resolve in this inspiring true story of wartime heroine Violette Szabo, based on the book by R. J. Minney. A young Englishwoman with a French mother, Violette married French soldier Etienne Szabo, but after his death in action she joined the British secret service. The film recounts her rigorous training, her resourcefulness after parachuting into Occupied France to work with the Resistance, her eventual capture and her ensuing ordeal in the hands of the Nazis.

There is as much intrigue, suspense and bravery in this as in solid, macho war dramas. But we also get graceful female appeal and poignant human touches, such as the little love poem from her husband which Vi uses for her secret code, a gentle and admiring love interest from her 'control' (Scofield), and the daring purchase of a Parisian frock for her little girl, which the child wears to Buckingham Palace to accept her mother's George Cross for valour. Director Gilbert creates a perfect closing scene to end the film with an affirmation that Violette's self-sacrifice had real meaning.

CHARLOTTE GRAY (2001)

Directed by Gillian Armstrong
Starring Cate Blanchett, Billy Crudup

It's 1943 and after her RAF lover is shot down intelligence agent Charlotte (Blanchett) parachutes into Occupied France. Her own agenda is to find her man, but involvement with distractingly dishy Resistance leader Julien (Crudup) draws her ever deeper into danger. Like *Captain Corelli's Mandolin*, this is a reverent, scenic but problematic adaptation of a bestselling novel (by Sebastian Faulks).

Charlotte is exceptional because she gets to combine brains with derring-do while sustaining a masquerade (becoming 'Dominique Gilbert' through dyed hair, smuggled underwear and learned social behaviour). And director Armstrong has always done her best work illuminating women who want more from their lives. But this romantic drama bites off more than any gal can chew!

The book puts most of the emphasis on Charlotte's internal journey. On film she is necessarily much busier foiling Nazis and collaborators, but ultimately that exposes how ineffectual her deeds have been while she's been exploring her identity and searching her heart. There is certainly chemistry between Blanchett and Crudup, but also a melodramatic phoniness that stops the film from being as moving and inspiring as it wants to be.

COLD MOUNTAIN (2003)

Directed by Anthony Minghella
Starring Jude Law, Nicole Kidman, Renée Zellweger

In the American Civil War wounded Confederate soldier Inman (Law) deserts and embarks on an epic journey back to his despairing sweetheart, Ada (Kidman), who is fighting hunger, ruin and terrorisation. While love can't possibly conquer all in this adaptation of Charles Frazier's novel, it certainly makes the going more romantic, as gorgeous Law and Kidman withstand a heap of suffering in a compelling story of heartache and hope. The story was inspired by Homer's *Odyssey*, as well as Frazier's own family history, with Inman encountering all manner of perils and Ada no simpering Southern belle, but a cultured contemplative who gets on with the labour of living.

As he did with *The English Patient*, writer–director Minghella beautifully reshapes the novel's structure, and thereby raises the emotional stakes. The sensitive leads are backed by interesting support, notably Oscar-winning Zellweger's rough-hewn farmhand. But the most memorable moment (apart from a damned fine spot of smooching) is the anguished soldier's cry, 'She's the place I'm going!' This is five-hanky drama with a love story to die for. All that's missing is the bodice-ripping soap operatics that made mini-series *North And South* a girl's closet favourite.

HANOVER STREET (1979)

Directed by Peter Hyams
Starring Harrison Ford, Lesley Ann Down

A rare romantic outing for Ford – which he made after he had appeared in *Star Wars* but before he became a megastar thanks to *Raiders Of The Lost Ark* – has him starring (and looking quite uncomfortable) as a cocky Yank bomber pilot stationed in England during the Second World War. While he's there he does his own bit for Anglo-American relations when he falls for beautiful married English lady Lesley Ann Down.

Of course, true love never runs smoothly, especially when one of the protagonists is already hitched, and matters for the lovers are further complicated when Harrison has to go on a dangerous mission with – yes, you guessed it – Down's unsuspecting husband (Christopher Plummer). It's all complete hokum, but enjoyable thanks to a breathy performance from Down, a stiff-upper-lipped one from Plummer, and an early, too-cute-to-be-true appearance by toddler Patsy Kensit as Down's cherubic daughter.

HEAVEN AND EARTH (1993)

Directed by Oliver Stone
Starring Hiep Thi Le, Tommy Lee Jones, Joan Chen

The third of Stone's Vietnam War cycle (after the decidedly more manly *Platoon* and *Born On The Fourth Of July*) gives us a Vietnamese point of view and the director's first female protagonist.

Newcomer Hiep receives strong support from Jones, a surprising Chen and a touching Haing S. Ngor in the true story of Le Ly Hayslip's arduous odyssey (chronicled in her two memoirs) from happy peasant child in a peaceful Buddhist village to Vietcong guerrilla, then from GI bride to liberated American entrepreneur.

Many critics couldn't get their heads around the notion of Stone getting in touch with his feminine side, and the film is a bit of a muddle. It's also stronger on the visceral and distressing than it is on the spiritual and emotional. But it's still affecting, and ends on a blessedly high note.

HEAVEN KNOWS, MR ALLISON (1957)

Directed by John Huston
Starring Deborah Kerr, Robert Mitchum

Delightful – if a war movie can be such a thing – drama with Mitchum as the gruff marine stranded with nun Kerr on a Pacific island overrun by the Japanese during the Second World War. It's a romance (of sorts) as their friendship grows: she becomes dependent on him for survival and he falls in love with her, baffled though he is that such a beautiful woman would choose a religious life.

In another director's hands, and with a less capable cast, this could have been an implausible disaster, but Huston delivers a moving adventure that's on a par with his earlier, more acclaimed *The African Queen* (another tale of misfits becoming friends). But most of the praise should go to the luminous, Oscar-nominated Kerr and the blustering Mitchum, who really are a delight.

IN LOVE AND WAR (1996)

Directed by Richard Attenborough
Starring Sandra Bullock, Chris O'Donnell

One wonders what Richard Attenborough was thinking when he chose O'Donnell to play a young Ernest Hemingway, the man who would go on to become one of the most celebrated figures in American literature. O'Donnell's acting skills are about as deep as a puddle, but since this whole movie is ill-advised, at least he fits right in.

It's the story of a love affair that takes place during the First World War. Hemingway is taken to a field hospital after he is shot in the leg, and there he falls for older nurse Agnes (Bullock), who at first spurns his advances. This relationship – only discovered following the real Agnes's death, when love letters she received from Hemingway were unearthed – formed the basis of the author's classic *A Farewell To Arms*, but here it is played like an adaptation of a Danielle Steel novel. O'Donnell tries to pull off 'brooding' but ends up with 'sulky'. Attenborough, who handled a real-life love story so brilliantly in *Shadowlands*, here seems far happier with the war scenes. Ultimately this is of interest only to die-hard Bullock and (if there are any) O'Donnell fans.

THE LAND GIRLS (1998)

Directed by David Leland
Starring Catherine McCormack, Rachel Weisz, Anna Friel

The Second World War is used as a backdrop for the life-and-love stories of three young women in this romantic drama from *Wish You Were Here* director Leland. It's 1941, and with Britain's young men off fighting, the Women's Land Army is formed to send women out to the country-side to work on farms until the men return. Snotty Stella (McCormack), whose fiancé is a naval officer, quirky Cambridge graduate Ag (Weisz) and flirty hairdresser Prue (Friel) are sent to the same farm, where they bond, work and chase after hunky young farmer Joe (Steven Mackintosh).

It's all perfectly innocuous stuff, and the three leads rise above their stereotypical roles and the clichéd script. But there's nothing here that hasn't been seen before – and done better – in films like *Yanks* (which had the added bonus of hunky Richard Gere) and a million TV movies.

LUCIE AUBRAC (1997)

Directed by Claude Berri
Starring Carole Bouquet, Daniel Auteuil

Departing from his grand epics of the land such as *Jean De Florette* and *Germinal* to dramatise events during the Nazi Occupation of France in the Second World War, Berri focused not on action heroics but on an intense love story.

Bouquet is Lyon Resistance fighter Lucie, whose passionate commitment to her husband Raymond (Auteuil) drives her to conceive an audacious bluff to save him when he falls into the hands of the Gestapo and the infamous Klaus Barbie. Lucie requires resolve and nerve for her rescue plan, not firepower.

Based on Aubrac's book *Outwitting The Gestapo*, this is a remarkable true story of the power of love over fear and betrayal. In typical Berri style it unfolds at a steady, deliberate pace that some may call plodding, but it is ultimately touching.

MRS MINIVER (1942)

Directed by William Wyler
Starring Greer Garson, Walter Pidgeon

A morale-booster for Blighty while England battled through the dark days of the Second World War. Louis B. Mayer remarked that Winston Churchill had written to him, '*Mrs Miniver* is propaganda worth a hundred battleships'. It also won six Academy Awards, including Best Picture and Best Actress, and was nominated for a further six.

Upper lips are suitably stiff and everyone is frightfully nice and polite in this drama about a housewife (Garson) keeping her family together during the early days of the war as the German bombs fall around them. Never mind that a bomb could fall on the house, there's a village flower show to prepare for! Her eldest son finds love, there are her two adorable younger children to think of, and numerous calamities arise, including the arrival of a downed German pilot who seeks refuge with the Minivers. Through it all we get a real sense of what it must have been like for those left at home to experience war on their doorstep.

The film belongs to Garson who broke Oscar records by delivering an acceptance speech of over five minutes. She's simply gorgeous – Richard Ney who played her eldest son despite only being ten years younger than Garson certainly thought so, as they became a couple and were married in 1943.

ODETTE (1950)

Directed by Herbert Wilcox
Starring Anna Neagle, Trevor Howard

Formerly celebrated as a musical star, the durable Dame Anna is superb in this umpteenth collaboration with her director–producer husband Wilcox. It's another authentically inspiring true-life story about a woman's resourcefulness. This one is adapted from Jerrard Tickell's book about the valiant Odette Churchill, a Frenchwoman recruited to return to her country as a spy for the British Special Operations Executive after her English husband is killed.

The story centres on her arrest, interrogation, torture and imprisonment in a concentration camp, where Marius Goring excels in the terrifying 'Ve haff vays of making you talk' department in a scene when Odette's toenails are torn out. The romantic interest with fellow-agent Captain Peter Churchill (Howard) was for real. The duo survived – thanks to Odette's cleverness in dealing with their captors – to be liberated, married and honoured by His Majesty for their heroism. As a result, Neagle was able to consult with Odette, enhancing the authenticity of her gripping performance.

PARADISE ROAD (1997)

Directed by Bruce Beresford
Starring Glenn Close, Pauline Collins, Frances McDormand, Julianna Margulies, Jennifer Ehle

Or *Tenko* meets *The Sound Of Music*. In 1942 a disparate group of European, American and Australian women and children attempt to leave Singapore following the Japanese invasion, only for their ship to be bombed and them to be taken captive. Once in the POW camp, some of the women – led by society belle Adrienne (Close) and mumsy missionary Margaret (Collins) – decide that the only way to survive the horror of their situation is to form a vocal orchestra. This is not as straightforward as it sounds, though, as they are forbidden by the Japanese to gather in groups, and have to hide the musical scores as they're banned from possessing pen and paper.

It's essentially a triumph-over-adversity tear jerker as the women (including *ER*'s Margulies as the spunky American and McDormand as the sullen German-Jewish doctor) battle to keep both body and spirit alive. Unfortunately, director Beresford handles every scene with a plodding predictability, and although the story is based on true events, there is an odd feeling of detachment to the whole affair. An impressive, classy cast is therefore wasted on an ultimately missable movie.

PEARL HARBOR (2001)

Directed by Michael Bay
Starring Ben Affleck, Josh Hartnett, Kate Beckinsale

One of the biggest blockbusters of 2001 also turned out to be one of the cheesiest, as action director Bay used one of the most famous events of the Second World War – the Japanese attack on American Pacific base Pearl Harbor in 1941 – as the backdrop for a laughable romantic story.

The plot is enjoyably ridiculous: pilot Rafe (Affleck) falls for pretty nurse Evelyn (Beckinsale) just before he is due to go off to war in Europe. When she hears he is missing, presumed dead overseas, she wastes no time in getting over her lost love by taking up with Danny (Hartnett), Rafe's best friend. But wouldn't you just know it, Rafe returns from the grave just hours before the Japanese attack to discover what the shameless hussy has been up to. In the real world, of course, she would get a good slap for not even mourning for a few months before hopping in the sack with another man (or in this case enjoying a fumble in an aircraft hangar filled with conveniently decorous parachutes rustling romantically in the breeze). But this is Mills & Boon-style fluff that has even more preposterous twists before the rousing finale.

However, the effects are amazing (almost to the point of being gratuitous) as Bay stages the attack with a million guns blazing, and there are some good performances from a supporting cast that includes Alec Baldwin, Tom Sizemore, Jon Voight and Cuba Gooding Jr. It's ultimately all tosh, of course, but with Affleck looking exceedingly delicious in his uniform, this is one of those bad movies that is also a guilty pleasure.

PLENTY (1985)

Directed by Fred Schepisi
Starring Meryl Streep, Charles Dance

A meticulous post-war drama adapted from David Hare's acclaimed play sees Streep's neurotic Susan Traherne provocatively cruel to her decent, remarkably tolerant husband (Dance) as she frets about the staleness of her life. You suspect her only motive for getting out of bed of a morning is to drift between a succession of dinner parties in her perfectly tailored fifties ensembles.

While many find Susan's chronic unhappiness a bore, Streep's subtly played emptiness is a profoundly sad contrast to the electric emotion of her wartime experiences in France, fighting with the Resistance and intensely loving a comrade in arms (Sam Neill, so who could blame her?). The terrible truth that some people have the time of their life in war – living on nervous excitement for a clear-cut cause, and subsequently viewing everything that follows as inevitably anticlimactic – has seldom been conveyed so sharply or with such bitterly ironic poignancy. An interesting cast includes Tracey Ullman, perfect as the best friend, Sir John Gielgud, Ian McKellen and Sting.

SEVEN WOMEN (1966)

Directed by John Ford
Starring Anne Bancroft, Sue Lyon, Margaret Leighton

Feuding warlords and bandit marauders make life hell for a group of women stranded and taken captive by cut-throats in a North China mission in 1935. This is an atypically women-orientated film from the great Ford in the twilight of his career. Although it's damned as dull by critical menfolk, it's particularly enjoyable for the hissing and spitting between Leighton's pious spinster and Bancroft's tough, cynical doctor with a shady past. Meanwhile, sweet young Lyon leads the children in Christian songs and terrified, pregnant Betty Field screams her head off.

Bancroft's insolent Dr Cartwright (dressed like Indiana Jones) swaggers wonderfully, blowing cigarette smoke in the missionaries' faces and sassing the rapacious brute whose downfall she brings about through her own noble sacrifice.

SHINING THROUGH (1992)

Directed by David Seltzer
Starring Melanie Griffith, Michael Douglas, Liam Neeson, Joely Richardson

This unintentionally hilarious slice of wartime hooey has to be seen to be believed. It's one of those rare movies that's so bad it's (almost) brilliant. Told in flashback as she is interviewed in old age by the BBC, Linda Voss (Griffith, delivering the most halting narration imaginable), recounts her participation in the war as a half-Jewish, German-speaking secretary working for American spymaster Ed Leland (Douglas). In a ridiculous plot twist, she finds herself replacing a top Berlin spy killed while shadowing smooth Nazi Franz-Otto Dietrich (Neeson).

Apart from the completely bonkers casting – Douglas and Griffith are far too contemporary in their appearance and acting style to be remotely plausible as wartime heroes – this is made even more laughable by terrible dialogue ('I know it was on a Friday that Ed and I said goodbye because the next day was Saturday ...'), a ludicrous plot and wooden turns from the majority of the cast. It's still worth watching, however, if only to see Douglas looking so uncomfortable, especially during the finale, when he has to play hero and save Griffith from the bad guys. Unmissable, for all the wrong reasons.

SOPHIE'S CHOICE (1982)

Directed by Alan J. Pakula
Starring Meryl Streep, Kevin Kline, Peter MacNicol

If you don't sob your way through this movie, check in to a hospital right away as there must be something wrong with you. Like *Love Story* and *The Way We Were*, this is a classic full-box-of-tissues weepy, an achingly powerful drama set in post-war New York.

Streep stars as Sophie, a Polish survivor of a Nazi concentration camp, who lives with the tempestuous Nathan (Kline, in his movie debut) in a Brooklyn boarding house. It is there that they befriend young writer Stingo (MacNicol), through whose eyes we learn about the couple, and Sophie relates to him the haunting visions of her horrific past, and eventually the choice she made that gives the film its title.

Based on William Styron's novel, the story was lovingly – if somewhat lengthily – adapted for the screen by Pakula, and it remains one of the director's most moving films. A great deal of the credit for its power, though, should go to Streep, who deservedly won an Oscar for her heart-rending performance.

SWING SHIFT (1984)

Directed by Jonathan Demme
Starring Goldie Hawn, Kurt Russell, Christine Lahti, Ed Harris

While husband Jack (Harris) is off fighting in the Second World War, housewife Kay (Hawn) takes a job at an aircraft factory against his wishes. There she meets boozin', cursin', screwin' free spirit Hazel (Lahti) and hunky trumpeter Lucky (Russell), with whom she eventually has an affair.

What could have been a by-the-numbers drama about a wartime romance is given much more depth by Demme, who delivers a moving film that vividly captures the mood of the time. His cast is also perfect:

Hawn delivers one of her best (and completely non-ditzy) performances, and she is well teamed with Russell (who became her real-life leading man during filming); Lahti, Harris, Holly Hunter (as another factory worker) and Fred Ward (as Lahti's lover) similarly all give memorable turns. A treat.

THREE CAME HOME (1950)

Directed by Jean Negulesco
Starring Claudette Colbert, Patric Knowles, Sessue Hayakawa

Adapted from Agnes Newton Keith's Second World War memoir, this prison-camp saga of British and American women fighting for their own and their children's survival after being captured by the Japanese in Borneo is among the best of its kind. Colbert, as the writer, and Hayakawa, as the cultured commandant, brilliantly develop a fascinating relationship amid the customary food squabbles and escape bids. Highlights include the women provoking their captors with an exultant conga line after spotting Allied planes overhead, a heart-wrenching sequence when the commandant tells Colbert about the A-bomb, and a nail-biting climax.

A TOWN LIKE ALICE (1956)

Directed by Jack Lee
Starring Virginia McKenna, Peter Finch

Based on Nevil Shute's novel, this gorgeous drama stars McKenna as English rose Jean, one of a group of British women in Malaya who watched their husbands and fathers rounded up and taken to camps by the Japanese in the Second World War. No camps are allocated for the women, however, so for months they are dragged across country by their captors, many dying along the way. During their journey Jean meets an Australian POW named Joe (Finch), who tells her about his home town of Alice Springs.

Finch and McKenna both won BAFTAs for their roles in this uplifting film about the courage of women, and, while the sheer Britishness of it all has dated somewhat, it's still worth a look.

THE WAR BRIDE (2001)

Directed by Lyndon Chubbuck
Starring Anna Friel, Brenda Fricker, Molly Parker

Anna Friel is Lily, a plucky young Londoner who falls for and marries a Canadian soldier during the Second World War. While he's still away at the front, Lily and their newborn daughter leave the bombs behind and travel to his Canadian home, which he's always described as a sprawling ranch. It transpires that it's actually a ramshackle farm in the middle of nowhere, and that his mother (Fricker) and sister (Parker) are in no mood to welcome the new arrivals with open arms.

A sweet slice of Canadian history, this feels a bit like a TV movie but benefits tremendously from a strong performance from Friel, and a superbly grumpy one from Fricker. Canadians may be slightly offended that they are portrayed as simple folk resistant to change who are in need of Lily's free spirit to do so, but as a fluffy *Yanks*-style war romance it's an entertaining diversion.

WATERLOO BRIDGE (1940)

Directed by Mervyn LeRoy
Starring Vivien Leigh, Robert Taylor

This sentimental favourite and multiple-hanky gem is a superior weepie describing heartbreak in the Great War. At the start of the next world war, once-dashing officer Taylor recalls meeting and falling madly in love with Leigh's delicate ballerina. When he's subsequently reported dead, despair drags her to the depths as a lady of the pavement (too bad she wasn't robust enough for work in an ammunitions factory), preparing us for memorable tragedy and a doozy of a last scene even as a happy miracle seems at hand. Leigh was never lovelier … and that's pretty darned lovely.

James 'Frankenstein' Whale had already made a version of the story in 1931 with Mae Clarke (and, in a minor role, a young Bette Davis), which is also tear-jerking and a bit raunchier, but sadly almost impossible to find.

YANKS (1979)

Directed by John Schlesinger
Starring Richard Gere, Vanessa Redgrave, Lisa Eichhorn, William Devane

Here comes a uniformed Richard Gere to sweep a girl off her feet …
again. But while *An Officer And A Gentleman* had its fair share of macho
moments (see page 87), *Yanks* is an unashamedly girlie film. And Gere
is at his cutest as the young romantic lead. He stars as Matt, a GI stationed in Yorkshire prior to the Normandy landings who falls for a
young local (Eichhorn) whose fiancé is away fighting. Their tentative
romance lies at the heart of the film, but we also see the locals' attitudes
to the peaceful American invasion (yes, the Yanks are overpaid, over-
sexed and over here), and a friendship that develops between Matt's
commander (Devane) and society lady Helen (Redgrave).

It's a chocolate-box romance, but Gere (who was thirty when the
movie was made) has never looked so scrumptious nor played such an
appealing romantic role.

Chapter 5: Let's Face the Music and Dance
Musicals and Dance Movies

With the possible exception of *The Rocky Horror Picture Show*, just about every musical and dance movie – especially all those brimming over with divine costume, dashing men and gorgeous women twirling about – is girlie. (And if you believe the clichés, quite popular with gay men too.) We could fill half this book with musicals alone, from the lavish MGM spectacles of the thirties and forties, like the Broadway Melody series and *Easter Parade* (1948) starring Judy Garland, to boisterous fifties productions such as *The Band Wagon* (1953) and *Seven Brides For Seven Brothers* (1954), while not forgetting virtually every film Gene Kelly, Busby Berkeley or Doris Day ever made.

Instead, we've picked those that are truly chick flicks. So you won't find *Coyote Ugly* (2000) here: it may have a female protagonist, but all that bumping and grinding by semi-naked women on top of a bar, and a distinctly unappealing male lead in the form of Adam Garcia, exclude it. *Saturday Night Fever* gets passed over too, as men loved that film just as much as women. (Apparently, white-suit sales rose dramatically in 1977, and they can't *all* have been bought by women who wanted their boyfriends to look like Travolta.) Ditto *Guys And Dolls* (1955), *Fame!* (1980), *On The Town* (1949) and anything featuring Elvis Presley. (As much as we love the King, there are too many women jiggling around in bikinis in most of his movies to class them as chick flicks.) And *The Wizard Of Oz* (1939) isn't here either. Yes, it's a musical, yes, the lead is a girl, but it's really a family film rather than a women's picture (unless you have a strange crush on the Tin Man, in which case you should keep it to yourself).

The most women-friendly of the musicals and dance movies tend to fall into one of three categories. First, there are those that began life as stage musicals. These tend to feature the big-skirted gowns and sweeping storylines of a period movie, and they're usually shot in sumptuous Technicolor.

Then there are the movies that are primarily romantic comedies or dramas with added songs and soft-shoe shuffles, like *Young At Heart* and *Flashdance*. Sometimes they can be musical remakes of a non-musical original, such as *High Society* (a reworking of *The Philadelphia Story*) and, of course, *West Side Story* (*Romeo And Juliet*). The weepier examples of the genre tend to be musical biopics, those films that tell the usually tragic true story of a singer's rise and fall. These get extra hankie points if there's an accidental death, drug addiction, or a rags-to-riches-back-to-rags plot.

The least successful of the genre (but we love some of them anyway) tend to be the music movies intended as star vehicles for singers who want (or more often *demand*) a film career. While Barbra Streisand, Frank Sinatra, Prince (well, in 1984's *Purple Rain* at least) and Bette Midler all successfully made the transition from vocalist to actor, many more attempts have failed and are of interest only to die-hard fans. Need we mention *Spice World* (1997), the teeth-grindingly awful Spice Girls flick that must have made co-stars Richard E. Grant and Alan Cumming cringe in embarrassment? Or *Xanadu* (1980), a fantasy love story with a musical number on roller skates that was meant to cash in on Olivia Newton John's star power after *Grease* and is notable solely for featuring Gene Kelly – presumably wishing he were somewhere else – in one of his last roles? And, worst of all, there's the entire film career of mums' favourite Cliff Richard, encompassing such crimes to humanity as *Expresso Bongo* (1960) and *Summer Holiday* (1963), which should never be liberated from the bargain video bin.

Instead of those, here are some of the loveliest, most memorable and sometimes silliest girlie musicals and dance movies from the last seven decades. Every type of music, from classical to jazz to pop to rock, makes an appearance. As does every dance move, from the *pas de deux* to whatever it is that Patrick Swayze is doing with his hips that speeded up our pulses during *Dirty Dancing*.

DIRTY DANCING (1987)

Directed by Emile Ardolino
Starring Jennifer Grey, Patrick Swayze

No one expected *Dirty Dancing* to become the phenomenally success-ful chick flick it is today. Made for a relatively modest budget of $6

million, the film went on to earn over \$150 million at the box office worldwide; it became one of the bestselling videos ever; and it spawned *two* chart-topping soundtrack albums, the first of which features the hit theme tune '(I've Had The) Time Of My Life', which won an Oscar for Best Song. Not bad for a movie filmed in a few weeks with a cast of virtual unknowns.

Grey, who at twenty-seven was playing a character a decade younger, stars as Frances 'Baby' Houseman, an idealistic teen who accompanies her vain younger sister Lisa (Jane Brooker) and their parents (Jerry Orbach and Kelly Bishop) to Kellerman's, an American holiday resort in the Catskills. It's a pretty boring way to spend the summer, until Baby stumbles across the 'dirty dancing' that some of the hotel staff practise when they are not teaching elderly ladies how to rumba. All the hip-grinding and sweatiness is enough to get any gal's pulse racing, but it accelerates to Formula One speed when Baby spots dance teacher/smouldering beefcake Johnny Castle (Swayze).

Part of the film's enduring appeal is that all women can identify with Baby, an average girl, who's not a princess, nor an ugly duckling who turns into a swan through the application of a bit of make-up, but a sweet, ordinary girl who still ends up sharing her heart (and his bed) with the movie's hunk. And, more to the point, if Baby can win Patrick Swayze, surely we all stand a chance, too.

Of course, Swayze himself is another reason why this film turns us all to mush. Fans of TV mini-series *North And South* already knew Swizel was dreamy, but here he got to show off his moves (he's the son of a choreographer and trained as a dancer). Even better, much of the time he dances topless, so we got the full benefit of his toned bod. (Is it just us, or is it getting hot in here?) Men may scoff at Patrick's lack of Oscar-worthy acting skills, but every woman melts as he turns the final dance with Grey into a declaration of love. And we all wipe away a tear as he memorably declares, 'No one puts Baby in a corner!' OK, it's a corny line, but that's why we love it.

Harking back to a simpler time, *Dirty Dancing* has it all – the dreamboat, the love that cannot last, the disapproving dad, numerous misunderstandings and, of course, the show-stopping dance finale. And it's all played out against a fabulous sixties soundtrack (The Ronettes' 'Be My Baby' and Otis Redding's 'These Arms Of Mine' among the songs), with the added bonus of Patrick warbling 'She's Like The Wind'. Ahhhhh.

42nd STREET (1933)

Directed by Lloyd Bacon
Starring Warner Baxter, Ruby Keeler, George Brent, Bebe Daniels, Dick Powell

The grandmother of all backstage musicals, this defined the genre: we have the director (handsome Baxter) whose life and career are riding on his new show, the wisecracking chorus girls (Ginger Rogers and Una Merkel), the lecherous producer, and the temperamental star (Daniels) whose romantic problems climax in an injury just before opening night. Best of all is the eternally appealing fairytale of the sweet little ingénue (Keeler) plucked from the chorus line to replace the lead after the immortal pep talk in the wings: 'You're going out there a youngster, but you've got to come back a star!' And, of course, she does.

Cute Keeler, making her film debut (although she was already a darling of Broadway's *Ziegfeld Follies* and the wife of superstar Al Jolson) and the first of seven musicals with the boyish, peppy crooner Powell, taps an absolute treat atop a taxi in one of the brilliant Art Deco Manhattan sets. But even she is eclipsed by Busby Berkeley's kaleidoscopic, groundbreaking dance numbers. Sassy and sensational.

AN AMERICAN IN PARIS (1951)

Directed by Vincente Minnelli
Starring Gene Kelly, Leslie Caron

The winner of six Academy Awards, including Best Picture, Minnelli's joyous musical was created as a vehicle for choreographer and star Kelly, and was built around a collection of the Gershwins' most enduringly popular songs (including 'I Got Rhythm' and ''S Wonderful'). Aspiring artist Kelly brings his athletic Yankee exuberance to Gay Paree, where he embraces *la vie Française* in a sanitised Montmartre, tap dances with street urchins, falls for the enchantingly gamine dancer and artists' muse Caron, and competes for her affections with suave French singer Georges Guetary while his jealous, wealthy patron 'The Older Woman' (Nina Foch) seethes.

Minnelli fills the movie with vitality, romance and a riot of colour. The sensational, innovative highlights are Kelly's original, eighteen-minute ballet to the title music, staged through sets that mimic the style of French artists (such as a can-can in a Toulouse-Lautrec poster brought electrifyingly to life), and the blissfully romantic Kelly–Caron dance to 'Our Love Is Here To Stay' on the banks of the Seine. *Absolument merveilleux.*

BEAUTY AND THE BEAST (1991)

Directed by Gary Trousdale, Kirk Wise
Voiced by Robby Benson, Paige O'Hara, Angela Lansbury

Most of Disney's 'human' animated movies (as opposed to those featuring cute animals) are pretty girlie – it's hard to imagine boys getting very excited over Cinderella unless Prince Charming carried a Uzi sub-machine gun – but this is the *crème de la crème*. It boasts gorgeous computer-generated backdrops and a truly modern heroine in Belle, rather than the simpering gals we were used to who tended to faint at the first sight of a good man (yes, that means you, Snow White and Sleeping Beauty).

We first meet the lady in question as she yearns for adventure away from her small French village, but that comes all too soon when her father is captured by a vicious beast. Belle offers to swap places with her dad, and so is imprisoned in the Beast's castle, complete with friendly talking clock, candelabra and teapot (Mrs Potts, voiced by Lansbury). Between songs such as the Busby Berkeley-esque 'Be Our Guest', they try to convince Belle that beneath his growling, shaggy exterior, the Beast might have a warm heart.

Hugely enjoyable, thanks to snappy one-liners and the great Alan Menken/Howard Ashman tunes ('Belle', 'Beauty And The Beast' and the hilarious 'Gaston' among them), this is a yummy love story based on a classic tale that may have been aimed at children but is wonderful enough to reduce most grown women to tears.

BELLS ARE RINGING (1960)

Directed by Vincente Minnelli
Starring Judy Holliday, Dean Martin

The effervescent, legendary comedienne Holliday reprised a role she had originated on Broadway for her last film before her tragically premature death from cancer. And she is adorable as the good-hearted girl who used to work in a bra factory before she found her true calling as confidante, agony aunt and fixer at the Susansaphone telephone answering service. One of the customers in need of her help is debonair Dino's playboy songwriter, and she's fallen in love with his voice, so she engineers a meeting. Naturally, what follows is ring-a-ding-ding!

Musicals had gone out of fashion when Minnelli's stylish gem was released, but the score has become a classic, including 'The Party's Over', 'Just In Time' and Judy's comic showstopper 'I'm Going Back To The Bonjour Tristesse Brassiere Company'. Sparkling fun.

CALAMITY JANE (1953)

Directed by David Butler
Starring Doris Day, Howard Keel, Allyn Ann McLerie, Philip Carey

If we could have only one Doris Day movie, this rip-snorting, thigh-slapping triumph of the tomboy heroine would have to be it. The liveliest of musicals exults in the rowdy adventures of boisterous sure-shot Calam, who chews 'baccy, bellies up to the bar with the boys, scares off Injuns and nurses an unrequited passion for a drippy cavalry officer while forever brawling with hunky Keel's Wild Bill Hickok. Of course, he is oblivious to her charms until she scrubs up and dolls up – to comically jaw-dropping effect – under the influence of beribboned saloon singer and roommate McLerie. But she quickly reverts to her irresistibly individual, raucous style and discovers real love by being her inimitable, buckskin-clad old self. And that gives us just as much satisfaction as the eternal Sammy Fain–Paul Francis Webster numbers, including 'The Deadwood Stage', 'I Just Got Back From The Windy City', the lovely Day–Keel duet 'The Black Hills Of Dakota' and Doris's Oscar-winning anthem 'Secret Love'. Whip-cracking fun.

CENTER STAGE (2000)

Directed by Nicholas Hytner
Starring Amanda Schull, Zoe Saldana, Peter Gallagher

This is one of those movies that's enjoyable because it's so terrible. Think *Fame* meets *Swan Lake* as a young woman gets into ballet school and then discovers it's tougher than she expected. All the clichés are here: the tough teacher (Gallagher) who may kick her out if she doesn't improve; the bitchy dancer who has inner problems; the young stud who may make her his next conquest; and the quiet pal you just know is going to be around to pick up the pieces.

What's a surprise is that this tosh is directed by Nicholas Hytner, best known for the justly acclaimed *The Madness Of King George*. Perhaps he was suffering from some madness of his own – especially during a dance number that involves the leads riding a motorcycle on stage in a scene reminiscent of one of the worst bits of *Grease 2*. Bet you don't see that at Sadler's Wells very often.

CHICAGO (2002)

Directed by Rob Marshall
Starring Catherine Zeta-Jones, Renée Zellweger, Richard Gere

Oscar-winning Zeta-Jones is Velma Kelly, a showgirl who has murdered her cheating husband. Zellweger is Roxie Hart, a wannabe singer who has killed her lover then tried to frame her husband for the crime. And *Chicago* is the all-singing, all-dancing tale of the two Windy City murderesses in the 1920s vying for the attentions of top lawyer Billy Flynn (Gere) based on the hit stage musical.

While this movie cannot rival the innovative flair of *Moulin Rouge!*, Marshall does a decent job of bringing the exhilarating stage show to the screen, complete with memorable song and dance numbers ('All That Jazz', 'Razzle Dazzle' and 'Mister Cellophane' among them). But then he has a very capable cast to help him. While Madonna, Goldie Hawn, Nicole Kidman and even Britney Spears were all mentioned as possible leading ladies in the years before filming began, Zeta-Jones and Zellweger are perfect as the two no-good good-time girls who use their jailtime to launch their musical careers. Gere (in a role John Travolta was once mentioned for) is equally impressive – he can actually sing (as the band leader), while Queen Latifah (as jail matron Mama Morton), John C. Reilly (as Roxie's dopey husband) and Taye Diggs are all terrific in supporting roles.

COAL MINER'S DAUGHTER (1980)

Directed by Michael Apted
Starring Sissy Spacek, Tommy Lee Jones, Beverly D'Angelo, Levon Helm

This musical-realist biopic of country superstar Loretta Lynn is about as good as they get. It's a rags-to-riches story so extraordinary it could only be true, although some of the more unpalatable facts of Lynn's tortured life are glossed over. Spacek, who does her own singing, gives an Oscar-winning performance as the girl who grew up in dire poverty, married at thirteen, churned out babies, hit the road with a guitar and a dream, and eventually conquered Nashville.

That the singer, songwriter and spangled queen of heartache didn't do it all on talent alone is appropriately reflected by a terrific supporting cast: Jones as rough-hewn, paternalistic husband Doo; D'Angelo, also doing her own singing, as Lynn's bosom buddy – the tragic Patsy Cline; and The Band's drummer/vocalist Helm, leaving a fine impression as Lynn's poor but loving father. The Lynn songbook is beautifully rendered, most memorably the autobiographical title song. Have a hanky to hand.

DANCE WITH ME (1998)

Directed by Randa Haines
Starring Vanessa Williams, Chayanne, Kris Kristofferson

Think *Strictly Ballroom* with a mambo beat and you'll know what to expect of this easy-on-the-eye (and even easier on the brain) dance drama from *Children of a Lesser God* director Haines.

Loose-hipped Chayanne plays Rafael, a Cuban who gets a job at a Houston dance studio, working for a man (Kris Kristofferson) he believes to be his father. There he meets competitive dancer Ruby (Vanessa Williams), and it's not long before they are steaming up the dance floor with their stunningly choreographed Latin numbers, complete with revealing costumes. Complications, jealousies and revelations abound, and supporting stars Joan Plowright and *Ally McBeal*'s Jane Krakowski pop up for pointless subplots. But forget the clichéd story and lacklustre performances and just enjoy those fast-footed salsa moves.

EVITA (1996)

Directed by Alan Parker
Starring Madonna, Jonathan Pryce, Antonio Banderas

There had been numerous attempts to bring Andrew Lloyd Webber and Tim Rice's stage musical to the screen, with Meryl Streep just one of the actresses in the frame for the lead role. In the end, of course, it was Madonna who got to play the role of Eva Duarte, the young woman who left her rural Argentinian home for the bright lights of Buenos Aires and eventually became the wife of dictator Juan Perón, and thus Argentina's First Lady.

With a wardrobe consisting of eighty-five different outfits, Madonna certainly looks the part, and, while her voice isn't too strong, her performance comes alive during 'Don't Cry For Me Argentina', 'Another Suitcase In Another Hall' and 'You Must Love Me' (a song written especially for the movie). Jimmy Nail (as the charmer who brings Eva to the big city) and Pryce (as Perón) lend solid support, but the discovery here is Antonio Banderas (as Che, the movie's narrator/social conscience). We always knew he was sexy, but the boy can sing, too!

FLASHDANCE (1983)

Directed by Adrian Lyne
Starring Jennifer Beals, Michael Nouri

Fame might have got us all wearing leg-warmers, but it was *Flashdance* that introduced the slash-neck sweatshirt and had millions of teenage girls practising removing their bras in a sexy manner from underneath it, as Beals does in the movie. She plays Alex, a steel welder by day (yes, really) who dances on stage at a 'flashdancing' club at night, and dreams of being accepted into ballet school.

While this daft scenario and the romantic subplot (featuring Nouri as Alex's boss and love interest) are pure chick flick, the raunchy gyrations at the flashdance club (basically a strip joint with artier dance moves and costumes) and juicy language drew in the blokes, too. As a result, the film and its rock soundtrack both became huge hits.

The dances have become iconic, with everyone from J-Lo to Geri Halliwell emulating the grand finale, when Alex finally gets her dance audition (actually performed by Marine Jahan and a *male* breakdancer) to the massive hit 'What A Feeling!'

FOOTLOOSE (1984)

Directed by Herbert Ross
Starring Kevin Bacon, Lori Singer, John Lithgow

From the moment pairs of feet stomp across the opening credits to the tune of Kenny Loggins's rockin' 'Footloose', you know this is going to be thumping, kitsch fun. And it is, from the classic teen-goes-against-the-establishment plot to the enthusiastic dance sequences and bestselling soundtrack.

Bacon became a star as Ren – and he was never cuter, with his upturned toilet-brush haircut and carefree attitude. He's the big-city teen who moves with his mom to a God-fearing town and then angers the locals with his love for the Devil's music. It seems that dancing and rock have been outlawed by the townspeople, led by Reverend Moore (Lithgow), because it leads to drinking and sex. So when snake-hipped Ren decides to organise a dance on the edge of town *and* date the Reverend's sulky daughter Ariel (Singer), it looks like he's going straight to hell, possibly propelled there by the local bully (Jim Youngs).

There's every teen-movie cliché here – even a 'chicken' race, as in *Rebel Without A Cause*, except here it's done with combine harvesters! – as Ren teaches his pal (Chris Penn) to dance, gets into fights and romances the girl but that's all part of the toe-tapping fun. *Sex And The City* fans should watch out for an unsophisticated Sarah Jessica Parker as Ariel's pal Rusty – if you can tear yourself away from looking at Bacon's wiggling ass, that is.

FUNNY FACE (1957)

Directed by Stanley Donen
Starring Fred Astaire, Audrey Hepburn

Unsurprisingly, since way back in 1927 he had starred in the original stage hit of the same name (same songs, completely different plot), the great Astaire as cynical fashion photographer Dick Avery (modelled on the great Richard Avedon), is very long in the tooth as romantic partner for enchanting Hepburn's Jo Stockton, who he transforms from a bespectacled intellectual he discovers in a Greenwich Village bookstore to top model and the toast of Paris. And she can barely sing or dance. How much do we care? They are both supremely graceful and the film has daft laughs (she's a beatnik interested only in getting to France to meet her philosophy hero), gorgeous colour, bags of 'swellegant' Fifties vogue (designed by Givenchy, flaunted by top models of the day) and a charming Gershwin score including ''S Wonderful' and 'He Loves And She Loves', immortalised in the wedding-dress dance number. Kay Thompson steals every scene in which she appears as Astaire's crazy-for-pink magazine editor. Very silly, but *très chic*.

FUNNY GIRL (1968)

Directed by William Wyler
Starring Barbra Streisand, Omar Sharif, Kay Medford

La Streisand was in her element and won an Oscar for her performance in this musical. It's based on the life of comedienne Fanny Brice, who rose from being an 'ugly duckling' immigrant from the Jewish Lower East Side of New York to become a star performing in the *Ziegfeld Follies* in the early 1900s.

Although this is a biopic – with a young and extremely dashing Sharif providing the romantic interest as playboy Nick Arnstein – that really just provides the framework for a series of luscious performances from Barbra. She belts out such standards as 'People' (as in 'Peeeeeeople … who need peeeeeople … are the luckiest peeeeeeople' etc) 'Don't Rain On My Parade' and 'My Man', and also showcases her flair for slapstick comedy: check out her hilarious turn as a roller-skating chorus girl who can't skate.

It's corny, of course, but thanks to memorable musical numbers (staged by Herbert Ross, who went on to direct the film's disappointing sequel, *Funny Lady*), Streisand's performance and her amazing voice, *Funny Girl* is still one of the most fun musicals ever made.

GIGI (1958)

Directed by Vincente Minnelli
Starring Leslie Caron, Maurice Chevalier, Louis Jourdan, Hermione Gingold

'Thank Heaven For Little Girls' probably played in Minnelli's mind as he finally took the Oscar for Best Director with this most scrumptious of his many fabulous musicals. There was a total haul of nine Academy Awards, including Best Picture, for this utterly charming, exquisitely dressed adaptation of Colette's *fin-de-siècle* story of a girl trained to be a Parisienne courtesan turning the tables on her tutors and the man-about-town who wants to make her his mistress. Caron is captivating as Gigi, maturing from coltish schoolgirl into breathtaking young beauty and innocently wielding the power to subdue debonair dish Jourdan's thunderstruck Gaston. And, although he's as old as the hills, thirties superstar Chevalier, in his triumphant comeback, winningly exercises the charm for which he was legendary.

Highlights include Gigi learning the things every upwardly mobile girl should know: about gems, clothes, posture, wines, cigars and eating quail. The perfect Lerner and Loewe score includes 'The Night They Invented Champagne' and Chevalier's trip down Memory Lane with ancient paramour Gingold, 'I Remember It Well'. To die for.

GLITTER (2001)

Directed by Vondie Curtis-Hall
Starring Mariah Carey, Max Beesley

This may look tempting when you're standing looking for a musical chick flick to rent. So we include it here as a warning. If ever there was a prime example of how *not* to make a musical, this is it. A vanity picture for pop songstress Carey, *Glitter* won her a Razzie (the awards that *dis*honour the worst achievements in film) for Worst Actress, and it was nominated for five more, including Worst Screen Couple (for Mariah's prominent cleavage).

A sort of biopic, very loosely based on Carey's own career, the film tells the story of Billie Frank (Carey), who is abandoned by her mother at an early age and raised in an orphanage. A decade later, in 1983, she and her friends (played by Da Brat and Tia Texada) are spotted by a record producer who wants them to sing back-up. Meanwhile, DJ Dice (Beesley, sporting an excruciating mid-Atlantic accent) spots Billie's true singing potential (and, presumably, the degree to which she stretches a tube top) and decides to make her his girlfriend and a star.

The sub-*Star Is Born* plot (his star fades as hers rises) is bad enough, but this poorly scripted drama is also littered with every musical cliché in the book, and is topped off with two terrible performances from Carey and Beesley (the only actor, one assumes who was desperate enough to accept such a role in the first place). Mariah fans may secretly love it (the soundtrack is packed with her songs), but for the rest of us this falls into the so-bad-it's-almost-good category.

GRACE OF MY HEART (1996)

Directed by Allison Anders
Starring Illeana Douglas, Matt Dillon, Eric Stoltz, John Turturro

Feminist filmmaker Anders's criminally neglected musical of art and heart is a fabulous romantic drama about a songwriter literally and metaphorically finding her voice. The magnificent Douglas stars as a frustrated talent (inspired by Carole King) who churns out chart-topping songs for others in the fifties and sixties. Her own dreams of making it into the spotlight are continually frustrated by industry fashions and her complicated love life. Among the men in her life are Turturro, as her musical mentor (modelled on Phil Spector); Stoltz, as her first husband and songwriting partner; and Dillon, brilliant as her second husband, the eccentric musical genius leader of a sixties surfing group (*à la* Beach Boy Brian Wilson).

Patsy Kensit and Bridget Fonda also put in useful appearances in a film packed with humour, poignancy, colourful period detail (combos, cars, frocks and coifs) and spot-on, original songs. The latter were commissioned from dream teams of vintage and contemporary composers (such as 'God Give Me Strength' by Burt Bacharach and Elvis Costello). Terrific, and tuneful.

GREASE (1978)

Directed by Randal Kleiser
Starring John Travolta, Olivia Newton John

A camp classic, *Grease* was for teenage girls in the late seventies what *Star Wars* was for boys at the same time.

Snake-hipped, slick-haired and skinny Travolta shines as Danny Zuko, hip leader of the T-Birds at fifties school Rydell High. He falls for sugary-sweet, out-of-town gal Sandy (Newton John) during the holidays and is then mortified when she turns up at Rydell, her goody-two-shoes image threatening to cramp his style.

This boy-meets-girl, boy-dumps-girl, boy-shows-his-manliness-and-wins-back-girl musical comedy drama has stood the test of time surprisingly well. At the heart of its enduring appeal are the timeless song-and-dance numbers, including 'You're The One That I Want', which features Newton John in trousers so tight that she had to be stitched into them. But fun set pieces (such as the 'Greased Lightning' dance routine that a million boys practised in their bedrooms and the Thunder Road car race), unashamed kitsch and perfect performances all play their parts, too. Among the terrific ensemble cast the standouts are Stockard Channing as bad girl Rizzo, Didi Conn as beauty-school dropout Frenchie, and Jeff Conaway as Danny's tough pal Kenickie.

Funny, sad, and packed with memorable songs – *Grease* is *still* the word.

GYPSY (1962)

Directed by Mervyn LeRoy
Starring Rosalind Russell, Natalie Wood, Karl Malden

This tells the story of legendary stripper Gypsy Rose Lee – the thirties burlesque queen who found wealth, fame, confidence and liberation in the art of undressing. It was adapted, with its knockout Stephen Sondheim–Jule Styne score ('Let Me Entertain You', 'Everything's Coming Up Roses', 'Funny'), from a bittersweet Broadway smash based on Lee's memoirs.

Wood is touching as the talentless child eager to please, serendipitously reinventing herself in a backstage striptease emergency. But Russell is a domineering wow as the ultimate pushy stage mother, dynamo Mama Rose, who prodded Gypsy and her spotlighted sister June around the vaudeville circuit throughout their childhoods. Perennially disappointed by life, frustrated, ambitious, living through her children and stubbornly blind to their own needs and dreams, Russell's fast-talking, tragi-comically conniving Rose is a marvel of making a monstrous mother into a sympathetic, engaging creature. No wonder, either, that this was remade in 1993 as a TV movie tailor-made for Bette Midler, in fine, bombastic fettle as Rose.

HIGH SOCIETY (1956)

Directed by Charles Walters
Starring Bing Crosby, Grace Kelly, Frank Sinatra, Celeste Holm

A musical version of *The Philadelphia Story* was the perfect vehicle for the first onscreen pairing of old-time crooner Crosby and his musical successor Sinatra.

Kelly – in her last screen role before she was whisked off by Prince Rainier to become Princess Grace of Monaco – stars as spoiled rich girl Tracy Lord, who is due to marry dull but dependable George (John Lund). The whole of East Coast society is gathering for their nuptials, including Tracy's first husband Dexter (Crosby), who wants to stop the wedding, and tabloid journalists Mike (Sinatra) and Liz (Holm), on hand to report on the social event of the season.

With jazz great Louis Armstrong (as himself) on hand like a Greek Chorus to bring us up to speed on the various romantic entanglements, this is a deliciously realised rom-com, filled with to-die-for fifties fashion (Kelly is luminous in adorable gowns in every scene), and Cole Porter songs that are presented in a low-key fashion rather than in the showy, elaborate way musical audiences of the forties and fifties had come to expect. Classics such as 'Who Wants To Be A Millionaire?' (sung by Sinatra and Holm as they admire the wedding gifts), 'Mind If I Make Love To You' (by a wistful, solo Sinatra) and the unforgettable

'Well Did You Evah' (Crosby and Sinatra, taking refuge from the pre-wedding party in the library) move the plot along just as well as the witty dialogue.

HONEY (2003)

Directed by Bille Woodruff
Starring Jessica Alba, Lil' Romeo, Mekhi Phifer

The great thing about this entertaining, surprisingly sweet hip-hop musical – *Fame* meets *Flashdance* with carefully nice, polite rappers – is that for its dancer heroine Honey Daniels (beautiful Alba), who overcomes caddish sexual harrassment to become a hot, respected choreographer for artistes including Missy Elliott, Ginuwine and Tweet, it's not about meeting Mr Right (although she does, almost by the way, in Phifer). Nor is it about becoming rich and famous. It's about having a dream, and working hard to achieve it. Then when she does, she uses her success to spread the love, bringing hope and a goal to the street kids in her community and mounting an ambitious dance programme in the 'hood in the time-honoured tradition of those Mickey Rooney–Judy Garland 'Let's put the show on here!' musicals of the late thirties and early forties. Totally girlie, it's positively inspiring stuff for pubescents and refreshingly cute for big girls.

THE KING AND I (1956)

Directed by Walter Lang
Starring Yul Brynner, Deborah Kerr

Even if you have never seen this film, chances are you know a few of the songs ('Getting To Know You', 'I Whistle A Happy Tune') or have seen some of the memorable moments on TV, like the gorgeous 'Shall We Dance' routine that has Kerr and Brynner gliding across the screen. Based on the Rodgers and Hammerstein stage musical, which itself was based on a straight play and the book *Anna And The King Of Siam*, it's the story of English widow Anna (Kerr), who is employed as a governess by the arrogant King of Siam (Brynner). Her job is to educate his large brood of children. East and West cultures clash until the English rose eventually melts the heart of the stern ruler.

The Oscar-winning Brynner is marvellous as the stubborn King, and Kerr shows just the right amount of strength as Anna, although in all of the songs her voice is dubbed by Marni Nixon. But the real star of this film is designer Irene Sharaff, who also won a Oscar for her costumes. Kerr's huge petticoated and hooped gowns are simply breathtaking, and were especially so for the actress herself: they weighed over thirty pounds each, and Kerr apparently lost almost a stone in weight through wearing them during filming.

KISMET (1955)

Directed by Vincente Minnelli
Starring Howard Keel, Ann Blyth, Dolores Gray

The Scheherazade music by nineteenth-century Russian composer Alexander Borodin, so beloved of ice dancers, lent its hauntingly familiar tunes to a gorgeous song score ('Stranger In Paradise', 'Baubles, Bangles And Beads', 'And This Is My Beloved') in this wonderfully fun, panto-like Arabian Nights musical. Men usually sneer, but it appeals to the part of us that likes dressing-up and fabulous fancies.

Keel is in fine voice as a charismatic but destitute poet and fast-talking teller of tall tales who stumbles into extravagant reversals of fortune. He takes ye olde Baghdad by storm and dices with scimitar-wielding dastards while sweet daughter Marsinah (Blyth), Cinderella-fashion, catches the eye of turbanned Caliph-in-need-of-a-Calipha Vic Damone. As the bodacious Lalume, Broadway star Gray's sizzling 'Not Since Nineveh' very nearly steals the show, but the harem costumes and the love songs are sooo dreamy.

LADY SINGS THE BLUES (1972)

Directed by Sidney J. Furie
Starring Diana Ross, Billy Dee Williams, Richard Pryor

The tragic life of legendary jazz singer Billie Holiday is perfect fodder for a movie biopic. The woman known as Lady Day worked as a maid in her teens and then as a prostitute at a Harlem brothel before being encouraged to sing professionally. Dogged by racism as her star began to rise, she became addicted to drugs, battled many personal demons, married three times, and died at the age of just forty-four.

This vehicle for Diana Ross (in her first and best film role) understandably infuriated jazz fans, who noted that many musicians Holiday worked with and met during her career (such as Benny Goodman and Count Basie) are not even mentioned. Similarly, there's barely any reference to her first two marriages; Williams plays Louis McKay, who was hubby number three. However, the depictions of her early life and later heroin addiction are surprisingly gritty. And while Ross's vocal cords are not in the same league as Holiday's, her attempts to catch an essence of the wonderful singer's stage presence are more successful.

LILI (1953)

Directed by Charles Walters
Starring Leslie Caron, Mel Ferrer, Jean-Pierre Aumont, Zsa-Zsa Gabor

Strictly speaking this charming romantic drama isn't a typical musical tune fest, but it won an Oscar for Bronislau Kaper's lilting score, the song 'Hi-Lili, Hi-Lo' plays an integral role in the tale (based on a story by Paul Gallico), and Caron has a magical dream sequence dance.

Lili (Caron) is a sincere, tender-hearted French orphan who attaches herself to a circus troupe. She falls in love with the flirtatious magician Marc (Aumont), but finds employment with bitter, twisted puppeteer Paul (Ferrer), who was a celebrated dancer before he was lamed during the war. Lili always forgets that the hostile, bullying Paul's four puppets aren't real people, so she talks and sings with them, to the delight of growing crowds drawn by her sweet naivety. Belatedly, she realises that the puppets are aspects of Paul's personality that he's too proud to reveal to her face to face. Simple, graceful and always touching.

FRED & GINGER

For decades, millions of moviegoing women had one fantasy in common: to dance with Fred Astaire (1899–1987). He wasn't handsome, but he did have style, grace and elegance. He also didn't have a great voice, but his expressive delivery and timing delighted the illustrious songwriters of the day, who all wrote for him. And when he danced, he made magic.

Astaire and his sister Adele were dance partners who became established musical stars on Broadway and in London's West End. After Adele retired, Fred took a screen test. Famously, his assessment read, 'Can't act. Slightly bald. Can dance a little.' In 1933, though, he was paired by RKO with a hoofer who had been playing sassy supporting roles, Ginger Rogers. They danced 'The Carioca' in *Flying Down To Rio* and suddenly everyone was talking about them. It marked the beginning of a ten-film partnership that illuminated the screen and caused Katharine Hepburn to comment: 'He gives her class and she gives him sex.'

Fred and Ginger benefited from RKO's taste for Art Deco production design. No expense was spared to set them off against dazzling black-and-white backdrops that featured shiny, reflective dance floors, chrome and deluxe settings. In the nine pictures they made for the studio, Astaire and Hermes Pan choreographed inventive, spectacular, funny and dreamy dance numbers that have never been equalled in romantic musical comedy. The very best are in:

TOP HAT (1935)

The typically piffling plot is merely an excuse for knockout numbers, including 'Top Hat, White Tie And Tails', 'Cheek To Cheek' and an army of dancers doing 'The Piccolino' through a highly stylised Venetian set.

SWING TIME (1936)

Dance instructor Ginger and penniless Fred team up and are on the verge of stardom and romance when his fiancée arrives in town. Showstoppers include 'The Way You Look Tonight', 'A Fine Romance', 'Never Gonna Dance' and Fred's classic 'Bojangles' routine.

SHALL WE DANCE (1937)

Dance team Fred and Ginger have to pretend to be married – don't ask! – to do proud the Gershwins' 'They Can't Take That Away From Me', 'They All Laughed' and 'Let's Call The Whole Thing Off'.

LITTLE VOICE (1998)

Directed by Mark Herman
Starring Jane Horrocks, Michael Caine, Brenda Blethyn, Ewan McGregor

Originally a hit West End play entitled *The Rise and Fall of Little Voice*, this movie version sees Horrocks reprising the lead role she took on the stage. She's the waifish ingénue L. V. (as in 'Little Voice') who, bereft following the death of her father, sits in her room and sings along to his Judy Garland, Marilyn Monroe and Shirley Bassey records.

Her bitchy, brassy mother Mari (Blethyn) is unaware of L. V.'s impressive vocal talent until her latest lover, sleazy talent agent Ray Say (Caine), overhears the singing and realises what a financial opportunity lurks in the upstairs bedroom. Ray and Mari hatch a plan to turn L. V. into a golden-egg-laying goose, and it seems her only friend is the local telephone engineer (McGregor), who has taken a shy shine to her.

Caine – paunchy and deliciously icky – and a mini-skirted Blethyn almost steal the show as the greedy, slimy and horrendously badly attired pair out to cash in on L. V. But this remains Horrocks's movie, and her gorgeous voice and talent for mimicry are just as impressive on screen as they were on stage.

MEET ME IN ST LOUIS (1944)

Directed by Vincente Minnelli
Starring Judy Garland, Margaret O'Brien, Mary Astor, Lucille Bremer

Ostensibly an affectionately nostalgic revel in Americana, Minnelli's episodic jaunt through a year in the life of an 'ordinary' family has them excitedly anticipating the 1904 St Louis World's Fair during a period of romantic and domestic turmoil. But it's intriguing that this is a female-dominated family whose preoccupation with the acquisition of husbands triggers most of the tearful hysteria and male anxiety.

Garland and Bremer are sisters Esther and Rose, who claim to belong to the 'nice girls don't let men kiss them until they're engaged; they don't want the bloom rubbed off!' school of thought. But their collusion on how to manoeuvre the hapless chumps they favour into commitment would terrify Machiavelli. The same goes for their bluff father (Leon Ames), who is putty in the hands of motherly Astor. Meanwhile, little Margaret O'Brien, who received a special Oscar for this film, precociously upstages everyone as naughty baby sister Tootie, as disturbing as she is cute.

Spirits are perked up no end by the great score, including the title song, 'The Trolley Song', 'The Boy Next Door' and 'Have Yourself A Merry Little Christmas'. It plays zing-zing-zing on your heartstrings.

MOULIN ROUGE! (2001)

Directed by Baz Luhrmann
Starring Nicole Kidman, Ewan McGregor

The third in Luhrmann's highly stylised 'Red Curtain' trilogy (following *Strictly Ballroom* and *Romeo And Juliet*) is a glitzy erotic fantasy played at a fevered pitch, and an outrageous mélange of opera, melodrama and music video. Two star-crossed lovers, McGregor's penniless bohemian writer Christian and Kidman's consumptive courtesan Satine, are irresistibly drawn together and steal a brief bit of bliss in turn-of-the-century Paris. Around them a three-ring circus is in full swing at riotous nightclub the Moulin Rouge, where Jim Broadbent's proprietor presides over dreams, schemes, the can-can and torrid tango dancing while Richard Roxburgh's fiendish British duke lecherously twirls his moustache and absinthe-fuelled artists, including John Leguizamo's Henri Toulouse-Lautrec, serve as a zany chorus.

You will either love or hate this, but no one can deny that the combination of energy, excess, spectacle and yearning is startling and heady. The same is true of some humorous casting (Kylie Minogue as the Green Fairy) and – contentiously – the contemporary song score, which includes a dramatic 'Roxanne', a magical 'Your Song' (to which our lovers dance among the stars) and the one original composition for the picture, 'Come What May'. *Ooh la la!*

MY FAIR LADY (1964)

Directed by George Cukor
Starring Audrey Hepburn, Rex Harrison

This musical adaptation of George Bernard Shaw's *Pygmalion* is a girlish treat. Hepburn, even when scrubbed down and dirty, looks divine; there are big, gorgeous frocks aplenty; and it's all peppered with Lerner and Loewe's fabulous songs ('On The Street Where You Live', 'I Could Have Danced All Night' and 'Wouldn't It Be Loverly' among them).

Hepburn, with singing vocals supplied by Marni Nixon, stars as Eliza Doolittle, the prettiest street urchin you ever saw, who is unsurprisingly spotted by snobby Professor Henry Higgins (Harrison) when selling flowers on a London street. He wagers a friend that he can take this common girl and in six months turn her into someone he can pass off as a member of upper-class English society. Eliza is instantly whisked off to his home to begin her studies.

Packed with terrific performances – including turns from Wilfred Hyde White, Stanley Holloway and Gladys Cooper – and played out on luscious sets, this is a sumptuous classic, filled with delicious dialogue.

NAUGHTY MARIETTA (1935)

Directed by W. S. Van Dyke II
Starring Jeanette MacDonald, Nelson Eddy

The first teaming of the screen's most successful singing partnership – an international sensation in the thirties – is the choicest bon-bon of their eight blockbusters. A spirited French princess (with a soaring soprano voice) escapes an unwelcome arranged marriage by donning the guise of a servant girl and setting sail for the adventure of the New World aboard a ship of prospective brides.

Adapted with enormous verve from a preposterous Victor Herbert operetta, the movie has abduction by pirates, sanctuary in a musical marionette theatre, romantic canoe rides up the bayou, bewigged French toffs lording it in eighteenth-century Louisiana, revolution in the air, a nicely comedic supporting cast (Frank Morgan, Elsa Lanchester), and charming Marietta's feisty relationship with egalitarian Eddy's rugged baritone Indian scout. What's not to like?

The succulent corn includes the number most identified with America's singing sweethearts, 'Ah, Sweet Mystery Of Life', which gets big laughs from modern cynics but endures as a sparkling landmark of high camp.

THE RED SHOES (1948)

Directed by Michael Powell, Emeric Pressburger
Starring Moira Shearer, Anton Walbrook, Marius Goring

Inspired by a Hans Christian Andersen fairytale, this visually stunning backstage melodrama broke new ground in marrying dance to story. And to this day it remains the ultimate ballet movie, adored by every little aspiring ballerina and everyone who relishes a gloriously coloured tragedy of art, love and betrayal.

Lovely redhead Shearer stars as Vicky Page, a young dancer who becomes the protégée of dictatorial dance company impresario Lermontov (Walbrook). As her star rises she is distracted from Lermontov's iron discipline by another of his prospects, struggling composer Julian (Goring). On stage she is a sensation in a new ballet, *The Red Shoes*, as the recipient of an enchanted pair of scarlet silk shoes that make her dance until she drops dead. Off stage she is bullied by both men, torn between her love and her dancing, until her desperation mirrors the heroine of the ballet.

The most celebrated in a string of exceptionally beautiful films by Powell and Pressburger, this was an Academy Award winner for its score and direction but is in every department a movie of grace, invention and magic.

THE ROSE (1979)

Directed by Mark Rydell
Starring Bette Midler, Alan Bates, Frederic Forrest

This movie gave the divine Miss M her first major film role and also garnered her a Best Actress Oscar nomination. She stars as Mary Rose Foster – loosely, but obviously, based on Janis Joplin – a burned-out rock singer, pumped up on booze and drugs, who wants to quit, against the wishes of her manager (Bates). He's determined that she must keep performing, and also tries his best to separate her from her latest flame (Forrest), the only person who seems to have her best interests at heart. It's a clichéd tale that works only because of Midler's ability to screech across the screen at full throttle, delivering a belter of a performance, most notably on stage as she thunders out 'Fire Down Below'.

Midler and director Rydell worked together twelve years later on *For The Boys*, a drama so nauseating that we can't bring ourselves to include it in this book, even though it was clearly conceived as a chick flick.

SAVE THE LAST DANCE (2001)

Directed by Thomas Carter
Starring Julia Stiles, Sean Patrick Thomas

A fun, if somewhat predictable, follow-your-dreams drama that rises above the average thanks to strong central performances. Stiles is Sara, the young ballerina who gives it all up when her mother dies in a car crash en route to her daughter's audition at the Julliard. Following the funeral, she moves to Chicago to live with her father and starts attending the predominantly African-American local high school. There she meets hunky Derek (Thomas), who teaches her funkier, hip-hop dancing and encourages her to fulfil her promise, while also providing a romantic shoulder to cry on.

There are two subplots – one featuring Derek's gangsta best friend, and the other his sister, a young single mother – but this works best when Stiles and Thomas share the screen, shuffling their shoes and impressing with their skilful hoofing. Actually, they both had doubles to dance for them, but who cares?

SELENA (1997)

Directed by Gregory Nava
Starring Jennifer Lopez, Jon Seda, Edward James Olmos

Before she became a singing star in her own right, Lopez played tragic Mexican-American singer Selena Quintanilla in this well-made biopic of her short life. A huge star in Latin America, Selena was poised to be the first female singer to cross over from the Spanish- to English-speaking US music charts when she was killed in 1995 – shot dead by the woman who ran her fan club – at the age of twenty-three.

Nava's film focuses on Selena's warm family upbringing and life, rather than on the events leading up to her well-documented death.

This introduces us to her father (Olmos), who also managed her career, and her husband, guitarist Chris Perez (Seda). Selena's father was executive producer of the movie, so don't expect any revelations, but Lopez is terrific as the singer, and looks uncannily like her, especially during the stage performances. However, she lip-syncs, as Selena's parents wanted only their daughter's vocals to be used in the film.

SHOW BOAT (1936)

Directed by James Whale
Starring Irene Dunne, Allan Jones, Paul Robeson, Helen Morgan

Jerome Kern and Oscar Hammerstein II's tuneful melodrama of life, love, loss and racism among show folk on a Mississippi riverboat was a landmark in American musical theatre for innovatively integrating songs with the narrative. And what songs: 'Ol' Man River', 'Can't Help Lovin' Dat Man Of Mine', 'Bill' …

Always a goldmine, the oft-revived show – in which women suffer an inordinate, operatic amount of sorrow in a popular musical – spawned three film versions. Whale did it best, with some new songs added by Kern and Hammerstein, and a superior singing cast including torch singer Morgan as tragic Julie and the legendary Robeson. Dunne's sweet Magnolia is swept off her feet by feckless gambler Gaylord Ravenal, experiences the vicissitudes of life with a wastrel and, though ill-equipped for it, has to cope with single motherhood. Meanwhile, the exposure of leading lady Julie's mixed-race heritage condemns her to abuse, abandonment and a despairing decline into dissolution. The passage of years takes the story from bustles and parasols into the Jazz Age.

The 1951 version starring Kathryn Grayson, Howard Keel and a luminous Ava Gardner (her singing dubbed by Annette Warren but at her best as a touching Julie) is plusher, in lush Technicolor. It upped the dance content, ditched some good numbers and compressed the time-frame, making the whole more sugary but still tearfully entertaining.

THE SLIPPER AND THE ROSE (1976)

Directed by Bryan Forbes
Starring Gemma Craven, Richard Chamberlain

A twist on the *Cinderella* tale, told from Prince Charming's perspective, this musical is so English it should be watched while eating scones with clotted cream and raspberry jam. Edward (Chamberlain), the prince of tiny Euphrania, is to be married off on the instructions of his father, the King (Michael Hordern). A bride-finding ball is arranged, and there Edward meets and falls in love with Cinderella (Craven). But instead of everything ending happily ever after, the King intervenes and insists Edward must marry a more suitable woman to cement a political alliance.

Much beloved by anyone who saw it as a girl, this is dreamily filmed and brims over with floaty costumes, soft focus, romantic shots of Craven and Chamberlain, picturesque Austrian scenery and lavish song-and-dance numbers, such as 'What Has Love Got To Do With Getting Married' and 'Protocolicorically Correct'. Best of all, it's a *Who's Who* of stalwart British stars, with Annette Crosbie (Fairy Godmother), Kenneth More (Lord Chamberlain) and Edith Evans (the sarcastic Dowager Queen) among the supporting cast.

THE SOUND OF MUSIC (1965)

Directed by Robert Wise
Starring Julie Andrews, Christopher Plummer

The Sound of Music has it all – nuns, children cute-as-kittens, evil Nazis and the breathtaking Austrian scenery that is shown to terrific effect from the opening scene of Julie Andrews singing 'The hills are alive ...' on a mountaintop, which was captured by a helicopter that apparently flew so close to her that it made her topple over.)

Andrews stars, of course, as Maria, who leaves her convent (much to the relief of the other nuns, driven insane by her incessant chirpiness and constant warbling) to become governess to the children of strict Captain Von Trapp (Plummer). As well as raising the kids, she encourages them to sing and perform together, and thereby gradually thaws the heart of her employer (*aaahhh*). However, just when you think they are all going to live happily ever after, up pop those pesky Nazis to force the family into a daring escape across the Alps.

It's incredibly sunny and bright and cheery, and certainly not to everyone's taste, but the infectious Rodgers and Hammerstein songs ('My Favourite Things', 'Sixteen Going On Seventeen', 'Edelweiss', 'So Long, Farewell' among them) are timeless, and even the most reluctant viewer will soon be singing merrily along with the adorable Von Trapps.

A STAR IS BORN (1954)

Directed by George Cukor
Starring Judy Garland, James Mason

There have been four versions of this classic drama about one couple's relationship with fame – George Cukor's 1932 *What Price Hollywood?*, 1937's William Wellman-directed tale, starring Janet Gaynor and Fredric March, and the most recent (1976) adaptation, starring Barbra Streisand and Kris Kristofferson (although Babs reportedly wanted Elvis Presley for the role) that spun off a huge-selling soundtrack album featuring the movie's Oscar-winning love song 'Evergreen'. But the best version of this story has to be 1954's three-hankie weepie, also directed by Cukor.

It's the classic tale of a couple's relationship with each other and with fame. Garland is the unfortunately monikered Esther Blodgett, an aspiring singer who meets and falls in love with Norman Maine (Mason), a movie star whose career is on a downward spiral. As her star meteorically rises – and her name is wisely changed to Vicki Lester – his falls, thanks to a mixture of bitterness and drink. Their crumbling marriage is captured achingly alongside an often witty satire about stardom and the ruinous influence of Hollywood.

Garland gives one of the most unforgettable performances of her career: it's impossible to keep dry-eyed as she sings 'The Man That Got Away'. But it is Mason – in a role that was reportedly turned down by major stars Montgomery Clift and Humphrey Bogart because they didn't want to tempt fate by playing an ageing, failing actor – who is scene-stealingly superb, believably and movingly unravelling before our eyes.

STRICTLY BALLROOM (1992)

Directed by Baz Luhrmann
Starring Paul Mercurio, Tara Morice

Luhrmann's eye-catching film debut sprang from an improvised play he had workshopped in Sydney, and from his boyhood involvement in Australia's competitive ballroom scene (which explains a lot!). Studly Mercurio's dance-crazy Scott was born to win championships. But his rebellious proclivity for spontaneity and fancy footwork that steps outside the rigid rules sends shock waves through the 'Come Dancing' hierarchy, which is depicted as grotesquely obsessive. Only Morice's adoring, mousy Fran, his pushy mother's least promising student, believes in him. Gee, do you think when she takes off her glasses and does her hair he'll make her his partner?

While there are no wild surprises in the deliberately familiar plot, the disarmingly bizarre, exuberantly garish execution is madly captivating. As is the joyful, triumphant passion of the two lead characters, drawn together with a slyly deployed, Latin-drenched soundtrack, including 'Love Is In The Air', Doris Day's recording of 'Perhaps, Perhaps, Perhaps', and 'Time After Time', to which our couple do a delicious *pas de deux* on the roof.

Lovers of this film should also check out the funny, heart-warming Japanese movie *Shall We Dance?* (1996), in which a depressed business-man experiences the liberation of nonconformity and the passion of the rumba when he secretly takes dance lessons.

SWEET DREAMS (1985)

Directed by Karel Reisz
Starring Jessica Lange, Ed Harris

This biopic charts country music legend Patsy Cline's (Lange) rise to stardom, from her early days singing in bars in the fifties, through her marriage to abusive husband Charlie (Harris), and up to her tragic death in a 1963 plane crash.

While Sissy Spacek sang all the songs when she played Loretta Lynn in *Coal Miner's Daughter* (see page 228), here Lange lip-syncs along to 'Crazy' and other classics rather than attempt Cline's distinctive sound;

but that doesn't detract from her performance, especially as the film focuses on Cline's tempestuous marriage rather than on her stage appearances. It's a bit of a soap opera as Charlie and Patsy fight, kiss and make up, then fight again, but utterly convincing turns from Lange and Harris make this a moving film, guaranteed to reduce even the toughest country music fan to a sobbing wreck.

THOROUGHLY MODERN MILLIE (1967)

Directed by George Roy Hill
Starring Julie Andrews, James Fox, Mary Tyler Moore, Carol Channing

Since there was a problem over the rights to the hit musical *The Boyfriend* (eventually filmed by Ken Russell and starring Twiggy), this alternative twenties spoof musical was created as a vehicle for Andrews. And we're lucky it was, as her pert personality and sweet soprano both shine in this cute, adorably costumed nonsense.

Ambitious, efficient Millie cuts off her curls, shortens her skirts and straps her bosom to become a red-hot *moderne*, but she still intends her secretarial job to land her tall, dark, handsome and rich boss Trevor (John Gavin). The scheme backfires, though, because he likes sweet, old-fashioned girls with curls, as personified by Moore's dizzy Miss Dorothy. Meanwhile, the girls' hotel manager (marvellous old Bea Lillie) is kidnapping young ladies for the white slave trade; Fox's tall, blond, handsome but poor (or is he?) Jimmy is ardently wooing resistant Millie; and Channing's madcap millionairess is throwing champagne jazz parties that promote romantic confusion and misunderstandings.

This is silly fun, with superb trappings (we love the cloche hats and Millie's witty accessories), an Oscar-winning score, a nostalgic collection of songs including 'Baby Face' and 'Poor Butterfly', and the amusement of the sixties' two favourite nice girls, Andrews and Moore, tap-dancing together.

THE CHICK FLICK MIX TAPE

These songs appeared in dramas and comedies rather than musicals, but they are forever linked to the movies for which they were recorded.

1 Everything I Do (I Do It For You) – sung by Bryan Adams (from *Robin Hood: Prince Of Thieves*)

2 Up Where We Belong – sung by Joe Cocker and Jennifer Warnes (from *An Officer And A Gentlemen*)

3 The Way We Were – sung by Barbra Streisand (from *The Way We Were*)

4 Take My Breath Away – sung by Berlin (from *Top Gun*)

5 Moon River – music by Henry Mancini (from *Breakfast At Tiffany's*)

6 Take A Look At Me Now – sung by Phil Collins (from *Against All Odds*)

7 Love Is A Many-Splendored Thing – music by Sammy Fain and Paul Francis Webster (from *Love Is A Many-Splendored Thing*)

8 Que Sera Sera – sung by Doris Day (from *The Man Who Knew Too Much*)

9 Alfie – sung by Cilla Black in UK, Cher on the US version (from *Alfie*)

10 Live To Tell – sung by Madonna (from *At Close Range*)

11 I Will Always Love You – sung by Whitney Houston (from *The Bodyguard*)

12 Show Me Heaven – sung by Maria McKee (from *Days Of Thunder*)

13 When You Say Nothing At All – sung by Ronan Keating (from *Notting Hill*)

14 Stay (I Miss You) – sung by Lisa Loeb (from *Reality Bites*)

15 Theme From *Mahogany* – sung by Diana Ross (from *Mahogany*)

16 Endless Love – sung by Diana Ross and Lionel Richie (from *Endless Love*)

THE TURNING POINT (1977)

Directed by Herbert Ross
Starring Shirley MacLaine, Anne Bancroft, Mikhail Baryshnikov, Leslie Browne

This starry ballet-shoe saga took its cue from a burning issue of seventies women's lib – the obstacles to 'having it all' – which it then surrounded with the time-honoured clichés of backstage soapers. Ex-dancer DeeDee (MacLaine) surrenders her talented daughter (Browne) to a New York company, where her old rival Emma (Bancroft) makes the girl her protégée. DeeDee gave up her career for marriage and motherhood (understandably, given that her husband is Tom Skerritt), and she has regrets. Emma gave up love for her dazzling career, and, wouldn't you just know it, she has regrets too. While the baby ballerina is becoming a woman with seductive rake in tights Yuri (the famously straight ballet stud Baryshnikov), the two old troupers' jealousies and resentments explode in a doozy of a hair-pulling catfight.

The terpsichorean element is a neat 'Best of Ballet' crash course. Notable dancers of the day such as Antoinette Sibley do their stuff in scenes from *Giselle*, *Le Corsaire*, Prokofiev's *Romeo And Juliet* and Tchaikovsky's *Swan Lake*, as choreographed by greats including Alvin Ailey, George Balanchine and Frederick Ashton. Subsequent tutu tales like *Center Stage* and *The Company* can't beat it.

THE UMBRELLAS OF CHERBOURG a.k.a. LES PARAPLUIES DE CHERBOURG (1964)

Directed by Jacques Demy
Starring Catherine Deneuve, Nino Castelnuovo

The New Wave romantic Demy and composer Michel Legrand's wistful musical drama is delicate, bittersweet and inimitably French. It's also, in spite of every word being sung, a realistic view of young love's rapture and despair.

Deneuve (aged only twenty, an exquisite bud that would blossom into France's great star of her generation) is Geneviève, who works in her widowed mother's umbrella shop and is pressed to encourage wealthy suitor Roland (Marc Michel). But Geneviève and young auto mechanic Guy (Castelnuovo) are already madly in love. Discouraged by his sweetheart's mother's objections, Guy leaves for the army and doesn't write, not knowing Geneviève is pregnant. What follows has the painfully poignant ring of truth, and is beautifully acted, even though the actors were lip-syncing throughout.

With its vivid colour palette restored to its original glory in 1994 by Demy's widow Agnes Varda, this is now as striking as ever. Disappointingly, Demy's song-and-dance follow-up, *The Young Girls Of Rochefort* (1967), which teamed Deneuve with her sister Françoise Dorleac and Gene Kelly, rapidly exhausted his idea for a new kind of musical since it's stronger on style than soul.

WEST SIDE STORY (1961)

Directed by Jerome Robbins, Robert Wise
Starring Natalie Wood, Richard Beymer, Russ Tamblyn, Rita Moreno, George Chakiris

Shakespeare's *Romeo And Juliet* was given the Leonard Bernstein musical treatment for this superb, Oscar-winning tale of doomed young love. Instead of the warring Montague and Capulet families, two gangs – the Puerto Rican Sharks and the Polish Jets – fight it out on the streets of New York. Meanwhile, Tony (formerly of the Jets) and Maria (sister of Sharks leader Bernardo) secretly fall in love.

Co-director Wise had originally wanted Elvis Presley for the role of Tony, which would have been something to see, but Beymer has great chemistry with Wood (as Maria), although their romance is overshadowed by the powerhouse supporting one between Anita (Moreno) and Bernardo (Chakiris). However, it's in the musical numbers and the dancing (staged by Robbins) that *West Side Story* truly comes alive, from the finger-snapping, angry, stunning ballet opener that introduces us to the rival gangs, to the romantic ballad 'Tonight' and the rousing 'America'. A classic.

WHAT'S LOVE GOT TO DO WITH IT (1993)

Directed by Brian Gibson
Starring Angela Bassett, Laurence Fishburne

Rock singer Tina Turner's rise to stardom, based on her autobiography

I, Tina, makes for a fascinating movie. Much of the credit for that, though, must go to Angela Bassett, who perfectly captures the fiery, ballsy star, both on stage and off.

As with all the best musical biopics, the road to fame for Turner was a very rocky one. Born Anna Mae Bullock, the young singer was spotted by performer Ike Turner, who promptly married her, moulded her and changed her name. The duo became stars, played Vegas and had hit records, but behind the scenes Ike allegedly became jealous of Tina's fame, grew addicted to coke, and began beating her.

Unlike most musicals, this contains some harrowing stuff, as Tina endures the beatings and struggles to escape from Ike's hold on her. Fishburne expertly avoids the trap of playing a one-dimensional 'bad husband', giving Ike real depth and showing both the good and the bad sides of his personality. Bassett is simply terrific, and completely convincing as Tina, even when lip-syncing to the singer's vocals.

WITH A SONG IN MY HEART (1952)

Directed by Walter Lang
Starring Susan Hayward, Rory Calhoun, David Wayne

This absorbing tear jerker, with its Oscar-winning score, launched a wave of terrific, schmaltzy musical biopics about female singing stars whose fame and wealth didn't buy them happiness. Setting the standard, here it's thirties and forties radio favourite Jane Froman's rise to stardom, her troubled love life and her painful comeback trail after being crippled in a plane crash. Luckily, she has everybody's favourite wisecracking nurse–confidante, Thelma Ritter, coaxing her out of her wheelchair. Hayward lip-syncs to Froman's recordings, including such classics as 'Blue Moon', the Gershwins' 'Embraceable You', Rodgers and Hart's 'I'm Through With Love' and a showstopping 'American Medley' for wartime troops.

If you like this, a trio of 1955 flicks should be right up your street. *I'll Cry Tomorrow* has Hayward back and magnificent (in Oscar-winning costumes, and this time doing her own singing) as Lillian Roth, a Jazz Age Broadway and Hollywood star ravaged by eight divorces and alcoholism. *Interrupted Melody* (an Oscar-winner for its script) stars a heart-rending Eleanor Parker as Australian diva Marjorie Lawrence, stricken by polio but overcoming suicidal depression by singing for

Allied troops in the Second World War. *Love Me Or Leave Me* (which won an Oscar for its story) features a sensational Doris Day as tough twenties chanteuse Ruth Etting ('Ten Cents A Dance', 'Shaking The Blues Away') and James Cagney as her abusive, gangster husband.

YENTL (1983)

Directed by Barbra Streisand
Starring Barbra Streisand, Mandy Patinkin, Amy Irving

Streisand's directorial debut was an unashamedly old-fashioned film, and of course featured the golden-voiced diva in the title role – even though Babs was 41 at the time and the part requires her to play a much younger woman.

It's Eastern Europe at the beginning of the twentieth century, and young Yentl wants to be a religious scholar and study the Talmud, something forbidden to women. When her father dies, she cuts off her hair, wears boys' clothes, stuffs a sock down her trousers and convinces a Jewish school that she is a man so she can satisfy her hunger for knowledge. Things get complicated, however, when she falls for one of the rabbi's students, the hunky Avigdor (Patinkin), especially as he has eyes only for Hadass (Irving) and thinks of Yentl as his (male) buddy.

Based on the story by Isaac Bashevis Singer, this is La Streisand's show from opening to end credits. As well as directing and starring, she produced, and she is the only person who gets to sing, despite the presence of renowned musical star Patinkin. Basically, if you love Barbra, you'll love this (especially when she sings 'Papa, Can You Hear Me?'). If you're not keen on her, this will be over two hours of utter torture.

YOUNG AT HEART (1954)

Directed by Gordon Douglas
Starring Frank Sinatra, Doris Day, Gig Young

An absolute must for female Sinatra fans, this tear-jerking musical features a handsome, vulnerable, yummy performance from the blue-eyed crooner. It's a reworking of 1938's non-musical *Four Daugh-*

ters, with sunny Doris Day (as Laurie), Dorothy Malone (Fran) and Elisabeth Fraser (Amy) as the musically inclined New England Tuttle sisters vying for the attentions of handsome Alex Burke (Young). He and Laurie seem best suited, but she takes pity on Alex's bitter and pessimistic pal Barney Sloan (Sinatra) who, even when she marries him, is convinced he is haunted by bad luck.

The cast – especially Day, Ethel Barrymore (as Laurie's wise Aunt Jessie) and Robert Keith (as the Tuttles' father) – make the dialogue sizzle. But Sinatra steals this romantic movie, especially when he sings the Gershwins' 'Someone To Watch Over Me' and nurses a self-pitying drink while delivering a moving version of 'One More For The Road'. An unashamedly glossy Hollywood production, but a glorious one for all that.

Chapter 6: Bad Girls
Sirens, Sinners and Wicked Ladies in Dramas, Action and Adventure

Bad girls and wicked women have been film favourites ever since Theda Bara became the first sex goddess of the screen. At twenty-five she burst to stardom as a sinful siren luring a man to his ruin in *A Fool There Was* (1915) with the immortal command, 'Kiss me, my fool,' which became a popular catchphrase. She had been born Theodosia Goodman, a tailor's daughter from Cincinnati. Her stage name was an anagram of 'Arab Death', and she claimed to be the love child of an Egyptian princess. Nicknamed 'The Vamp' (short for vampire), Bara exploited her artificially exotic, decadent persona to the hilt, thrilling audiences with her sultry impersonations of notorious seductresses *Cleopatra*, *Salome* and *Carmen*.

In the twenties audiences derived vicarious enjoyment from the restless abandon of such liberated flappers as Louise Brooks, a bobbed icon as the sexually insatiable Lulu in *Pandora's Box* (1928), and Clara Bow, the It Girl with cupid-bow lips. In the thirties Mae West made screen history by humorously exploiting the stereotype of the man-eater, and she was loved for it. At the same time, the great actresses and women's women of the day (and for all time) – including Bette Davis and Barbara Stanwyck – successfully disdained typecasting, slipping between long-suffering heroines and meaty villainesses with impressive élan. Davis's electrifying performance as the nasty, vulgar, avaricious woman in *Of Human Bondage* (1934) made her a star, and over the years women most admired her when she played women at their worst: arrogant, selfish, wilful, but also thrillingly spirited and self-sufficient. She was top of every casting director's list if they wanted a wild, conniving tease (*Jezebel*, 1938), an adulterous murderess (*The Letter*, 1940), a ruthlessly corrupt matriarch (*The Little Foxes*, 1941), a husband-stealing sociopath (*In This Our Life*, 1942), good and evil twins

(*A Stolen Life*, 1946, and *Dead Ringer*, 1964) or a homicidal hag (*Whatever Happened To Baby Jane?*, 1962). Stanwyck, meanwhile, was a remarkably versatile leading lady, but her performances as controlling, hard-as-nails women really set the standard for duplicitous dames, as embodied in *Double Indemnity* (1945).

Movies would be much poorer without the gold-diggers, spider women and murderesses. Alongside the artistic dramas and heightened melodramas, the 'women behind bars' mini-genre sprang up with its own set of clichés established in *Condemned Women* (1938). It reached its zenith with Susan Hayward's Oscar-winning performance in *I Want To Live!* (1958), gave Britain's platinum-blonde bombshell Diana Dors her finest hour in *Yield To The Night* (1956) and was still being mined when Miranda Richardson was haunting as the last woman hanged in Britain, Ruth Ellis, in *Dance With A Stranger* (1985) and Sharon Stone deglamorised herself on Death Row in *Last Dance* (1996). Wild good-time girls, thrill-seeking young 'skirts' and troubled teens have also made regular appearances, from Clara Bow's and Joan Crawford's frenzied tabletop displays in the twenties, through *Gun Crazy* (1949), *High School Hellcats* (1958), to modern satire and drama like *Heathers* (1989) and *Thirteen* (2003).

However, most of the cinema's 'bad' female archetypes are the products of male fantasies and/or male anxieties. Pre-eminent among them is the *femme fatale* of the *noir* thriller (such as Lana Turner in 1946's *The Postman Always Rings Twice*). There is also the whore with a heart of gold, a familiar presence in Westerns (such as Marlene Dietrich's saloon singer Frenchy in 1939's *Destry Rides Again*). The 'bunny boiler', an epithet originating with Glenn Close's psychotic stalker in *Fatal Attraction*, has inspired numerous imitators appealing to male-ego issues, like Alicia Silverstone's fixated nymphet in *The Crush* (1993).

Then there are the maids/secretaries/nannies from hell. Our favourite ridiculous male fixation is the unfulfilled wife/career woman with a sordid secret life turning tricks (Catherine Deneuve in Luis Buñuel's great 1967 shocker *Belle De Jour*; Kathleen Turner in Ken Russell's 1984 kinkfest *Crimes Of Passion*). And in an era of increasingly violent screen women there are the cold-hearted likes of Sharon Stone's icepick-wielding flasher in 1992's *Basic Instinct* (decidedly not a women's picture despite the plethora of lesbian psychokillers tripping over each other in Joe Eszterhas's misogynous script). We must, though, admit to a particular admiration for Bond girl Xenia Onatop (Famke Janssen in 1995's *GoldenEye*), who cracks men like walnuts between her thighs.

Women protagonists such as the female serial killer (notably Charlize Theron's Oscar-winning go as Aileen Wuornos in 2003's *Monster*) or the obsessive admirer (like another Oscar winner, Kathy Bates's unforgettably 'cock-a-doody' nurse and captor Annie in 1990's *Misery*) do not in themselves a women-oriented picture make. No, we prefer female rebels, sinners, shooters, sickos and transgressors whom we can recognise, identify with closely, sympathise with, or at least understand. Many of our 'bad girls' are not even bad at all but are simply perceived as such. Others are driven by cruel circumstance, poor parenting or, like Thelma and Louise, abuse and fear into breaking taboos or laws. Some are wronged and misunderstood, others troubled and unhappy. But some – Suzanne in *To Die For*, Julie in *Jezebel*, Eve in *All About Eve* – *really* are nasty girls! We like them too, because we know exactly where they're coming from.

THELMA AND LOUISE (1991)

Directed by Ridley Scott
Starring Susan Sarandon, Geena Davis, Harvey Keitel, Michael Madsen, Brad Pitt

One of the all-time-great and most influential chick flicks, this female buddy movie with its Oscar-winning script by Callie Khouri is full of spot-on observations and glories in magnificent performances from its two stars. A feminist manifesto for the 1990s, Scott's self-discovery-on-the-road movie is in the tradition of the male buddy movie as epitomised by *Butch Cassidy And The Sundance Kid* and its many imitators. But, astonishingly, this was the first major Hollywood film modelled on *Butch And Sundance* in which the pals were gals.

And what gals! When Sarandon's worn-down waitress Louise and Davis's bullied mousewife Thelma take off for a girls' weekend away from their cares (synonymous with their men), an encounter with a drunken, foul-mouthed, would-be rapist in the car park of a honky-tonk sparks rage and memories of past abuses. A sudden act of violence sends the sickened, terrified women on the run from a murder charge across the American Southwest. But it is also a flight from the joylessness and inequality of their lives, and turns into a

wild, cross-country spree with sexy stud muffin Pitt thumbing a lift and an army of lawmen in pursuit. That their route to unattainable freedom and fulfilment goes way over the top in a 'Bonnie and Bonnie' scenario of escalating disaster and crime is less troublesome than it ought to be, thanks to Davis and Sarandon raising hell and cracking wise in a womanly, utterly captivating style.

For a refreshing change, it's the male actors trailing in their wake who play the ciphers: Thelma's odious husband (Christopher McDonald), Louise's commitment-phobic fella with a Peter Pan complex (Madsen), the Nazi redneck cop, the lewd trucker, the seductive thief (Pitt and his six-pack in their breakthrough role), and even Keitel's understanding detective who is a tad paternalistic in his concern for the 'ladies'. However, few men dared to raise any objections as angry women in cinema audiences cheered and screamed their encouragement as Thelma and Louise violently and hilariously took charge.

One cannot but share these women's exultation as they answer 'the call of the wild', speeding along the highway in a convertible T-bird, chugging Wild Turkey bourbon, swapping delightful one-liners and harmonising with the radio on their exhilarating bid for freedom. Scott's most important contribution is simply unleashing the women's personalities while using stunning, desolate landscapes as a mythic backdrop for their daring odyssey.

The ultimate, significant difference that makes this buddy movie feminine is that when Butch and Sundance go out they are holding guns; when Thelma and Louise are indelibly freeze-framed, pedal to the metal in *their* crazy act of defiance, they are holding hands.

ALL ABOUT EVE (1950)

Directed by Joseph L. Mankiewicz
Starring Bette Davis, Anne Baxter, George Sanders

'Fasten your seatbelts. It's going to be a bumpy night.' At the top of her game (and that's dizzyingly high), Davis delivers one of a succession of unforgettable lines in the most fabulously sophisticated, sizzling picture of theatre bitchiness ever made. Elegantly costumed and with a cocktail ever at hand, Davis's tempestuous Broadway grande dame Margo Channing is pitted against Baxter's cunning Eve, a wide-eyed waif with a swell sob story who is brought in from the rain claiming to be Margo's biggest fan. Around the two women a marvellous ensemble (including arch Sanders as a vicious drama critic, Thelma Ritter as a wisecracking maid, and young Marilyn Monroe as a wannabe actress) swap scintillating barbs and witty repartee. But the fascinating core is the ruthlessly ambitious, back-stabbing Eve's sly progress from pathetically grateful charity case to protégée until she is revealed to be a viper at Margo's breast, taking over the star's lover, friends and career.

Six Academy Awards, including Best Picture, were virtually demanded, and it still holds the record for the most Oscar nominations to actresses from a single film (Davis, Baxter, Ritter and Celeste Holm). Over half a century on, it remains brilliant.

ALL THIS, AND HEAVEN TOO (1940)

Directed by Anatole Litvak
Starring Bette Davis, Charles Boyer

The epitome of the classic 1940s women's picture – grand, weepy, adapted from a period novel, gorgeously costumed amid extravagant sets – this proves that sometimes wickedness is in the eye of the beholder.

A mysterious new French teacher (who else but queen of the genre Davis?) arrives at a girls' school in New York but is unmasked by her hostile, sneering pupils as prototypical celebrity slut 'The Notorious Mademoiselle D', the other woman in an infamous, criminal sex scandal. Shaken Mademoiselle then tells the girls her side of the story. As Henriette Deluzy Desportes, she became governess to the children of the noble Duc de Praslin (suave Boyer). Alas, the nasty, neurotic Duchesse (Barbara O'Neil, best known as Scarlett's mother in *Gone With The Wind*, here playing the world's scariest mother) suspects an affair and inevitably prompts one by her obsessive jealousy and hysteria. Murder, suicide and a sea of tears ensue. Of course, Mademoiselle isn't really bad at all; she has just been painted that way. Nowadays, one suspects schoolgirls would be thrilled to have a scarlet woman as their teacher.

ANGEL FACE (1952)

Directed by Otto Preminger
Starring Robert Mitchum, Jean Simmons

Poor, hunky Bob Mitchum was particularly vulnerable to scheming *femmes fatales* and doomed relationships in a genre littered with the corpses of male patsies undone by duplicitous dames. This cool and artful drama, a particularly cynical late entry in the field, has him as simple working stiff Frank, conflicted between the Good Woman (fiancée Mary, played by Mona Freeman) and the Bad Girl (Diane, as portrayed by Simmons). Diane is ravishingly beautiful, rich and very bad indeed, seductively selecting Frank to receive her favours and, if he'd be so kind, dispose of her stepmother. Naturally, the scheme goes awry, putting the couple under suspicion in a *Postman Always Rings Twice* kind of way with inevitably fateful consequences.

What makes this somewhat different for women is the appropriately angelic Simmons, cast against type to deceptive and chilling effect. Her death angel is without conscience but with undeniable class and, atypically, it is love – twisted and obsessional though it is – that supersedes her greed, sense and self-interest.

THE BAD SEED (1956)

Directed by Mervyn LeRoy
Starring Nancy Kelly, Patty McCormack

Maxwell Anderson's controversial but dramatically compelling play fed the hot 'nature versus nurture' debate of the day. It opted for heredity over environment in a chilling story of a child supposedly born to be a sociopath.

When she can no longer ignore a string of fatal accidents curiously connected to her young daughter, Kelly's archetypal Fifties suburban mommy is horrified to learn she herself is the adopted offspring of a murderess, and that McCormack's engaging, affectionate, ultra-girlie little Rhoda is a monster in pigtails. The latter confesses her misdeeds in a uniquely riveting mother–daughter confrontation. Ten-year-old McCormack is hair-raising, switching from sweetie to psycho: 'You won't tell anyone, will you, Mommy?' can be heard as either a plea or a subtle threat. What's great is pondering what Mommy's going to do about it!

Alas, filmmaker LeRoy was forced to concoct a 'happy' ending and a quaintly cute end credits sequence. But the potent, if ridiculous, concept and the performances (Kelly and McCormack were reprising the roles they'd originated on Broadway) are mesmerising.

THE BELLES OF ST TRINIAN'S (1954)

Directed by Frank Launder
Starring Alastair Sim, Joyce Grenfell, George Cole

Based on Ronald Searle's cartoons, this was the first film to introduce cinema audiences to the naughty girls of St Trinian's School. It was followed by three sequels within a decade and a later attempt to resurrect the franchise in 1980. Like the *Carry On* movies, this is a terrific slice of British camp. Alastair Sim plays the school head*mistress*, then steps out of the tweeds to take the role of her bookie brother, who smuggles his daughter into the sixth form so she can pick up racing tips from a schoolmate whose father is a racehorse owner. Gambling, drinking and general misbehaviour are the order of the day – as the headmistress notes, 'In other schools girls are sent out quite unprepared into a merciless world, but when our girls leave here, it is the merciless world which has to be prepared.'

As a depiction of how we all wish our school years had been, this is witty, silly and peppered with hilarious performances from a cast of truly great comic character actors, including Grenfell, Cole (as spiv Flash Harry), Irene Handl, Beryl Reid, Joan Sims and Sid James.

THE BLUE ANGEL (1930)

Directed by Josef von Sternberg
Starring Emil Jannings, Marlene Dietrich

Directed and sensationally lit by her German Expressionist Svengali von Sternberg, nascent sex goddess Dietrich gives a masterclass (make that a mistressclass) in how to destroy a man. Schoolteacher and model of rectitude Jannings finds his way into the Blue Angel, a tawdry club, where he falls under the spell of Dietrich's chanteuse, Lola Lola. The true spider woman, she ensnares him, enslaves him, chews him up and spits him out when she gets bored. And, dahhhhling, she's so easily bored by men. By that time, he's been humiliated and ruined in exchange for a pair of her knickers.

Shot simultaneously in German and English versions, its international success propelled Dietrich to Hollywood, where she and Sternberg made six more films together. These were all variations on the *Blue Angel* theme and turned Marlene into the mythic mystery woman. Even those who have never seen this film will be familiar with its great iconic image of her perched on a chair in an insolent, come-hither-if-you-dare pose, wearing a top hat and stockings with that little strapless number in between. And who hasn't heard Dietrich drawling her signature tune, 'Falling In Love Again'? It screams decadence, Weimar Berlin and sexual power – and has been mimicked numerous times, from Liza Minnelli's wannabe vamp Sally Bowles in *Cabaret* to Madeline Kahn's side-splittingly spot-on send-up in *Blazing Saddles*.

THE BRIDE WORE BLACK (1968)

Directed by François Truffaut
Starring Jeanne Moreau, Michel Bouquet, Jean-Claude Brialy

When the bride's (Moreau) husband is gunned down on the steps of the church on their wedding day, her first impulse is to kill herself. But after her mother-in-law stops her, she switches into cool, composed, calculated mode and sets about hunting down, charming and dispatching the five men responsible in a macabre variety of perfect murders. You go, girl!

Truffaut's dark, spirited homage to Hitchcock (even to the extent of including a dramatic score by Hitch's favourite composer, Bernard Herrmann) is adapted from a story by twisted mystery writer Cornell Woolrich. Flashbacks to the fateful church scene and the revelations of how and why the bride found her targets – male archetypes that include the idle fat cat, the corrupt politician and the practised Lothario – maintain the suspense and excitement while the indomitable Moreau grimly pursues her revenge quest.

Other adaptations of Woolrich novels include *No Man Of Her Own*, *Phantom Lady* and *Rear Window*. He anticipated *Kill Bill* by several decades.

FIVE COCKTAILS FOR WOMEN WHO MEAN BUSINESS

THELMARGARITA

$1^1/_2$ oz. tequila
$^1/_2$ oz. Triple Sec
$^1/_2$ oz. lemon or lime juice
Rub the rim of a chilled cocktail glass with lemon or lime peel, and dip the rim lightly in salt. Shake the tequila, Triple Sec and juice with ice. Strain into the glass. Add a twist of lime.

MARGO'S MARTINI

2 oz. gin
$^1/_2$–1 oz. dry vermouth
Shake the gin and vermouth with ice and strain into a martini glass. Add a green olive.
For a vodka martini, substitute vodka for the gin and add a black olive or a twist of lemon.

ANGEL'S KISS

Creme de cacao
Double cream
Fill a liqueur glass three-quarters full with creme de cacao. Float double cream on top of the liqueur to the rim. Add a maraschino cherry.

THE BRIDE WORE BLACK RUSSIAN

$1^1/_2$ oz. vodka
$^3/_4$ oz. Kahlua
Shake the vodka and Kahlua with ice and strain into a chilled whisky glass filled with ice cubes.
For a White Russian, add $3^1/_2$ oz. of cream or milk.

JEZEBEL'S JULEP

Fresh mint sprigs
1 tsp. sugar
$1^1/_2$ oz. bourbon
Soda water
Stir a few mint leaves mixed with the sugar and a splash of soda water in a chilled highball glass. Fill the glass with crushed ice and pour in the bourbon. Decorate with mint, a slice of orange and a slice of lemon.

THE CRAFT (1996)

Directed by Andrew Fleming
Starring Robin Tunney, Fairuza Balk, Neve Campbell, Rachel True

Girls can be wicked when they get together. And that was never more amply demonstrated than here, where four teenagers cast spells and plot torments for the schoolmates who have dubbed them 'the bitches of Eastwick'.

Nancy (Balk), Bonnie (Campbell) and Rochelle (True) are social outcasts at school who recognise that new girl Sarah (Tunney) may be the fourth witch they need to complete their teen coven. Soon the quartet are changing their hair colour by magic, levitating and inflicting pain on their fellow-students, but before you can say, 'Abracadabra!' everything gets out of hand and the girls start to turn on each other.

While one can't help wondering why the girls don't do more with their magic (like conjure up a million dollars or turn Brad Pitt into their sex slave, for example), this is a fun look at teenage girls discovering their dark side and is especially watchable for a deliciously nefarious performance from Balk.

LES DIABOLIQUES (1954)

Directed by Henri-Georges Clouzot
Starring Simone Signoret, Vera Clouzot, Paul Meurisse

This is an oft-imitated and truly terrifying thriller from France's morbid master of suspense Clouzot. Sensuous Signoret is the earthy, sexy mistress and Mme Clouzot is the frail, browbeaten wife who put aside their personal antipathy – as only Frenchwomen would – to collaborate in the murder of sadistic Meurisse. However, that proves an arduous, sloppy, protracted business in a film that is a classic model of the 'slow burner'. Set largely in a dreary, cash-strapped, provincial private school where he's the headmaster and the women teach, the atmosphere is one of quietly simmering emotions that boil over spectacularly when wronged women go bad. Things really start to zing after the physically and emotionally exhausted women dump the bully's body in the murky school pool. Spooky goings-on and the disappearance of the body shred their nerves and alliance, setting the stage perfectly for some massive shocks.

Hollywood's 1996 remake, *Diabolique*, with Sharon Stone, Isabelle Adjani and Chazz Palminteri, is well cast but totally lame, except that Stone's feline wardrobe – all animal prints – was very desirable.

DROP DEAD GORGEOUS (1999)

Directed by Michael Patrick Jann
Starring Kirsten Dunst, Denise Richards, Ellen Barkin, Kirstie Alley

A mockumentary about what really goes on at those glorious feasts of American excess: beauty pageants. Amber (Dunst) and Becky (Richards) are two of the teen contestants prepared to go to any lengths to win the crown. This may explain why entrants are dropping like flies and one has the extreme misfortune to blow up. Meanwhile, their scary mothers (Barkin and Alley, respectively) are just as bitchy in their quest to push their daughters to triumph.

The comedy is broad (witness Becky's 'talent' portion of the competition in which she sings 'Can't Take My Eyes Off You' to a certain religious icon) and the script witty, but the best reason to watch this is provided by Barkin. Playing the last word in trailer-trash, complete with beer can melted into her hand following an unfortunate fire, she hilariously steals the movie from everyone around her.

LA FEMME NIKITA (1990)

Directed by Luc Besson
Starring Anne Parillaud, Jean-Hughes Anglade, Tchéky Karyo, Jean Reno

Wild street punk Nikita (Parillaud) kills a cop in a drug-crazed heist and is condemned to death. But her execution is faked when she is snatched by a covert government organisation, who tame and train her into an assassin. Karyo is her rather charismatic spymaster, Bob, Jeanne Moreau puts in a welcome appearance as her soignée instructor in etiquette and grooming, and Reno enjoys a great turn as the dispassionate 'cleaner' who sorts out a massacre. All this is raw, vivid and highly influential in the development of tough-cookie action fare. The heart is engaged when Nikita is finally released into the world and falls for Anglade's decent, ordinary guy, putting her transformed self in a tricky, conflicted spot when deadly duty calls.

The Assassin (1993) – the inevitable, glossier, pointless Hollywood remake – starred Bridget Fonda as the bad girl. Director Besson and Reno did better themselves in their American debut, the slick sort-of-sequel *Léon* (1994). A snazzy spin-off TV series starring Peta Wilson, created by Joel Surnow, ran for four seasons and laid the groundwork in style and paranoid tone for his later TV phenomenon *24*.

LA FILLE DE L'AIR (1992)

Directed by Maroun Bagdadi
Starring Beatrice Dalle, Thierry Fortineau, Hippolyte Girardot

Dalle seized her best role since *Betty Blue* (which is hot but so not a women's film) in this tense, dramatic thriller of love outside the law. It's based on the true story of Nadine Vaujour, who made headlines in 1986 when she piloted a helicopter to pluck her husband from a French prison yard.

The movie provides a fascinating portrait of a basically ordinary woman who cherishes normality – raising her children, working, redecorating her home – but is accustomed to and accepting of the violent crimes of her lover and his sidekick, her brother. Stoically giving birth in prison, cheerfully marrying in the presence of an armed police guard, Dalle's Brigitte (renamed to allow the film to take fictional liberties) rebelliously, even bravely, strikes her blow for *l'amour* despite the sorry consequences.

Bagdadi could be accused of sympathising with criminals and making a heroine out of a woman who has no regard for society's rules. But, as one character says of Brigitte, she is 'one hell of a chick'.

THE GOOD GIRL (2002)

Directed by Miguel Arteta
Starring Jennifer Aniston, Jake Gyllenhaal

Friends star Aniston finally dropped her cute TV persona to star as thirtysomething Justine. She's a discount-store assistant stuck in a predictable marriage to house painter Phil (John C. Reilly), who spends most of his time stoned with his pal Bubba (Tim Blake Nelson). It's hardly surprising, then, that Justine looks for affection elsewhere, and finds it in the arms of Holden (Gyllenhaal), a teenage co-worker who has named himself after the lead character of his favourite book, that ode to teenage angst *The Catcher In The Rye*. Soon, despite Justine's initial guilt, they are having sex in the local motel, the shop's store-room and her car, until one day Bubba spots them. From that point on, just about everything in Justine's life (including her obsessed toyboy himself) starts to unravel.

Aniston's spot-on dowdy performance as the nice wife gone bad is terrific, and she's surrounded by a talented cast, most notably Gyllen-haal and Reilly (best known for his roles in *Boogie Nights* and *Magnolia*). Both funny and oddly touching, it's a little film well worth seeking out.

HEARTBREAKERS (2001)

Directed by David Mirkin
Starring Sigourney Weaver, Jennifer Love Hewitt, Jason Lee

Mother and daughter Max (Weaver) and Page (Hewitt) are con artists, working together to fleece unsuspecting wealthy men. Max marries them, then Page seduces them, so the poor unfortunate bloke agrees to a hefty divorce settlement before watching the pair disappear into the sunset with the loot. Unfortunately, their last scam ended with them being discovered by the businessman (Ray Liotta) they tricked, so Max and Page head for the rich pickings of Palm Beach. There they spot wheezing tobacco millionaire William Tensy (Gene Hackman), and Max starts working her magic on him. Meanwhile, Page explores the sights and falls for local lad Jack (Lee), causing problems for their grand scheme.

Thanks to terrific performances from the leads, this is a huge improvement on the similar comedy *Dirty Rotten Scoundrels*, in which Michael Caine and Steve Martin also conned the rich and stupid. Weaver and Hackman, especially, are hilarious – watch out for a superb visual gag about his smoking – while Nora Dunn is eye-wateringly funny as Tensy's sinister housemaid, and Liotta displays a previously untapped knack for comedy.

CLASSIC FEMMES FATALES

Some of the best bad girls are *femme fatales*, but they tend to crop up in movies that could never be defined as chick flicks. Nevertheless, here are a few of the pouting, plotting, wanton women we love.

BARBARA STANWYCK in DOUBLE INDEMNITY (1944)

Drooling Fred MacMurray doesn't stand a chance against scheming siren Barbara as they plot to kill her husband and make off with the insurance money in this classic *film noir* from Billy Wilder.

LANA TURNER in THE POSTMAN ALWAYS RINGS TWICE (1946)

Platinum-blonde Turner oozes seduction as Cora, the wife of a roadside restaurant owner, who begins an affair with drifter Frank (John Garfield) and then plots her husband's murder with his help. The 1981 remake, starring Jack Nicholson and Jessica Lange, also sizzled (in part thanks to the memorable kitchen-table sex scene).

SUE LYON in LOLITA (1962)

Pouting fourteen-year-old Dolores (Lyon) leaves middle-aged writer Humbert Humbert (James Mason) a gibbering wreck in Stanley Kubrick's adaptation of Nabakov's controversial novel. Avoid the nasty 1997 remake unless you want to see Jeremy Irons being pervy.

KATHLEEN TURNER in BODY HEAT (1981)

William Hurt looks like a deer caught in the headlights as Kathleen Turner's sexpot Matty seduces him with her trademark smoky voice ('You aren't too bright. I like that in a man') and a lack of clothing due to a Florida heatwave. Then she asks him to murder her rich husband (Richard Crenna).

GLENN CLOSE in FATAL ATTRACTION (1987)

Described as a metaphor for AIDS, Close's Alex went from Dan's (Michael Douglas) enthusiastic one-night stand to bunny-boiling psycho woman ('I won't be *ignored*, Dan!') after she was rejected and he returned to his wife (Anne Archer). A cautionary tale for any man considering an affair, we think …

LINDA FIORENTINO in THE LAST SEDUCTION (1994)

Fiorentino's sultry Bridget tricks hapless Mike (Peter Berg) after she seduces him up against a chainlink fence and also double-crosses seedy Clay (Bill Pullman) in John Dahl's delicious thriller.

HEATHERS (1989)

Directed by Michael Lehmann
Starring Winona Ryder, Christian Slater

Ryder has never been better than in this super-sharp black comedy set in the back-stabbing world of high school. She's Veronica, the only member of bitchy clique the Heathers who isn't actually called Heather. Tired of being the butt of the Heathers' jokes, she sets about turning the girls against each other, but things take a deadly turn after she befriends brooding loner J. D. (Slater, out-Nicholsoning Jack Nicholson) and they decide to dispatch each of the Heathers, passing their murders off as suicides.

Packed with memorable and often macabre scenes, this also brims over with terrific dialogue, from the innovative put-downs ('Did you have a brain tumour for breakfast?') and Veronica's pensive diary entries ('Are we going to prom or to hell?') to the finest cinematic expression of surprise ('Well, fuck me gently with a chainsaw'). Extremely nasty, deliciously wicked, it's one of the best teen movies ever made.

HEAVENLY CREATURES (1994)

Directed by Peter Jackson
Starring Melanie Lynskey, Kate Winslet, Sarah Peirse, Diana Kent

Oddball New Zealander Peter Jackson (and his wife and collaborator Fran Walsh) took a notorious fifties murder case that shocked his country – the true story of two teenaged girls, Pauline Parker and Juliet Hulme, who beat Pauline's mother to death – and spun it into an imaginative picture of adolescence, the intense friendship between a misfit and a rebel, and the strange fantasy world these girls created. By turns gruesome and captivating, informed by the girls' own diaries, it's beautifully played by young discoveries Lynskey (as Pauline, the dumpy Mario Lanza fan) and Winslet (as Juliet, the feverish fantasist who in real life went on to become a successful crime novelist under the pen name Anne Perry).

Excitingly directed with a brilliant eye, it has sympathetic insight into a relationship that develops from fun to desperately unhealthy, and Jackson showed startling ingenuity in creating the macabre but stunning 'other world' of the girls' imaginings. This is also the picture that convinced people Jackson was the man – and how! – to adapt J. R. R. Tolkien's *The Lord Of The Rings*.

HIGH HEELS AND LOW LIFES (2001)

Directed by Mel Smith
Starring Minnie Driver, Mary McCormack

In this comedy adventure, Thelma and Louise wannabes Shannon (Driver) and Frances (McCormack) are the two pals who overhear a conversation about a robbery and decide that the money would be rather handy. So they set about blackmailing one of the dumber-than-dumb thieves, little knowing that he works for a particularly nasty bad guy, who himself works for the even more sinister Kerrigan (a hilarious turn from Michael Gambon).

This film starts extremely slowly, but once the gals realise the situation is more complicated than they first imagined, the pace picks up considerably. Director Smith picks up the pace in the second half with a mad and funny shoot-out, but unfortunately that merely highlights the lack of such amusement in the first hour. Then, just as it looks like we could be heading towards a fulfilling climax, the movie abruptly ends. You are left wondering if the filmmakers ran out of money or just out of ideas.

I WANT TO LIVE! (1958)

Directed by Robert Wise
Starring Susan Hayward, Simon Oakland

Barbara Graham (Hayward) might be bad, but that doesn't mean she's guilty of the crime she's imprisoned for in this terrific drama based on true events. There's no denying that she's a lady of loose morals, as they used to say, having left a string of lovers and a heroin-addicted husband in her wake. And she's committed her fair share of petty crimes. But when she is arrested along with two men for the murder of a little old lady, Barbara protests her innocence. However, her past counts against her and she finds herself sentenced to death for the crime.

The second half of this film, as a psychiatrist and journalist try to save Barbara and we watch the countdown to her execution in the gas chamber (repeatedly postponed due to a series of last-minute appeals), is harrowing stuff. Hayward deservedly won an Oscar for her superb portrayal of a woman unravelling before our eyes. There was also a tacky but enjoyable TV movie based on the same story, which starred ex-*Bionic Woman* Lindsay Wagner as Graham.

KILL BILL VOLUME 1 (2003) and VOLUME 2 (2004)

Directed by Quentin Tarantino
Starring Uma Thurman, Daryl Hannah, David Carradine

It's unlikely *Reservoir Dogs* director Tarantino will ever make a *real* girls' movie, but his two-part ode to martial arts, Japanese B-movies and 'muse' Uma Thurman deserves inclusion because it features a cool, kick-ass chick in the lead. And it's full of bad girls who delight in killing, torturing, maiming and bitching. Cool.

Thurman stars as pregnant former hit-woman The Bride, who – along with her bridal party – is gunned down on her wedding day by Bill (David Carradine) and his team of hit men and women. Left for dead, she spends years in a coma before waking up and swearing revenge on those who shot her, her fiancé and everyone else. So she heads off to track down Lucy Liu's O-Ren Ishii, Vivica A. Fox's Vernita Green and the other three assassins responsible.

Although the two volumes were filmed as one long movie, which was cut in half later, they are very different. The first is notable for impressively staged and realised set pieces, including the famous fight in the House of Blue Leaves. The second has more development of character and dialogue and less blood-splattering moments. In both, hats are tipped to spaghetti Westerns, forties melodramas, *film noir* and kung-fu B-movies, and they are surprising, funny, even shamelessly sentimental. Oh, and very bloody too.

THE LADY EVE (1941)

Directed by Preston Sturges
Starring Barbara Stanwyck, Henry Fonda

Regarded by many as the great Sturges's masterpiece, this witty, sophisticated, madly sexy movie was the last classic screwball romantic
comedy of Hollywood's Golden Age. Fonda's naive dolt Charles Pike,
heir to the Pike's Pale Ale fortune, is seduced at sea by Stanwyck's
worldly adventuress Jean Harrington, a cynical con artist and gold-
digger who plies her trade on ocean liners with her rascal of a father. To
her surprise, though, she falls for her latest patsy, but when he learns
she's a bad girl he scrams.

Bent on revenge, she reappears in his life, masquerading as aristocratic English heiress Lady Eve. He falls for her all over again, even
though his testy valet is adamant she's 'the same dame'. On their
wedding night she humiliates him with a fictitious, fabulously sordid
account of her sexual history and her expectation of a whopping
divorce settlement. Dumbfounded, dismayed, destroyed, he trips off
the train and falls on his face into the mud. Nitwit to the end, he sets
out to find Jean and falls repentantly into her arms, ecstatic to have
escaped the awful Eve. Rarely does a screen heroine get to have her cake
and eat it as deliciously as this vixen, scoring neat vengeance on the
man who spurned her and still getting to keep him (because, after all,
he *is* lovely) right where she wants him.

LAST DANCE (1996)

Directed by Bruce Beresford
Starring Sharon Stone, Rob Morrow

Found guilty of murder, Cindy Liggett (Stone) has spent twelve years
on death row waiting for a date for her execution. When it is finally set,
she is visited by an idealistic lawyer (Morrow), newly employed by the
Clemency Board, who has to try to get her sentence commuted to life
imprisonment. Although Cindy, ready to die, doesn't want his help
and he seems to suffer from a huge helping of naivety and a bad
haircut, it's not long before the pair are gazing wistfully at each other
through the cell bars.

In the right hands, this could have been a sensitive love story, but instead cliché follows cliché. Stone gives it all she's got, but Morrow is lost in a role too complex for his talents. Like the couple's romance, this inferior female version of *Dead Man Walking* is both unbelievable and ultimately doomed to failure.

MAE WEST (1892–1980): 'GOODNESS HAD NOTHING TO DO WITH IT'

A boxer's daughter from Brooklyn, Mae was on stage from the age of five, graduating to burlesque billed as the Baby Vamp. At fourteen she had worked her way up to vaudeville and Broadway revues dancing the shimmy. In 1926 she wrote, produced, directed and starred in a play called *Sex*. It got her ten days in jail for obscenity … and a Hollywood deal. Curvy and brassy, she swaggered one step ahead of the censors, titillating fans as the dominatrix of the double entendre and overpowering the likes of Cary Grant in saucy smashes such as *She Done Him Wrong* (1933), in which she invited him to 'come up and see me' and introduced the song 'Frankie And Johnny'.

Women loved her just as much as men did, for her wit, vivacity and insolence, and by 1935 she was the highest-paid woman in America. Lifejackets became popularly known as 'Mae Wests' after her famous bosom. At fifty, she retired from the screen, but in her sixties she was still a nightclub star surrounded by hunky himbos. Late in life she caused a stir as a lascivious little old lady in *Myra Breckinridge* (1970) and *Sextette* (1978).

Her cynical one-liners celebrating and sending up sex are lore: 'A hard man is good to find'; 'To err is human, but it feels divine'; 'I used to be Snow White, but I drifted'; 'Is that a pistol in your pocket or are you just glad to see me?'; and, in response to 'Goodness, what beautiful diamonds!', 'Goodness had nothing to do with it, dearie.'

THE LETTER (1940)

Directed by William Wyler
Starring Bette Davis, Herbert Marshall, Gale Sondergaard

There have been at least four screen adaptations of W. Somerset Maugham's play of murder in Malaya among the whisky-and-soda-swilling colonial plantation set, but none of the others can hold a candle to Wyler's brooding mood piece of vintage *noir* melodrama.

Davis is Leslie Crosbie, who guns down her lover in the opening scene, then puts on a splendid act playing the faithful wife bravely defending her honour from the rapacious cad. Her decent rubber-planter husband Robert (Marshall) wants to believe her, and the expat crowd rally around with supportive outrage, but one woman knows the truth. It emerges that the dead man had an exotic native wife (a creepily enigmatic, glittering-eyed Sondergaard), who is not only miffed at being widowed, but has an extremely compromising letter written by Leslie to the man she loved, lost and coolly plugged full of lead.

The implications are deadly, the atmosphere is electric, and the resolution is as unforgettable as the opening. Davis portrays duplicity and desperation brilliantly, eliciting surprising sympathy for her jealous, vengeful *femme fatale*.

THE MAN IN GREY (1943)

Directed by Leslie Arliss
Starring Margaret Lockwood, James Mason, Phyllis Calvert, Stewart Granger

One of Gainsborough Pictures' tastiest costume melodramas, this made Mason a star as the elegant, eponymous cad, and boosted Granger's status as a matinée idol. But it's largely Lockwood's show as the poor, calculating Hester.

After Calvert's sweetly innocent heiress Clarissa has married Mason's cold-hearted rake and produced the desired heir, she is naively eager to open her heart, sumptuous home and purse-strings to supposed bosom buddy Hester. The callous hubby and the shameless hussy gauge each other's measure in one lusty glance, but Hester is a woman who wants to have it all, so she hatches a scheme to promote Clarissa's seduction by Granger's roguish Rokeby. When that fails, nothing less than murdering her only friend will do.

This spiffy Regency bodice-ripper set up a Lockwood–Mason rematch in *The Wicked Lady* (see page 288) and established her as the loveliest villainess women love to hate.

MEAN GIRLS (2004)

Directed by Mark S. Waters
Starring Lindsay Lohan, Lacey Chabert, Rachel McAdams

Heathers meets *Beverly Hills 90210* in this smartly scripted and thoroughly entertaining tale of spiteful schoolgirls.

Cady (Lohan) is a pretty, bright teen who has been home-schooled all her life. So the cliques and machinations of an American high school come as something of a shock when she starts attending North Shore High and discovers the most popular girls are the 'Plastics', a trio of snide, fashion-obsessed bitches led by Regina (McAdams). After befriending two social outcasts, Janis (Lizzy Caplan) and Damian (Daniel Franzese), Cady infiltrates the Plastics to report back on their antics to her new pals, but she finds herself torn between the nice kids and the lure of the lip-glossed, boy-mad cool girls.

Saturday Night Live comedienne Tina Fey's script is hilarious – as is her cameo as a bumbling teacher. Every teen horror is here, from an amorous sports coach to the pitfalls of religious home-schooling ('On the third day, God created the rifle to shoot the dinosaurs … and the homosexuals'). And the cast is fabulous too, from Lohan's innocent teen to McAdam, Chabert and Amanda Seyfried as the trio of witches who rule the school.

MILDRED PIERCE (1945)

Directed by Michael Curtiz
Starring Joan Crawford, Jack Carson, Zachary Scott, Eve Arden, Ann Blyth

Gunshots crack and a dying man gasps, 'Mildred!' In this flashback classic, Mildred (Crawford) confesses to murder and recounts how she toiled from waitress to prosperous restauranteur to meet bad daughter Veda's (Blyth) demands for the finer things in life. Mildred's neurotic indulgence and the ungrateful Veda's precocious appetites inevitably boil over into sexual betrayal and rage when they both fall for Scott's conniving cad.

A definitive forties women's picture and a seething domestic soap opera, *Mildred Pierce*, adapted from a breathtakingly perverse novel by James M. Cain, is also a superbly nasty *noir* that wreaks havoc with the era's ideals of mom and apple pie. Throbbing melodrama doesn't come with more conviction. Even to those usually turned off by the tough Crawford (who won an Oscar), Mildred is tragically compelling in her pathological indulgence. Meanwhile, Blyth (aged only seventeen) is sneeringly sensational as the *fille fatale*. Curtiz's masterly deployment of actors and technical elements (such as cinematographer Ernest Haller's expressive shifts from sunny suburbia to shadowy nightmare) is intoxicating.

MOLL FLANDERS (1996)

Directed by Pen Densham
Starring Robin Wright, Morgan Freeman, Stockard Channing

This version of Defoe's classic tale – 'inspired by' the book rather than adapted from it – has some choice moments as our eighteenth-century heroine goes from man to man in an attempt to survive.

Born in prison to a mother hanged soon after, Moll (Wright) grows up in a convent before an unfortunate incident with a knitting needle causes her to be cast out onto the streets, where she makes her living as a prostitute. Unlike the novel, the story is told in flashback by a mysterious character (Freeman's Hibble) as he takes Moll's daughter on a journey. This is just one of many diversions from the book: in the original, Moll marries five times in a search for love and security; here she marries only once. It's played far more slowly and seriously than you'd expect, but Wright gives a moving performance, and there's good support from Channing as a bordello owner and John Lynch as the love interest.

Kim Novak had previously starred in 1965's bawdy *The Amorous Adventures Of Moll Flanders*, but our favourite adaptation of the novel is the fun British TV mini-series featuring *ER*'s Alex Kingston.

NO MAN OF HER OWN (1950)

Directed by Mitchell Leisen
Starring Barbara Stanwyck, John Lund, Lyle Bettger

Stanwyck is the no-class fallen woman Helen Ferguson, whose shady boyfriend (Bettger) has abandoned her, pregnant and broke, in New York. When a young couple she's just met aboard a train are killed in a crash, she assumes the identity of the dead woman and descends on the late husband's family, who've never met 'Patricia'. Only too happy to embrace the alleged widow and her baby, the affluent suckers give her a taste for life in their clean, comfy, upper-middle-class Midwest. Then the brother of Patricia's dead hubby falls in love with her (despite nerve-racking incidents like her forgetfully signing a cheque with her real name). What seems to be shaping up into a classic weepy melodrama shifts gear into a compelling *noir* thriller when Bettger's bad ass ex turns up, bringing bags of blackmail, irony and suspense to clandestine meetings in dark places. Stanwyck makes bad sympathetically desperate in a hanky-twisting intrigue (adapted from a Cornell Woolrich story).

There have been two remakes: an OK French version, *I Married A Shadow* (1982), starring Nathalie Baye; and a *comedy* starring Shirley MacLaine and Ricki Lake, *Mrs Winterbourne* (1996).

ORIGINAL SIN (2001)

Directed by Michael Cristofer
Starring Antonio Banderas, Angelina Jolie

Angelina Jolie's cleavage heaves even more than usual in this hilariously hokey bodice-ripper set in turn-of-the-century Cuba.

It's steamy stuff, but the plot is just plain daft. Cuban plantation owner Luis (Banderas) buys himself an American mail-order bride, but, instead of the expected subservient missus, he ends up with scheming thief Julia (Jolie). There are numerous twists and turns as the pair try to outwit each other once she has fleeced him of his fortune, but it's really just an excuse for a few sweaty sex scenes featuring the two appealing leads. (These were so raunchy that Mrs Banderas, Melanie Griffith, insisted on being present while they were being filmed.)

Unintentionally one of the funniest films of the last few years, this requires much suspension of disbelief (for a start, why would a man who looks like Banderas need a mail-order bride?), but it's so terrible that it's great fun.

THE QUICK AND THE DEAD (1995)

Directed by Sam Raimi
Starring Sharon Stone, Gene Hackman, Russell Crowe, Leonardo DiCaprio

It's the Old West, and Ellen (Stone) is the stranger who rides into Redemption looking for revenge. Herod (Hackman) is the corrupt leader of the town, and there's soon to be a gunfighting tournament with him, young buck Kid (DiCaprio) and reluctant gunslinger Cort (Crowe) the main contenders for the title. Until our Shaz turns up, that is.

While this is really a boys' Western, directed by Sam '*The Evil Dead*' Raimi and filled with moody glares, shoot-outs and numerous Old West clichés, it possesses lots of girlie appeal too, thanks to Stone's tough-chick performance. But the main reason for recommending it is the two-hunks-in-one-movie casting of the then barely known Crowe and a very young, pre-*Titanic* DiCaprio, who was picked especially for the role by producer Stone.

THE RAINS CAME (1939)

Directed by Clarence Brown
Starring Myrna Loy, Tyrone Power

This epic tear jerker sees Loy shagging her way through the fictional Indian province of Ranchipur before finding true love and (sob!) dying soon after.

Loy stars as bored Englishwoman Lady Edwina, who is trapped in a loveless marriage but keeps herself amused with a series of affairs. Her heart finally melts, however, when she meets dedicated doctor Rama Safti (Power). When a dam breaks and floods the city, bringing malaria in its wake, she pitches in to help. Truly, she's a changed woman, but not even that can save her in an era when hussies always got their come-uppance in the end.

Both Loy and Power tug at the heartstrings, but even they are out-shone by the special-effects team, who manage to create earthquake, flood and pestilence on a Hollywood lot. Terrific stuff.

SET IT OFF (1996)

Directed by F. Gary Gray
Starring Queen Latifah, Jada Pinkett, Vivica A. Fox, Kimberly Elise

It's girls-with-guns time again as four friends take to robbing banks to wreak revenge on the system that has let them down. Each has her own reason for donning a mask and toting a gun: Stony (Pinkett) wants to escape the projects where her brother was mistakenly shot dead by the police; Tisean (Elise) needs the cash so she can get custody of her child from Social Services; Frankie (Fox) is lashing out after being fired from her job at a bank; and Cleo (Latifah) wants the money so she can have a good time.

Director Gray successfully handles the robberies action and the mounting tension within the group as one hold-up leads to another and the women disagree about when they should cut and run. Unfor-tunately, too many heist-movie and sisters-doin'-it-for-themselves clichés are thrown into the mix, but thanks to solid performances – especially from Latifah and Pinkett – and a sizzling soundtrack (includ-ing songs by Seal, En Vogue and Chaka Khan), this is still a very watchable and often tense drama.

SUNSET BOULEVARD (1950)

Directed by Billy Wilder
Starring Gloria Swanson, William Holden, Erich von Stroheim

'I am big! It's the pictures that got small.' So hisses the screen's great killer queen, Norma Desmond, denying that she 'used to be' big in pic-tures. When on-his-uppers screenwriter Joe (Wilder's favourite actor William Holden, jumping in where Montgomery Clift decided not to tread) evades car repossessors by swerving into the drive of a decaying mansion on Hollywood's storied Sunset Boulevard, he discovers he has strayed into the strange, cobwebbed world of faded silent screen star

Norma Desmond (authentic silent screen star Swanson in a triumphant comeback and *tour de force*). Norma isn't so much bad as she is monstrous, and completely mad.

The audacious, wickedly witty Wilder opens the film on Joe's dead body floating in Norma's swimming pool and the murdered man narrates the story as a flashback, so we know immediately things are not going to go well. Megalomaniac Norma is bent on a comeback and keeps handsome Joe as gigolo–script doctor for her hopeless Salome project. He feels pity, shame and eventually rage as her delusions and violent jealousy take her away into a glamorous la-la land where she is forever desirable and adored in the spotlight. This is just magnificent in its mix of cruelty, tawdry tragedy, hilarity and Hollywood exposé. After the first screening of *Sunset Boulevard*. the great Barbara Stanwyck knelt and kissed Swanson's hem, early and classy recognition that Gloria's Norma Desmond is forever a wonder to behold.

THIRTEEN (2003)

Directed by Catherine Hardwicke
Starring Holly Hunter, Evan Rachel Wood, Nikki Reed

This could be subtitled 'Every Parent's Worst Nightmare'. The young teenage girls presented here aren't the airbrushed cuties we're used to seeing in movies, who respect their parents and are just looking for love and acceptance from the Porsche-driving dudes at school. Instead, they are alarmingly realistic: mean, bored, destructive, scheming and, quite frankly, scary. What makes them even more terrifying is the knowledge that *Thirteen* was co-written by one of the stars, then-thirteen-year-old Nikki Reed, and is based on her own experiences. In true Hollywood style, she told Hardwicke – her father's girlfriend at the time – about her problems, and the director suggested it might be cathartic to write them down.

Tracy (Wood) seems like a normal, likeable girl until she befriends troubled (but ultra-cool) teen Evie (Reed). Before Tracy's single mum (Hunter) realises what is happening, her previously strait-laced daughter is shoplifting, drinking, getting high, having body piercings and generally behaving like a foul-mouthed slut, while Evie takes up seemingly permanent residence in Tracy's room.

Sure, these girls have problems (Tracy's mum is an alcoholic struggling to make ends meet; Evie's is entirely absent) but they are bad because they want to be. And in the hands of Wood and Reed they are convincingly so. Both young actresses screech, hit and pout their way across the screen, while Hunter delivers a performance of quiet desperation in the midst of this riveting hormonal horror.

TO DIE FOR (1995)

Directed by Gus Van Sant
Starring Nicole Kidman, Matt Dillon, Joaquin Phoenix

Kidman was a revelation in this wicked black comedy, based on Joyce Maynard's book – which, alarmingly, was in turn inspired by a true story.

The tightly wound Suzanne Stone (Kidman), who lives in a burg called Little Hope(!), will do anything to be on TV, because 'you're nobody if you're not a celebrity'. Since this pre-dates *Big Brother*, Suzanne claws out a low-end niche as her local TV channel's weathergirl, but her scruple-free ambition is limitless. Soon she's teased three nitwit, misfit teens, led by Phoenix's infatuated Jimmy, into murdering her easy-going, too unremarkable husband Larry (Dillon), an Italian-American whose ethnicity provides an early joke that sets up the film's final irony. Illeana Douglas is also terrific as Larry's sister, who has Suzanne sussed and enjoys her come-uppance with a memorable variation of dancing on someone's grave.

Gifted with priceless dialogue (written by Buck Henry, who plays the slacker assassins' teacher), Kidman presents self-absorbed Suzanne as a dazzlingly perfect characterisation, from her meticulous hair, make-up, clothes and mannerisms – all emblematic of the bimbo TV presenter – to her perky ruthlessness.

VALLEY OF THE DOLLS (1967)

Directed by Mark Robson
Starring Barbara Parkins, Patty Duke, Sharon Tate

Jacqueline Susann's racy novel of three women in Hollywood popping pills, sleeping around and trying to become starlets shocked America when it was first published, especially as Susann – once an actress – claimed it was based on her own experiences. But it went on to become a bestseller and the inspiration for this kitsch (check out the gravity-defying hairdos) movie.

The women and the men who live in the valley of the dolls ('dolls' being pills) are bitchy, scheming and back-stabbing. Neely (Duke) finds fame but gets hopelessly hooked on drink and drugs – leading to one of the movie's silliest moments when, in a mental ward, she sings a duet with another star who is there battling a terminal disease. Anne (Parkins), meanwhile, is the country girl turned supermodel who loses her cheating husband to one of her friends, and Jennifer (Tate) goes from Hollywood wife to porno star to pay the bills.

It's seedy, tacky and camp – a scene in which Duke rips off the wig of Broadway star Helen Lawson (Susan Hayward) in a catfight is typical – and would be on no one's 'best movie' list, but that's all part of its trashy appeal. A toned down 1981 TV movie was also made, starring Veronica Hamel and Catherine Hicks.

WHITE PALACE (1990)

Directed by Luis Mandoki
Starring Susan Sarandon, James Spader

Sarandon's Nora is the kind of bad girl we love – she smokes, she drinks, she curses and she hasn't done the housework in months. No wonder uptight widower Max (Spader) falls for her in this drama about two complete opposites who come together and discover they share secret pain.

Nora is a fortysomething waitress at White Palace, a greasy burger bar where Max goes to complain about an order for a party he's attending. They later meet again in a bar and end up horizontal at her place. An affair begins but he's not about to introduce this brassy older woman to his snobbish friends, and seems hung up on their social differences. As she eloquently notes: 'We get naked with each other and touch each other and you get inside of me, and you can't tell me how much rent you pay?' And what on earth is she doing with a guy who gives her a Dustbuster as a present, anyway?

Sarandon has never been better as tough-talking but vulnerable Nora, while Spader is at his sexiest. There's also great support in this wittily scripted drama from Jason Alexander and Eileen Brennan.

A WOMAN'S FACE (1941)

Directed by George Cukor
Starring Joan Crawford, Melvyn Douglas

Crawford is Anna Holm, a scheming, bitter woman cut off from society due to the scar on her face. Caught up in a blackmailing and murder plot being planned by her nefarious lover, Anna is offered the chance of having surgery to remove the scar by kindly doctor Segert (Douglas), but will her new face change the woman within?

A huge hit when it was released – cinemagoers flocked to the film after posters announced Crawford was playing a 'female monster' and a 'scar-faced she-devil' – this is almost *film noir* as Cukor lights his leading lady with a sinister glow and Crawford gets to breathe life into a truly nasty character. Along with her leading role in *Mildred Pierce*, it is one of her best performances, and there is delicious support from Conrad Veidt as her charmer of a lover.

OUTLAWS AND FUGITIVES

BAD GIRLS (1994)

Directed by Jonathan Kaplan
Starring Madeleine Stowe, Drew Barrymore, Mary Stuart Masterson, Andie MacDowell

It's *Young Guns* in skirts as prostitutes Cody (Stowe), Sweetpea (Masterson), Eileen (MacDowell) and Lily (Barrymore) saddle up in the Old West after Cody is sentenced to hang, then head for Texas with the law in hot pursuit.

Desperately silly – how did the women learn to shoot and ride; and why do they only ever get smudges of mud on their cheekbones, as if it were blusher? – this gets by on mountains of charm from the leads (especially Barrymore) as the girls are shot at, kidnapped, leered at and robbed on their way to new lives. There's the obligatory women-bathing-in-a-pond scene to keep male members of the audience happy, while we girls get to marvel at the hopelessly inauthentic fashions: bustiers, stockings and suspenders, and outfits that helpfully co-ordinate with their horses.

BANDIT QUEEN (1994)

Directed by Shekhar Kapur
Starring Seema Biswas

The woman portrayed in this film, Phoolan Devi, had already spent twelve years in prison and was facing possible further charges when it was made, prompting her to threaten to set herself on fire publicly if the film was released. It was, and she didn't.

While her concern was understandable, this colourful Indian feminist epic recounts Devi's exploits by casting her in the light of a right-on heroine of the oppressed. A poor, lower-caste girl sold into marriage at eleven, she fled the abuse of her husband and his mother and was subsequently drafted by a gang of robbers. Provoked by a horrific gang rape and the murder of her bandit lover, she embarked on a bloodthirsty revenge quest that Tarantino couldn't have dreamed up and which electrified the whole of India.

Involving, distressing and one of a kind, the film relies on a remarkably strong central performance by Biswas. The real Phoolan Devi was assassinated in 2001.

BIG BAD MAMA (1974)

Directed by Steve Carver
Starring Angie Dickinson, Tom Skerritt, William Shatner

Okay, this Roger Corman production set in the Great Depression is a cheap and cheerful, shameless exploitation flick (think *Bonnie And Clyde* meets *Lolita*). And it enjoys cult status with men who can't get enough of the enthusiastic nude scenes, in which Dickinson definitely outshines Shatner. But it's also tons of girls-on-top fun that came with the endearing tag line 'Men, Money and Moonshine – When it Comes to Vice, Mama Knows Best'! This is the acme of B-movies bedecked with gun-crazy gals with no hang-ups whatsoever.

Dickinson's feisty Mama Wilma, bravely bearing up after the loss of her husband, likes her love triangle with Shatner's gambler Baxter and Skerritt's bank robber Diller, who surprisingly also has the energy to indulge in threesomes with Mama's precocious offspring, Polly and Billy Jean. Mama is similarly fond of bootlegging, bank robbery, kidnapping (the hostage is such a spoiled bitch you're not overly concerned) and machine-gunning a swathe through rural America.

Sexy, bloodthirsty and very funny, this movie miraculously sidesteps the ugly nastiness of Corman's *Bloody Mama* (1970), but beware the sorry sequel, *Big Bad Mama II* (1987).

BONNIE AND CLYDE (1967)

Directed by Arthur Penn
Starring Warren Beatty, Faye Dunaway, Gene Hackman

Bored Bonnie Parker (a star-making performance by Faye Dunaway) impulsively goes on the run with bank robber Clyde Barrow (Warren Beatty) and finds the thrills she seeks as half of the Depression's most famous fugitive couple. Her big disappointment in this lifestyle choice is that crime makes her hot and Clyde is impotent.

Yes, we know men like this film, and controversy raged around the graphic violence and the glamorisation of notorious criminals, who in real life were nothing like as attractive as their sexy, anti-establishment screen counterparts. But women equally have always responded to the movie. Along with its highly influential, trend-setting realism, bloodletting and social comment, it has the fresh air of frank sexuality and humorous energy that director Penn (Sean's uncle, by the way) and producer Beatty admired in the French New Wave and blew into American filmmaking. And a pronounced aspect of its phenomenal success was its triggering (to coin a phrase) a fashion craze *à la* Dunaway's Bonnie, an instant icon who ushered back long tight skirts and the comeback of stockings while the menfolk ran around pretending all they were excited about was the new cinema.

Dunaway's resolutely sixties hairstyle, her carefully angled berets and carelessly chic neck scarves, the insouciant poses with cigarettes and guns, the sexual aggression, may not belong in the Depression-era Southwest, but they all evoke images of Parisienne actresses. And they make her a standout presence in a vivid picture.

DOUBLE JEOPARDY (1999)

Directed by Bruce Beresford
Starring Ashley Judd, Tommy Lee Jones

Judd is sent to prison for the murder of her husband (Bruce Greenwood, whose character is amusingly named Nicholas Parsons) but discovers he is alive and well, having faked his own death and framed her (the bastard). So she beefs up in prison in readiness for the moment when she is freed. Then she can murder him for real and get away with it, because, apparently, you can't be tried for the same crime twice. Meanwhile, marshal Jones does his damnedest to stop her.

A daft but addictive drama that has echoes of those woman-hell-bent-on-revenge TV movies that usually star Cheryl Ladd, this made a fortune at the box office and turned Judd into a star as women flocked to the cinema to watch Judd get her own back on the behalf of all wronged wives. Jones does his sub-*Fugitive* performance by numbers, but it's still fun, thanks to Judd's tough-cookie turn.

ENOUGH (2002)

Directed by Michael Apted
Starring Jennifer Lopez, Billy Campbell, Juliette Lewis, Noah Wyle

Singer–actress–diva J-Lo gets to kick some butt in this drama, in which she plays a wife who discovers her too-good-to-be-true husband is exactly that. Not only has Mitch (Campbell) been cheating on Slim (Lopez), but when she expresses her distaste at his nocturnal activities, he beats her up and leaves her sprawled on the floor while their young daughter cries in the other room.

Like the similarly themed *Sleeping With The Enemy* (see page 94), ludicrous plot twists hack away at the film's credibility. But at least this movie explains why the wife has stayed with the husband: it begins with them meeting, when he appears normal, handsome and pleasant, and the beatings don't start until well into their marriage. And the audience has every reason to cheer her on when Slim toughens up and returns home to give the sleazeball a taste of his own medicine. Go, girl!

KANSAS CITY (1996)

Directed by Robert Altman
Starring Jennifer Jason Leigh, Miranda Richardson, Harry Belafonte

Altman's 'jazz memory' of his home town in the Thirties meticulously recreates the atmosphere of hot jazz, coolly sinister gangsters, racial segregation and political corruption. He presents a swirl of mood vignettes around the slender story of tough little tootsie Blondie (Leigh), who kidnaps a drug-addled socialite (Richardson) and pressures her captive's politically connected husband to effect the release of her no-good hoodlum husband.

Those wanting the dense plotting of Altman's masterworks may be disappointed: the film was panned and rapidly disappeared from the screens. But the period evocation is rich, the musicianship superb, and both lead actresses brilliant. Richardson's dipsy, neurasthenic dame is a marvellous foil for Leigh's wisecracking wannabe moll, who has styled herself on Jean Harlow and acquired her dress sense, mannerisms, turns of phrase and limited ideas from the movies she loves.

THE WICKED LADY (1945)

Directed by Leslie Arliss
Starring Margaret Lockwood, James Mason

'I never could resist anything that belonged to somebody else,' smoulders Lockwood's Barbara Worth after she steals her best friend's beau in this deliciously lurid tale based on the novel *The Life And Death Of The Wicked Lady Skelton*.

The biggest box-office hit in Britain in 1946 (partly due to Lockwood's oft-displayed cleavage, one assumes, which sent American censors into a tizzy), it's the racy tale of an ambitious woman who eventually turns to gambling and highway robbery. She also finds time to romance a highwayman (Mason) on her days off. While all the men in her life (even Mason's smouldering bandit) have some sort of moral code, Barbara herself breaks every rule in the book, so she must receive her come-uppance before the end credits roll.

Still sexy after all these years, this movie has stood the test of time better than Michael Winner's ill-advised 1983 remake starring Faye Dunaway, Alan Bates, Denholm Elliott and Oliver Tobias.

Chapter 7: Working Girls
Lawyers, Waitresses, Doctors, Cops and Teachers

The roles women play in films don't often accurately reflect their working status in the real world. But it's interesting to consider the progress of women as they have been presented on the screen. It used to be extremely rare for women to play anything, apart from the odd wisecracking reporter with shoulder pads, that was much higher up the career scale than nightclub chanteuse or ambitious secretary sleeping her way up the corporate ladder – check out Barbara Stanwyck in the immortal *Baby Face* (1933). Now lady doctors and lawyers, however unlikely (Cher?), are a commonplace – though we hate when they appear in court with bare legs and minimal, if excellent, lingerie under their well-tailored suits so they can head from the courtroom straight into a quickie with the leading man, tsk, tsk.

Early stereotypes of women in film were simple. Basically they were mother, angel and whore. If the women were employed – a necessity only for the poorer, lower classes – nice girls were typically seamstresses, teachers or nurses. Nasty girls, therefore, were found in saloons and nightclubs as chanteuses. Occasionally a woman who had inherited money, a publishing empire or a ranch might boss people around, in which case she was a domineering matriarch. The chief business of the screen's sex goddesses was the ruin of men, while saintly homebodies mended socks, bandaged wounds and put dinner on the table. The odd biopic of a queen or a scientist (and there was pretty much only one of them – Marie Curie) invariably focused on their love lives more than the business of state or the lab work. Gradually, women both good and bad were depicted as secretaries and saleswomen because these were a way to meet men. And the 'inspirational teacher' mini-genre was always a good niche for ageing actresses, like Bette Davis in *The Corn Is Green* (1945).

Of course, middle-class women were not in the workforce in significant numbers or diverse occupations before the Second World War. It would be a mistake, though, to think that women were never depicted as professionals or get-up-and-go gals before Women's Liberation. In the early thirties Katharine Hepburn, Rosalind Russell and Jean Arthur were glamorously demonstrating the possibilities, playing aviatrixes, reporters and lawyers. Then war sent millions of men overseas. British and American women went into the factories, 'manned' the farms, and even played professional sport. The delightful Ann Sothern, whose films are now all but forgotten, made ten popular B-movies between 1939 and 1947 that turned her character Maisie into a household name. She started as a good-hearted chorus girl but through a series of topical adventures and wildly varied jobs – from maid to special agent – she put people's lives to rights and aided the war effort (as in 1943's *Swing Shift Maisie*, which saw her working in an aircraft factory). More than the lavish dramas of the time, her light-hearted escapades embraced the changing role of ordinary women. And there was no going back to the kitchen for many of them, although fifties films tried desperately to idealise the homemaker.

It was in the sex comedies of the swinging sixties and a flowering of realism in the seventies that women were finally truly recognised as people of diversity and myriad abilities who wanted or needed to work, whether as magazine editors or mill hands. Eventually mainstream pictures, many of them based on real-life stories, acknowledged that women's work can have dramatic interest and impact: Sally Field as a labour organiser in *Norma Rae* (1979) or Meryl Streep as a nuclear-plant whistle-blower in *Silkwood* (1983).

A development for which Sigourney Weaver and *Alien* (1979) director Ridley Scott can take bows is establishing the action woman (although blaxploitation heroine Pam Grier's vengeful nurse *Foxy Brown*, introduced in 1974, has her devotees). When Warrant Officer Ripley kicked alien butt in outer space, Weaver shattered the myth that a woman couldn't headline a blockbuster, and three successful sequels proved the iconic attraction of a tough cookie. Hot on Ripley's heels came the toned biceps of Linda Hamilton's Sarah Connor in *Terminator 2: Judgement Day* (1991), Anne Parillaud's *La Femme Nikita* (1990), Angelina Jolie's *Lara Croft: Tomb Raider* (2001), Carrie-Anne Moss's Trinity in the *Matrix* trilogy (1999–2003) and, exploring the sadistic depths of Girl Power, Demi Moore's *GI Jane* (1997). Even Meryl Streep flexed her muscles in *The River Wild* (1994). We also live in a new age of female cops and FBI agents: Jamie Lee Curtis in *Blue Steel* (1990), Debra

Winger in *Betrayed* (1988), Angelina Jolie in *The Bone Collector* (1999) and *Taking Lives* (2004), Ashley Judd in *Twisted* (2004), Sandra Bullock in *Murder By Numbers* (2002), Jennifer Lopez in *Out Of Sight* (1998) and *Angel Eyes* (2001). And the two great law-women of our time: Jodie Foster's Clarice Starling in *The Silence Of The Lambs* (1991) and Frances McDormand's heavily pregnant, no-nonsense police chief Marge Gunderson in *Fargo* (1996) – both Oscar-winning roles. These are not chick flicks, but we're glad the better ones are there.

For our own favourite working girls, we've chosen a variety of women, from waitresses to politicians, who speak to women, not because of the job they do but because they are seen juggling their professional and personal lives, just as most of us have to do.

HIS GIRL FRIDAY (1940)

Directed by Howard Hawks
Starring Cary Grant, Rosalind Russell

This splendid, sensationally funny comedy is still unrivalled for snappy repartee and precision timing, and it rejoices in scintillating performances from Grant and Russell.

Ben Hecht and Charles MacArthur's classic comic newspaper play *The Front Page* has been filmed successfully both before and after this version (in 1931, and in 1974, with Jack Lemmon and Walter Matthau directed by Billy Wilder). But astute and witty director Hawks gave it a startlingly simple twist that proved a stroke of genius. He turned ace reporter Hildy Johnson into a woman (and he didn't even have to bother changing his/her name). *Et voilà*, he wrought the fastest-talking battle-of-the-sexes romantic screwball comedy ever, scripted by Hecht and Charles Lederer.

Hildy (Russell, whose mother was a fashion editor) is the star reporter of a city paper edited by unscrupulous, aggressively charming Walter Burns (Grant). He also happens to be her ex-husband. When Hildy announces that she's quitting the news game to marry a meek, nine-to-five square (Ralph Bellamy), Walter's incredulity and dismay launch him into conniving overdrive. As the wily Walter quickly calculates, scoophound Hildy just can't resist one last big scoop, and he persuades her to postpone her departure until she's done an exclusive interview with a condemned man on the eve of his execution.

In no time at all, Hildy is up to her absurdly jaunty hat in a hot jailhouse escape and an exposé of crooked city politics. Allied with Walter in regular telephone briefings and copy dictation, but largely on her own at the jail, resourceful Hildy hides the escaped prisoner she has come to believe is innocent. She gets the goods on nitwit politicians and the police department. She runs rings around the male reporters in the press room (a wealth of great character actors who act as a gum-chewing, poker-playing, smoke-wreathed chorus of cynicism). And she *never* stops talking. Even Hawks's other comic masterpieces, *Twentieth Century* and *Bringing Up Baby*, can't match *His Girl Friday* for machine-gun-speed patter, with Grant and Russell engaging in a dizzying display of wisecracking, retort and reportage in a plot that attains farcical heights amid a visual style that sports more shoulder pads than the Dallas Cowboys.

Russell's stylish, sophisticated, sarcastic Hildy Johnson – for whom the intoxication of news gathering proves as essential as oxygen – made girls want to be journalists, imagining themselves as well-tailored, quick-witted, smooth-talking and indispensable.

Switching Channels (1988), starring Kathleen Turner, Burt Reynolds and Christopher Reeve, updated the scenario to a satellite TV news station. It did so rather well, too, but not as hysterically.

WORKING GIRL (1988)

Directed by Mike Nichols
Starring Sigourney Weaver, Harrison Ford, Melanie Griffith

A forties-style comedy with an eighties slant, *Working Girl* remains one of the best, and funniest, looks at women in the workplace.

Tess McGill (Griffith) is turning thirty. She's a secretary at a broker-age firm who has big, brassy hair, big, brassy accessories and a big, brassy voice. She rides the Staten Island ferry every day to work and dreams of something more. Her opportunity comes when she lands a new job as secretary to the new boss of the mergers and acquisitions department, Katharine Parker (Weaver). First the two women get along fine, but when Katharine goes on a skiing trip and ends up in traction for weeks, Tess discovers a computer file that reveals her boss was going to take one of her ideas and pass it off as her own. The bitch!

So begins a charade as Tess cuts back her bouffant hair, tones down the make-up, borrows her absent boss's clothes and assumes the role of an executive so she can see her idea to fruition before back-stabbing Katharine's return. During this deception she encounters Jack Trainer (Ford), a broker who works with her, unaware she's really a lowly secretary.

Ford is terrific in his funniest role as the confused man who wants a horizontal as well as a business relationship with Tess. And Weaver is hilarious as the woman we love to hate. Joan Cusack (as Tess's best friend) and Alec Baldwin (as her philandering boyfriend) lend fabulous support, but this is Griffith's film from the opening frame to the end credits. Part Cinderella, part self-made Eliza Doolittle, she's smart, sexy ('I have a head for business and a bod for sin,' she memorably tells Jack at their first meeting), funny and tough, and in MIke Nichols's terrific comedy drama she gets the best role of her career.

THE ACTRESS (1953)

Directed by George Cukor
Starring Spencer Tracy, Jean Simmons

Actress, playwright and screenwriter Ruth Gordon (immortal on screen as satanic old Minnie in *Rosemary's Baby*) adapted her own autobiographical play into this film. It is an affectionate tribute to her father and an insight into a stagestruck girl turning her fantasy into reality in small-town New England at the turn of the century. Irascible father Clinton Jones (Tracy) is a retired seaman whose life of hardship and poverty has not prepared him for a daughter (Simmons as Ruth Gordon Jones) with a wild, unrealistic dream of going on the stage. Only her passionate persistence wears him down, especially when she sacrifices budding romance with Anthony Perkins's nice, prosperous suitor in favour of an insecure, socially frowned-upon profession. The film is undeniably stagey and wordy, but Tracy and Simmons are sympathetic and engaging.

ADAM'S RIB (1949)

Directed by George Cukor
Starring Spencer Tracy, Katharine Hepburn, Judy Holliday

This choice battle-of-the-sexes comedy has been an inspiration for countless imitations dealing with combative but sexually combustible couples. Of the nine Tracy–Hepburn vehicles, it's arguably the best, still crackling with wonderful performances, witty dialogue and a spirited discussion of double standards and sexual stereotypes. It was written by Tracy and Hepburn's great pals, the married team of Ruth Gordon and Garson Kanin.

When sweet, ditsy blonde Doris Attinger (a sensationally funny Holliday in the debut role that launched her meteoric career) is charged with the attempted murder of her two-timing husband, proto-feminist attorney Amanda 'Pinkie' Bonner (Hepburn) agrees to defend her. But Amanda's husband, Adam 'Pinky' Bonner (Tracy), is the prosecuting attorney, and their courtroom rivalry quickly extends into the bedroom.

Director Cukor gave Hepburn free rein for her outrageously crafty showboating in court – forever an inspiration to lady lawyers-to-be – while Tracy frothed with indignation at her tactics and principles. Highlights include brainy Amanda's cross-examinations and the spectacle of Adam tearfully getting in touch with his feminine side to worm his way back into his wife's good graces. While some of the arguments seem quaint now, the sophistication is undiminished.

BABY BOOM (1987)

Directed by Charles Shyer
Starring Diane Keaton, Sam Shepard

Keaton has always seemed capable of taking care of just about *anything*, even when she's at her most ditsy. So she seems an unlikely choice for the role of a yuppie businesswoman who finds herself failing to juggle her career and relationships when she inherits a baby from a distant relative.

The movie is not as warm, fuzzy and coochie-coo-ish as you might expect, thanks to a believably harassed performance from Keaton and strong support from Harold Ramis, Sam Wanamaker and Pat Hingle. It veers into cute cuddly-bunny territory only when Keaton heads to the country and falls for humble village veterinarian Shepard.

BLACK WIDOW (1987)

Directed by Bob Rafelson
Starring Debra Winger, Theresa Russell

Russell is terrifically sexy as the elusive serial killer who changes identities, personalities and seduction techniques as quickly as she marries and murders a string of wealthy men (Dennis Hopper among them). She is intelligent, cunning and ruthless. Now that's what we'd call a very bad girl. But what makes this thriller so intriguing and a notch above the usual female-killer flick is its focus on Winger's more recognisable, workaday character. Her lonely Alex is a smart but lowly Justice Department data analyst, longing for a field assignment they will never give her. Sniffing a connection between the various millionaire mortalities, she is patronised, insulted and disbelieved by male colleagues but defiantly, obsessively, follows her instincts, developing a consuming fascination with the confident killer.

The contrast of sleek *femme fatale* with funky, frizzy-haired lawwoman when Alex makes contact with her target – and desperately tries to imitate her style – creates extraordinary tension in a uniquely feminine battle of wits.

BROADCAST NEWS (1987)

Directed by James L. Brooks
Starring William Hurt, Albert Brooks, Holly Hunter

The leading men are rival TV news reporters – Hurt the handsome, nice-but-dim Tom and Brooks the clever, sweatily untelegenic Aaron – but a smashing Hunter is the real star as Jane Craig. She's their writer and producer at the network's Washington news bureau. Writer–director James L. Brooks turned this into an authentic look inside the workings of television news gathering and reporting, but he is also appealingly insightful about people in stressful professions sidelining their personal lives. Marketed as a comic love triangle, it's actually a terrific, though ultimately rather painful, study of a smart, feisty, controlling woman and the price she pays in her relationships for her obsession with and satisfaction in high-pressure work well done. Look out for the scene in which Jane edits a piece nail-bitingly close to its onair deadline, and for Jack Nicholson's wonderful cameo as the network's illustrious New York anchorman.

KATHARINE HEPBURN (1907–2003): THE INDEPENDENT WOMAN

The redoubtable Katharine Hepburn was a screen goddess for over sixty years of her life, and remains an enduring icon after her death: the graceful, arrogant *grande dame* of spunky defiance, for ever her own woman, and always a survivor.

'Kate' was raised and highly educated by remarkable, progressive parents who urged her to 'go out and make life interesting'. She certainly did that, for herself and for the rest of us. The winner of a record four Academy Awards and nominated another eight times, the partner on and off screen of Spencer Tracy for twenty-seven years (they made nine films together between 1942 and 1967), she never took Hollywood seriously and wore her fame lightly. She said what she thought, did what she wanted, strode around in trousers when that was considered shockingly unladylike – and did it all with class. And she commanded respect from the moment she made her screen debut (as John Barrymore's daughter in *A Bill Of Divorcement*) at twenty-five, prepared to fight for the roles she wanted and scorn those she didn't.

Hepburn won her first Oscar for her third film, as an aspiring actress in 1933's *Morning Glory*. The next three came when she was past fifty: for 1967's *Guess Who's Coming To Dinner?*; as conniving, imperious Queen Eleanor in 1968's *The Lion In Winter*; and for 1981's *On Golden Pond*. In between she was radiant in period films like *Little Women* (1933), *Alice Adams* (1935) and *A Woman Rebels* (1936). She crossdressed in *Sylvia Scarlett* (1935), and sparkled in the classic comedies *Bringing Up Baby* (1938), *Holiday* (1938) and *The Philadelphia Story* (1940). She found unlooked-for love later in life in *The African Queen* (1951), *Summertime* (1955) and *The Rainmaker* (1956). She went magnificently crazy in *Suddenly Last Summer* (1959), *Long Day's Journey Into Night* (1962) and *The Madwoman Of Chaillot* (1969). Best of all, she was an inspirational role model eager for challenges as headstrong women taking on men at their own games – whether as an aviatrix (1933's *Christopher Strong*), a political commentator (*Woman of the Year*), a lawyer (*Adam's Rib*) or a professional athlete (1956's *Pat And Mike*). None of these films has dated, because she doesn't.

THE CHILDREN'S HOUR (1961)

Directed by William Wyler
Starring Audrey Hepburn, Shirley MacLaine, James Garner

Karen Wright (Hepburn) and Martha Dobie (MacLaine) are college friends and dedicated teachers who run their own private girls' school. The business is going swimmingly, and Karen is engaged to Garner's dishy doctor Joe, when a malevolent pupil lies that she's seen Karen and Martha engaged in sexual behaviour. Shock and horror all round as the school, the women's careers, their friendship and Karen's marriage plans face ruin amid a sinister atmosphere of bigotry and suspicion. Who'd be a teacher?

This adaptation by Lillian Hellman of her famous play was actually the second film version undertaken by Wyler, who had made the looser, determinedly non-lesbian *These Three* with Merle Oberon, Miriam Hopkins and Joel McCrae in 1936. The veteran Hopkins, who played Martha in that movie, appears in *The Children's Hour* as Martha's interfering aunt Lily. Another great 'women's pictures' trouper, Fay Bainter, plays the influential, morally outraged Mrs Tilford, while a young Veronica Cartwright is the pilfering pupil too frightened to tell the truth. The earlier, more conventional love-triangle film probably has more ardent admirers. But Hepburn and, especially, MacLaine (whose character, it emerges, really *is* in love with her best friend) are excellent as women doing honourable work that counts for nothing when their private lives are targeted.

CLOSE TO EDEN / a.k.a. A STRANGER AMONG US (1992)

Directed by Sidney Lumet
Starring Melanie Griffith, Eric Thal

We simply couldn't resist including this unintentionally hilarious police drama. Griffith stars as Emily Eden, a cop who goes undercover in the Hasidic Jewish community of New York City to investigate a disappearance. Because, if anyone could pass as a Hasidic Jew, it's Melanie, right?

Desperately silly – Emily is supposed to be a trigger-happy, tough-as-nails cop, whereas Melanie looks like she'd faint if she broke a nail – this has a romantic subplot as Emily falls for one of the suspects (Thal), despite having a wounded cop boyfriend (Jamey Sheridan) at home. (However, in a recut version of the film, he is barely mentioned.) But no amount of romance can paper over one of the daftest conclusions ever committed to film as Emily figures out whodunnit about an hour after the audience has.

COMA (1978)

Directed by Michael Crichton
Starring Geneviève Bujold, Michael Douglas, Richard Widmark

A cracking medical thriller based on Robin Cook's bestselling novel. Dr Susan Wheeler (Bujold) starts to think something strange may be going on at the hospital where she works when seemingly healthy patients suffer complications during routine operations and end up in comas. Can she trust hunky doctor Mark Bellows (Douglas, in his first major big-screen role) or anyone else at the hospital? And why are all the coma patients taken to a heavily guarded medical facility?

Extremely creepy stuff from director Crichton (who went on to write the novel on which *Jurassic Park* was based), this gets honorary chick-flick status because it's Bujold, not Douglas, who crawls through ventilation shafts, gets chased by heavies, and takes all the risks.

THE CONTENDER (2000)

Directed by Rod Lurie
Starring Joan Allen, Gary Oldman

When the Vice-President dies, President Jeff Bridges gets the chance to appoint a female senator (Allen) as his replacement in this engrossing political tale. Of course, as we all know, in politics things are never that easy, and there is a conniving opponent (Oldman) waiting in the wings to humiliate her and bring her name into disrepute (she's got quite an interesting past to hide).

Written and directed by former film critic Lurie, this is thoroughly gripping stuff that accurately depicts the inner jealousies and back-stabbings of government with humour and tension. We'll forgive him the somewhat cop-out final scene because the rest is so good, populated with a *Who's Who* of talented actors, including Christian Slater, Sam Elliott, William Petersen and Philip Baker Hall. And with Bridges giving us the sexiest President the United States is ever likely to have, it becomes unmissable.

COPYCAT (1995)

Directed by Jon Amiel
Starring Sigourney Weaver, Holly Hunter

In a nice twist of casting, little Holly Hunter's the tough cop determined to track down a killer no matter what the cost. She's even prepared to enlist the help of skittish criminal psychologist and agoraphobic Sigourney Weaver, who's been having a little trouble getting out and about after nearly being the victim of an obsessed murderer herself.

It turns out the killer is copying well-known murders from the past, and the two women team up to catch him (any male cops, friends, etc. are dispatched a.s.a.p. so the sisters can do it for themselves). Along the way, a few ludicrous yet rather obvious plot twists are thrown in, Sigourney gets to run around in her knickers and tough-but-cute Holly shouts a lot, but at least they get to prove that gals can catch bad guys and look good in heels *at the same time*. Not in the same league as the atmospheric *Se7en* or *Manhunter*, perhaps, but this is still a fair addition to the genre.

DANGEROUS MINDS (1995)

Directed by John N. Smith
Starring Michelle Pfeiffer, Courtney B. Vance

It's *To Sir With Love* for the nineties in this based-on-a-true-story drama. Pfeiffer, in a leather jacket and specs, replaces Sidney Poitier as the teacher inspiring inner-city kids to stop shooting each other and learn the poetry of the two Dylans (Thomas and Bob, that is).

A surprise hit – aside from Pfeiffer, the cast is made up of a group of unknown actors and school kids – *Dangerous Minds* had audiences queuing round the block. There were two main reasons for this: they wanted to see Michelle getting down and dirty as an ex-marine; and they wanted to hear the chart-topping soundtrack, which includes tracks by Wendy & Lisa, and 'Gangsta's Paradise' by Coolio. In fact, it often seems like you are watching a feature-length rap video, as every inner-city *Boyz 'N The Hood*-style cliché is trotted out over the music while our plucky gal tries to solve problems like gang involvement drives and teenage pregnancy. It says something about Pfeiffer's talent that she somehow makes this rather preachy and formulaic film thoroughly watchable, but even she can't stop you wincing at the feelgood ending.

DREAM WIFE (1953)

Directed by Sidney Sheldon
Starring Cary Grant, Deborah Kerr

While scarcely among the more sparkling romantic comedies graced by Grant, this relic is fascinating for the attitudes expressed about a woman's role. It's also interesting for the rarefied professional status accorded Kerr's character in the Eisenhower era of 'the little woman'. She is Effie, a high-powered diplomat about to marry Grant's globe-trotting businessman, Clem. But he is exasperated that international crises requiring her talents invariably take precedence over his dinner plans. He wants a doting housewife who will make breakfast. She says he can pay someone to do that. Dumping Effie, Clem takes up the ruler of an oil-rich Middle Eastern kingdom's offer of his beautiful, subservient daughter, who has been trained to be a perfect (i.e., silent, compliant and adoring) wife. Assigned as liaison between the parties, Effie cannily orchestrates the emancipation of the bride-to-be while wising up Clem on the desirability of a smart, accomplished woman.

ERIN BROKOVICH (2000)

Directed by Steven Soderbergh
Starring Julia Roberts, Albert Finney, Aaron Eckhart

Julia Roberts won a Best Actress Oscar for her role as real-life Erin Brokovich, a brassy, uneducated mother of three who convinces lawyer Ed Masry (a suitably gruff Finney) to hire her despite her lack of qualifications. His faith is rewarded when she turns up evidence that a huge power company has knowingly polluted a whole town with carcinogenic chemicals, instigating a major lawsuit.

Striding around in mini-skirts and low-cut tops that reveal a whopper of a cleavage (apparently courtesy of a specially constructed push-up bra that should have been given an end credit), Roberts powers through every scene. Spitting out choice dialogue ('As long as I have one ass instead of two, I'll wear what I like, if that's all right with you!'), she revels in the first film that proved she was more than just a pretty face and a big smile. Fascinating stuff. Watch out for a brief cameo from the real Erin as a waitress.

FRANKIE AND JOHNNY (1991)

Directed by Garry Marshall
Starring Al Pacino, Michelle Pfeiffer

He's a short-order cook newly released from prison; she's a dowdy waitress who's supposedly given up on men for good. Played by Pacino and Pfeiffer, it's hard to believe these two beautiful people would find it difficult to find love, but the story is touching as Johnny admits he doesn't want to be alone while Frankie tries to convince herself that she does.

Based on Terrence McNally's play *Frankie and Johnny at the Clair De Lune*, this comedy drama was justifiably criticised for its casting when it was released. Frankie isn't supposed to be pretty – Kathy Bates had played the part on stage and lobbied for the film role – and Pacino has too much star power to convince as one of life's losers, but they both give solid performances. There is also fine support from Hector Elizondo, Nathan Lane (as Frankie's obligatory gay pal) and Kate Nelligan.

GORILLAS IN THE MIST (1988)

Directed by Michael Apted
Starring Sigourney Weaver, Bryan Brown

This is the true story of Dian Fossey, a physical therapist whose life-long dream of working in Africa was triumphantly (and eventually tragically) realised when she made herself the world's leading primatologist ... and an eccentric, reclusive researcher with many enemies – one of whom murdered her.

Apted's film departs radically from the traditionally cuddly depictions of women anthropologists/zoologists/whatevers bonding with animals. This is a driven, warts-and-all drama of a woman with a lot of rage. Fossey recklessly took on tribesmen, poachers and the government in Central Africa when her study of mountain gorillas became an obsessive mission to protect them. Weaver conveys this passion compellingly, especially when Fossey rejects her photographer lover (Brown) for the sake of her more beloved gorillas. You might think that this was Apted taking liberties for dramatic effect, but it really happened.

HEART LIKE A WHEEL (1983)

Directed by Jonathan Kaplan
Starring Bonnie Bedelia, Beau Bridges

There aren't many pictures catering for women who feel the need for speed, so this biopic of groundbreaking professional drag-racer Shirley Muldowney (Bedelia) is a curiosity – and happily not at all bad. Into the thrill of fast cars since childhood, Shirley does what's almost unthinkable for a screen heroine: she walks out on her unsupportive husband and their teenage son (played by young Anthony Edwards a decade before *ER*) to fight for a place on the hot-rod racing scene. She crashes, she burns (horribly), she tosses out her cheating lover (Bridges) even though he's her mechanic, and she proves she has the right stuff to compete on the dangerous dragster circuit. Women who choose their work over love and family, striking out on their own to fulfil themselves, are so often unsympathetically portrayed that this is a refreshing change of gear.

A LEAGUE OF THEIR OWN (1992)

Directed by Penny Marshall
Starring Tom Hanks, Geena Davis, Madonna, Lori Petty

While the men are off fighting in the Second World War, farm girls, housewives and any women who can throw a ball are recruited to play in the newly established All American Girls Baseball League in this comedy drama from *Big* director Marshall. Among them are sisters Dottie (Davis) and Kit (Petty), who are assigned to the Georgia Peaches team with good-time girl Mae (Madonna), tough-cookie Doris (Rosie O'Donnell) and drunken has-been coach Jimmy Dugan (Hanks).

It's a cute look at a little-known part of American sporting history, packed with well-tuned performances (yes, even Madonna's) from the girls, who all did their own stunts and had the bruises to prove it. (When the actresses auditioned they had to show they could play baseball as well as act.) Hanks gives one of his best comedy performances, especially when he memorably points out to one weepy player in his charge that 'There's no crying in baseball!'

LEGALLY BLONDE (2001)

Directed by Robert Luketic
Starring Reese Witherspoon, Luke Wilson, Selma Blair

Fans of dumb-blonde comedy *Clueless* will get a kick out of this similar tale in which fluffy, flaxen-haired dimwit Elle (Witherspoon) decides to get into Harvard Law School so she can show the boyfriend who has just dumped her that she's just the sort of smart girl he wants to marry.

Watching fuchsia-pink-clad Elle totter through the revered halls among all the tweed-wearing preppies is enough to produce a few giggles on its own, and there are more when she tries to survive at the brainy college by using her knowledge of *Cosmo*, fashion and skincare rather than the law. Why did the heads of the school let her in, you may wonder – because she sent them a video of herself wearing a skimpy bikini, of course. Like Elle, the film is sunny and funny without ever being too clever. Bright entertainment that's perfect for a dull winter's evening, this was followed by a so-so sequel in 2003.

THE LONG KISS GOODNIGHT (1996)

Directed by Renny Harlin
Starring Geena Davis, Samuel L. Jackson

Yes, this is an action movie, but it's a strangely girlie one. Samantha (Davis) is a suburban schoolteacher and single mother suffering from amnesia who enlists the help of private investigator Mitch (Jackson) to unearth her true identity. It turns out she's actually Charly Baltimore, a highly trained secret-agent assassin whose memory suddenly returns, and who has to battle both personalities to use Charly's skills to rescue the kidnapped daughter Samantha wants back.

Perhaps the message here is that, ladies, you can have a career *and* be a mum … although we're not sure how many mothers are knife-wielding hit-women. But really it's all just an excuse for Davis to kick some male ass, toss out some *Die Hard*-style quips and flex her toned upper arms. Silly, but unquestionably entertaining.

MISS CONGENIALITY (2000)

Directed by Donald Petrie
Starring Sandra Bullock, Michael Caine, Benjamin Bratt, William Shatner

With the notable exception of Chandler Bing (who had a fixation with this flick on *Friends*), only women normally relate to this utterly predictable but very amiable comedy.

Bullock's determinedly frowzy FBI agent is forced to go undercover as a contestant in a beauty pageant. In the hands of Caine's camp pageant consultant she is tweezed, waxed, creamed, primped, bullied, buffed and styled to the max – although she never masters the stilettos – all to unmask the fiend behind a terror threat on the Miss United States contest. The fun cast includes camp icon Shatner and glacial beauty Candice Bergen letting their hair down hilariously as the pageant organisers. But it's Bullock's show, and she's in engaging form whether bonding with the bimbos, performing her absurd contribution to the talent section, or springing into action against the criminal.

MONA LISA SMILE (2003)

Directed by Mike Newell
Starring Julia Roberts, Julia Stiles, Kirsten Dunst, Maggie Gyllenhaal

It's *Dead Poets Society* with big skirts as Art History professor Roberts attempts to teach a group of fifties twinset-and-pearls-wearing college girls that their time in higher education is not just a means to meet well-bred, rich future husbands. They could actually *learn* something, and pursue careers other than 'homemaker'. Unfortunately, director Newell thinks the way to get this message across is to pack the film with lingering shots of the luscious college campus and Roberts's patented smile. Then he throws in a few caricature students – the upper-class meanie (Dunst), the sexy booze-swiller (Gyllenhaal), the gullible wallflower (Ginnifer Goodwin) and the smart but unhappy one (Stiles).

The story is as predictable as the reviews in teen magazines that described this movie as – *eek!* – 'inspiring'. And, while its heart is in the right place, you can't help but be disappointed that such a crop of female acting talent has been wasted in such a clichéd and dull-as-tweed film.

MUSIC OF THE HEART (1999)

Directed by Wes Craven
Starring Meryl Streep, Aidan Quinn, Angela Bassett

Streep plays Roberta Guaspari, a real divorced mother with no work experience who marched into a poor Harlem school with fifty violins and set about transforming disadvantaged little desperadoes into disciplined, motivated musicians. OK, it's a shock that horror-film luminary Craven is having a stab at the inspirational-teacher genre; but he himself was a teacher, he loves classical music, and he admired a documentary on Guaspari. Aside from the director, though, this is a surprise-free zone that would have been a typical TV movie if it had starred Donna Mills rather than Streep. But she is as splendid as ever as Guaspari, growing in confidence from abandoned wife to warrior educator, battling for arts funding to schools and pumping darling pupils with American mantras like 'Stand strong!'

NINE TO FIVE (1980)

Directed by Colin Higgins
Starring Jane Fonda, Lily Tomlin, Dolly Parton, Dabney Coleman

Workers uniting has seldom taken a more drastically crazy turn than when three secretaries revolt against their odious, chauvinist-pig boss, Frank (Coleman). Judy (Fonda) is the timid housewife entering the workforce and gaining confidence. Violet (Tomlin) is the competent assistant denied promotion because she is a woman. And kind Doralee (Parton) is reviled because she's the victim of Frank's lying sexual boasts. The women team up to take Frank captive in his own home, and while he's literally tied up they cover for his absence, running his department better than he did.

Hilarious, this was timely, and a fun screen debut for the vivacious Parton (who had a hit with the title tune), but Tomlin is the sharpest of the trio, and enjoys some great speeches about bigotry and harassment in the workplace. Male bosses would eye secretaries more warily ever after.

NORMA RAE (1979)

Directed by Martin Ritt
Starring Sally Field, Beau Bridges, Ron Leibman

Textile-worker Norma Rae (Field) braves ostracism, arrest and threats as she attempts to unionise the Alabama cotton mill where she, her family and friends have long endured poor pay and dangerous conditions. Based on the true story of Crystal Lee Jordan, this multi-award-winning drama was one of the first mainstream pictures to centre on an ordinary working-class mother, here defying her culture's belief that organised labour spells 'troublemakers'.

Former *Flying Nun* Field won a role turned down by Jane Fonda and several other 'serious', A-list actresses after writer–director Ritt saw her in *Sybil* (see page 111). She prepped for her role by working in a factory, and gives a ferocious, Oscar-winning performance of guts and gumption. Her finest moment, nervously switching off her machine, standing on her work table and raising a sign that reads, 'Union' (prompting a strike and her arrest), became emblematic.

THE NUN'S STORY (1959)

Directed by Fred Zinnemann
Starring Audrey Hepburn, Peter Finch

Being a nun may be a vocation rather than a profession, but the dilemma for Gabrielle Van Der Mal (Hepburn, just as luminous in a habit as in Givenchy), once she becomes Sister Luke, is that her dedication to medical practice continually conflicts with her religious vow of obedience. The story is enlivened by the flattering attentions of Finch's handsome surgeon in the Belgian Congo. But at the heart of it is Sister Luke's struggle – despite her unshakeable faith – to comply with humility to orders when she is naturally spirited and intellectually gifted. The outbreak of the Second World War and her impulse to aid the Resistance bring about her inevitable spiritual crisis.

Zinnemann's film, adapted from the book by Kathryn Hulme, is fascinating in its details of everyday life in a cloistered convent and an African mission, in the training and routines of nuns who teach, care for the mentally ill and run hospitals in dangerous places. A terrific ensemble, including Dames Edith Evans and Peggy Ashcroft, give genuine depth to the women underneath the veils.

THE PRIME OF MISS JEAN BRODIE (1969)

Directed by Ronald Neame
Starring Maggie Smith, Robert Stephens, Pamela Franklin, Celia Johnson

Muriel Spark's audacious novel about an inspirational teacher whose self-delusion and misjudgement exert a powerful but damaging spell on the girls under her influence is a doozy of a tale. Adapted into a play and this film by Jay Presson Allen, it is perfectly realised by Maggie Smith's vibrant, Oscar-winning portrayal of Miss Brodie. She is a liberated history teacher in thirties Edinburgh who expounds to enthralled adolescent girls on life, art and passion while having affairs with fellow-teachers, including artist Teddy (Stephens, Smith's husband in real life). Unhappily, and calamitously, Jean is also a zealous Fascist, which vindicates both the headmistress's (Johnson) concern and Miss Brodie's ultimate betrayal by her protégée, Sandy (Franklin). To her credit – and dramatic appeal – the woman certainly knows how to live, live, live and how to infuse her admirers with that ardour.

THE PRINCE OF TIDES (1991)

Directed by Barbra Streisand
Starring Nick Nolte, Barbra Streisand, Blythe Danner

Pat Conroy's epic novel about a dysfunctional Southern family was deftly translated to the screen under the surprisingly subtle direction of Barbra Streisand, who was notoriously overlooked in the nominations for a Best Director Oscar, despite the movie itself being up for Best Picture (it lost out to *The Silence Of The Lambs*).

Babs – who can comfort herself with the knowledge that she was the first person to receive a Grammy, a Tony, an Oscar (for *Funny Girl*, followed by a Best Song gong for 'Evergreen', the theme to *A Star Is Born*) and an Emmy as well as the Cecil B. De Mille Lifetime Achievement Award – also stars here as the New York psychiatrist helping Nick Nolte to come to terms with his twin sister's attempted suicide.

Streisand sensibly stays on the sidelines (although the camera lingering occasionally on her stockinged legs and talon-like fingernails does provide some unwelcome distraction) and allows her gruff co-star to shine. And Nolte rises to the challenge, giving one of the best and most moving performances of his career as the man wrestling with his family's demons and his growing attraction to his sister's psychiatrist. Note to nepotism buffs: Jason Gould (Streisand's son from her marriage to Elliott Gould) also features as, of course, Streisand's on-screen son.

PRIVATE BENJAMIN (1980)

Directed by Howard Zieff
Starring Goldie Hawn, Eileen Brennan

Spoiled rich girl Judy Benjamin (Hawn) understandably freaks out when her husband (Albert Brooks) keels over and dies on their wedding night. On a whim, she signs up for the army. Unsurprisingly, GI Jane she is not, so her flighty manner soon incurs the wrath of Captain Lewis (Brennan) in this armed forces comedy.

This was a breakthrough role for Hawn. She had previously been a co-star in *Cactus Flower* and *Shampoo*, but this was the first film in which she took the lead, to startlingly successful box-office effect. It's really just a showcase for her kookiness, as Judy bumbles her way through various aspects of military life. And it's fun, although the addition of Armand Assante as Judy's love interest spoils the whole premise that army life has strengthened her to the extent that she no longer needs the security of a man.

SECRETARY (2002)

Directed by Steven Shainberg
Starring Maggie Gyllenhaal, James Spader

A relationship drama in which the relationship in question is a sado-masochistic one (definitely not a movie you should watch with Granny then).

Lee (Gyllenhaal) is a young woman who cuts herself for pleasure and in times of stress. On her release from a mental hospital she lands a job as a secretary for local lawyer Edward Gray (Spader). Soon their relationship develops from boss–employee to master–servant as Gray notices Lee's masochistic tendencies and explores his own sadism. (She delivers his post in her mouth because she is handcuffed.)

While S&M is at the core of this 'romance', the cast (especially Spader, who expands upon the sexually tortured character he played in *sex, lies, and videotape*) and director Shainberg inject the film with enough humour and emotion for you never to have to feel you are watching a sordid tale. And Gyllenhaal's performance is so bold that it's impossible to view Lee as a victim. The end result is a sometimes slight but often compassionate film that's the oddest little love story you're likely to find.

SPEECHLESS (1994)

Directed by Ron Underwood
Starring Geena Davis, Michael Keaton

A nineties twist on forties-style screwball comedies has Keaton and Davis as two insomniac political speechwriters, who meet, fall in love, and then discover they work for opposing candidates. So begins a war of words as the pair accuse each other of seduction for political gain. Meanwhile, the arrival of her ex-boyfriend (a delicious turn from Christopher Reeve as war correspondent 'Baghdad Bob', who never seems to take off his bullet-proof vest) and the interference of his ex-wife (Bonnie Bedelia) further complicate an already complicated relationship.

Both political satire (with some sharp stabs at the media) and comedy romance, this smart film never received a UK cinema release, but it is well worth seeking out for the two lead performances, especially Keaton's.

SPELLBOUND (1945)

Directed by Alfred Hitchcock
Starring Ingrid Berman, Gregory Peck

Dr Anthony Edwardes (Peck), the new director of a psychiatric hospital, arrives to take up his post. His unexpected youth and good looks soon have earnest, glacial psychiatrist Dr Constance Peterson (Bergman) experiencing an unnerving erotic awakening, notably in an extraordinary Freudian dream sequence designed by Salvador Dali. Had he been old and ugly, Edwardes might have been on his own in this singular romantic thriller from the master of suspense. But when he's unmasked as an amnesiac impostor with galloping paranoia, Dr Peterson protectively springs into analytical overdrive to discover his identity and the fate of the real Dr Edwardes. This is probably the first murder mystery cracked by a woman through dream interpretation.

THE THRILL OF IT ALL (1963)

Directed by Norman Jewison
Starring Doris Day, James Garner

The first and more delightful on-screen pairing of Day and Garner (they also starred together in *Move Over Darling*) is a battle of the sexes between husband and wife. He's successful doctor Gerald Boyer and she is his missus Beverly, who is happy and contented to be a housewife and raise their cute kids. That is, until she tells an anecdote about the children and the product Happy Soap to the chairman of the company that makes it during a dinner party. The big boss is so enchanted that he asks her to appear in commercials promoting the soap, and Beverly instantly becomes a television celebrity with no time to be a home-maker, much to Gerald's annoyance.

A kitsch sixties classic, as Beverly cooks dinner in her sparkling kitchen, scrubs her too-good-to-be-true children and rarely has a hair out of place (even when the swimming pool fills with soap suds), this is fluffy fare but utterly lovely for it.

UP CLOSE AND PERSONAL (1996)

Directed by Jon Avnet
Starring Robert Redford, Michelle Pfeiffer

Pfeiffer is the driven woman who dyes her hair platinum blond and scales the career ladder from weathergirl to respected TV journalist, falling in love with weather-beaten mentor Redford along the way.

Originally based on real-life TV anchorwoman Jessica Savitch, a reporter renowned for her ambition who died in a car accident at the age of thirty-six, it was almost a decade before the story made it on to the screen, by which time most of the similarities to Savitch's life had been removed. Pfeiffer certainly plays a tough cookie, but with its soft focus, swirling music and a theme song by Celine Dion ('Because You Loved Me'), the film concentrates on her romance rather than on her career. In a way, though, that's perfectly understandable, because Redford (at fifty-nine) is still gorgeous.

Looking scarily similar to Pfeiffer (complete with bleached hair), Angelina Jolie tackled a similar role in the more comedic *Life Or Something Like It* in 2002.

VERONICA GUERIN (2003)

Directed by Joel Schumacher
Starring Cate Blanchett, Gerard McSorley, Ciarán Hinds, Brenda Fricker

This is the true story of Irish journalist Guerin (Blanchett), who was murdered in the course of her investigations into Dublin's gangster drug lords. It's particularly interesting because Blanchett's powerhouse performance doesn't pull any punches, and the film is far removed from the sentimental sanctimoniousness that one might have expected. Guerin is as foolhardy confronting ruthless thugs, naive for mixing with a treacherous snitch (Hinds), thoughtless of the jeopardy into which she is placing her family, and egotistically arrogant about her crusading articles as she is undeniably courageous by undertaking such an important job.

In contrast, the earlier, more fictionalised account of Guerin's life and work, *When The Sky Falls* (2000), starring the superb Joan Allen and approved in draft form by Guerin before her shocking death, falls into the trap of making her just too saintly for a journalist.

VIGIL IN THE NIGHT (1940)

Directed by George Stevens
Starring Carole Lombard, Brian Aherne, Anne Shirley

This is a terrific medical melodrama, based on the novel by A. J. Cronin. At a Manchester hospital, nurse Anne Lee (Lombard) takes the blame for a fatal mistake made by her sister Lucy (Shirley) and ends up losing her job. After securing a post at another hospital, she meets dashing Dr Prescott (Aherne), but a lecherous boss, an understaffed and ill-equipped facility and an epidemic all conspire against them.

Lombard – better known for her comic roles – shows she's just as accomplished when not wisecracking, while Hollywood's approximation of northern England is surprisingly realistic. Watch out for a young Peter Cushing in an early role.

WOMAN OF THE YEAR (1943)

Directed by George Stevens
Starring Spencer Tracy, Katharine Hepburn

This, the first Tracy–Hepburn collaboration, is a smart, tart comedy about the still relevant womanly ambition of 'having it all'. Tracy's Sam is a sportswriter for a New York paper. Hepburn's Tess is a political columnist, commentator and activist. He likes baseball and beer. She likes the arts and wine. His friends are boxers and barflies. Hers are international statesmen and socialites. Nevertheless, they fall in love with sizzling haste, and marry in a chaotic little ceremony squeezed in between her pressing engagements. It all goes horribly wrong because she's never home. The final straw is her well-meaning acquisition of a refugee child whom she then neglects. Accusing her of not being a real woman, Sam splits.

It comes as a huge relief to us that her repentant incursion into his kitchen to cook the most disastrous breakfast ever is *not* how the issue is resolved. Wisely, Sam doesn't expect Tess to become what she can never be. He just wants her to get in touch with her feelings and find some balance between her professional and personal lives. Easier said than done, as working women everywhere know.

Incidentally, Vincente Minnelli's comedy *Designing Woman* (1957), which starred Gregory Peck as a sportswriter who marries Lauren Bacall's fashion designer, is not a remake. However, it tries hard to recreate the chemistry and deals with the same theme as *Woman Of The Year*.

WOMEN ON THE VERGE OF A NERVOUS BREAKDOWN (1988) a.k.a MUJERES AL BORDE DE UN ATAQUE DE NERVIOS

Directed by Pedro Almodóvar
Starring Carmen Maura, Antonio Banderas, Julieta Serrano

Spanish writer–director Almodóvar's absorption with women's experiences and emotions reached deliriously comical heights in this, his international breakthrough film. But it wouldn't be as hysterically melodramatic if the protagonist Pepa (played by Almodóvar's principal muse Maura) were not an actress, exaggeratedly playing life large.

On discovering her lover has abandoned her for another woman, Pepa overreacts with high histrionic abandon, breaking down at the studio where she dubs foreign-language movies and preparing a gazpacho with an overdose of barbiturates. Then she makes the further discovery that her cheating lover's mentally ill wife is planning to kill him, and she determines nobly to intervene. Before she can save his hide, however, her apartment becomes crowded with an odd assortment of desperate and desperately talkative friends and unwanted visitors caught up in increasingly bizarre circumstances.

Original, colourful, stylised, this is an affectionate homage to women who live life like it's a performance.

Chapter 8: The Ties that Bind
Mothers, Children, Sisters and Gal Pals

If the clichés about the male psyche are to be believed, you just need to say the word 'relationship' to a man and he'll run a mile. We girls, of course, have the opposite reaction. We *love* relationships. We want to have them, talk about them and, best of all, watch other people's, both happy and sad.

We've already covered romantic relationships – be they tortuous or funny, fabulous or tragic – in previous chapters. Here, it's the turn of movies that celebrate (or denigrate) other types of relationship: those between mothers and their children, between sisters and other siblings, and those special friendships between women who aren't related but stick together through thick and thin. We've even thrown in a few relationship movies that seem to revolve around the dinner table.

Naturally, there are many 'relationship' movies that cannot be described as chick flicks, no matter how much we wanted to include them. The father/son/brother relationship between Tom Skerritt, Craig Sheffer and a blond and simply divine Brad Pitt in *A River Runs Through It* (1992) makes men cry just as much as women, as does Kevin Costner's with his late father in *Field Of Dreams* (one of our archetypal 'Male Weepies' in Chapter 2). Usually, movies that deal with a mother's love or that of a female child tend to be more girlie than those between boys and their dads, though we do recommend you check out *The Yearling* (1946), *At Close Range* (1985), *Flesh And Bone* (1993), *Frequency* (2000) and *The Great Santini* (1979) to see how men deal with parental angst (usually through sport or by shooting someone).

The films that men tend to hate most aren't those that deal with family. After all, they're often humorous looks at a subject we can all relate to; and many, like *Parenthood* (1989), *The Daytrippers* (1995) and *Life Is Sweet* (1990), broadly appeal to everyone. No, with the exception of ballsy, ass-kicking *Thelma And Louise* (see page 258), the movies that are truly chick flicks are those that feature gal pals. In these, girls and women are friends to the end, while men are sidelined and at best peripheral to the plot.

You'll notice that most of the movies that fall into the 'gal pal' category are relatively recent, with many of them made in the last twenty years. You could chalk this up to a cinematic type of feminism – more women are making movies or have elevated positions at movie studios, so inevitably more films with central female characters are being made. At the same time, actresses like Ashley Judd, Sandra Bullock, Julia Roberts, Drew Barrymore and Meryl Streep have big box-office appeal, and often their own production companies, which means that their pet projects now tend to get made. This luxury was not available in the past to Doris Day or Bette Davis.

Most importantly, this surge of girlfriend chick movies is down to you and all the other women who go to the cinema with their best girlfriends, rather than a boyfriend/husband, women who want to sit back and watch a movie in which love, friendship, long-lost hot summers and sisters doing it for themselves are the main themes, rather than murder plots or alien invasions. And here they are. Enjoy!

FRIED GREEN TOMATOES AT THE WHISTLE STOP CAFE(1991)

Directed by Jon Avnet
Starring Kathy Bates, Mary Stuart Masterson, Mary-Louise Parker, Jessica Tandy, Cicely Tyson

1991 was a red-letter year for the chick-flick renaissance with *Thelma And Louise* redefining the buddy picture, and this pleasing adaptation of Fannie Flagg's bestseller *Fried Green Tomatoes At The Whistle Stop Café* proved just as significant. Featuring an impressive line-up of actresses, it was so popular that it sparked a new enthusiasm for ensemble chick flicks about bonding and self-awakening. A sprawling Southern saga that spans more than fifty years, it centres on a plucky knock-her-down-and-she'll-always-get-up-again gal, but there are also emotional subplots aplenty. The end result is a tearful comedy drama which contains echoes of *Driving Miss Daisy*, *Steel Magnolias* and *The Color Purple.*

In the present day, frumpy, dumpy mousewife Evelyn Couch (Bates) meets doughty little old biddy Miz Ninny Threadgoode (Tandy) in a nursing home and begins to pay her weekly visits. An Alabama Scheherazade, Ninny captivates Evelyn and keeps her coming back with instalments of the story of wild, boyish Idgie (Masterson) and gentle Ruth (Parker), a vibrant pair who shared high spirits, heartache and home cooking at their small country-town café in the thirties.

Ninny's account reveals how Idgie and Ruth's friendship gave them the strength to ride out tragedy, abuse, peculiar regional cuisine (such as the breaded, fried, unripe tomatoes of the title), the Depression, brutal racist attacks on their loyal friend Big George (Stan Shaw) and a long-running murder mystery. Inspired by feisty Idgie's antics half a century earlier, Evelyn takes charge of her life, her weight, and her slob of a husband, ringing the changes with hilarious vigour. Her growing confidence brings about one of our favourite moments in the film. Two insolent slappers steal Evelyn's parking space in their flashy car and jeer, 'Too bad, lady, we're younger and faster.' Enraged, she repeatedly slams into their car and crows, 'Too bad, girls, I'm older and have more insurance.'

The Depression-era tale is very nostalgic, heart-warming ... and mouth-watering, as Idgie and Ruth cook up a storm. They are kindly to the hungry and homeless, love Idgie's old nanny Sipsey (Tyson) and her son George, and stand tall against violent, sexist and racist rednecks even as darker events threaten, progressing to a courtroom climax. Thank heavens for the murder intrigue and the strong performances (Masterson, in particular, is a peach), because it's all a bit much and could get cloying without them. The lesbian element is so discreet as to be barely detectable beyond Idgie's snappy trews and tie.

What is unreservedly entertaining is what Bates carves out of the film. Formerly dreary Evelyn raises her consciousness, lowers her cholesterol and starts speaking her mind in fine tribute to, and celebration of, the empowering pleasure of friendship between women.

EVE'S BAYOU (1997)

Directed by Kasi Lemmons
Starring Smollett, Samuel L. Jackson, Lynn Whitfield, Debbi Morgan

Eve's Bayou is a handsome Louisiana property where a descendant of the original Eve, her ten-year-old namesake (Smollett), is our narrator. She's also the troubled witness to a strange, tragic and spellbinding sequence of events one summer.

Daddy (Jackson) is a doctor, an elegant charmer and a compulsive womaniser. Mother (Whitfield) maintains her poise and grace, suffering his philandering in silence. And sexy Aunt Mozelle (Morgan) is cursed in love and gifted with psychic vision. When Eve unwittingly opens a Pandora's box of guilty secrets she takes us through heartbreaking, humorous and mesmerising episodes of sex, lies and voodoo.

This assured writing–directing debut by actress Lemmons (Clarice's buddy in *The Silence Of The Lambs*) is a superior Southern Gothic drama, an imaginatively structured and visualised story of family, sisterhood, secrets and selective memory, steeped in Creole culture, folklore and atmosphere.

EVELYN (2002)

Directed by Bruce Beresford
Starring Pierce Brosnan, Aidan Quinn

When his wife leaves him to raise his kids alone in Ireland in 1953, unemployed painter and decorator Desmond Doyle (Brosnan) knows life isn't going to be easy, but he's prepared to do the best he can for the children he loves. However, the Irish courts learn Desmond is bringing up his two sons and daughter Evelyn without a mother, so his children are taken away and placed in orphanages. Desmond then finds he has no legal right under Irish law to have them returned to him. But he's prepared to fight the system all the way, which he does with the help of his friend Bernadette and a principled legal team.

It's fascinating subject-matter for a drama and is bolstered by a talented cast: young Sophie Vavasseur, who is a treat as Evelyn; *ER*'s Julianna Margulies as Bernadette; and Quinn, Stephen Rea and Alan Bates as Desmond's lawyers. Director Beresford (best known for *Driving Miss Daisy*) occasionally piles on the schmaltz, but if you can forgive him that, this is an enjoyable, ultimately feelgood movie.

HANGING UP (1999)

Directed by Diane Keaton
Starring Meg Ryan, Diane Keaton, Lisa Kudrow

Based on Delia (sister of *When Harry Met Sally* Nora) Ephron's novel about three sisters dealing with their almost senile father (Walter Matthau), this never develops into the 'family bonding' movie you expect it to be. Instead, it's a pretty lifeless and clichéd tale about the relationship between just one of the siblings (Ryan) and her dad.

While Matthau gets some choice lines, you'll yearn for more scenes like the deliciously bitchy one when the three girls turn on one another, each blaming the others for just about everything. Unfortunately, even if you manage to persevere through the full ninety-minute running time (it feels much longer!), you'll be rewarded with just a bit of weeping and groaning. It will be coming from the poor unfortunate you dragged to this, as well as the three sisters on screen.

HOME FOR THE HOLIDAYS (1995)

Directed by Jodie Foster
Starring Holly Hunter, Robert Downey Jr, Anne Bancroft

Anyone who dreads clan gatherings will laugh with recognition at director Foster's cute domestic-crisis comedy featuring a dysfunctional family who have grown ever further apart. Hunter drags her heels to the old family home to eat, argue, eat, cry, eat, laugh and eat some more with parents (Bancroft and Charles Durning) who still treat her like a stubborn child, the sister who chose marriage and children but seethes with resentment at Hunter's independence, and the hilariously irresponsible brother (Downey Jr) who arrives with another fella (Dylan McDermott). Unexpected romance in her home town gets her out of the house and combines with an amusing string of embarrassments and horrors that remind you why you left home in the first place.

HOW TO MAKE AN AMERICAN QUILT (1995)

Directed by Jocelyn Moorhouse
Starring Winona Ryder, Ellen Burstyn, Anne Bancroft

And we complain about men who can't commit! Ryder plays Finn, a graduate student who is unable to settle on a thesis subject or set a wedding date with her fiancé, until she spends an illuminating summer with her offbeat gran and great aunt (Burstyn and Bancroft). They and their sewing-circle gal pals ponder patchwork-quilt patterns and betrayals of the heart while initiating Ryder in the tribal rituals of women's handicrafts and life wisdom by sharing family histories of love, loss and life down through the generations.

A *Who's Who* of female American acting talent, from Claire Danes and Samantha Mathis to venerable Esther Rolles (plus poet Maya Angelou and guest Britons Jean Simmons and Kate Nelligan), do their stuff, nicely stitching together tales of joy, pain and fulfilment. But ultimately it's an Americanised, somewhat inferior version of *The Joy Luck Club*, adapted from Whitney Otto's novel.

JACK AND SARAH (1995)

Directed by Tim Sullivan
Starring Richard E. Grant, Samantha Mathis, Judi Dench

It's *One Man And A Baby* time as Jack's (Grant) wife dies in childbirth, leaving him holding the baby in this bittersweet comedy. Refusing the help of his mother (Dench), Jack instead hires inexperienced American waitress Amy (Mathis) as nanny to baby Sarah.

You know from reel one that the trio will find lurve, despite Amy being a selfish opportunist rather than a suitable substitute mom. By reel two you won't be bothered anyway, as the movie flits uncomfortably between tragedy and comedy: Jack mourns his wife one minute and then goes shopping with Sarah in a Jiffy bag (don't ask) the next.

Grant, Dench and Eileen Atkins (as the mother-in-law) give the best performances and get the sharpest lines, but even these three talents can't save what is a very uneven, if well-meaning, film.

MARVIN'S ROOM (1996)

Directed by Jerry Zaks
Starring Meryl Streep, Leonardo DiCaprio, Diane Keaton

Streep and Keaton give sterling performances as Lee and Bessie, two sisters who haven't spoken in over a decade, in this drama based on the play of the same name. They are reunited when Bessie is diagnosed with leukaemia because only Lee or one of Lee's two children could provide a possible match for a bone-marrow transplant. The reunion is strained, however, as Lee feels guilty that for years she has left Bessie to look after their ailing father Marvin (Hume Cronyn). Meanwhile, the presence of Lee's eldest son Hank (DiCaprio) – who has just been released from a mental institution, where he was staying after setting fire to his mother's house – adds to the tension.

It's comforting to see that some families are even more dys-functional than our own, and, with the quality support of Robert De Niro and Dan Hedaya, this is funnier and warmer than you might expect.

MEN DON'T LEAVE (1990)

Directed by Paul Brickman
Starring Jessica Lange, Arliss Howard, Joan Cusack, Chris O'Donnell

Unfortunately, Beth's (Lange) husband has left – well, actually he's died – and she is now trying to cope with raising her two sons alone. Forced to move from the suburbs to an apartment in Baltimore, she has to readjust to her new life and begin dating again. She meets a musician (Howard), while her eldest son (O'Donnell, in his first movie role) falls for an older neighbour (Cusack). A drama about how it is possible to pick up the pieces after a catastrophe, this is an often moving film, and features a terrific central performance from Lange.

MERMAIDS (1990)

Directed by Richard Benjamin
Starring Cher, Bob Hoskins, Winona Ryder, Christina Ricci

Cher looks utterly fabulous as Mrs Flax, small-town floozy and crazy, mixed-up single mom, who wriggles through this cute mother–daughter comedy drama in backless stilettos, breath-defying pedal-pushers and teased hair. This is mortifying to teen Charlotte (Ryder), who's Jewish but wants to be a nun … until she spots the convent's muscular handyman. Meanwhile, Lou (Hoskins) tirelessly woos Mrs Flax. He's no oil painting, but he's the perfect man: he's nice, he cooks, he's good in bed and, be still my heart, he owns a shoe store.

Set nicely in 1963, this coming-of-age tale has sweet, eccentric amusements in the mother–daughter tug-of-war, not to mention Mrs Flax's odd notions of what constitutes dinner. It veers slightly into TV kitchen-sink drama when near tragedy for the adorable kid sister (the tiny Ricci) brings conflicts to a head. Still, the leads are all genuinely appealing, with Ryder acting her bobby sox off.

MIAMI RHAPSODY (1995)

Directed by David Frankel
Starring Sarah Jessica Parker, Mia Farrow, Antonio Banderas

This Woody Allen-style film for girls begins innocently enough with Parker contemplating marriage to her long-term boyfriend (*Ally McBeal*'s Gil Bellows). Then she discovers her mother (Farrow) is sleeping with the Cuban nurse (Banderas) who is looking after her grandmother; her father (Paul Mazursky) is having an affair with his travel agent; her brother (Kevin Pollack) is cheating on his pregnant wife with a supermodel (Naomi Campbell); and her just-married sister wants to meet up with her ex-boyfriend for a quickie. Not exactly a family brimming over with role models for monogamy, then.

Hot and humid Miami provides a suitable backdrop for all this infidelity, as our heroine tries to decide whether to wed her dependable man or succumb to the temptations of her mother's Latin lover. It's genuinely funny, and Antonio has never been dreamier.

THE NEXT BEST THING (2000)

Directed by John Schlesinger
Starring Madonna, Rupert Everett

Yet more proof, as if it were needed, that Madonna has better taste in music than movies. Her real-life buddy Everett delivers as good a performance as he can under the circumstances (the script is awful) as Madge's gay pal, who, after an alcohol-fuelled night, also ends up as the father of her unborn baby. The ensuing gay dad/yoga-mad straight mum scenario might have worked as a comedy but, astonishingly, halfway through, the movie tries to get all serious. It turns into a *Kramer Versus Kramer* for the new millennium as the pair fight for custody of the sprog. You have to wonder why either of them would want her, though, as she is extremely annoying for one so young.

Only worth having if you intend to take the disc or videotape and smash it into small pieces, thus removing at least one copy of Madonna murdering Don McLean's 'American Pie' (the film's theme song) from the planet.

ONCE AROUND (1991)

Directed by Lasse Hallström
Starring Holly Hunter, Richard Dreyfuss, Danny Aiello

Our families can be our greatest supporters, but also the people who criticise us the most. Renata (Hunter) learns this when she brings her older, flamboyant new boyfriend Sam (Dreyfuss) home to meet her close-knit, disapproving Italian family.

Dreyfuss is a scream as the obnoxious fiancé, but the film works so well because of the humour added by the family: Aiello as Renata's dad, Gena Rowlands as her mum and Laura San Giacomo as her sister. Hunter enjoys herself in a meaty role as the woman determined to stand by her decision and her man in the face of astute family opposition.

ORDINARY PEOPLE (1980)

Directed by Robert Redford
Starring Donald Sutherland, Mary Tyler Moore, Judd Hirsch, Timothy Hutton

Redford's graceful, compassionate directorial debut tackles the impact of a son's death on his family. It's a sincere, restrained and intimate personal drama that makes some viewers queasy with its emphasis on people getting in touch with their feelings. But it took Academy Awards for Best Picture, Direction, Supporting Actor (Hutton, at nineteen, the youngest actor ever to win an Oscar) and Alvin Sargent's sensitive screenplay, adapted from Judith Guest's novel.

Schoolboy Conrad (Hutton) is suicidally depressed after the accident which he survived but which killed his older brother. There is no understanding for him from his cold mother Beth (TV sitcom sweetheart Moore, cast very much against type and giving an astonishingly brave performance). She is a ruthlessly ladylike control freak, obsessed with appearance, incapable of expressing love and intolerant of emotional mess. It falls to concerned father Cal (Sutherland) and a committed psychiatrist (Hirsch) to get through to the anguished boy, and Cal is eventually forced to make a painful reassessment of his family.

All the leads are compelling, and Elizabeth McGovern made a charming debut as Conrad's awkward girlfriend.

PARADISE (1991)

Directed by Mary Agnes Donoghue
Starring Don Johnson, Melanie Griffith, Elijah Wood, Thora Birch

When his mother can't cope during the break-up of her marriage, she sends young Willard (Wood) down South to her old friend Lily Reed (Griffith) for the summer. In Lily and her husband Ben (Johnson) the boy finds a couple whose grief at the loss of their own child has driven a wedge between them. But as the hopeless duo warm to Willard he becomes the means by which they are drawn back together. Willard also makes friends with neighbour Billie (Birch), whose own family troubles lead the two children into misadventure and climactic jeopardy that have the desired effect of prompting happy endings.

While the poor, darling kids have far more sorrowful grown-ups to contend with than is either fair or reasonable, their summer experience is touching, and all the performances are sympathetic and winning. Johnson and Griffith (then married) often got bum critical raps, but together and separately here they are both understated and moving.

THE PARENT TRAP (1998)

Directed by Nancy Meyers
Starring Lindsay Lohan, Dennis Quaid, Natasha Richardson

This classic tale of manipulative twins was originally made in the sixties, with cute-as-can-be Hayley Mills taking the double lead. This time Lohan plays Hallie and Annie, who were separated shortly after birth when their parents split up. Hallie has grown up in California with her vineyard-owning dad Nick (Quaid); Annie has been raised by her mother Elizabeth (Richardson), who designs wedding gowns in London. Unaware of the other's existence, the pair finally meet at summer camp and then scheme to switch places so that each can meet the parent they've never known, and perhaps reunite the couple before Nick marries gold-digger Meredith (Elaine Hendrix).

While the movie is quite slow for a family film, it's saved by a thoroughly engaging cast and two fabulous performances from Lohan, who carries every scene without ever being annoying.

PIECES OF APRIL (2003)

Directed by Peter Hedges
Starring Katie Holmes, Patricia Clarkson, Oliver Platt

Dawson's Creek's Katie Holmes proved she is more than just an ex-teen TV star in this warm comedy drama, but even she was outshone by Patricia Clarkson, who earned a deserved Oscar nomination.

April (Holmes), the funkily dressed black sheep of her middle-class family, is living in a run-down New York apartment block with her boyfriend Bobby (Derek Luke). She has spent her life being criticised by her now terminally ill mother (Clarkson), so the pressure is on as she prepares a Thanksgiving dinner for the whole family that is driving over to see her.

Writer–director Hedges has made an often funny, sometimes moving indie film. The laughs come from April's disastrous preparations while her parents, grandmother and siblings bicker in the car and worry about what gastronomic delights will greet them when they finally arrive. It may be only eighty minutes long, but this sweet, observant film captures much of the angst, love and frustration we all know in our own families.

PLACES IN THE HEART (1984)

Directed by Robert Benton
Starring Sally Field, Lindsay Crouse, Ed Harris, John Malkovich, Danny Glover

Writer–director Benton's tribute to his own mother won him an Oscar for his screenplay and Field her second for Best Actress (prompting her famous, much-mocked outburst, 'You like me! You really like me!'). But credit where credit's due: she deserved it for her heartfelt performance as Edna Spalding, a young widow in the thirties South struggling fiercely for her children and their home. With the odds against them bringing in the cotton crop in time, the extended family she's made of migrant worker Moze (Glover), bitter, blind war veteran Mr Will (Malkovich) and her troubled kinsfolk (Crouse, Harris) pitch in with blood, sweat and tears. There are also the matters of a tornado, brutal racial attacks and betrayals to contend with in a beautifully made drama of forgiveness, grace and hope.

PLAYING BY HEART (1998)

Directed by Willard Carroll
Starring Sean Connery, Gillian Anderson, Dennis Quaid, Gena Rowlands

Writer–director Carroll delivers a passionate, funny and thoroughly enjoyable drama of love in all its forms, performed by a stellar cast. Connery and Rowlands are the long-married couple dealing with new and old secrets; Anderson is the businesswoman afraid to commit to a relationship; Madeleine Stowe and *ER*'s Anthony Edwards are two adulterous lovers; Jay Mohr is dying of AIDS; and Angelina Jolie is the party girl in hot pursuit of the surprisingly reluctant Ryan Phillippe. It's powerful, touching stuff, but with enough sharp humour and spot-on performances for it not to be dismissed as just a chick flick.

WHAT A GIRL WANTS (2003)

Directed by Dennie Gordon
Starring Amanda Bynes, Colin Firth

This is a sweet, if rather implausible, teen comedy drama that tells the tale of Daphne (Bynes). She's a sixteen-year-old American, living with her mother (Kelly Preston), who has always dreamed of meeting the father she has never known. Determined to find him, she hops on a plane to London, where she learns that Dad is Lord Henry Dashwood (Firth, tongue firmly placed in cheek), an aristocrat and politician who is about to marry the scheming Glynnis (Anna Chancellor) and take on her equally conniving daughter Clarissa (Christina Cole).

Young girls will enjoy Daphne's adventure as her American ways raise eyebrows in polite English society, and there's a sweet little romance with a local musician (Oliver James) thrown in for good measure. Grown-ups can snigger at the way the Brits are portrayed as snobby, badly dressed socialites who prefer their antique chandeliers to their children. It's all complete nonsense, of course, but as pre-teen *Cinderella* stories go, this one (loosely based on the Rex Harrison movie *The Reluctant Debutante*) is suitably fizzy and enjoyable.

YOU CAN COUNT ON ME (2000)

Directed by Kenneth Lonergan
Starring Laura Linney, Mark Ruffalo, Matthew Broderick

Single mum Sammy's (Linney) calm existence is disrupted by the arrival of her wayward younger brother Terry (Ruffalo) in this bittersweet comedy drama. Orphaned as children, Sammy has been her brother's anchor, staying in their small home town with her young son (Rory Culkin). But Terry's reappearance isn't what she had imagined – he takes her eight-year-old to a bar, for starters – and her peaceful life is further complicated by the attentions of her smarmy boss (Broderick).

The dialogue in this little film is so realistic that you feel as if you are eavesdropping on conversations between real siblings, and lovers, and parent and child. Linney is superb as the woman constrained by her circumstances; Broderick is a hoot as her married lover; and Ruffalo shines as the irresponsible brother. Superb in every way.

 MOVIES FOR THE MUNCHIES

An old TV jingle declared that 'Nothin' says lovin' like somethin' from the oven'. Well, food preparation is certainly an expression of love that's popular in films about family relationships. Couples, chums and extended clans chew over their emotional issues while the camera hungrily circles the dinner table. We've already discussed *Simply Irresistible*, and we won't linger here on the delicious *Big Night* (1996), although we do recommend it for showing men how to cook eggs perfectly. We must also reluctantly pass on the world's greatest noodle movie, the Japanese comedy treat *Tampopo* (1986). And we are indebted to Francis Ford Coppola and Martin Scorsese for invaluable spaghetti Bolognese tips in *The Godfather* (1972) and *GoodFellas* (1990).

For the foody movies that follow, we recommend that you have a toothsome bite before or yummy snacks readily to hand; otherwise you'll be drooling in torment as the heroines (and one hero) sling skillets and life wisdom in these delicious entrées in the menu mini-genre.

BABETTE'S FEAST (1987)

Directed by Gabriel Axel
Starring Stephane Audran, Birgitte Federspiel, Bodil Kjer

Danish writer–director Axel's Oscar-winning adaptation of an Isak Dinesen story is a gorgeous drama of self-sacrifice and love sweetened with generous amounts of charm and humour. In a remote nineteenth-century Jutland village two sisters – one a beauty, the other a talented singer – decline marriage and a musical career to care for their venerable pastor father and his austere Protestant congregation. Years later, the impoverished ladies (Federspiel and Kjer) take in French Catholic refugee Babette (Audran), who becomes their devoted if enigmatic housekeeper. Several more years later, Babette wins a lottery and uses the windfall to repay her employers' loving kindness by preparing a mighty, sumptuous, seven-course feast for them and their flock, whose lifelong inhibitions are drowned in champagne. The banquet proves a wondrously life-altering experience by the time the mystery of Babette's past is served up with her magnificent *baba au rhum*.

CHOCOLAT (2000)

Directed by Lasse Hallström
Starring Juliette Binoche, Lena Olin, Johnny Depp, Judi Dench

In this charming adaptation of Joanne Harris's magical bestseller, free-spirited single mother and chocolatier Binoche sets up shop in a repressed provincial French town in the fifties. She is soon concocting mouth-wateringly sinful sweeties that transform the lives of those who succumb to temptation. Depp's seductive gypsy affects an oddly Oirish accent – like we care – while the conservative town mayor and all-round meany (Alfred Molina) is so unbelievably twisted that he does his worst to run Binoche, her engaging little daughter, the gypsies *and* chocolate out of town. Can any man be that sad?

This movie drew heavy critical fire for the clashing accents of its multinational cast, but we still want to know what's in the bon-bons that make a bored man amorous! And, as in *Babette's Feast*, a celebratory meal makes you groan and drool with desire.

EAT DRINK MAN WOMAN (1994)

Directed by Ang Lee
Starring Sihung Lung, Kuei-Mei Yang, Chien-Lien Wu, Yu-Wen Wang

Writer–director Lee's densely plotted, character-rich dish of family dynamics, emotional complications and culinary skills celebrates the two basic requirements in life: sex and food. Taiwanese master chef Mr Chu (Lung) is the cantankerous widowed father of three daughters, with whom he has difficult relationships. His artistry ranges from death-defying techniques in veggie slicing to the carving of intricate designs into a melon for use as a soup tureen, and his fastidious, ritualised family meals are elaborate acts of love that substitute for his inability to express it verbally. Outside their home, all four principals are engaged in busy spirals of frustration, desire and romance that produce a series of bombshell revelations back at the dinner table. Lee artfully keeps the flavour of life simmering up to a resolution that is as satisfying, and as beautifully presented, as Mr Chu's steamed deer in a pumpkin pot. Sweet and sour, poignant and hilarious.

If you love Mexican food, the English-language remake set in LA, *Tortilla Soup* (2001), starring Hector Elizondo as the taciturn paternal chef, is good and tasty but not quite as delicious.

LIKE WATER FOR CHOCOLATE (1992)

Directed by Alfonso Arau
Starring Lumi Cavazos, Marco Leonardi, Regina Torne

Passion is on the boil in this marvellous binge of magical realism adapted from Laura Esquivel's bestseller, a captivating fairytale of romance, revolution and recipes set in early twentieth-century Mexico. Beautiful Tita (a radiant Cavazos) is born in the kitchen of her wealthy family's ranch, and she is destined to spend the rest of her life there, catering to all her relatives and especially to the monstrous mother who forces her to remain single so that she may care for her. When unhappy Tita has to prepare the wedding feast for her sweetheart and her sister, her gift for putting her feelings into her cooking begins to reveal itself: her tears fall into the batter and all the guests gorging on cake become upset. This unique culinary talent shapes the family's fates in wildly unexpected ways through forty emotional years of hearty eating and lust-inducing recipes, such as quail in rose-petal sauce. Bittersweet and wickedly funny, it's a tastebud-tingling blend of cookery tips, dreamlike images and vast charm for a loving celebration of women and the work they do.

WHAT'S COOKING? (2000)

Directed by Gurinder Chadha
Starring Alfre Woodard, Mercedes Ruehl, Joan Chen, Lainie Kazan

Set in Los Angeles on Thanksgiving Day, when it is a sacred obligation for Americans to stuff a turkey and themselves, this comedy explores four ethnically diverse (but excruciatingly universal) families through confrontations, revelations and catastrophes that accompany mouth-watering food preparation. It's hard to choose which spread is the most tempting, but Ruehl's Hispanic household has the spiciest fun. The Jewish family serve up the most hilarious one-liners (along with the noodles) as lesbian daughter Kyra Sedgwick and her partner Julianna Margulies drop a bombshell. Joan Chen's Vietnamese clan experience the most tense drama, incinerating the turkey while contending with hostile teens. But the African-Americans are the easiest to identify with, as an interfering mother-in-law stirs up a debate about oyster/shiitake mushroom stiffing into a marital crisis for Woodward and Dennis Haysbert. A hearty celebration of multiculturalism and family.

SISTERS AND GAL PALS

AGNES OF GOD (1985)

Directed by Norman Jewison
Starring Jane Fonda, Anne Bancroft, Meg Tilly

Tilly is the Agnes of the title, a nun who is discovered with a dead newborn baby in her room. Anti-Catholic psychiatrist Dr Livingston (Fonda) is sent to solve the mystery, and what a mystery it turns out to be. For a start, no one knows how the baby died; but there's also the question of how Agnes had a child in the first place, especially as the only man the nuns come into contact with is elderly Father Metineau. Could it have been an immaculate conception? Agnes isn't telling: a naive innocent before this, she now has amnesia about the whole affair. And the convent's mother superior (Bancroft) doesn't go out of her way to help Livingston in her investigation either.

The mystery is never fully resolved, which makes for frustrating viewing, but seeing the well-matched Bancroft and Fonda butting heads is a treat.

ANITA AND ME (2002)

Directed by Metin Huseyin
Starring Chandeep Uppal, Anna Brewster

Based on Meera Syal's bestselling novel, this comedy drama tells the story of teenager Meena (Uppal), the daughter of the only Punjabi family in an English village in the seventies. It focuses on her friendship with the outgoing Anita (Brewster), the often foul-mouthed daughter of an equally plain-speaking mother (Kathy Burke) who moves in next door.

While this is packed with the clichés you'd expect from a movie that reminisces about a summer friendship between two unlikely pals, it's saved by two great central performances from the girls, and a dash of humour from a supporting cast that includes Syal herself and Lynn Redgrave. As culture-clash comedies go, it isn't a patch on *Bend It Like Beckham*, but anyone who can still remember the days when *Jackie* was every young girl's bible and glam rock was (almost) cool is sure to have a laugh or two.

BAGDAD CAFÉ / a.k.a. OUT OF ROSENHEIM (1987)

Directed by Percy Adlon
Starring Marianne Sägebrecht, C. C. H. Pounder, Jack Palance

German tourist Jasmin (Sägebrecht) rows with her husband in the middle of the Mojave Desert, stomps off to a failing truckstop café, and stays. Shocked by the dirt and disorder, the hefty *Hausfrau* sets about the place to the bemusement of lean, mean owner Brenda (Pounder), her chaotic household and her eccentric regulars – including the Native American cook, a tattoo artist and a retired Hollywood set decorator (Palance, a particular hoot), who admires Jasmin's ample beauty. Jasmin's loosening up (literally, as she lets her hair down and ditches her corset), the bond that develops between her, Brenda and the others, and the witty transformation of the diner into a nightly cabaret with Jasmin as the star-turn illusionist contribute to a charming, offbeat delight, written by Adlon and his wife Eleanore. It inspired a short-lived spin-off TV series starring Whoopi Goldberg.

THE BANGER SISTERS (2002)

Directed by Bob Dolman
Starring Goldie Hawn, Susan Sarandon

Ever wondered what happens to groupies when they hit middle age? According to this comedy, seventies rock fans either end up like Suzette (Hawn), tending bar wearing skimpy tops and reminiscing about falling asleep under Jim Morrison, or they chose to be like Lavinia (Sarandon), erasing all memory of her past and settling into suburban domestic bliss, complete with carefully co-ordinated silk suits and neurotic children.

In the best comic tradition, though, Lavinia's life is destined never to be so prim again when her old pal Suzette turns up out of the blue after a couple of decades' absence. All the pairing-of-opposites clichés are explored, but in the deft comic hands of Hawn and Sarandon (who should be given more funny roles if this is any guide) the film raises more than a few chuckles and proves that it's not just Mick Jagger who can still rock into his fifties.

BEND IT LIKE BECKHAM (2002)

Directed by Gurinder Chada
Starring Parminder Nagra, Keira Knightley, Jonathan Rhys Meyers

Eighteen-year-old Asian Londoner Jess (Nagra) wants to be a football star, just like her hero David Beckham. The trouble is, her traditional parents don't agree, and they can't understand why she doesn't want to train to be a lawyer, learn to cook traditional meals and marry a nice Indian boy. So when Jess is spotted playing footie in a park by Jules (Knightley) and is asked to turn out for the local women's team, the Hounslow Harriers, she decides to keep her ball-kicking activities to herself. She's equally tight-lipped about her crush on the team's coach, Joe (Meyers).

A light-hearted movie that boasts romance, comedy, culture clashes and, of course, football, *Bend It Like Beckham* also has the distinction of being the first football movie in history that women actually went to see. Funny and sweet, it's a feelgood film about gal pals and first loves, and so much more than a bunch of sweaty people kicking a ball around.

BLACK NARCISSUS (1947)

Directed by Michael Powell, Emeric Pressburger
Starring Deborah Kerr, David Farrar, Sabu, Jean Simmons, Flora Robson, Kathleen Bryon

In a breathtakingly beautiful adaptation of the Rumer Godden novel, a group of Anglican nuns are sent to the Himalayas to establish a convent school and mission clinic in an abandoned harem palace. They are under the charge of pretty young Sister Clodagh (Kerr), whose sternness masks her religious uncertainty. High in the mountains, the thin air, exotic surroundings, beguiling native ways and rugged, dissolute expatriate neighbour Mr Dean (Farrar) really start to get to the sisters, and not in a good way.

An Oscar winner for its art direction and ravishing cinematography, this intense psychological drama of women confined together is mesmerising as old memories, doubts, crises of faith, hysteria and eroticism assail the community. Bryon's performance as Sister Ruth, jealously succumbing to lust and insanity for a heart-stopping climax, is unforgettable.

BOYS ON THE SIDE (1995)

Directed by Herbert Ross
Starring Whoopi Goldberg, Mary Louise Parker, Drew Barrymore

Who needs men when you've got gal pals? Gay nightclub singer Jane (Goldberg), shy Robin (Parker) and young Holly (Barrymore) share laughter, tears and secrets on the road to Los Angeles. They become friends who stick together through the good times (Holly finally finds a decent man, as played by the yummy Matthew McConaughey) and the bad (Robin looks a bit peaky, doesn't she?).

Ross, who also directed *Steel Magnolias*, is great at teasing outstanding performances from his leading ladies, and he certainly does so here, with both Goldberg and Barrymore providing many of the laughs. It does get syrupy in places, but thanks to a largely fun script and the delightful cast, you'd really love to take a road trip with these girls.

THE BREAKFAST CLUB (1985)

Directed by John Hughes
Starring Molly Ringwald, Emilio Estevez, Ally Sheedy, Judd Nelson, Anthony Michael Hall

Five teenagers are sentenced to a Saturday detention and despite their differences, have formed some kind of bond by the end of the day in this comedy drama.

The actors who would soon be dubbed the 'brat pack' here play a quintet of American high-school stereotypes: there's the jock (Estevez), the heavy-eyelinered weirdo (Sheedy), the stuck-up princess (Ringwald), the nerd (Hall) and the rebel (Nelson). They are all trying to entertain themselves under the watchful eye of anally retentive teacher Vernon (Paul Gleason). Truths are revealed, grudges are aired, and each classmate (and each actor) gets his or her moment to shine.

Much imitated both in films and on TV (an episode of *Dawson's Creek* memorably paid homage to it), this teen movie – complete with the Simple Minds song written specifically for it, 'Don't You Forget About Me', and a bestselling soundtrack – remains a classic slice of the eighties and a favourite of young girls everywhere (some of whom weren't even born when it first came out).

CALENDAR GIRLS (2003)

Directed by Nigel Cole
Starring Helen Mirren, Julie Walters

Whereas *Bridget Jones's Diary* may have been aimed at twenty- and thirtysomething women, this British comedy drama is for a slightly more mature female audience. Loosely based on true events, it's the story of how a group of Women's Institute members in North Yorkshire rallied together to raise money for the local hospital (where one of the ladies' husbands died of leukaemia) by posing for a nude calendar. Since they were all over fifty, the calendar was very tasteful – iced buns, vases of flowers and other props hid any naughty bits – but what was intended to sell a few copies in nearby villages went on to be a bestseller, outselling the raunchier ones featuring Cindy Crawford and Britney Spears.

Events leading up to the calendar's printing are a hoot, with Mirren, Walters and co-stars Penelope Wilton and Annette Crosbie providing many of the laughs. But things turn sour when the WI members become stars and head to Los Angeles to promote the calendar where petty jealousy causes them to fall out. Worth watching for the first hour, then fast-forward to the feelgood finale.

CAREER GIRLS (1997)

Directed by Mike Leigh
Starring Katrin Cartlidge, Lynda Steadman

Leigh's follow-up to *Secrets And Lies* (1996) is a tale of two girlfriends, former college flatmates getting reacquainted after six years of estrangement, and centres on a pair of brilliantly eccentric but natural performances. The nervous Annie (Steadman) travels back to London to catch up with hardened Hannah (Cartlidge) and tags along during her hunt for a new flat. Through strange encounters and recollections of their ghastly, riotous and emotional student days together, the women take stock of their lives and loves, their jobs and, eventually, what they mean to each other.

It's bizarrely funny – as in a scene featuring a rendezvous with an estate agent who doesn't remember either of them but dated them both in college – and bittersweet, with eighties flashbacks that ring cringe-making bells for those of us who were around at the time. We love the friends' way of seeking life counsel: they chant, 'Miss Brontë, Miss Brontë' and open a copy of *Wuthering Heights* at random as others would consult the *I Ching*. Interestingly, the score is co-composed by actress Marianne Jean-Baptiste (the star of *Secrets And Lies* and TV's *Without A Trace*).

CIRCLE OF FRIENDS (1995)

Directed by Pat O'Connor
Starring Minnie Driver, Chris O'Donnell, Saffron Burrows, Alan Cumming

Minnie Driver has never been better than as Bernadette 'Benny' Hogan, a pudgy young girl (the actress piled on thirty pounds for the role) in

1950s Ireland who finds love for the first time when she goes to college in Dublin and meets hunky Jack (O'Donnell). Although their romance is central to the plot, so is Benny's friendship with school pals Eve (Geraldine O'Rawe) and the conniving Nan (Burrows), who fancies the local rich landowner (Colin Firth) and falls pregnant in an attempt to trap him into marriage. Hearts are broken, friendships are betrayed, while the marvellous Alan Cumming creeps around in the background as the slimy man with designs on Benny. A sweet tale, based on Maeve Binchy's novel.

CRIMES OF THE HEART (1986)

Directed by Bruce Beresford
Starring Diane Keaton, Jessica Lange, Sissy Spacek

Three Oscar-winning actresses come together in Beth Henley's adaptation of her own Pulitzer Prize-winning play. Although the trio differ wildly, they strike up a remarkably believable blood relationship as three giggly, gossipy, secretive and scandal-prone sisters who are – through heredity – completely crackers.

The Magrath girls are reunited in their Southern family manor when the youngest, Babe (Spacek), shoots her husband, because he's peeved about her affair with a teenager. Lenny (Keaton) has had her love life blighted by a gynaecological problem, but sexpot wannabe singer Meg (Lange) makes hay with whoever is to hand (on this occasion an old flame played by Lange's real-life partner Sam Shepard).

A sardonic but deeply affectionate comedy of sisterhood, this is a complete reversal of the familiar Southern Gothic melodrama of woe, and all of the women are fabulous (including Tess Harper as their permanently scandalised cousin next door).

CROSSROADS (2002)

Directed by Tamra Davis
Starring Britney Spears, Dan Aykroyd

Not a movie version of the naff TV soap, but the first starring role for pop tartlet Britney Spears. Britney – whom we first meet lip-synching

Madonna songs into her hairbrush dressed in her undies – isn't bad as studious Lucy, who reunites with childhood pals Kit (Zoe Saldana) and pregnant Mimi (Taryn Manning) to honour a pact they made as tots to go in search of their destinies after their high school graduation. Travelling with Mimi's hunky friend Ben (Anson Mount), they intend to head to LA to enter a singing competition, dropping Lucy off in Arizona on the way where she intends to find her long-lost mother (Kim Cattrall).

But, as in similarly fluffy films like *Flashdance* and *Coyote Ugly*, the plot is largely irrelevant. Of greater importance are getting to see Britney in her lacy undies and flashing her toned midriff at every opportunity (if you're a teenage boy); Britney winning (surprise, surprise) a karaoke competition singing 'I Love Rock 'N' Roll' and scribbling down 'poetry' that of course will end up as a song about her innermost feelings; and, for those who know of the pop poppet's real-life pledge to remain a virgin until she's married, the sniggersome dialogue before and after her deflowering on screen. A surprisingly enjoyable coming-of-age adventure.

CRUSH (2002)

Directed by John McKay
Starring Andie MacDowell, Imelda Staunton, Anna Chancellor

The three leads play single, fortysomething friends who meet for chocolate and gin every Monday. They call themselves the 'Sad Fuckers Club' (the movie's original title) and ruminate on who is the most pathetic when it comes to men.

However, when rural schoolmistress Kate (MacDowell) meets her twenty-five-year-old ex-pupil Jed (Kenny Doughty) at a funeral and ends up having sex with him in the graveyard, she understandably doesn't share this information with Molly (Chancellor) and Janine (Staunton). They assume she's having a clandestine fling with the far more reliable (and older and stuffier) Gerald (Bill Paterson). When they finally learn her secret, they think she's humiliating herself with young Jed and decide to do something about it.

There's some terrific humour in the women's conversations and those between Kate and her young lover. But one can't help thinking that her friends aren't as supportive or as nice as they should be: they plot ways of getting rid of Jed, which isn't very sisterly. And a surprisingly tragic twist in the plot turns what could have been a thoroughly uplifting comedy into a rather depressing one.

DANCING AT LUGHNASA (1998)

Directed by Pat O'Connor
Starring Meryl Streep, Catherine McCormack, Kathy Burke, Brid Brennan, Sophie Thompson, Michael Gambon

Brian Friel's stage hit transferred gracefully to the screen with an outstanding ensemble of actresses. They play a poor but proud, loving but exhausted quintet of sisters in rural Ireland in the thirties. Scarcely able to fend off starvation, they care for their darling but frail and loopy brother (Gambon).

They face even more consternation when the youngest sister (McCormack) takes in her irresponsible sometime-lover (Rhys Ifans), who is flitting through for some bonding with the young illegitimate son who is the sisters' collective shame and joy. He arrives just in time for the pagan Gaelic festival of Lughnasa – with its traditional bonfires, trysts and liberal consumption of alcohol. The five women seize the day and let their hair down just this once for a communal moment of exaltation before their enclosed world changes forever.

The cast etch memorably colourful, touching characters in this tender tale. Nothing much happens, but it does so beautifully.

DIVINE SECRETS OF THE YA-YA SISTERHOOD (2002)

Directed by Callie Khouri
Starring Ashley Judd, Sandra Bullock, Ellen Burstyn, Maggie Smith

When Sidda (Bullock) falls out with her drunken Southern mother Vivi (Burstyn), the latter's lifelong friends, the Ya-Yas, get together to convince Sidda that her mother isn't all that bad. They accomplish this by telling her the secrets of Vivi's colourful past in this movie based on the bestseller of the same name.

A hybrid of a plethora of touchy-feely films with long titles – *How To Make An American Quilt, Fried Green Tomatoes At The Whistle Stop Café,* et al. – this features every cliché from tangled mother–daughter relationships, tragic romance and the value of lifelong female friendship to that old favourite, 'a few choice homilies and a glass of iced tea are the solution for everything'.

On the plus side, this does have an impressive cast who give the movie some class and the occasional welcome injection of acid wit. Burstyn and Judd especially do their best as the present-day and flashback versions of Vivi. Unfortunately, director Khouri – best known for her brilliant script for the ultimate chick flick *Thelma And Louise* – mostly seems to have forgotten that we gals like a little strength and sassiness with our sugar.

ENCHANTED APRIL (1992)

Directed by Mike Newell
Starring Josie Lawrence, Miranda Richardson, Polly Walker, Joan Plowright

This slow, elegant film focuses on two unhappily married English ladies in the 1920s, Rose (Richardson) and Lottie (Lawrence). They rent an Italian villa for a month with glamorous Lady Caroline (Walker) and crotchety widow Mrs Fisher (Plowright) in order to escape from their husbands. Friendships are forged and cemented among the quartet against a backdrop of beautiful Italian countryside, but their idyll is shattered when the husbands (Alfred Molina and Jim Broadbent) pay a surprise visit.

Surprisingly funny for a period costumer, this looks scrumptious and features warm performances from the sparky female cast – especially Walker and Lawrence.

THE FIRST WIVES CLUB (1996)

Directed by Hugh Wilso
Starring Goldie Hawn, Bette Midler, Diane Keaton

This 'get even and get everything' comedy is a lot of fun, not least for the sight of a trio of expert comediennes going through their paces as wronged women on the rampage.

Three university buddies are reunited in middle age at the funeral of a fourth friend (Stockard Channing), who committed suicide after her husband ditched her for a younger, thinner woman. Over a tearful lunch, they launch Operation Hell's Fury as payback for their friend's and their own humiliations. Midler's Brenda is the hefty *Hausfrau* who becomes supercharged with empowerment. Keaton's gentle Annie learns to express her anger. And Hawn is sensational as movie-star Elise, a vain lush desperately denying her decline with vodka and cosmetic surgery. But she possesses a fortune that enables the threesome to pull off retribution against ex-husbands and their obnoxious trophy wives (including Sarah Jessica Parker) in a scheme so sneaky the FBI would admire it. And there are some fabulous one-liners.

GAS FOOD LODGING (1992)

Directed by Allison Anders
Starring Brooke Adams, Ione Skye, Fairuza Balk

Writer–director Anders's hard early life explains her affinity with resilient women. This, the first of her superb chick flicks, is the story of an abandoned wife and mother, Nora (Adams), and the two daughters she is struggling to raise in a trailer park. It provides a resolutely low-key, realistic, but poetically passionate slice of life.

While Nora slaves in a diner, seventeen-year-old rebel Trudie (Skye) seeks escape from their dreary New Mexico town with slutty disillusionment. Younger sister Shade (Balk) is a hopeful dreamer hooked on Mexican melodramas at the local cinema. An encounter with their deadbeat dad (James Brolin) and Trudie's short-lived romance with an English rock hunter (Robert Knepper) who leaves her pregnant only exacerbate the awful but truthful screaming matches in the trailer.

While there are no neat happy endings here, life goes on in its mostly trying but sometimes terrific and tender way, keenly observed and beautifully detailed.

GHOST WORLD (2001)

Directed by Terry Zwigoff
Starring Thora Birch, Scarlett Johansson, Steve Buscemi

Misfit best friends Enid (Birch) and Rebecca (Johansson) leave school craving independence but find their options for jobs, college, entertainment, romance and even hipness severely limited. Drifting between the mini-mall and the TV, they pour scorn on all around them until Enid develops a pitying fascination for oddball Seymour (Buscemi).

Adapted from one of the most interesting and successful underground graphic novels of the nineties (by Daniel Clowes, who co-scripted the movie with Zwigoff), this captures sarcastic teen angst and the collapse of modern culture, no less, with sharp humour and painfully recognisable, authentic characters. Eighteen-year-olds Enid and Rebecca are sneering, smart-aleck soul sisters to *Catcher in the Rye*'s Holden Caulfield, and their search for a place in the world is a brightly cartoon-coloured but melancholy comedy whose tone is dangerously balanced between edgy satire and sulky despair.

As they are defiantly, obnoxiously disconnected themselves, we are not expected to love these girls. The keenly observed awfulness of everything and everyone around them is irresistible, though, while half-baked feminista political correctness – in the shape of Enid's hippy art teacher (a hilarious Illeana Douglas) – provokes richly ludicrous incident. A world away from the *American Pie* school of filmmaking, this is 'teen comedy' of startling sophistication and depth – as well as some horribly funny bits.

GIRLS' NIGHT (1998)

Directed by Nick Hurran
Starring Julie Walters, Brenda Blethyn, Kris Kristofferson

Best friends Jackie (Walters) and Dawn (Blethyn) work in the same Northern factory, and share their winnings at bingo every Friday night. Dawn is a quiet wife and mother. Jackie is loud and tarty, and has her legs wrapped around the bingo-hall manager at the very moment when Dawn realises she's just won the £100,000 National Jackpot. Ever the good mate, Dawn gives Jackie her cut, but when the cancer Dawn thought she had beaten years before returns, Jackie uses the cash to take them on the trip of a lifetime to Las Vegas.

There's no denying that this is major tugging-at-the-heartstrings stuff aimed at the *Shirley Valentine* market, but with a sharp script from Kay Mellor (best known for her TV series such as *Band Of Gold*), unsentimental direction and superb lead performances, it never becomes the cloying disease-of-the-week movie it could have been.

HANNAH AND HER SISTERS (1986)

Directed by Woody Allen
Starring Woody Allen, Michael Caine, Mia Farrow, Barbara Hershey, Dianne Wiest

What is for many the best Woody Allen film of all and an Oscar-winner for his screenplay begins and ends with Thanksgiving dinners at which the serene, stable Hannah (Farrow) nourishes and nurtures her difficult clan. Between the holiday gatherings around the groaning table, a dizzying round of relationships are forged and disintegrate. Hannah's husband Elliot (Caine in an Oscar-winning performance of agony and ecstasy) guiltily falls desperately in love with her sister Lee (Hershey), who lives with a tortured artist (Max von Sydow). Insecure third sister Holly (Wiest, dynamite and also an Oscar winner) does her neurotic worst to self-destruct in a blur of bad choices. Meanwhile, Hannah's ex-husband, the hypochondriac Mickey (Allen), keeps everyone abreast of his latest life-threatening ailment.

Allen and his all-star cast keep the romantic comedy, angst, smart one-liners and genuine emotional poignancy in perfect balance right through to the heart-warming, family-as-a-united-front conclusion.

I CAPTURE THE CASTLE (2003)

Directed by Tim Fywell
Starring Romola Garai, Bill Nighy, Rose Byrne

Based on Dodie Smith's novel of the same name, this focuses on the teenage life and first romances of young Cassandra (Garai), who lives with her eccentric family in an almost condemned castle in 1930s Suffolk. Her father (Nighy) is an author who has had writer's block for over a decade (which explains why they have no money and haven't paid their landlord for two years), while her sister Rose (Byrne) spends her time wishing for a handsome and wealthy man to take her away from the crumbling walls and leaking pipes. Her prayers seem to be answered when two American brothers come to call, having inherited the nearby mansion. Rose soon sets her sights on the elder, Simon (Henry Thomas), despite his brother Neil's (Marc Blucas) obvious interest in her, and unaware that Cassandra has fallen for Simon herself.

A sweet tale of growing older and wiser, this drama works well thanks to the perfect casting of Byrne, and especially Garai, who is in virtually every scene and injects each one with memorable warmth.

LE DIVORCE (2003)

Directed by James Ivory
Starring Kate Hudson, Naomi Watts

A rare contemporary movie from Merchant–Ivory, who are better known for their period costume dramas like *A Room With A View* this isn't quite as successful as their previous endeavours.

American Isabel Walker (Hudson) travels to Paris to visit her pregnant sister Roxy (Watts). She arrives on the very day that Roxy's French husband chooses to walk out on her. This is just one of a series of sub-plots that also includes Isabel's affair with an older French politician, the arrival of an unhinged American (Matthew Modine) who is married to Roxy's husband's lover, and the origins of a piece of art owned by the Walker family.

Although it's adapted from Diane Johnson's comic novel, the humour in the film is less evident than it is in the book. Instead, most of the movie has the feel of one of Merchant–Ivory's period dramas performed in modern clothes; that is until the last reel, when they throw in some jokey narration and a few whimsical scenes. But these merely seem out of sync with the rest of the film.

LOVELY AND AMAZING (2001)

Directed by Nicole Holofcener
Starring Emily Mortimer, Brenda Blethyn, Catherine Keener, Jake Gyllenhaal

The Marks women have cornered the market in insecurity. Young actress Elizabeth (Mortimer) is so concerned about her body that she asks her arrogant actor lover (Dermot Mulroney) to critique her while she stands naked in front of him. Her mother, Jane (Blethyn), isn't much better – she is about to enter hospital to have extensive cosmetic surgery. Meanwhile, Jane's eight-year-old adopted black daughter Annie (Raven Goodwin) desperately wants to straighten her hair so she will look more like her white sisters, and Jane's married daughter Michelle (Keener) embarks on a fling with a teenage boy (Gyllenhaal) partly to boost her self-esteem.

Both humorous and painful – Michelle being arrested for her under-age affair has a bit of both – this is a realistic, honest look at how a mother's insecurities and hang-ups can be passed on to her daughters. It features marvellous central performances from Mortimer and especially Keener, with the latter bravely depicting a woman who is pretty unlikeable in her misery.

MI VIDA LOCA / a.k.a. MY CRAZY LIFE (1993)

Directed by Allison Anders
Starring Angel Aviles, Seidy Lopez, Jacob Vargos

Drawing on the lives of her Hispanic neighbours in the Echo Park area of Los Angeles (and recruiting young locals to the ensemble), writer–director Anders vividly explores the world of girl gangs with hot tempers, cool tattoos, complex relationships and a hard reality. When Sad Girl (Aviles) becomes pregnant by cocky drug dealer Ernesto (Vargas), to the fury of her childhood friend and love rival Mousie (Lopez), the knives are out in a bitter enmity that divides the girls 'n the 'hood. Vibrant beauties with street names like Giggles, Whisper and La Blue Eyes clash and commiserate, swap blows, share sorrows and dare to hope for more, redefining the terms 'family' and 'community' in a sector of society where the men are typically behind bars or buried by twenty-one. Keep your eyes peeled for a young Salma Hayek.

ME WITHOUT YOU (2001)

Directed by Sandra Goldbacher
Starring Anna Friel, Michelle Williams

Anna Friel and Michelle Williams play two mates growing up in London during the seventies and eighties in this drama about friendship, bad fashion choices and men. Pals since childhood, their relationship is severely tested at college when they both start sleeping with a hunky lecturer (Kyle MacLachlan). What's most puzzling about the relationship between the two friends – and is ultimately the film's undoing – is that Williams puts up with it all, even though Friel's character is a slutty cow who uses and abuses her pals at every opportunity.

However, there are some great comic moments thanks to Williams, MacLachlan and Trudi Styler (as Friel's boozy mum), and the two leads have fun in the godawful fashions of the era. So it may not be the best example of a friends-to-the-end flick, but it's a must for anyone who once turned a bin-bag into a punk skirt or sported horrid fingerless lace gloves from Chelsea Girl because she thought it looked cool.

MOONLIGHT AND VALENTINO (1995)

Directed by David Anspaugh
Starring Elizabeth Perkins, Whoopi Goldberg, Kathleen Turner, Gwyneth Paltrow

After her husband is run over while jogging, grieving young widow Perkins is roused out of her shock and slowly brought back to life by best buddy Whoopi, dotty younger sister Paltrow and bossy ex-stepmother Turner, none of whom will leave her alone. What really does the trick, though (it would work for us, too!), is hiring dishy house painter Jon Bon Jovi to do up the house. (Valentino, incidentally, is his dog.)

The story, by Neil Simon's daughter Ellen, doesn't ring terribly true, with its quirky moods and odd quartet of divas, although it is actually semi-autobiographical. But we don't really mind because Perkins is superb, Turner is a scream, Bon Jovi makes a pleasing, natural acting debut, and the young Paltrow almost steals the show as the neurotic, wraith-like sibling who unexpectedly finds a romance of her own (with Jeremy Sisto).

MYSTIC PIZZA (1988)

Directed by Donald Petrie
Starring Annabeth Gish, Julia Roberts, Lili Taylor

This was Roberts's eye-catching big break after a couple of earlier false starts. She plays Daisy, the sexy, rebellious one among a trio of pizzeria waitresses in this coming-of-age romantic drama that's aimed squarely at girls.

Sensitive, academic Kat (Gish) is smitten with a married man; spunky Jojo (Taylor) is on the verge of marriage to a good-natured local fisherman (Vincent D'Onofrio). Along with Daisy, they develop a mutual support system to overcome life's disappointments during a summer in the seaport of Mystic, Connecticut.

Julia's legs and auburn mane are flaunted throughout, which snares the Ivy League boy (Adam Storke) for Daisy and created a buzz around the actress herself. But all the women in this movie are good, including Conchata Ferrell, who as the girls' employer dispenses life wisdom along with the mozzarella. Look out for a young Matt Damon as Storke's brother in the snobby family dinner scene.

NOW AND THEN (1995)

Directed by Lesli Linka Glatter
Starring Demi Moore, Melanie Griffith, Rosie O'Donnell, Rita Wilson

Their names may be high on the credits, but it's misleading to say that this film 'stars' Moore (who co-produced), Griffith, O'Donnell and Wilson (a.k.a. Mrs Tom Hanks). In fact, they've just been drafted in to play the grown-up versions of four young girls at the top and tail ends of this slight coming-of-age drama.

It's the summer of 1970, and tomboy Roberta (Christina Ricci), bra-stuffing flirt Teeny (Thora Birch), tubby Chrissy (Ashleigh Aston Moore) and occult-obsessed Samantha (Gaby Hoffman) have the whole of the holidays to become friends, hold seances and discover boys. Unfortunately, none of this sub-*Stand By Me*-for-girls stuff is very thrilling unless you actually *are* a twelve-year-old girl, and the few scenes of the friends all grown up and reunited do little to improve a well-meaning but fluffy-as-candyfloss tale.

PASSION FISH (1992)

Directed by John Sayles
Starring Mary McDonnell, Alfre Woodard, David Strathairn, Vondie Curtis-Hall, Angela Bassett

What appears as if it's going to be a worthy but depressing account of a woman's struggle to come to terms with paraplegia becomes something much more in the hands of writer–director–editor Sayles. This is a witty, perceptive, compassionate exploration of the ways life has of never going to plan.

TV soap star May-Alice (a magnificent McDonnell) is paralysed in a freak accident and retreats to her remote family home in Louisiana's Cajun country to drown herself in tears and booze. But she meets her match in quiet nurse Chantelle (Woodard), who is emotionally crippled by her own life crisis and spoiling for the power struggle that takes the women from bitching and bullying to bonding. Their gradually evolving friendship opens them both to some of the happier surprises that life still has in store.

The film's title comes from a charming folk tale recounted in the bayou, underlining the theme that even 'damaged' people can find something to hope for. Moving and amusing, this is an uplifting, emotionally satisfying and accomplished film, with plenty of Cajun *joie de vivre* and zydeco music.

THE SPITFIRE GRILL (1996)

Directed by Lee David Zlotoff
Starring Alison Elliott, Ellen Burstyn, Marcia Gay Harden

Percy (Elliott), freshly released from jail, arrives in a small town in Maine hoping to start a new life. She lands a job working for tough-on-the-outside Hannah (Burstyn) at the Spitfire Grill, and while customers speculate on Percy's past and why she was in prison, she befriends her fellow-waitress Shelby (Harden) and comes to the rescue when Hannah can no longer run the diner.

Preposterous by the end (there's a plot twist involving a rapidly churning river), this is still an enjoyable drama about gals supporting one another over a plate of carbohydrate-heavy food in the *Fried Green Tomatoes* vein.

STEEL MAGNOLIAS (1989)

Directed by Herbert Ross
Starring Sally Field, Dolly Parton, Shirley MacLaine, Daryl Hannah, Olympia Dukakis

Ross's multiple-hanky version of Robert Harling's award-winning play is a slick, entertainingly comedic yet tear-jerking drama of Southern belles. (The title is the author's homage to the strength underneath soft, feminine exteriors.) They range from the rich, the eccentric and the difficult (MacLaine and Dukakis) to the poor, meek and bespectacled (Hannah), who all gather in jolly Parton's small-town Louisiana beauty parlour.

The flashy female ensemble swap sassy one-liners and share solidarity through their travails with hairstyles and their exasperations with the men in their lives (who include Tom Skerritt and Sam Shepard). Most cruelly, they congregate for the saga of an anxious, devoted mother (Field) and her doomed-to-kidney-failure daughter (Julia Roberts, who received an early Oscar nomination for her showy supporting role), who vows, 'I'd rather have half an hour of wonderful than a lifetime of average,' when she insists on marrying and trying for a baby.

Prestigious, quintessentially women's fare, it's not quite up there with the all-time greats but it's good stuff.

TEA WITH MUSSOLINI (1998)

Directed by Franco Zeffirelli
Starring Cher, Judi Dench, Joan Plowright, Maggie Smith, Lily Tomlin

Director Zeffirelli draws on his own childhood growing up in the Fascist Italy of the 1930s here. Presumably the young boy Luca (Baird Wallace) is based on Zeffirelli himself, but he is not the central character of the film. Rather, his are the eyes through which we see an eccentric group of women who raise him after his mother dies and his father leaves him at an orphanage.

Corseted as if they have just walked off the set of a Merchant–Ivory drama, Dench, Plowright, Smith, Tomlin and Cher all give boisterous performances as the gaggle of women who gather over tea to gossip, while acting as Luca's unofficial minders and teachers during a troubled time.

WAITING TO EXHALE (1995)

Directed by Forest Whitaker
Starring Whitney Houston, Angela Bassett, Loretta Devine, Lela Rochon

Users, abusers and losers troop through the lives of four sassy women whose friendship keeps them going during their searches for Mr Right. Houston acquits herself well, while Bassett's more painful story of a faithless husband and her explosive revenge benefits from her dramatic intensity. And voluptuous Devine strikes a stinging comic blow for the big girls. The men – including Gregory Hines, Dennis Haysbert, Mykelti Williamson and Wesley Snipes – are easy on the eye, too.

Whitaker's directorial debut bubbles with earthy good humour and has obvious appeal in showcasing African-American actresses, who are still excluded from too many mainstream women's pictures. We just wish that white women weren't trashed quite so heartily as man-snatching villainesses in a film – based on a bestseller by Terry McMillan – that otherwise is a giggle which speaks to all modern working women looking for love.

WALKING AND TALKING (1996)

Directed by Nicole Holofcener
Starring Catherine Keener, Anne Heche, Todd Field, Liev Schreiber, Kevin Corrigan

This little independent comedy – adapted in part from writer–director Holofcener's diary – addresses the resentment women feel when their girlfriends neglect them for men.

Approaching the big Three-Oh, Amelia (Keener) comes over all needy when her best pal Laura (Heche) moves out to get married and seldom answers her incessant calls. But when self-absorbed Laura gets commitment jitters she turns to Amelia, who has been venting her stress and distress on ex-boyfriend Andrew (Schreiber).

We can't help noticing that modern chick flicks rely heavily on gals gabbing too much. The angst-ridden lot here talk – on the phone, over coffee – far more than they walk or do anything else. But at least the chatter is very funny, not least Andrew's long-distance phone-sex relationship, when he can manage to get away from Amelia's neurotic prattle for a minute or two.

WHERE THE HEART IS (2000)

Directed by Matt Williams
Starring Natalie Portman, Ashley Judd, Stockard Channing, Sally Field

Pregnant teen Novalee Nation (Portman) is abandoned by her no-good boyfriend in the parking lot of a Southern shopping mall while they're en route to California. Penniless, she makes a secret nest in the Wal-Mart superstore, where she gives birth to baby Americus. Her story makes attention-grabbing headlines and has several consequences, one of which is the unexpected reappearance in her life of her feckless, selfish mother (Field). Helping Novalee through the fallout and encouraging her efforts to make a new life for herself are serial single mom Lexie (Judd), religious but lusty Sister (Channing) and shy librarian Forney (James Frain).

This adaptation of Billie Letts's bestseller is all over the place, with a kidnapping, a tornado and an unnecessary music-business subplot. And Portman is far too refined in look, manner and sensibility to pass for trailer trash. But the gals have spirit, and it's sweet.

WOMEN TALKING DIRTY (1999)

Directed by Coky Giedroyc
Starring Gina McKee, Helena Bonham Carter

Ellen (McKee) is a strait-laced Scot with a compulsive gambler (James Purefoy) for a husband, while Cora (Bonham Carter) is a spiky-haired single mum trying (and usually failing) to make ends meet. The pair meet in an Edinburgh pub and form a friendship that carries them through bad relationships, debts, children and drink, but is threatened by a secret that one of them can't reveal without destroying the other.

Deliciously comic (Bonham Carter, especially, really lets her hair down) and oddly moving, this is effective because the leads make you believe that these two very different people could really be friends, and that their friendship can withstand all the quirks – and the men – that life throws in their way. The bewitching pair are supported by Eileen Atkins, James Nesbitt, Richard Wilson and Kenneth Cranham (the last two as a cuddly gay couple), and although these characters aren't as well developed as they could have been, they add colour to an already bright and fun film.

THE WOMEN (1939)

Directed by George Cukor
Starring Norma Shearer, Joan Crawford, Rosalind Russell

Anita Loos's adaptation of Claire Boothe Luce's screamingly bitchy hit play provides a wickedly funny melodrama for a sensational all-female cast. And that extends not only to the 130 actresses – including most of MGM's women stars, like Paulette Goddard, Joan Fontaine and Marjorie Main – but to the dogs and horses, too! The human characters love, lose, fight, go through divorces and reconciliations, and gossip like mad throughout.

Refined Mary Haines (Shearer) is devastated to learn – thanks to the relentlessly malicious Sylvia (Russell) – that her beloved husband Stephen is having an affair with vulgar, gold-digging salesgirl Crystal Allen (Crawford). With friends like hers, Mary doesn't need enemies. Humiliated, she puts her pride before all and heads for Reno, where a gang of gals bond at a dude ranch while awaiting their divorce decrees.

After Stephen has married home-wrecker Crystal, Mary puts on a brave face. But on hearing that Crystal is cheating, pussycat Mary sharpens her claws and orchestrates the mass catfight of the century in a nightclub powder room to reclaim her man. All this *and* a Technicolor fashion show – in the middle of a black-and-white film – make *The Women* simply divine.

A musical remake, *The Opposite Sex* (1956), pits June Allyson against Joan Collins and misses the fur-flying point entirely by including men.

ALL ABOUT MY MOTHER (1999) a.k.a TODO SOBRE MI MADRE

Directed by Pedro Almodóvar
Starring Cecilia Roth, Marisa Paredes, Candela Pena, Penelope Cruz

When health worker Manuela's (Roth) teenage son Esteban is killed, she journeys to Barcelona in search of his father, becoming embroiled with transvestite hookers (one of whom is the man she seeks), lesbian actresses and a pregnant nun.

Writer–director Almodóvar's Oscar-winning film is his familiar heady mix of comedy, melodrama and soap opera, with pointed homages to *A Streetcar Named Desire* and *All About Eve*. The actress Huma (Paredes), whose autograph Esteban was trying to get when he was run over, hires Manuela as her personal assistant and carer for her junkie co-star lover Nina. Tranny pal Agrado (Antonia San Juan) holds an angry audience captive by relating her life story. And saintly Sister Rosa (Cruz) is taken in by Manuela to await childbirth. But for the first time, and in spite of all the craziness, Almodóvar's love for women enfolds his ensemble in admiration, tenderness and mercy. This movie goes straight to the heart … with a touch of hilarity.

ANGIE (1994)

Directed by Martha Coolidge
Starring Geena Davis, Stephen Rae, James Gandolfini

Angie (Davis) is a frank, sassy free spirit in this bittersweet comedy with heartache, adapted from Avra Wing's novel *Angie, I Says*. She's sure there's something better than a man like her father, whom she blames for her unhappy mother's desertion, or her Tarzan boyfriend, Vinnie (Gandolfini). So when she becomes pregnant, Angie's impulse is to bolt anywhere away from the life others have planned for her. But the baby brings with it unforeseen difficulties for which Angie is unprepared physically and emotionally.

This is a game effort to address the resentments and rebelliousness of contemporary working women who don't aspire to having it all but would like at least some of it on their own terms. Davis also makes a likeable go of a character with some mean and foolish streaks who learns with pain that the price of her self-fulfilment is responsibility.

ANYWHERE BUT HERE (1999)

Directed by Wayne Wang
Starring Susan Sarandon, Natalie Portman

This adaptation of a bestseller by Mona Simpson has much in common with the superior *Tumbleweeds*, released the same year, but squeaks by mainly on the appeal of its stars.

Adele August (Sarandon) abandons her family and the Wisconsin home where she feels stifled, dragging protesting daughter Ann (Portman) to Beverly Hills for a new, more fulfilling and glamorous life. Adele is an irresponsible mother and a dreamer who plans a movie career for her daughter. Ann is the sensible one who wants to do well in school and escape the feckless sexpot to whom she is biologically shackled. It's an anecdotal story filled, naturally, with disappointments and disputes, but Sarandon is fun in an appalling kind of way and Portman shines with precocious poise.

AUNTIE MAME (1958)

Directed by Morton Da Costa
Starring Rosalind Russell, Forrest Tucker, Coral Browne, Peggy Cass

Adapted from Patrick Dennis's autobiographical novel celebrating the madcap aunt who raised him (later made into the smash-hit musical *Mame*), this adorably entertaining wheeze gives Russell one of her most captivating roles and a gobsmacking wardrobe.

Socialite party girl Mame Dennis (Russell) is amazed when her estranged brother's will names her guardian of young orphan Patrick (Jan Handzlik and later, as a young man, Roger Smith). But she tackles motherhood with the same happy zest as she does everything else, her motto being 'Live, live, live!' Patrick's education is as colourful as Mame's circle of friends (notably Browne, a scream as hammy actress

Vera Charles), admirers (Tucker as Beauregard Burnside, the Southern plantation owner Mame eventually marries) and disciples (Cass as Mame's mousy secretary Agnes Gooch). It's full of fun, style, cocktails and witty zingers.

BLUE SKY (1994)

Directed by Tony Richardson
Starring Jessica Lange, Tommy Lee Jones, Powers Boothe, Carrie Snodgress, Amy Locane

Alex's (Locane) coming of age in the fifties and early sixties is painful, as she's shunted from one army post to another and witnesses the difficulties of her parents. Mother Carly (Lange in spectacular, Oscar-winning form) is loving but unpredictable, promiscuous and frankly nuts, a source of constant embarrassment and worry to her children and husband Major Hank Marshall (Jones, also outstanding). The nature of Carly's trouble is never clarified – manic depression? – but in a wild siren phase she attracts the lustful attentions of Hank's commanding officer, General Johnson (Boothe), who assigns Hank to dangerous, politically sensitive, distant duty. Ironically, ultimately it is Hank who is committed to a mental hospital to silence him, and surprisingly it is Carly who fights like a cornered tigress to save the family.

Richardson's last film, belatedly released four years after it was made and little seen, ambitiously seethes with sex, nuclear politics and military misdeeds, but at its rewarding heart is a complex love story, superbly acted.

CARRIE (1976)

Directed by Brian De Palma
Starring Sissy Spacek, Piper Laurie, Amy Irving, John Travolta

Technically, a blood-splattered chiller based on a novel by horrormeister Stephen King can't really be classified as a chick flick. But *Carrie* deserves an honorary mention for the relationship that's at the core of the film, between teenager Carrie White (Spacek) and her obsessively religious mother (Laurie).

Carrie is a social outcast, mainly thanks to her strict mother, who represses and torments her daughter, forcing her to say her prayers in the closet. It also doesn't help that Carrie has telekinetic powers, which come to light whenever she is traumatised – ultimately, and famously, resulting in her fiery destruction of the school gym during prom night after she is humiliated and doused with pig's blood by some of her evil classmates.

Both Spacek and Laurie deservedly received Oscar nominations for their performances, and the latter's depiction of one of cinema's worst ever parents remains creepy to this day.

CENTRAL STATION / a.k.a. CENTRAL DO BRASIL (1998)

Directed by Walter Salles
Starring Fernanda Montenegro, Vincius de Oliveira

Impoverished and embittered, retired teacher Dora (Montenegro) sits in Rio de Janeiro's train station, writing letters for illiterate 'trash', as she calls her clients, which she then throws away. When a little boy (de Oliveira) whose mother has died needs to write to the father he has never known, Dora sells him and buys a TV. This is one hard old bag!

However, after being rebuked by a friend, she impulsively rescues the child and embarks with him on a cross-country quest, ostensibly to find his father but really to rediscover herself. Her transformation and her growing affection for the boy on the road are neither predictable nor sweet, but subtle and superbly carried off by Montenegro. Hers was the first Brazilian performance to receive an Oscar nomination.

THE DEEP END OF THE OCEAN (1999)

Directed by Ulu Grosbard
Starring Michelle Pfeiffer, Treat Williams, Whoopi Goldberg

At her high-school reunion, Beth (Pfeiffer) leaves her three-year-old son Ben in the care of his older brother Vincent. But Ben disappears and can't be found. Nine years later, the still-grieving family moves house and, by sheer accident, Beth realises a boy who lives a few blocks away is her missing son.

A whole-box-of-hankies weepy about the effect of losing a child and then finding him again, this feels like two separate films. The first is about a family coping with grief; the second about the disruption caused when a loved one unexpectedly reappears. Dad Pat (Williams) thinks life will somehow become normal, son Vincent is scarred by the knowledge it was his fault his brother disappeared and has become a tearaway teen, Beth is obsessed by the return of her boy and Ben – who has grown up believing his kidnappers are his family and his name is Sam – has to come to terms with his strange situation.

The plot may sound like that of an improbable TV movie, but thanks to superb performances from Pfeiffer, Williams and Goldberg (as the detective investigating Ben's disappearance), this is a realistic, moving portrait of a family and a mother's love for her son.

THE GOOD MOTHER (1988)

Directed by Leonard Nimoy
Starring Diane Keaton, Liam Neeson, Jason Robards

Anna (Keaton) *is* a good mother. But her ex-husband (James Naughton) decides to fight her for custody of their young daughter after little Molly tells him on one of her weekend visits what has been going on at home since he moved out. It seems Anna has a hunky new Irish boyfriend named Leo (Neeson), and one night when he was staying over (and making love to Anna), Molly walked in on them. To make matters look even worse, on another occasion, when they were left alone in the house together, the curious Molly asked Leo if she could see and touch his penis. Knowing that Anna believes in family openness, he let her. Oops.

Such a sensitive issue is bungled somewhat in this drama. Anna's ex is portrayed as evil for wanting to snatch away her child, rather than as a (justifiably) concerned dad. We're also never shown what happened between Leo and Molly, so it is hard to sympathise with Leo, Molly's dad or even Anna, who herself doesn't know for sure what occurred. The best moments are those that don't actually concern the central custody battle – Anna and Leo's romance, Anna's visit to her grandparents (Ralph Bellamy and Teresa Wright). That's a shame, because with a better script this could have been a powerful showcase for Keaton's considerable talent.

HIDEOUS KINKY (1999)

Directed by Gillies MacKinnon
Starring Kate Winslet, Said Taghmaoui, Bella Riza, Carrie Mullan

In Marrakech in 1972, scatty hippy Julia (Winslet), wreathed in a cloud of hashish smoke and draped in fetching Pre-Raphaelite casbah tat, has dragged her little girls (Riza and Mullan) on her quest for spiritual enlightenment and personal freedom. Raising children on ideals and oranges isn't enough, however, and eventually Julia is torn between self-actualisation and her maternal responsibility to two children who crave normality.

Winslet is delightful, warm, vulnerable, untogether but brave in a slight but sweet adaptation of Esther Freud's autobiographical novel (Freud was one of the daughters, not the mother). Poverty, the elusiveness of mystical fulfilment and Julia's relationship with a charming Arab rogue (Taghmaoui) make for a funny, sad and anxious odyssey with enchanting, natural children, a colourful backdrop and a trippy soundtrack.

HOPE FLOATS (1998)

Directed by Forest Whitaker
Starring Sandra Bullock, Harry Connick Jr

Bad title, not much better movie. Bullock, who in her role as executive producer had a hand in the casting of Connick Jr, stars as Birdie. In the best scene of the film, she learns on a Ricki Lake-style talk show that her husband has been unfaithful. As a result, she decides to return to the small home town where she was once a beauty queen to get over the pain with her mother (Gena Rowlands) and young daughter at her side.

There's far too much moping and sobbing before she realises that the boy next door (Connick Jr) is now rather hunky, and director Whitaker seems to think that over an hour of wallowing is more interesting than the few amusing scenes of budding romance and bickering between mother and daughter.

MOTHERS IN PERIL

Numerous thrillers feature plots involving women in danger, but scarier still are those in which mums (and their kids) are being stalked, haunted or otherwise terrorised. These aren't exactly chick flicks, but we felt we had to celebrate the ballsy mothers who (sometimes) beat the bad guys, save the day and get more screen time than the men in these dramas.

ROSEMARY'S BABY (1968)

Husband and wife Guy (John Cassavetes) and Rosemary (Mia Farrow) move into a swish New York apartment and are befriended by their elderly neighbours. But things take a decidedly nasty turn when Rosemary starts having horrible dreams and Guy becomes remote and mean. Rosemary then discovers she is pregnant and starts to worry that the building's other residents have some sinister plan for her unborn baby. Roman Polanski's chiller is still one of the creepiest movies ever made.

THE STEPFORD WIVES (1975)

Forget 2004's fluffy remake, this original film version of Ira Levin's novel (he also wrote the book on which *Rosemary's Baby* is based) is far superior. Joanna (Katharine Ross) moves to the quaint town of Stepford with her husband and kids only to discover the other wives there are just a little too perfect and well behaved. Something mysterious is happening at the local men's club that Joanna's husband has just joined and she soon realises that staying in Stepford may be bad for her health.

THE JUROR (1996)

Demi Moore is the mum selected to sit on the jury of a big Mafia trial, while Alec Baldwin gets to chew up the scenery as the mysterious figure who threatens to end her son's life if she doesn't get her fellow-jurors to vote 'not guilty' in this daft thriller. Naturally, with this being in Demi's *GI Jane* period, it ends with her getting tough and taking the law into her own hands, but it's worth a look for a suitably gruff performance from *The Sopranos'* James Gandolfini as Baldwin's fellow-hitman.

THE ASTRONAUT'S WIFE (1999)

A similar idea to *Rosemary's Baby*, this wasn't as successful, but it does feature fun, tongue-in-cheek performances from Johnny Depp and Charlize Theron (who even sports a Mia Farrow-style crop). He's an astronaut who's been acting a little peculiar after returning to Earth following his latest mission. She notices but tries not to worry when he molests her and she ends up pregnant. Could there be something wrong with the babies? Like they'll be born with two heads and have the ability to speak Martian?

THE OTHERS (2001)

This is a terrific, old-fashioned scary movie. Nicole Kidman stars as Grace, a young mother living with her two children in a rambling mansion on Jersey at the end of the Second World War. Confined to the house because her children are allergic to sunlight, and with no news as to whether her soldier husband is alive, Grace has just her three spooky servants for company until her daughter reveals she has been talking to a ghostly presence in the house. Atmospheric and chilling stuff.

PANIC ROOM (2002)

Divorced mum Jodie Foster and her diabetic daughter move into an impressive New York house that comes complete with a panic room. Gee, do you think they are going to need it? Slow to start, this thriller from David '*Se7en*' Fincher gets tense when bad guys Forest Whitaker, Jared Leto and Dwight Yoakham invade the dark maze of a home and Foster gets to kick some burglar ass.

INDOCHINE (1992)

Directed by Régis Wargnier
Starring Catherine Deneuve, Vincent Perez, Linh Dan Pham

The ravishing Deneuve received an Oscar nomination for her performance in this gorgeous, four-hanky wallow that crosses *The Killing Fields* with a soap opera. Spanning some twenty years in Indochina, from French colonialism in the thirties through revolution to independence in the fifties, it follows the entwined fates of rubber-plantation owner Eliane (Deneuve), her cherished adopted Vietnamese daughter Camille (the exquisite Linh Dan Pham) and Jean-Baptiste (Perez), the handsome naval officer they both love. Deneuve brings her celebrated cool to Eliane's chic decadence when she's dreamily adrift in an opium den or playing with her toyboy. But maternal resolve kicks in when the young lovers become revolutionaries and flee.

This sweeping epic of a mother and daughter in love and war is long, slow and somewhat removed as the four French screenwriters muse on collective colonial guilt. But as grievous events pile up it becomes increasingly gripping, and the authentic locations are as magnificent as the women.

THE JOY LUCK CLUB (1993)

Directed by Wayne Wang
Starring Kieu Chinh, Tsai Chin, France Nuyen, Ming-Na Wen, Tamlyn Tomita

Every mother and daughter should see this marvellous distillation of women's hopes and hurts across the generations, adapted by Amy Tan and Ronald Bass from Tan's phenomenally popular novel. Experiences every woman will understand are explored through the relationships of four Chinese mah-jong-playing bosom buddies and their very American daughters. The older women recount spellbinding tales of their early lives in China (depicted in exotic, tragic and magical period sequences). The younger ones relive their stories of childhood, careers, love, expectations and disappointments, each one heading to a classic, amusing and tearful mother–daughter confrontation that brings new understanding.

Visually evocative, it moves between thirties China and nineties California with skill, symmetry and lashings of tears. The eight stories are interwoven beautifully, with scads of fabulous actresses playing the characters at different ages with wit and wisdom that resonate beyond cultural boundaries. Other imitative chick flicks have tried to build a multi-plotted, multi-layered collection of individual stories into a sweeping, emotional mosaic of life, but none has achieved it as wonderfully as this.

LIGHT IN THE PIAZZA (1962)

Directed by Guy Green
Starring Olivia de Havilland, Rossano Brazzi, Yvette Mimieux, George Hamilton

In this sweet, tender drama, adapted by Julius *'Casablanca'* Epstein from a novel by Elizabeth Spencer and beautifully filmed in Florence, we meet well-heeled American mother Meg Johnson (de Havilland) and her daughter Clara (Mimieux) who are on holiday in Italy. Clara is retarded, but her beauty, happy nature and childlike innocence captivate handsome, rich and carefree Fabrizio (Hamilton), who dogs the inseparable mother and daughter and in no time is desperate to marry the angelic girl. The stunned Meg guiltily thinks it over. Since Fabrizio and his set are not exactly rocket scientists themselves, preoccupied as they are with film stars, fashion and frivolity, she decides, 'Why not?' But Meg will have to exercise her own charm on Fabrizio's wary papa (Brazzi). Wonderful performances and the delicate treatment make this a dewy-eyed heartwarmer.

LOSING ISAIAH (1995)

Directed by Stephen Gyllenhaal
Starring Jessica Lange, Halle Berry

Lange and Berry both deliver gut-wrenching, powerhouse performances in this drama as they face each other across a courtroom. Drug-addicted Khalia (Berry) abandons her young baby son Isaiah. Then – breaking all the rules – social worker Margaret (Lange) and her husband (David Strathairn) adopt him. A few years later Khalia, now straightened out, wants her baby back, and enlists the help of a lawyer (Samuel L. Jackson) to plead her case.

This would be mid-afternoon TV-movie material if it were not for the classy cast, which also includes Cuba Gooding Jr and La Tanya Richardson (Jackson's real-life wife) and subtle direction from Gyllenhaal (Maggie and Jake's dad).

MASK (1985)

Directed by Peter Bogdanovich
Starring Cher, Sam Elliott, Eric Stoltz

This warm and winning dramatisation of a true story features a bravura turn from Cher as biker-chick Rusty Dennis, the mother of teenager Rocky (Stoltz). Although afflicted with a rare, horribly disfiguring and inevitably fatal condition, Rocky is bright, sensitive, loving and well nicknamed, since he is Rusty's rock. She – despite her lowbrow taste for drink, drugs and footloose rebels like Gar (Elliott) – is also a hell of a great mom, fighting for Rocky's right to as much schooling, normality and living as he craves. He in turn is a source of strength in her dark, vulnerable downturns, thanks to the self-confidence and unconditional, unpitying love she has fostered.

This is far more uplifting and entertaining than it is distressing, but remains deeply affecting, from Rocky's experience of first love with blind Diane (a young Laura Dern) to the devoted camaraderie he inspires in the wild biker gangs who are his and his mom's 'family'.

MOMMIE DEAREST (1981)

Directed by Frank Perry
Starring Faye Dunaway, Diana Scarwid

The best dysfunctional families are the famous ones, and you can't get much more dysfunctional – or notorious – than the relationship between actress Joan Crawford (Dunaway) and her adopted daughter Christina (Mara Hobel as a child and Scarwid as an adult) and son Christopher. (Crawford actually had four adopted children but only these two are mentioned in the film.)

Based on Christina's book, this has become a camp classic thanks to Dunaway's powerful performance as the tough mother who terrorises her kids. She forces them to give away their own birthday presents, angrily hacks at Christina's hair and throws a legendary tantrum about the wire coat-hangers in her closet.

When the movie was released, it was considered something of a disaster – winning five Razzies, the bad-movie awards – but it's delicious fun as Dunaway savages everything in her path, depicting

Crawford as a perfectionist, an egomaniac and neurotic. Hilariously bonkers stuff.

POSTCARDS FROM THE EDGE (1990)

Directed by Mike Nichols
Starring Meryl Streep, Shirley MacLaine

Based on Carrie 'Princess Leia' Fisher's novel, which itself was loosely based on her relationship with her mother, Debbie Reynolds, this is an acerbic, episodic comedy of one woman's struggle with fame, family and addiction in Hollywood.

Suzanne (Streep) is a drug-addicted actress, forced to live with her mother (MacLaine) after emerging from a detox centre. The men in her life don't make recovery any simpler (especially a philandering boyfriend played by Dennis Quaid), but it is Mom who is enough to drive any woman back to drink and drugs. She's an outgoing, flirting boozer who upstages her daughter at every turn (including twirling around at Suzanne's seventeenth-birthday party while not wearing any underwear).

Although it's littered with sharp dialogue between mother and daughter, the movie is a tad uneven, but it benefits from two stunning performances from Streep and MacLaine.

THE RECKLESS MOMENT (1949)

Directed by Max Ophuls
Starring James Mason, Joan Bennett, Geraldine Brooks

Ophuls's *noir* classic of privileged small-town domesticity blasted by dark secrets is rooted in mother love that will stop at nothing. After failing to break up her daughter Bea's (Brooks) unfortunate, disreputable affair, Lucia Harper (Bennett) finds herself standing over the corpse of Bea's lover. Fearing the worst, she covers up the crime to protect her family. Enter dashing villain Martin Donnelly (Mason), whose blackmail threats ensnare Lucia in an ever-deadlier, nerveracking conspiracy that tests her devotion and resolve, even when Martin develops feelings for her that suggest a possible way out. Beware the 'ordinary' housewife when her blood is up!

Masterly direction and the two stars make this timeless.

The Deep End (2001), starring a superb Tilda Swinton and *ER*'s Goran Visnjic, is based on the same novel (Elizabeth S. Holding's *The Blank Wall*) but updates the action. Swinton's indiscreet child is a gay teenage musical prodigy led astray in sunny Lake Tahoe, Nevada. In this deliberately ironic setting, his mother's frenzied, furtive labours to dispose of the body and evade her tormentors meet with persistently unpleasant twists.

RIDING IN CARS WITH BOYS (2001)

Directed by Penny Marshall
Starring Drew Barrymore, Steve Zahn

With a different director at the helm, this true story based on Beverly D'Onofrio's memoirs could have been tremendous. It's the fascinating tale of a young girl whose life plan is altered irrevocably when she falls pregnant at fifteen, and the two leads – Barrymore (as Beverly) and Zahn (as Ray, the drop-out father of her baby) – are both superb.

Unfortunately, Marshall prefers mush to grit, so whenever she shoots a scene in which something unpleasant happens, she seems to feel obliged to follow it with a cute moment. And that's a problem, because Beverly's life was never cute. Her dreams of becoming a writer are dashed when she falls pregnant, marries Ray and has to bring up her son in a run-down house. The film follows her as she endures an unhappy life over the course of twenty years, framed by the journey she takes in the present day with her adult son (Adam Garcia), to visit Ray and get the permission she needs from him so she can publish her memoirs and finally become the writer she always dreamed of being.

STELLA DALLAS (1937)

Directed by King Vidor
Starring Barbara Stanwyck, Anne Shirley, John Boles

Brassy Stella (Stanwyck) is a toughie who snares well-born Stephen (Boles) when he's at a low point in her mean New England home town, and they have a daughter together. However, his fortunes revived, Stephen returns to New York and divorces Stella to marry a better class of woman. It scarcely matters to Stella, whose life revolves around her adored little Laurel (Shirley), with whom she braves painful social snubs. But when mother treats daughter to a vacation at an exclusive resort where her vulgarity and tarty clothes embarrass the girl, Stella decides Laurel will have a better life with her father, so she pushes her away with feigned indifference.

Celebrated for its heart-rending climax, this remake of a 1925 film version of Olive Higgins Prouty's bestseller gave Stanwyck her favourite role, and the one she thought her best work. It's hard to argue with her, since she finds remarkable dignity rather than cheap pathos in her martyr mother, and even Stella's unattractive qualities are imbued with an endearing vitality. A third version, *Stella* (1990), is greatly inferior, despite a game performance from Bette Midler.

STEPMOM (1998)

Directed by Chris Columbus
Starring Susan Sarandon, Julia Roberts, Ed Harris

Lucky Luke (Harris) has the gorgeous Jackie (Sarandon) for an ex-wife and the equally ravishing Isabel (Roberts) as his girlfriend in this fluffy drama about fractured family life.

The girls are naturally not quite as happy with this situation: Jackie doesn't exactly encourage her two children to like Daddy's new girlfriend; while Isabel has to deal with their disapproval of her relationship with Luke. Things change, however, when Jackie is diagnosed with cancer and she realises she may need Isabel's help.

Clearly primarily a vehicle for the two actresses (Harris doesn't get much of a look-in), this has them yelling at each other, weeping or bonding, but it's none the worse for that. Roberts puts in one of her better performances as the career girl caught up in a family that's not her own, but Sarandon steals the movie as the woman coping with jealousy, bitterness, grief and anger at her situation.

TUMBLEWEEDS (1999)

Directed by Gavin O'Connor
Starring Janet McTeer, Kimberley J. Brown

Southern mom Mary Jo (McTeer) doesn't have much luck with men. And every time a relationship goes bad, she skips town with her twelve-year-old daughter Ava (Brown) in tow, in this tough-chick flick based on Angela Shelton's childhood memoirs.

While this is a superior drama, it's also an often funny account of a four-time-married mother and her outspoken daughter, and features a superb performance from British stage actress McTeer. She was nominated for an Oscar, while the movie itself won the Filmmakers' Trophy at the Sundance Film Festival. Director O'Connor co-stars as one of the many men Mary Jo allows into her life.

TWO WOMEN / a.k.a. LA CIOCIARA (1960)

Directed by Vittorio De Sica
Starring Sophia Loren, Eleanora Brown, Jean-Paul Belmondo

Widowed shopkeeper Cesira (Loren) decides to escape the bombing of Rome in 1943 and flees with her precious twelve-year-old daughter Rosetta (Brown) to the countryside where she was born. Their journey is a harrowing one of hunger and horrors, but they make it to the village and become attached to ardent anti-Fascist Michele (Belmondo) while they struggle through to Liberation. When the worst seems to be over, Cesira and Rosetta embark on the daunting trek back to Rome, but in a ruined church they are ambushed by Moroccan Allied soldiers who beat them, gang rape them throughout the night and leave them for dead. Mute from her ordeal, Rosetta is sullenly slipping away from Cesira, who must find a way to reach her.

Agonising grief, rage, maternal ferocity and the will to survive are evoked with titanic power by an unforgettable Loren, who made film history as the first person to win the Best Actress Oscar for a foreign-language performance.

Dream Dates

Some actors simply don't play romantic leads in girlie movies very often, so they aren't featured in this book as much as we'd like. If the celluloid man of your dreams is more macho than mooning, here are some of the best (in terms of the actor's cuteness) non-chick-flick movies where you can find him.

MARLON BRANDO
Desiree • *Guys And Dolls*
Sayonara

SEAN CONNERY
Dr No • *Marnie*
The Wind And The Lion

RUSSELL CROWE
Gladiator • *LA Confidential* • *Master And Commander: The Far Side Of The World*

TOM CRUISE
Cocktail • *Jerry Maguire*
Mission: Impossible 2 •
Top Gun

MATT DAMON
The Bourne Identity •
Good Will Hunting •
The Rainmaker

JAMES DEAN
East Of Eden • *Rebel Without A Cause* •
Giant

JOHNNY DEPP
Edward Scissorhands •
Pirates Of The Caribbean (with the added bonus of Orlando Bloom) •
What's Eating Gilbert Grape

CLARK GABLE
Mutiny On The Bounty •
Red Dust • *San Francisco*

HARRISON FORD
Blade Runner • *Raiders Of The Lost Ark* • *Witness*

STEVE MCQUEEN
The Great Escape • *The Thomas Crown Affair* •
The Towering Inferno

PAUL NEWMAN
Butch Cassidy And The Sundance Kid • *Hud*
The Long Hot Summer

BRAD PITT
Ocean's Eleven (with the added bonus of George Clooney ... and Matt Damon ... and Andy Garcia) • *A River Runs Through It* • *Troy* (with the added bonus of Orlando Bloom)

WILL SMITH
Bad Boys • *Independence Day* • *Men In Black*

DENZEL WASHINGTON
Crimson Tide • *Devil In A Blue Dress* • *Much Ado About Nothing* (with the added bonus of Keanu Reeves)

Index of Films

Page numbers for the main entries for films are in bold type.